PRESIDENT CHARLES BRADLAUGH, M.P.

'His place in the history of the nineteenth century will be very distinct, more distinct, perhaps, than that of any single figure to be met with in its annals.'

Obituary to Charles Bradlaugh in the *Yorkshire Evening Post*, 30 January, 1891.

By the same author

100 Years of Freethought

President Charles Bradlaugh, M.P.

DAVID TRIBE

ELEK BOOKS
LONDON

ISBN 0 236 17726 5

First published in the United Kingdom
by Elek Books Limited
2 All Saints Street, London N1

Printed in Great Britain by
Unwin Brothers Limited

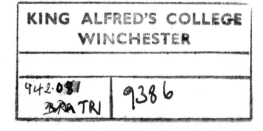

CONTENTS

		Page
	Introduction	9
1	Early Years	12
2	The Queen's Shilling	28
3	The Iconoclast	38
4	The Battles Begin	58
5	On the Threshold	87
6	Long Live the Republic	118
7	The Femme Fatale	157
8	Kicked Out	191
9	Indian Summer	251
	Postscript	292
	Appendices	300
	Notes	323
	Bibliography	371
	Index	376

ILLUSTRATIONS

	Page
The Youthful Iconoclast	165
Annie Besant	166
The Great Question of the Day	199
'Kicked Out'	200
Bradlaugh and the Bigots	233
Exit Caliban	234
Bradlaugh in later years	283
The Oaths Bill	284
The Northampton Statue	295

Two great political waves chased each other up the beach of Victorian England: the middle-class revolution and the working-class revolution. Below the tide-line eddied frantic cross-currents, whipped by the winds of inflation and recession. Perhaps the most interesting and certainly the least charted of these currents was the republican movement. Had an economic squall of exceptional ferocity sprung up, or the sands of the ruling classes been less cohesive, the whole beach might have been washed away and a republic carved out in its place. Of those figures that could have withstood the surges, a Canute *exēcutant*, no one was in a stronger position than Charles Bradlaugh. But the monarchy and the establishment triumphantly stayed put, and the republican movement is today a mere handful of pages, or sentences, in a social history. Yet, glimpsed through the political upheavals of the twentieth century and the collapse of kingship in most parts of the world, it grows in fascination as the years pass. With it grows interest in the popular leaders at its head. Had their personalities been different the outcome might have been very different. If Bradlaugh had possessed the egomania of a Danton or the ruthlessness of a Robespierre, to whom he was often likened, existing institutions might have been swept bloodily away. But in the uniquely bland political climate of Britain perhaps such a personality could never have become a popular leader.

The republican activities of Bradlaugh were not his only claim to consideration. Perhaps they were not even his most controversial or, as events transpired, his most important. Insofar as he features today in school history texts and journalistic reminiscence, it is as a footnote to a chapter on constitutional history. His was the last great battle in the removal of civil disabilities from the holders of heterodox opinion, and the last epic parliamentary struggle for the rights of constituents. By comparison, the modern fight of the 'reluctant peer', Anthony Wedgwood Benn, was a very tepid affair, and the celebrated campaign of John Wilkes in the eighteenth century a rather squalid one. The relative unfamiliarity of Bradlaugh to the general public today, not so many decades since the 'Bradlaugh affair' convulsed Britain and sent shock waves round the world, is something of a mystery. Or is it so mysterious?

Though not a rabble-rouser, he roused enough people to make him politically memorable. One is thus forced to conclude that in his case the religious and 'reverent agnostic' lobbies have organized something resembling a conspiracy of silence. Like Wilkes, Bradlaugh dared to defy the government and the élite of his day. Though this inevitably aroused the same number of powerful enemies, the political situation had changed appreciably by late Victorian times. If the republican movement had not throttled throne and Lords, it had certainly clipped their wings. It was not simply Bradlaugh's philippics that caused his exclusion from the House of Commons. Many radical leaders were more vociferous. It was his atheism. Now, atheism was no novelty in Victorian, or indeed in Georgian, England. There were a great number of unbelievers around, some of them in high places. Scepticism was acceptable so long as you followed David Hume's advice and did not discuss it in front of the servants. Bradlaugh, on the other hand, was a proselytizing atheist, who, if he did not shout his unbelief from every housetop in the realm, certainly used most of the town halls and market squares. This was unforgivable.

And there was something even worse, which ignited bitter enmity even among many of his old freethought friends. He was the champion of birth control. As such he became the victim of perhaps the most notorious obscenity prosecution of the nineteenth century, if not of any period, at a time when the subject was almost literally unmentionable. But 'victim' is hardly the right word. As with everything else he did, the indictment was not simply bad luck, the product of publishing inadvertence. He positively flung the offending publication in the faces of authority and challenged them to prosecute. And they were so much taken aback that the gauntlet was not immediately taken up.

Bradlaugh's life was not only a succession of swashbuckling incidents that left his contemporaries gasping. It laid the foundation of lasting political and social change. He deserves at least a portion of the credit for obtaining the rubber-stamp House of Lords and monarchy, the freedom of speech and publication, the planned families, the television satire, even the 'permissive society'—though no one would more have deplored the most florid aspects of it—we enjoy today. His greatest genius was for organization. The flood of pamphlets he poured out and the numerous court cases in which he figured were not pursued as passing sensations but as offshoots of deep-rooted campaigns for lasting ideological and social change. If he made people look back to the infamous conduct of earlier scions of the House of Brunswick, he made them look forward to averting such iniquities in the future. If there were never at any one time more than 10,000 actual members of the freethought and considerably fewer for the family planning organizations he was instrumental in establishing, society's attitude to both issues has changed appreciably since his day, and largely through his influence. For not only did he make myriads of silent converts and marginally stir the great apathetic masses, he forced the opposition to rethink their basic positions and rephrase their apologetics.

Though in Parliament he became a highly successful 'organization man', his organizing genius took the form of benevolent autocracy. While lacking advantages of environment and, on the face of it, heredity, he proved a natural leader in any undertaking he engaged in. When not the main speaker at the countless public meetings and rallies he attended, he was wont to preside. Apart from the surviving organizations with which his name is imperishably associated, movements for land law reform, or electoral reform, of radical or working men's education and social life, even curious ephemera like the Bimetallic League, thought it important to have Bradlaugh as their president or vice-president or to lose him so as to safeguard respectable opinion. Had the Republic of Great Britain been proclaimed it would have seemed quite natural to have had Bradlaugh as its first President, and in his later days only extreme socialists would have been loud in protest. He would by the way, have made an excellent President.

CHAPTER ONE — EARLY YEARS

'Until 1848 my life needs little relation' — *The Autobiography of C. Bradlaugh*, 1873.

East Anglia was long the battleground of England. It first came to prominence in Roman times under Boudicca (Queen Boadicea). Then came successive waves of Angles, Saxons, Jutes and Danes. Descendants of these sturdy conquerors and colonizers carved out for themselves great estates on the one hand and yeoman rights on the other. During the wool trade of the later Middle Ages the land prospered. When it declined in the sixteenth century worried landowners started to enclose the common lands and provoked the rebellion of the tanner, Robert Kett, and his brother, William. A different kind of revolt produced Oliver Cromwell and his Ironsides a century later.

One of the counties, that with its half-timbered houses and autumn gold seems quintessential not only of the region but of England, is Suffolk; and it is here that the family of Bradlaugh,[1] *alias* Jacob, may be traced from as far back as the sixteenth century, centring on Ipswich, Woodbridge, Wickham Market, Kelsall (now Kelsale), Brandeston and Laxfield. They were freeholders and copyholders, craftsmen and merchants. From the last named village, still isolated and lazily straggling, and mainly famous for the Puritan, William Dowsing, a physical iconoclast of the Civil War period, surfaces what appears to be Charles Bradlaugh's direct line in the sixteenth century. Yeoman George Jacob *alias* Bradlowe and his wife Margaret produced a son whose death is still commemorated by a stone in the old vestry of the parish church. His brother Thomas's family moved a few miles away to Brandeston. They remained good churchpeople, and in 1749 a celebrated new peal[2] of bells was rung by Thomas Bradlaugh, father and son, at Brandeston Church.

Probably it was younger brothers of one or other of these who established a forge[3] on the Brandeston Hall estate on the outskirts of the village. Here there was established a pattern that has continued, with few breaks, to the present century, whereby John became the blacksmith and his brother, James, the gunsmith. One apostate

12

James, however, born in 1780, moved to the bright lights of London in 1807 and established a business at 4 Parson's Court, Bride Lane, off Fleet St. He does not seem to have been enticed into journalism but stuck to his trade till his early death from tuberculosis in 1811, a few months after the birth of his son Charles. Charles was Bradlaugh's father.

The independent Bradlaugh line has known both crests of high tension and depressions of great calm and unadventurousness. A cousin of the Brandeston Bradlaughs was this century convicted of manslaughter for felling his wife's lover with a claw hammer. In a less spectacular way James Bradlaugh tore up long-established family roots. Conversely, his son appears to have been almost entirely a creature of circumstances. While apprenticed to a law stationer Charles was loaned to Messrs Lepard & Co., City solicitors. They were so pleased with his services that they arranged to cancel his indentures and appointed him their confidential clerk, a position he retained to his death. In an equally haphazard way he met and married a nursemaid, Elizabeth Trimby, a woman of stronger personality than himself though of completely conventional and commonplace mind. They settled down in a four-roomed terrace house at 31 Bacchus Walk,[4] a newly-built street in Hoxton. Their income was about thirty shillings a week, their rent about £10 a year, the district in the first wave of old East End's push to the north-east, and their way of life inside the penumbra where the working met the lower middle class,[5] as close to classlessness as one could get in nineteenth-century England.

It was in this undistinguished setting that Charles Bradlaugh Junior, 'a young eagle in a barn fowl's nest',[6] was born on 26 September 1833. His parents were not unduly concerned about his immortal destiny and it was not till 8 December that he was baptized.[7] The next child, Elizabeth, was born in June 1835, and the family steadily grew to seven, two of whom died in early childhood, in the accepted Victorian manner. As the family began to grow and the district to densify, they moved to Birdcage Walk,[8] off the Hackney Road to the east, where the father, a keen gardener, was able to grow dahlias in the long back garden. He was also a keen fisherman and often used to walk to Temple Mills, a part of the River Lea in the Hackney Marshes, then unpolluted. Young Charles was soon able to accompany him and participate in their only shared interest. Whether or not they were close on these occasions, they were not communicative, and the son later observed: 'I never had the opportunity of judging his tastes or thoughts'. [9]

Soon the garden was required for more intensive development and the family moved half a mile further east to Elizabeth Street,[10] Bethnal Green. This was the peak of the father's striving and from here on life defeated him. From 1801 to 1831 the population of England increased by 50 per cent, while the population of Middlesex increased even more.[11] This pattern continued. With galloping population growth came galloping inflation, broken by crises of recession. Bradlaugh Senior was lucky to stay in constant employment, but his weekly income, which never amounted to more than two guineas, was unable to keep pace with rising prices and rents. Accommodation was at a premium and tenements were divided and re-divided. Other difficulties confronting him were the growth of his own family (before there were family benefits) and the increasing chore of walking to and from work involved in moving further from the City (before there was metropolitan public transport). Whatever his faults—and commentators have tended to exaggerate them in a way his son never did—he was a hard-working, conscientious man who used his meagre talents as best he could to help his family. For a few extra shillings he exercised his considerable penmanship in evening work at home or the office and his fishing expertise in writing articles for dreary journals. He even did some newspaper sketches and short stories. But his efforts failed to stem the flow of poverty. The family made a final move, this time back into the built-up area, to a four-roomed dingy terrace house, 13 Warner Place (South),[12] Bethnal Green, one degree above a slum.

Bethnal Green was, and is, a somewhat more cosmopolitan district than Hoxton. The main industries were silk weaving and cabinet making, the origins of many of the weavers being French Huguenot.[13] What cheerfulness there was centred on the taverns, and drunkenness and brawling were rife. It was a period of great harshness before the development of the modest Victorian conscience of the 1850s. Indeed it was not till Henry Mayhew's *London Labour and the London Poor* (1851-62) that anyone thought the running sore of what was becoming the richest city in the world worthy of diagnosis. From his impressionable years Bradlaugh was to experience the conditions that gave him an abiding interest in social welfare, housing and sanitation, the temperance movement and the population question.

While possessing a natural gaiety, which shone throughout his life in the family circle or with intimates, and in flashing sallies at the

14

expense of some religious or political opponent, he early found that life was not much of a laughing matter. His father worked and struggled all his life and what was there to show for it? What was the rottenness at the heart of the greatest empire in the world? More importantly, what could be done to cure it? As a boy he lacked tin soldiers; but he did not spend his time in envious sulking. He made his own out of steel nibs. And, with the help of his 'gentle, sweet-natured'[14] sister Elizabeth, to whom he was always affectionately close, he cut out newspaper figures for enactments of *The Miller and His Men*. Otherwise he seems to have led a solemn and somewhat isolated life, scarcely a childhood at all, painfully conscious of his responsibilities as the eldest child.

When he was seven he was sent to the handsome brown brick and stuccoed school newly opened in Abbey Street[15] near St Matthew's parish church. This was a British School,[16] a Quaker foundation, but the pupils were apparently made to tremble more in the name of the master than in the name of the Master. In Bradlaugh's unconscious this regimen was associated rather with the Church of England than with the Society of Friends and he later recalled the establishment as a National School.[17] He could not have stayed there long. Concerned at ruler wounds whose scars were obvious enough to be recorded when he entered the army ten years later, his parents removed him, at considerable financial sacrifice, to a nearby private school and then to Marshall's boys' academy in Coldharbour Street,[18] off Hackney Road. By eleven his formal education was complete. Apart from religious knowledge he had acquired little beyond the three Rs, but those he had learnt well.[19]

Outside school he showed a precocious interest in the social and political ferment of his time. The year of his birth was one of great exultation and great bitterness.[20] The Great Reform Bill of 1832 was hailed as a triumph for 'the People'. In reality it strengthened the Whigs, who 'for the divine right of kings . . . had virtually substituted the divine right of the Revolution families'.[21] The new manufacturers joined the old landowners and merchants in what they were pleased to call, in the electoral address of the Birmingham Union, 'a great, a glorious, and a bloodless victory' which 'it has pleased Almighty God to grant to this nation'.[22] Wealthy Nonconformists found room with Anglicans under the parasol of the establishment. The percentage of adults with the vote rose from five to 7.1, an increase of a bare quarter of a million. By 'the People', Lord Brougham explained, he meant the middle classes. Whereupon the new haves blandly thanked

15

the masses who had aided the political unions in forcing through the Bill, and told them they could now go home as their job was done. Supporters of the National Union of the Working Classes declined dismissal in this lordly way. Soon they had injury added to insult when the 'Reformed Parliament' found seats for men even wealthier than before. Possessing 'very powerful interest out of it',[23] they tried unsuccessfully to block Shaftesbury's first Factory Bill. For the masses it was a moment of truth. At this point 'there is a sense in which the working class is no longer in the making, but has been made'.[24]

Other events in 1833 interestingly foreshadowed Bradlaugh's later career. Slavery was abolished in the British Empire just two months before the death of William Wilberforce. The year also saw the death of a famous Indian reformer, Raja Ram Mohan Roy,[25] and of Hannah More,[26] the establishment's answer to Thomas Paine. Trouble in Ireland evoked a repressive Coercion Bill and a conciliatory Irish Church Bill. Within the Church of England, alarmed by the recent political upheaval, sprouted the conservative Oxford Movement. Five years before, Nonconformists, and four years before, Roman Catholics had lost most of their civil disabilities, but a proposal to extend rights to the Jews passed only the Commons, not the Lords. The Quaker Joseph Pease claimed the right to affirm instead of taking the oath on assuming his parliamentary seat, citing in his support an Act of 1749 which allowed Quakers this alternative in courts of law. The matter was referred to a Select Committee, which decided in his favour; and the House then allowed him to affirm.

Popular discontent simmered away. In 1838 it produced the People's Charter, which was launched by a General Convention of the Working Classes with a petition of 1,280,000 signatures the following year. Favoured London sites for boosting agitation were Clerkenwell Green and, a little later, Victoria Park.[27] By the south-west boundary of the park was the main speakers' site, Bonner's Fields.[28] Here the Chartist orators gathered. But even before this area was opened up in his part of London, Bradlaugh had become interested in the Chartist cause. Probably stimulated by reading a volume of William Cobbett[29] lying among his father's meagre assortment of books, at the age of ten he crept 'after much hesitation, and with great trepidation'[30] into a chandler's shop and bought a copy of the Charter with a precious halfpenny.

When he left school he first became an office or errand boy, at five shillings a week, with his father's firm of solicitors at 9 Cloak Lane,

16

near Cannon Street. At the age of fourteen his potential had been recognized sufficiently for him to become wharf clerk and cashier to Messrs Green, Son, & Jones, coal merchants at Britannia Fields, City Road Bridge.[31] His spare time was spent at political meetings. After some falling away the Chartist movement was gaining fresh impetus, and Bradlaugh was deeply impressed at this time on first seeing its 'moral force' leader, William Lovett.[32] The following 'year of revolutions' saw the great fiasco of Kennington Common on 10 April 1848. At a supporting rally in Bonner's Fields Bradlaugh made his political debut with a short speech. He was also present at another Chartist fiasco the following Whit Monday. Over a thousand constables, a third of them with cutlasses, the first Life Guards and 400 Pensioners came to quell an anticipated insurgence in Victoria Park. Some random charges were made and Bradlaugh was struck with a truncheon. But rain and advance intelligence of police preparations kept away the speakers, while a cloudburst washed away whatever crowd or enthusiasm remained into the surrounding taverns.

The following year saw Chartism declining fast towards its fall. But Bradlaugh's personal life took a dramatic new turn. In 1840 a daughter church of St Matthew's, St Peter's,[33] had been consecrated near his home and an assistant curate from the original parish instituted as priest-in-charge. Nothing of him survives but an illegible tombstone in the churchyard and a neat prim hand in the registers of both churches, but he has gained a minor celebrity in the annals of British Christianity and freethought. For spokesmen of both ideologies have attributed to the Rev. John Graham Packer a key role in determining Bradlaugh's later career.[34] Though not themselves churchgoers, his parents dutifully sent their children to the local Sunday school. Charles's high moral earnestness and intelligence early marked him out as a student teacher, and when the Bishop of London announced a forthcoming confirmation he was, as the most apt scholar, charged to make a special study of the Thirty-Nine Articles so that he could meet the main barrage of episcopal questions. Ever painstaking in what he did, the boy went one better and sought out the Articles' biblical credentials. Whereupon, to his shocked amazement, he discovered not only a general discrepancy but even internal discord among the several Gospels. How could this be if the Bible were the Word of God and the Church of England the Church of God? It is the sort of thing that adult Christians, especially in our day, take in their stride, but this conscientious boy thought there must be some explanation which had escaped him. So he 'ven-

17

tured to write the Rev. Mr Packer a respectful letter, asking him for aid and explanation'.[35] This request, unique in the pastor's experience, so riled him that he wrote at once to the parents of the errant lamb denouncing this display of 'atheism' and suspending him from his Sunday school duties for three months.

Far from atheistic at the time but sensitive at being in disgrace, he absented himself entirely from the church over this period. Home was not a congenial alternative on these idle Sundays, for the reverend gentleman with misplaced though conscientious zeal followed up his salvo. He took to visiting the family regularly and eventually shamed the elder Bradlaugh into regular churchgoing. In the meantime he persuaded him to adorn the living-room with improving texts, the one chosen for the wall opposite Charles's chair being 'The fool hath said in his heart, There is no God'. Glad to escape this constricting atmosphere, the boy slipped off to Bonner's Fields on his day of rest. Politics flourished there as usual, but the Lord's Day was particularly marked by freethought orators. They were always pleased to answer questions or stage impromptu debates, and to these invitations the young Bradlaugh, who considered himself a good Christian, was happy to respond. Though they were scathing with smart alecs they were always kind to genuine seekers after truth, and took quite an affectionate interest in their encounters with the gangling but fluent and deeply sincere youth. Just as he was patently fast growing out of his shabby clothes, so they felt he might as quickly grow out of his youthful creeds. They found his inchoate political ideas similar to their formulated ones, and another interest they had in common was teetotalism. This came to the notice of Packer and the faithful and disturbed them as much as his incipient scepticism.

One of these heretics was James Savage. His brother John had gained some celebrity at the time of Bradlaugh's birth through raising the cry of 'no taxation without representation', refusing to pay taxes and having his goods distrained. They were rescued and returned to him by a sympathetic populace. James was also an old friend of George Jacob Holyoake, a well-known Chartist and Owenite Socialist. In 1842 Holyoake had briefly edited the first atheist journal, *The Oracle of Reason,* and then served six months for blasphemy on suggesting, at a meeting in Cheltenham, that while the people were distressed it would be wise to put the Deity on half-pay. Presently Savage invited Bradlaugh to an indoor debate, a great honour for one so young, on 'The Inspiration of the Bible'. The youth defended the good book with considerable eloquence but went away sadly feeling he had lost the debate. Then there ensued a period of bitter internal dialogue. He later described 'how he flung himself down and prayed aloud to God, if God there were, to give him light and help, and how no answer came from the void above him, from the empty air around'.[36]

His new friends brought him into contact with 'infidel literature', among which was *The Diegesis; being a Discovery of the Origin, Evidences, and Early History of Christianity, never yet before or elsewhere so fully and faithfully set down*. No doubt Bradlaugh was struck by the following sentence in the Prolegomena:

> 'To suppose that belief or unbelief can either be a virtue or a crime, or any man morally better or worse for belief or unbelief, is to assume that man has a faculty which we see and feel he has *not*; to wit, a power of making himself believe, of being convinced when he is *not* convinced, and not convinced when he *is*; which is a being and not being at the same time, the sheer end of "all discourse of reason".'[37]

This seemed to Bradlaugh so much to the point in their conflict that he at once sent the book off to Packer with a request for comments. The response was immediate. A hasty conference was convened with the youth's father and employers and an ultimatum was given to him to change his opinions within three days or lose his situation. Just before the time ran out he left both job and home.

We can now see the incident in some sort of perspective. In a physical sense it disrupted Bradlaugh's life, gave him at a most impressionable age a bitter taste of what happens when Christian bigotry and reverent agnosticism work hand-in-glove, cut off his links with orthodoxy and threw him into the willing arms of his new freethinking friends. One of Bradlaugh's biographers declared in 1880 that 'had the Rev. Mr Packer shown a little more self-control and discretion, Bradlaugh might never have been a Freethinker, and the thousands of persons whose opinions were changed through his influence might have remained Christians to this day'.[38] At that time respectable Victorian opinion sympathized with his father and cleric as wrens who had raised a monstrous cuckoo in their nest, but a few years later, when their assessment of Bradlaugh had changed, they turned on Packer for alienating so worthy a youth through his wicked lack of Christian charity. Certainly a modern psychologist might have foretold the results of this essay in human relations, but it is also true that there is a school of Freudianism which interprets atheism as 'rebellion against the father-figure.' It is, however, pretty certain that Bradlaugh would have thought himself into freethought whatever his circumstances, and would have written and lectured on it. But it is arguable that his activities might have lacked those aspects of a crusade which they were to assume.

Packer later gave his own version of the rift, blaming Bradlaugh Senior: 'Bradlaugh . . . incensed his father to a great degree; but whether he turned him out of his house I do not know, most certainly he did not do so at my instigation or suggestion. On the contrary, I endeavoured to reclaim the young man, and to pacify his father.'[39] To this the son replied: 'Mr Packer says it was not "at his instigation or suggestion"; but it occurred after his visits, and was never spoken of before.'[40]

Packer's indignation can be understood, especially in the light of the Victorian convention that little boys—and big boys—should be seen and not heard. The *Diegesis* was, at least in Britain, as novel as its author claimed. Somewhat turgidly it set out to prove, among other things, 'the monks of Egypt the fabricators of the whole Christian system'.[41] It is also possible that the parson knew more than Bradlaugh of some incidental notoriety. The author was the Rev. Robert Taylor, a former surgeon and clergyman, who had proclaimed his apostasy in the *Times*, founded a Christian Evidence Society nominally 'for the suppression of infidelity and scepticism by means of rational discussion alone'[42] but where he took malicious delight in acting as devil's advocate against all comers, lectured like a bishop in full canonicals at his own deistic chapel and the heretical Blackfriars Rotunda, and spent three years in gaol for blasphemy. It was hardly the most tactful thing Bradlaugh could do to forward his curate of souls a manifesto from such a writer, and later afforded his hostile brother, William Robert, the opportunity of observing: 'This action on the part of my brother, therefore, would scarcely betoken the true humility of an anxious inquirer, but rather the spirit of braggadocio.'[43] This it was not. But neither perhaps was the threat what it seemed. He later reflected it 'was never intended to have been enforced'.[44]

Adrift in the world with little education and few prospects, the youth took shelter for the first week with an old Chartist whose kindness he never forgot and for whom in later years, till the old man's death, he gave an annual benefit lecture. Then he moved to less crowded though no more affluent accommodation. By a remarkable coincidence, just up the road from his father's house, at number 1, lived the second family of the pioneer of British atheism and the foremost promoter of British republicanism in the early nineteenth century. This was Richard Carlile. For his republication of Paine's *Age of Reason* and other heretical writings, his political journals and his refusal to pay church rates, he had served in all nine years and four months in gaol, been fined thousands of pounds and had five Fleet Street[45] premises successively closed down. Two years after this astonishing career began in 1817, he made a compact with his wife Jane, with whom he did not get on, to separate as soon as he could afford a settlement. This was not until 1832. In the meantime she had joined him in gaol for two years, more in pursuit of business than out of any devotion to either her husband or heresy, together with his sister and many of his shopmen. They had all been released in the twenties, but soon Carlile was imprisoned[46] again, together with Robert Taylor, his companion on 'an infidel mission'.

Thrilled by this epic of courage, Eliza Sharples, an attractive and cultivated young woman from a prosperous Lancashire family, where she was 'surrounded with every luxury, with a carriage at my command and everything that the heart could desire',[47] came to London to carry on the Blackfriars Rotunda, which Carlile was running before his arrest. When he was released from prison, two years later, they formed a liaison[48] which lasted till his death in 1843, just after he had paid a visit of encouragement to Holyoake in Gloucester Gaol. In his later years he offended many of his former admirers by drifting into mysticism and calling himself a Christian, while his Christianity was of so unorthodox a nature that it failed to attract a respectable following. Nor did the liaison commend itself to many. No provision was, therefore, made for Eliza and her three young children, and they drifted into wretched penury. After a time the legend of his heroic days was revived but few wanted to be reminded of the common law widow and family. An application on the family's behalf was made to Holyoake, 'at the time Mr Holyoake was lecturing upon the life and character of Richard Carlile',[49] but he ignored it. In 1849 another application was made to Holyoake, and she herself, desperate for influence to be exerted in obtaining situations for her children, wrote to Thomas Cooper, a well-known freethought[50] and Chartist poet and lecturer of the time. Whether as a result of these exertions or not, a few months later she was installed with the help of local freethought friends in a rambling house at the corner of Warner Place, where a coffee room was established for her to manage and at the back of which a temperance hall was built.

Here it was that Bradlaugh had had his debate with Savage.

It was a remarkable but not a particularly happy household. If Eliza had a sweeter temper than Jane she had much less capacity for business, and the coffee room languished. Poverty had made her self-pitying, lamenting the youthful comforts she had thrown away and her children's blighted hopes. Bradlaugh had to share a bed with Julian, 'a quiet steady sedate truthful boy' of fifteen. Then there was Hypatia, 'so called after the beautiful and philosophic Hypatia so celebrated for her wisdom and learning in the City of Alexandria that the priests jealous of her influence and being no friend to their chicanery waylaid her, dragged her into their church and at the foot of their sacred altar scraped the flesh off her bones with oyster shells'. Hypatia Carlile was 'a delicate girl of thirteen only fit for needlework', who had stitched collars twelve hours a day for two shillings a week and so become 'prematurely a woman subdued in spirit by too early knowledge of care and anxiety'. Theophila was a year younger, 'entirely free of superstition . . . born to lead, a very Nelson of a woman'.[51] After these descriptions it is a little surprising to find Bradlaugh pictured by a biographer as 'falling hopelessly in love' with Hypatia and not Theophila; but he 'sighed in vain'.[52] Packer and a scurrilous Congregationalist, the Rev. Brewin Grant, spread rumours consummating their relationship.

With now a little more security than in the garret she had left, Eliza was desperately anxious to improve the children's meagre education. She had set her heart on the Post Office for Julian, millinery for Hypatia and a school for Theophila. Bradlaugh gladly joined in their orgies of study, books being propped up round the breakfast table. An old friend of Richard Carlile's taught them French, inviting himself to dinner so as to have the excuse of providing a joint to supplement the family's usually frugal vegetarian diet. Savage taught Bradlaugh Hebrew. Other friends gave him 'an imperfect smattering of other tongues'.[53] Then there was the university of hard knocks on the platform. Bradlaugh spoke and debated regularly, often on temperance, at the Warner Place hall, another temperance hall over stabling at 2 Philpot Street,[54] off Commercial Road, the Wheatsheaf in Mile End Road, and Bonner's Fields. Here his youthful appearance earned him the name of 'baby'[55] and his ability drew substantial crowds.

Public debate 'in the "high and palmy days" of Owenism and Chartism, and the hazy horrors of Red Republicanism . . . went on fast and furious'.[56] Through it Bradlaugh made many lifelong friends.

22

The most important of these was Abraham Hooper, a plasterer by trade, who kept a coffee house in Beehive Passage, Leadenhall Market, off Leadenhall Street, and was so highly thought of that he was later given the Freedom of the City of London. To Hooper Charlie was 'the young enthusiast' and 'the boy'.

Bradlaugh also thought of authorship. Stimulated by his confirmation researches he went on to produce, in May 1850, an *Examination of the four Gospels according to Matthew, Mark, Luke and John, with Remarks on the life and death of the meek and lowly Jesus*. In his Preface he needlessly apologized for its presentation, 'it being written at my place of business (not having enough time elsewhere)', and modestly hoped it would be read if only for the quotations from Taylor, Paine and Cooper. Unlike Taylor, he thought he could 'prove that there did exist a man named Jesus who was called *Christos* the good man'.[57] Though he set out to 'demonstrate to any one that the 4 Gospels as we have them are a jumble of nonsense and contradiction', the work is remarkably free of the usual exaggerations, if not of the apostrophizings and struggling jokes, of juvenilia. He then proceeded to an *Hypothesis of the life and death of the Therapeutan*[58] *Monk Jesus by some called Christ*. Finally, there was his *Reply to Brindley's Reply*,[59] a refutation of the farthest ranging contemporary apologetics seeking to promote Christ as the consummation of Old Testament prophecies.

These theses were never published. Neither were his verses at the back of the manuscript volume. They are in the rhetorical manner of the early Shelley and Ebenezer Elliott, 'the Corn Law Rhymer', to whom he was first attracted:

> Progress, for thee the muse I court,
> For thee I'll strive and fight;
> Each onward step is dearly bought
> To freedom's cheering light.

And again:

> For what do they keep down the humble and poor,
> For what keep the bayonets bright,
> For what oppress the labourer more and more
> But to keep up their pow'r and might?

Carlile, 'crushed with iron hand/Because he dared to break the band/ Of Ignorance and Crime', is the only person referred to, but some pages are missing. Perhaps they contained poems written in honour of Louis Kossuth, who had led a short-lived Hungarian independence uprising the previous year and then fled to England, and Giuseppe

Mazzini, architect of the Young Italy republican movement and the Italian Risorgimento (resurrection), who had a similarly brief triumph in Rome at about the same time. These tributes were 'printed on a fly sheet of paper' and were perhaps his first publications, though they became 'scattered and out of print, much to Bradlaugh's satisfaction',[60] in his lifetime. Though he never pretended to poetic talent he always had a facility with words and a resonance with the lyrical imagination; but his personal taste in literature had to be subordinated to ideas, ideals and the cause of human betterment. Not for him the parnassian, the private or the apocryphal.

The first publication of which we have any record was in prose, and strictly prosaic. It was produced shortly after the *Examination of the Four Gospels* and advertised as being on sale for one penny at 1 Warner Place 'and all booksellers'. The dedication of *A Few Words on the Christians' Creed*, in a manner brilliantly pioneered by Carlile and followed by other beleaguered writers of the century, was to the Rev. J.G. Packer himself, 'the Incumberer of St Peter's, Hackney Road'. Packer was still on the warpath. One stormy night he persuaded Bradlaugh senior to seize a board advertising one of Charlie's lectures in the nearby temperance hall and bring it home under his Inverness cape—until the monthly nurse persuaded him to take it back to avoid a prosecution. The clergyman also warned his flock against the hazards of local infidelity to such good effect that on one occasion when the screams of a baby seemed to flood from the hall a cry went up among the populace that a pagan sacrifice was taking place and the building was stormed. In his pamphlet Bradlaugh compared the Lord God with 'the bigoted parsons of the present day', pointed out the absurdity of the orthodox Trinity and Incarnation, and concluded with the challenge:

> 'To those readers who approve of this, I beg leave to ask their assistance in the work of progress by their acting as well as talking among their fellow-men. To those who disapprove, I say, "Answer it".'[61]

If it did not receive an answer it at least provoked a counterblast in the *British Banner*,[62] which was Bradlaugh's first press notice.

But what really made his reputation was a lecture at Philpot Street in October 1850 on the 'Past, Present, and Future of Theology'.[63] He had begun to frequent the publishing bookshops, particularly the radical ones. Among the most notable of these was that run by James Watson at 3 Queen's Head Passage, Paternoster Row, near St Paul's.

In the twenties Watson had moved to London from Leeds to replace the drain on Carlile's fast-vanishing shopmen and then served twelve months for issuing Elihu Palmer's *Principles of Nature*.[64] Ten years later he went to prison for another six months for selling Henry Hetherington's unstamped *Poor Man's Guardian*. In the upsurge of revolution that spread from Europe in 1848 he was in the vanguard of republican publishing. At Watson's shop Bradlaugh met his printer, the younger brother of George Jacob Holyoake. Austin Holyoake[65] was gradually being weaned away from his early religious beliefs through printing his brother's *Reasoner*,[66] the premier infidel weekly. He took Bradlaugh along to the Literary and Scientific Institution at John Street, near Fitzroy Square, which up till a few years before had been Branch A1 of the Halls of Science established by Robert Owen. It was at that time the main West End centre of freethought and radicalism, and here the youth was introduced to the celebrated G.J.Holyoake. Disappointed in his natural and spiritual fathers, endowed with a great sense of tradition, enthusiastic over ability, especially that exercised in the popular cause for little material reward, and displaying almost personal gratitude to anyone who had gone to gaol in defence of free speech, Bradlaugh was most deferential. Holyoake warmed and agreed to take the chair at the youth's lecture at Philpot Street. It was announced that 'a Collection will be made after the Lecture for the Benefit of C. Bradlaugh, victim of the Rev. J.G. Packer, of St Peter's, Hackney Road'.[67] The advent of Holyoake to the humble East End hall was a considerable boost to the youthful lecturer's reputation, and his address was a great success. In later years the chairman recalled that 'he spoke with readiness, confidence and promise'.[68] And a member of the audience recorded: 'After the lecture, discussion was invited. Two gentlemen, one a clergyman, the other a City missionary, responded to the invitation, but only to get worsted in the encounter.'[69]

Reference to the collection emphasized Bradlaugh's precarious financial situation. Already he had more than enough admirers to supply the modest wants of so valuable a propagandist. Holyoake graciously opened the columns of his paper to reports of his outdoor forays, in which the pattern of his life was already set:

'When I first came out, I attracted a little extra attention on account of my having been a Sunday School teacher, and, therefore, had more opposition than some of our other friends; and as the Freethinking party did not muster quite so well as they do now, I met with some very unpleasant occurrences. One Monday evening in particular I was well stoned, and some friends both saw and heard several Christians urging the boys to pelt me. As, however, the attendance of the Freethinkers grew more regular, these minor difficulties vanished. But more serious ones rose in their place.'[70]

His opponents began applying to the police to have him moved on. They insinuated themselves with the freethinkers so as to gain personal details about infidel speakers, thus adding an air of truth to later untrue charges, tore down his bills and even applied for a warrant against him. On that occasion the magistrate refused to grant it. Bradlaugh was not always to be so lucky in his dealings with the courts.

But the youth was far too proud to accept the charity of his friends. He had come across the essay on 'Self-reliance' by Ralph Waldo Emerson, the American Unitarian minister who had become a pantheistic essayist and poet, and copied out large parts of it. Its message was:

'To believe your own thought, to believe that what is true for you in your private heart, is true for all men—that is genius. Speak your latent conviction, and it shall be the universal sense . . . Whoso would be a man must be a nonconformist . . . What I must do, is all that concerns me; not what the people think . . . For nonconformity the world whips you with its displeasure . . . Trust your emotion . . . Fear never but you shall be consistent in whatever variety of actions, so they be each honest and natural in their hour . . . The soul is raised over passion . . . Virtue is the governor, the creator, the reality . . . Insist on yourself; never imitate . . . And so the reliance on Property, including the reliance on governments which protect it, is the want of self-reliance . . . Nothing can bring you peace but yourself. Nothing can bring you peace but the triumph of principles.'[71]

All this had rather more to do with his platform than with his professional life; but not unnaturally he believed no really self-reliant man could be out of a job.

At first he set up in high spirits as a coal merchant, printed business cards and even popped one under his father's door. The difficulty, however, soon came home to him that without capital or business connections not only was he unable to extend credit after delivery, but he was obliged to collect cash before he could put through an order. Most potential customers were too cagey for this

26

and he came to depend on a dangerously small number of regulars. One of these was a baker's wife who lived at the corner of Gold-smith's Place,[72] Hackney Road. As this was opposite Warner Place she had presumably seen Bradlaugh moping around, making furtive contact with his sister Elizabeth, and felt sorry for him. But soon she heard of his lecturing notoriety and challenged him with being an infidel. His diplomatic evasions were fruitless, and with a shuddered 'I should be afraid that my bread would smell of brimstone' she terminated the contract. The loss of ten shillings' commission was a crippling blow to a meagre business, but he tried to struggle on for some months more. Eventually he abandoned the coal trade and undertook the sale on commission of sixpenny buckskin braces for one of his admirers, T.J. Barnes of Goswell Road. It was probably a tactful way to support the young fellow, for he was given breakfast and dinner and sold very few braces.

Despite this kindness he fell into debt to the tune of £4 15s and grew increasingly despondent and sensitive. Once he rushed out of a coffee house when a friend's older brother ordered a meal for him. A subscription was organized and that too offended him. On 15 December 1850, after his Sunday lecture in Bonner's Fields, he was invited home by the sons of an admirer. At dinner he suddenly lifted his arms above his head and said, 'Mr Record, how do you think I should look in regimentals?' Samuel Record replied: 'My boy, you are too noble for that.'[73] The family thereupon began a collection for him. Four days later he walked out of their lives.

'Anyone who will travel through Ireland, and see our barracks . . . will see a coercive law as onerous as the Curfew law.'
– Charles Bradlaugh at a lecture at Steinway Hall, New York,
on 6 October 1873.

Almost aimlessly he set off, without a word to anyone, to find some
way of shedding his burden of debt. The East End he knew to be
barren, so he turned westward. Eventually, he reached Charing Cross.
There on a poster was an advertisement for smart young men for the
East India Service, offering a bounty of £6 10s. Enough to pay his
debts, and leave something over for books. He was soon directed to a
local bar where the recruiting sergeants gathered. Bracing himself
against the unaccustomed stench of liquor, he marched into a cellar
and found a fat and beery sergeant who looked after the East India
Service. In a fatherly way he was led to the recruitment centre and
signed up. To his indignation he then found himself in the 50th
Foot, a home regiment. His sergeant had previously borrowed a man
from his colleague in this regiment and Bradlaugh was the repay-
ment. Astonishingly more vocal than the average recruit he broadcast
his protest at this confidence trick to all who would listen and many
who would not. At last he found a sympathetic ear, that of the
medical officer. He explained that Bradlaugh was signed up for the
home service and this was irreversible, but he could use his influence
to get the youth into any local regiment he preferred. At this time
Bradlaugh had no particular interest in India and was perhaps un-
consciously relieved at not having to drop his old life so far behind
him. Allowing himself to be pacified, he looked out of the window
and selected what appeared to him to be the smartest uniform. It was
the scarlet, blue and gold of the 7th (Princess Royal's) Dragoon
Guards, popularly known as the 'Black Horse', 'Strawboots' or the
'Virgin Mary's Bodyguard'.[1]

He sent a message concerning his whereabouts to his grandmother,
who dispatched his anxious aunt Mary round to his parents to break
the news. His brother William later described how Bradlaugh Senior
at once went and 'had an interview with him at the depot at Westminster; and as my brother was determined to remain in the service,

28

my father obtained permission from the commanding officer for my brother to spend Christmas Day at home, on condition that my father himself brought my brother back to his quarters at night'.[2] Some sort of reconciliation was patched up, to the relief of them all. William declared that 'my father and brother kept up a regular correspondence all the time'[3] he was away. For he soon had orders to leave England. The 7th Dragoon Guards were then stationed in Ireland.[4]

It was on the voyage across to Dublin that Bradlaugh met his new barrackroom mates. It was a traumatic experience. He had been brought up among young toughs, but not in any intimate relationship, and his associates in recent years had been earnest, book-loving fellows like himself. Fortuitous events had driven him, and others like him, into the army but they were not the staple intake. A generation later, when steps had already been taken to introduce some sort of professional standards into the services, Dr Cameron, Inspector-General of Military Hospitals, complained: 'We are enlisting the very scum of society.' A Radical London paper echoed this:

> 'We may judge of the association into which respectable recruits are forced, by the fact that in 1873 no fewer than 2,025 men were discharged from the British Army as "bad characters", being an increase of 342 upon the preceding year, while the average number constantly in the hospital was nearly 4,000. In 1874 there were advertised for nearly 7,000 deserters.'[5]

The position was exacerbated by unhygienic barracks in garrison towns where booze and brothels were the only amenities, vicious sentences for minor infringements of discipline,[6] and cynical disregard by most of the officers and chaplains. Hair-raising tales by deserters and those who left less dramatically, did not advance recruitment among sober artisans, and it was desperate young chaps who tended to be brought in. Finding, in too many cases, already brutalized material to deal with, the officers, mostly young gentry who had bought their commissions and were simply marking time till the family estates or a wealthy marriage came their way, deemed a brutal regimen the only appropriate treatment. Left to their own devices, the men relaxed with more than the usual horseplay of youth.

Bradlaugh and his mates were still in civilian clothes. Unwisely turning up in his Sunday best, he cut a ludicrous figure in a silk hat and black suit fraying at the edges and shuffling up his overgrown ankles. With hairless cheeks, boyish appearance, pallor and emaciation from recent malnutrition, he looked a vulnerable as well as a ridiculous butt, ripe to be roughed up. They started on the hat. Finding that, weak and dispirited and beginning to feel sick from a stormy crossing, he did not retaliate, they turned to his other possessions. These were in a sealed box. They broke it open, perhaps hoping for some secret spirits. To their astonishment, apart from a few personal effects all they found were a Greek lexicon and an Arabic vocabulary, which soon figured in a wild game of football.

Then it became apparent that the ship itself was in difficulties. Its goods had been badly stored and in the rolling and heaving began to move. Fearing a disaster and being short-handed the captain asked the young dragoons to help him shift the cargo, promising them five pounds for their labour. All of them, even the sick ones, turned to with a will and the day was saved. As the storm abated, however, so did the captain's generosity, and he had to be pressed to honour his agreement. Finally he sought to escape his full liability by giving five shillings each to three or four of the strongest recruits in the hope that they would quell the rebellion. The stratagem might have worked had not Bradlaugh, moved more by collective injustice than by harsh treatment to himself, recovered his spirits and launched into a magnificent harangue denouncing the captain for his mendacity and threatening a letter to the *Times*. It had its effect and the captain paid up. Bradlaugh's fellows saw that learning had its uses, gained a new opinion of him and plied him with herrings and biscuits which they had filched from the ship's stores.

After a three day voyage the ship reached Dublin, serene and lovely centre of English Protestant power in Ireland. The recruits were whisked off at once to Newbridge Barracks, Kildare, where the regiment was stationed. At the routine interview with his commanding officer, Lieutenant-Colonel C.F. Ainslie, he was coolly looked up and down and then asked 'And what do you think you are fit for?' It was not an auspicious beginning. Before his uniform arrived he was set an undemanding task, white-washing the Quartermaster's room. Having nothing but what he stood up in he set to work in his black suit. It did not remain so long. The Quartermaster's daughter came in and, struck by his absurdly pathetic black and white figure, lean and forlorn, she slipped out and returned with a glass of port to invigorate him. What was her astonishment when, wildly gesticulating with his paintbrush, he refused it and delivered her a passionate lecture on teetotalism.[7] It was clear that this was no ordinary recruit.

The uniform arrived and with it drill. Here he was a dismal flop. Though he had led the hard life of an East End boy of the period, he had no experience of organized sport. Dull, repetitive movements bored him with their seeming purposelessness. But his greatest challenge as a cavalryman was coming to terms with horses. As his Paymaster Sergeant said of him, he was 'no horseman, and had a very unhappy time of it in the riding school as a recruit. He was not particularly well built for riding, nor had he in his boyhood been accustomed to the care of horses.'[8] It was necessary to be able to vault into the saddle without the aid of stirrups, and with the encumbrance of a sword at one's side and spurs on one's ankle, which caused the horse to start forward if they accidentally touched it. His animal soon noticed his nervousness and complicated his task by unpredictable evasive action. His riding master, Blinkhorne, he regarded at the time as 'the personification of the Demon'.[9] For he 'was compelled to ride until the blood ran down his legs, and before these wounds had time to heal he had to be on horseback again'.[10]

This difficulty was a regimental as well as a personal problem. For appearance's sake, 'at the General's inspection and on other special occasions of that kind he was employed as a barrack-room orderly, or with the cooks, and so escaped appearing on parade'.[11] In a culinary capacity he was little more successful. When he served the potatoes underdone the men 'pelted him with his produce'.[12] The distinction he had earned on board ship was rather set back by his poor showing on the exercise ground. Through his love of tea and books his comrades called him 'Leaves', and the more aggressive of them continued to plague him. Sometimes ingenuity came to his aid. He detected those who persistently stole his hair oil by mixing a foul-smelling liquid with it. But in the end it was physical rather than moral force that established his position.

Despite his own contributions the food was ample and sustaining, if unimaginative, and the regular exercise was also developing his body.[13] One day, when he had been teased by a leading boxer of the corps, he thought it time to challenge him to a fight. Seconds were found for both young men and the contest began. The usual excited crowd gathered round, though no one thought the issue was in doubt. Leaves was badly knocked about but stayed on his feet. His adversary got over-confident and left himself unguarded. On the advice of a second Leaves struck out, with more strength than skill, and his opponent went down. The contest dragged on to Homeric lengths. Leaves was further battered, the other man again floored. The challenger was just wondering whether he could in all decency sue for peace when 'to his intense surprise and delight his adversary suddenly threw up the sponge!'[14] His reputation among his fellows suddenly rose. Because of the clumsiness he had not yet grown out of, but partly perhaps as a tribute to his usual amiability, the general verdict was: 'You are bound to go down if Leaves hits you, but you're a fool if you get in the way of his fists.' The teasing stopped and they began to make use of his special talents. He found himself much in demand in the composition of letters, notably love letters requiring particular delicacy. Inevitably it was asserted in later years that he became something of a 'barrackroom lawyer' but his superiors denied this.[15]

After a few months it was announced that the regiment was moving to the Portobello Barracks, Dublin. It was the custom not to supply coals for the last couple of days before a move and the soldiers were allowed to scrounge wood. Bradlaugh was unaware of this custom and turned up without any. When taxed by his mess-mates with thus letting the side down he crossed the barrack-yard in broad daylight, unchained the normally vicious guard-dog of the 17th Lancers and bore its kennel off in triumph. An inquiry was held but everyone was so impressed not even the Lancers gave him away. When established in Dublin his main off-duty interest was lecturing at French Street temperance hall between the well-known radical James Haughton and the Rev. Dr Spratt, a Roman priest whom he recalled as 'the good old father'.[16] Sometimes he was given leave for these performances, sometimes not. Then his mates knotted their blankets together to let him out. It was not always possible to return by the same way and he then had to report and submit to arrest. The punishment for this unusual offence was kept nominal, for Bradlaugh usefully lectured the men on teetotalism in the barracks when not crusading abroad. A more serious misdemeanour, recalling his pre-army days, occurred in the local Rathmines Church. The vicar on one occasion observed that he did not imagine the guardsmen in his congregation could understand the felicities of his sermon. Leaves at once wrote him a letter not only evincing understanding but pointing out numerous errors and illogicalities. The following Sunday disparaging reference was made to this letter from the pulpit, whereupon 300 swords came crashing to the floor in disapproval. An inquiry was ordered and Bradlaugh summoned to appear, but the unexpected arrival of the Duke of Cambridge crowded it out.

After almost a year in Dublin the regiment tranferred to Ballin-collig, a village five miles from Cork. Leaves was by this time mastering his cavalry skills, becoming tolerably proficient with sword[17] and on horseback. But his clerical ability had proved so useful and his conscientiousness so obvious that he was appointed orderly room clerk. In this capacity he was able to give special help to Major Arthur Cavendish Bentinck, father of the Duke of Portland, in making up his regimental returns, and was lent the officer's fishing tackle. His teetotalism did not prevent his being on good terms with the Quartermaster's family, and together with his 'amiability of dis-position'[18] commended him to Regimental Sergeant Major David Scotland, a deeply sincere Christian. His colonel had an equally high opinion of him. He was once entrusted with the job of escorting to the nearest town a particularly violent prisoner in handcuffs, and here his own trust served him well. The man requested that the handcuffs be removed till they reached their destination. Bradlaugh agreed and they proceeded without incident. On arrival the man demonstrated that he could snap the bands at will.

There were two occasions when the colonel gave him valuable support. A local landowner built a gate across a right-of-way, which was opened to the gentry but shut against the soldiers and Inniscarra peasants. After investigating the legal position Leaves led a party which broke up the gate, writing on it 'Pulled up by Charles Bradlaugh, C. 52, VII D.G.'. When the landowner complained to Ainslie he was advised to check up on the position as the private was usually sure of his facts. No prosecution occurred. The next com-plaint 'was even more critical'.[19] Bradlaugh ordered an insolent new officer, who swore at him, out of the orderly room. Soon the officer returned with the CO. A courtmartial was in sight. When asked for an explanation the private requested the officer to repeat his words. This he faithfully did. Whereupon Bradlaugh told the colonel his accuser's memory must be at fault as could not have used language so unbecoming an officer and a gentleman. With a dry 'I think Private Bradlaugh is right; there *must* be some mistake', Ainslie left the room.

After the right-of-way incident the local peasants plied him with produce. But feelings between them and the dragoons were not usually amicable. When the regiment was stationed at Dublin they were challenged to turn up during the roystering Donnybrook Fair.[20] At six foot one and a half inches Leaves was the shortest of the sixteen men, armed with shillelaghs, who were picked to uphold the honour of the Seventh. Protecting themselves with their left arms and lashing out with their right they just managed, black and bloodied, to plunge into the fair and fight their way out. But the rain of blows on this guard arm 'set up a tendency to erisypelas in the arm . . . perhaps as dangerous as a broken head'. [21] Such an incident need not have involved malice on either side, but Bradlaugh was already coming to see, and soon saw more graphically, just why the Dragoon Guards were stationed in Ireland: to suppress the peasantry. [22]

There was one particular incident that burned into Bradlaugh's brain and remained alight to make him, through thick and thin, a champion of Ireland and the Irish for the rest of his life. He was one of a troop sent to protect the law officers and agent from Dublin who had come to make an eviction near Inniscarra. As the mud huts were vacated they were knocked down. A woman rushed out of one of the hovels into the rain and sleet. She flung herself on the ground before the officer in charge, Captain Beauchamp Walker, a martinet with his men, whom Bradlaugh confessed in 1873 he had 'not yet quite forgiven'. [23] She asked that her house might be spared. Her husband was dying of the fever and wished to expire in the place where he was born. Saying he had his orders and was pressed for time, the captain ordered the man to be carried out and he died in the sleet as the soldiers demolished his home. Three nights afterwards, while Bradlaugh was on sentry duty, there was a cry outside and the guard found the woman dying in delirium with one dead baby in her arms and another clinging to her nipple. Addressing an American audience years later he asked:

> 'If you had been brothers to such a woman, sons of such a woman, fathers of such a woman, would not rebellion have seemed the holiest gospel you could hear preached?' [24]

There was one thing which made this existence bearable. In August 1851 a student teacher had come to Ballincollig. This was James Thomson. Just a year younger than Bradlaugh he was also there through force of circumstances. He had been sent as a boy to the 'Model School' of the Royal Military Asylum, Chelsea, and the authorities had determined for him the uncongenial career of an army schoolmaster. At that time he was 'wonderfully clever, very nice-looking, and very gentle, grave, and kind'.[25] He was probably a repressed homosexual, but he fancied himself passionately in love with a fourteen-year-old girl of 'dreamy earnestness of expression',[26]

Matilda Weller, daughter of an armourer sergeant. It was not long before the aloof and studious Private Bradlaugh was transferred from Dublin, and the two at once became firm friends. As Leaves strode to and fro on guard duty, or as they both relaxed off duty, they would discuss politics, social questions, religion, the whole world of ideas. In most of these subjects Bradlaugh set the running, but in literature he found his superior. Thomson had a great talent for lyrical verse, which, as he had no ambition, he simply handed across to his friend as he churned the stanzas out. It was one of those intense platonic friendships of the late teens that neither man ever forgot. There are also brief references in Bradlaugh's letters to an Irish 'sweetheart',[27] but he saw her infrequently.

Then something happened which made Bradlaugh think again of home. A message came that his father was gravely ill.[28] He was granted compassionate leave but Bradlaugh Senior died on 24 August 1852 while his son was still on the way from Ireland and was buried in St Peter's churchyard. William later painted the improving picture of his 'big soldier-brother' collapsing in the hallway with the repeated cry, 'If I could only have knelt by his coffin and asked his forgiveness!'[29] This is almost certainly embroidered, but years later Bradlaugh upbraided Packer with dividing him 'from a kind father, and from a home in which I had been well — if not fondly — treated'.[30] When he returned to Ireland, the following month, he went down with rheumatic fever and at the same time his beloved grandmother Mary Bradlaugh died. Meanwhile the firm in which the confidential clerk had drudged for twenty-one years recorded his devoted service in the *Times* and J. Lepard, the senior partner, wondered what he could do to help the family, short of actually paying a pension to the widow.

In January 1853 Thomson returned to Chelsea, where he heard in July of the early death of Matilda Weller. There he wrote of

'Old memories hidden but cherished
In a heart-nook deep and calm;
They have not faded and perished
Like the old friends they embalm.'[31]

Bradlaugh's loneliness increased. After his brother's death William spread the libel, not without a grain of truth, that he kept up 'a regular correspondence with his mother, constantly informing her of the hatred he had towards his captain, saying that unless she obtained his discharge he would put a bullet through this officer'.[32] Lepard was having some difficulty in getting William and Harriet, the youngest Bradlaugh children, into the British Orphan Asylums at Clapham Rise. Elizabeth wrote to Charles to see if his well-connected officers could help. He wrote back:

> 'You have a great deal more to learn of the world yet, my dear Elizabeth, or you would not expect to find an officer of the army a subscriber to an Orphan Asylum. There may be a few, but the most part of them spend all the money they have in hunting, racing, boating, horses, dogs, gambling, and drinking, besides other follies of a graver kind.'[33]

In June his great-aunt Elizabeth Trimby, who had promised to purchase his discharge but never got round to it, died leaving almost £79 to his mother. While she was trying to make up her mind what to do, Elizabeth wrote to ask how much his discharge would actually cost. He replied that the total, including his passage home, would be £32 13s 6d. 'I would not wish to rob you and mother like that . . . though I would do anything to get from the army'.[34] The only way he could really support his family, whose responsibility they were to an eldest son, was by gaining more remunerative employment, whilst in the army he was expected to suppress riots during the coming elections in Ireland. His mother was about to open a nursery school, but she was herself dogged by ill health. At length Lepard intervened. He ascertained from Bradlaugh's adjutant that 'his conduct has been extremely good and I beg also to add that he is always considered to be a clever, well-informed and steady young man'.[35] In fact 'he was about to be promoted for good conduct to be a sergeant'.[36] Bradlaugh's mother confessed 'it was by Mr Lepard's wish that my son should be purchased off. I do not regret its being done. He is very steady and a strict teetotaler, has been so 5 years.'[37] Bradlaugh 'gave a loud "hurra" from pure joy'[38] when he heard in October he would be bought out; and on the 14th, with a 'very good' character from Ainslie, his discharge was confirmed.

It would be quite wrong to regard his army service as three lost years. If he emerged almost as poor financially as he had entered, he was greatly enriched in physical development, in knowledge of the world, in learning to adapt to strange circumstances and every manner of men, and in first-hand experience of the real effects of British imperialism. In James Thomson he had for the first time found an intellectual equal on which to hone ideas. And the drill, which at first he despised, came to be faced as a needed discipline. In later years his public meetings and demonstrations were organized with military precision. As Bradlaugh came well out of his relationship with the army, so in a sense did it. For a brutal and un-imaginative period, his officers handled this unusual and in some respects difficult recruit with considerable insight and flexibility. No one appreciated this more than he. He always looked back on his army days with a certain affection and nostalgia, and of all the groups whose rights and improved conditions he took especial pleasure in championing, none was higher than that of servicemen.

CHAPTER THREE — THE ICONOCLAST

'I have deemed that I attacked theology best in asserting most the fulness of humanity.

I have regarded iconoclasticism as a means, not as an end.' — *National Reformer*, 28 February 1863.

On his return to London Bradlaugh found many changes in the course of three years. Besides his father, grandmother and great-aunt, Eliza Sharples Carlile was dead. Her children and many of his old freethinking friends had emigrated to America. Packer had so harried the Warner Place Hall that one trustee left London, the mortgage was foreclosed and the building 'fell into other hands'.[1] The political excitements of 1848-50 had quite died away.[2] British republicanism had died in its crib despite the efforts of the revolutionary wood-engraver and mystic, William James Linton.[3] In 1851 Kossuth came to England to a great reception, but nobody showed any inclination to emulate his rising or its defeat. Just before his arrival Chartism was able to report a mere 742 members, paying and non-paying. Linton declared: 'Let us *hope* that this is indeed the last of Chartism. What use is there in endeavouring to galvanize the corpse?'[4] Yet another corpse was Owenism. Its socialist message had grown reedy with repeated failures of its 'utopian' settlements, and its 'rational religion' struck most people as neither rational nor religious. By 1850 it had six branches and an income of £2 5s 3d. As a substitute Grey suggested a pioneering scheme of State socialism, to be backed by the government to the tune of fifty millions, in order to 'regulate the "monetary system" ';[5] but it attracted little favour.

At this stage G.J. Holyoake decided a new movement was needed. He had long been on the fringe of politics and remained so throughout his life. Indeed, in 1852 he was involved in an abortive plot to replace Palmerston with Derby as Prime Minister. But he had little real flair for politics and the nation was going though one of its periodic phases of disillusion with politicians of whatever complexion. Ideologically, he had been brought up in the Congregationalism of Carrs Lane, Birmingham, but had drifted away and quickly turned from deism to atheism under the influence of Charles Southwell, who founded the *Oracle of Reason*. His views never changed thereafter, but his circumstances did. From Gloucester Gaol, where he often wrote in total darkness, he emerged chastened and more cautious. Moreover, by 1851 the well-known atheists were disappearing. Hetherington died in 1849. Francis Place, the 'radical tailor' of Charing Cross Road who stage-managed the Great Reform Bill, was now an old man. Southwell was little heard of. Watson was not as active as before. On the other hand, under the influence of Lovett, liberal Christians were becoming more socially conscious than previously. In other popular causes in which Holyoake was interested, notably the co-operative movement, Christian Socialism was beginning to crowd out the original non-religious inspiration. Holyoake, who in difficult times 'sought the company of men of a higher social rank than himself, who he thought would be of his own intellectual level and who would therefore appreciate him',[6] was on intimate terms with the proprietors of the Daily News and other leading radical papers. These patrons of posts in newspaper promotion, management and journalism, on which Holyoake was setting his sights, had little taste for public atheism, whatever their private views. So, with their encouragement, he formulated the idea of a movement with the social aims of Owenism but without either its early theological debunking or its later canting compromises, the political aims of Chartism without its working-class prejudices or bogus land schemes, and the moral aspirations of Christian Socialism without being tied to an incredible creed. Holyoake also hankered after the leadership of a national movement and deemed that the best way to gain this was to found his own.

In the forties he had launched a Society for the Promulgation of Naturalism and a Society of Theological Utilitarians, but neither got properly off the ground. For his new movement he rejected, for one reason or another, established names like 'realism' and 'moralism'.[7] Under the influence of the lawyer and publisher, William Henry Ashurst,[8] the name he finally selected was 'secularism'. It was launched at the end of 1851 at a 'Free discussion Festival' in one of the Owenite Halls of Science, 58 City Road,[9] a tiny place just down from the heretics' graveyard of Bunhill Fields and across from Wesley's Chapel. At a second 'festival' in 1852 a Society of Seculars was formally proclaimed. Up and down the country those Owenite groups that had not disbanded became secular societies. To these Bradlaugh returned. Though he was unashamed of atheism he welcomed the positive implications of 'secularism', which were very similar to those of 'humanism' today. The new movement struck him as viable, and he was more concerned to consolidate what existed, if it were suitable, than to invent something else. So he threw himself into the cause of secularism. He found, however, a very different atmosphere among the freethinkers of England from that which he had left. There had meanwhile condensed a cloud of internal strife which was to billow round him for the rest of his life.

The Victorians have somehow lingered on in the popular mind as smug, courtly and hypocritical. Yet close study shows that, outside the underground artistic movement, it is our century that is mealy-mouthed. One of the byproducts of the moral earnestness and capacity for prodigious strivings of the Victorians was an intense argumentativeness[10] that needed little provocation. While Bradlaugh was in Ireland, his hero Holyoake had become the centre of controversy. It transpired that the main reason why Southwell was now little heard of was that in the *Reasoner* Holyoake had what was not just the chief but the only freethought weekly. Reports of Southwell's meetings were excluded because of his 'personal reflections'[11] on the Christian Socialists. Another happy result of this policy was that Holyoake came to appear the only active freethinker in Britain and, aided by Southwell's erratic temperament, supplanted him in the £30,000 will of a wealthy sceptic Samuel Fletcher. Anxious to avoid a public row, the founder of the *Oracle of Reason* wrote privately to his successor accusing him of 'senseless shortsighted egotism'.[12] Holyoake showed no such reticence. In his journal he attacked one[13] of his rival's pamphlets as a 'fourpenny wilderness'[14] and its author as 'a shuffling, inexplicit, ill-worded, disparaging, sarcastic, biting, reproachful, overbearing and disagreeable sceptic'.[15] Southwell produced *Another 'Fourpenny Wilderness'* commending Holyoake's 'art of damaging an opponent, and at the same time concealing from the vulgar eyes his disposition to damage, amid a heap of stereotyped cants about doing the respectful'.

By this time Holyoake had other substantial critics. The first was Robert Cooper,[16] the leading Northern freethinker and Owen's favourite disciple. At the first free discussion festival he commented that 'freethinking was in danger of becoming Conservative' through Holyoake's 'carefulness'.[17] Privately Thornton Hunt, son of the poet Leigh Hunt, declared Holyoake's moral orthodoxy 'as despotic as a religious orthodoxy'.[18] Its next target was the great American supporter of the abolition of slavery, William Lloyd Garrison, whom Holyoake accused of 'fighting in the grosser form'.[19] Angered that the father of secularism should keep his strictures for the opponents of slavery and not for its practitioners, his old colleague Linton moved in to the attack, calling him a 'professor of polite politics'[20] and a time-server who had 'shuffled out of atheism when his respectable patrons preferred a less obnoxious title'.[21] Savage also turned on him as 'a "secular" Kaiser' and 'secular Pope'.[22] Holyoake was a complex personality who genuinely imagined himself to the last as a great popular leader. But he was unwilling to suffer the opprobrium and penury which such a position entailed. He was also a snob, secretly ashamed of his humble origins. So he tagged himself on to middle-class supporters. They kept him in tolerable comfort but had little use for him except as a 'representative working man'. Thus he hovered uncomfortably between two worlds, exercising his talent for making 'enemies of friends without making friends of enemies'.[23]

It is speculative how much of this saga had come Bradlaugh's way, or whether full knowledge of it might have influenced his later career, but on his discharge he was more concerned about the immediate challenge of finding a job. This proved no easy task, despite his army reference, and his mother grew restive. But when he was offered the post of time-keeper with a Fulham builder at a pound a week, she objected to his working at such a distance from home. One day in December he wandered into the office of a solicitor, Thomas Rogers, at 70 Fenchurch Street. Rogers had no vacancy for a clerk but asked Bradlaugh if he could recommend someone as an office boy at ten shillings a week. He at once recommended himself 'till he can get something better'.[24] At the end of three months he got a five shilling rise. Of this period a critic later declared: 'The first of the Common Law Procedure Acts was then coming into operation; in the applications made at Chambers there was an opportunity for adroitness and astuteness; and Bradlaugh was quick to profit by the chance.'[25] Rogers recognized his talents and after nine months made him manager of the common law department. As a solicitor to several building societies [26] he was probably influential in helping Bradlaugh to supplement his income by acting as secretary to a society at Hayfield Coffee House, Mile End Road. But the indefatigable young man also found time to return to his old propaganda. Anonymous letters were sent to Rogers, who simply asked that his clerk should 'not let his propaganda become an injury to his business'.[27] So he adopted the name 'Iconoclast'.

Bradlaugh's legal knowledge served the radical freethought movement better than the oratory, not to mention the bickering, of his older colleagues. In 1852 a hall was built in Goldsmith's Row,

Hackney Road, by the subscription of a number of poor men, and, indeed, the owner of the land himself contributed. When the building was finished it was dedicated at a meeting presided over by Robert Cooper and addressed by Holyoake. Whereupon the 'freeholder' asserted that his wife really owned the land, and he was unable to create a lease. Finding that the secularists had no redress in law, Bradlaugh offered a penalty rent; but this was refused. So he organized a party of men who overnight demolished the building stone by stone. Where the law had no remedy direct action did.

More auspicious developments were then under way in Bradlaugh's world. William Maccall, a Unitarian minister who had left the church to become a prolific pantheist writer and reformer, sketched *The Outlines of Individualism* [28] as a new creed. Taken up by John Stuart Mill, Herbert Spencer, Samuel Smiles, and in a modified form by Bradlaugh himself, it was to become a dominant strand of Victorian thought. In November 1853 Holyoake announced a 'New Secular Book Depot, No 147, Fleet Street', [29] to be conducted by Holyoake & Co., Booksellers and Publishers. With the help of a subscription he had just taken over the business of his publisher and potential rival, Watson, and acquired his copyrights, books and premises as a Central Agency. Then a friend promised Holyoake £1,000 and, recalling the palmy days of Carlile, he decided to move into 'the street'. A first-floor room at 147 became the committee room of the London Secular Society, whose president was first Watson and then Holyoake, and whose secretary was J.P. Adams, organizer of the East End propaganda. Printing presses were moved in to 'strive to put the classics of freethought into the hands of the people'. [30] Readers of the *Reasoner* might have gained the impression that this had never happened before, though only the year before Edward Truelove, for nine years secretary of the John Street Institution, had opened a bookshop at 240 Strand and begun publishing the Reformer's Library. But people were impressed by the Fleet Street House and the discords simmered down. After being shown the *Reasoner* account books, Southwell was convinced its editor was not making a fortune and graciously replied: 'I wish, ever have wished, to be on friendly terms with you.' [31] By the end of the year the House had become the centre of a German freethought organization, and Owen 'came especially to give us his benediction'. [32]

That Christmas Bradlaugh met the Hooper family for the first time. They lived at 21 Anglesea Street, near the Abbey Street school. All of them were radicals and freethinkers except the mother, whose god was respectability. Her husband was republican, teetotal, non-smoking, rough but good-natured. Their eldest daughter Susannah Lamb, belatedly baptized by the redoubtable Packer, was two years older than Bradlaugh and known for her 'kindness of heart and gentility of nature'. [33] She had few intellectual gifts but shared her father's radical views and was anxious to learn. Before long Bradlaugh was courting her in person and by letter, where he found love lyrics by James Thomson invaluable. Honestly he admitted the source. And he wrote his own. Much as he liked Bradlaugh, Abraham Hooper was a little anxious about his financial position and told him bluntly he was not 'a very saving character'. [34] Charles was living at home now and helping to support his family, though the youngest two safely got into Orphan Asylums early in 1854 and Elizabeth was working. But having 'never had any real chance in life', [35] she had minimal earning power. By November 1854 Bradlaugh described his prospects as bright. He was then earning £65 a year from Rogers and £35 from the building society, and chasing a job offering £150 plus. Admitting his tendency to extravagance, he likened it to Susannah's own. Shortly afterwards Hooper gave his blessing and the couple started to make plans. Charles suggested that as his mother intended to let the two upstairs rooms it would be more economical if, on their marriage, Susannah and he moved into them at ten shillings a week rather than support two households.

At this time relations were again less than harmonious among Bradlaugh's secular colleagues. Robert Cooper had made accusations similar to Southwell's: his articles and reports of his meetings were not being inserted in the *Reasoner* and his pamphlets were kept from view at 147 Fleet Street. In his defence Holyoake retorted that Cooper's writings were 'a rhetorical bore'. [36] The reply was not published. Whereupon Cooper told Holyoake that 'he had borne such treatment too long' [37] and launched a rival paper, *The London Investigator*. In the opening number he said that secularism 'need not shroud itself in refined obscurities' or lead people 'into a maze of ambiguity and incertitude'; and, with a lightly veiled innuendo, 'We aim to be a Reasoner but not a Trimmer'. [38]

Meanwhile, at his solicitor's office, Bradlaugh was learning the ramifications, limitations and benefits of the law. Especially when he entered the courts for the first, but far from the last, time as a plaintiff. In the course of his business he had been sent to demand certain account books in the possession of another solicitor. As they were not given up he seized them himself and bore them off, but was given in charge. Not getting an apology, he brought an action for wrongful imprisonment and won £30 damages. Soon afterwards he made legal arrangements of another sort. They had religious over-tones. On 5 June 1855 Iconoclast went to church. No doubt it was Mrs Hooper's wish that it should be a white wedding. Banns had been published in the usual way, and apparently in St. Philip's, [39] Stepney, nobody knew of any contrary 'cause, or just impediment'. Mrs Bradlaugh Senior was one of the witnesses, and the couple moved into Warner Place with friendly intentions on both sides. Poverty did not however help relations in the kitchen and Susannah soon wanted to move. After a few months the couple went to live at 4 West Street, [40] Bethnal Green.

During this period Bradlaugh was involved in a popular cause which brought him minor celebrity. It was in the zone where politics overlapped religion to embrace social conditions and civil liberties — a zone which Iconoclast was to make peculiarly his own. The issue was the Lord's Day laws. They were as illogical then as now, and involved more vital issues. Lord Robert Grosvenor had attempted to revive the 1677 Sunday Observance Act with his Sunday Trading Bill. [41] This was more than a triumph for the sabbatarians and an irritation for everyone else. It struck a mortal blow at the large class of street traders who could find no other employment, and it was worse than an inconvenience to the working masses who had no other day on which to buy provisions and cheap clothes and visit the barber. John Leno, 'the working-man poet', fomented an agitation which roused Dickens's sympathy and quickly fired the poor of London. On Sunday 24 June a demonstration was organized in Hyde Park. No speeches were allowed but thousands jeered the nobility as their carriages promenaded up and down Rotten Row, and one or two peers were intimidated into getting out and walking to save their coachmen from Sunday employment.

A yet larger demonstration was called for the following Sunday and the authorities took fright. After consultation with the Home Secretary, Sir George Grey, the Commissioner of Metropolitan Police issued a decree banning the event. Bradlaugh saw one of the posted bills and decided:

> 'The tenor of it seemed to me to be forbidding the assemblage, and I had not heard then, and have not heard now, that Sir Richard Mayne has any power to forbid my going into the Park; therefore I went.' [42]

Accompanied by Hooper he found a large and orderly crowd already gathered. After a time hooting and groaning broke out and some noblemen's horses shied. Whereupon the police, spoiling for a battle, charged with truncheons flailing. Women were knocked down and trampled over. Bradlaugh observed to his father-in-law: 'It is lucky they are no sisters of mine, or else they would stop to pick them up.' But there was little he could do. Then he saw a short man by himself being hit by four or five policemen as he pleaded, 'For God's sake, do not hit me — take me!' Bradlaugh rushed across. Pushing one truncheon back he roared, 'The next man that strikes I will knock him down!' The police were so astonished they put away their truncheons and marched the man off as he had asked. An operation commenced to clear the park. As he was walking away Bradlaugh was needlessly prodded on with a truncheon. 'Do not do that, friend,' he expostulated; 'you have no right to do it, and I am stronger than you are.' The officer beckoned to two colleagues, who came over with weapons at the ready. When they were within reach Bradlaugh seized them, saying to the first policeman: 'If you attempt to touch me, I will take one of those truncheons, and knock you down with it.' And to demonstrate that this was no idle threat he took possession of both of them. A nasty scene was probably averted by a group of bystanders rushing over and bearing him off on their shoulders in triumph. When they put him down they wanted him to be their leader and organize the demonstration, but Bradlaugh remembered from his army days the hazards of impromptu operations and declined.

A Royal Commission was appointed to investigate the affair and he was one of eighty-six witnesses for the complainants. His laconic replies in examination and cross-examination were already typical:

'They found that you were rather a strongish man?—They would.' In the course of the hearing a mounted policeman showed contempt for Bradlaugh's professed ability at unhorsing, but did not accept his invitation to experiment. Stuart Wortley, the chairman, treated him with every courtesy, and he later recorded: 'I was very proud that day at Westminster, when, at the conclusion of my testimony against the authorities, the Commissioner publicly thanked me, and the people who crowded the Court of Exchequer cheered me . . . This was a first step in a course in which I have never flinched or wavered.'[43] In the mid-nineteenth century there were many lacunae in the law that have since been filled. Bradlaugh was not the first lawyer, lay or qualified, to espouse the popular cause in England, though such men were commoner on the Continent.[44] The physical force Chartists, for example, had had Ernest Jones, a qualified barrister. Most of them had spent some time in gaol. Bradlaugh was as prepared to face prison as the next man, if it were necessary, but realized he would be much more useful outside. He saw that if it were possible for the rich to drive a coach and horses through the law, it was equally possible for the poor to lead through a platoon of workers. In this instance, protesting that he had all along been concerned to rest 'the overtaxed thousands of the metropolis', [45] Lord Grosvenor withdrew his Bill. A new National Sunday League [46] to circumvent the sabbatarians was organized, and Bradlaugh became secretary of its East End branch at the Hayfield Coffee House. His lecture at Hoxton in mid-July on 'Sunday Trading and Sunday Praying' marked the beginning of his career as an acknowledged political lecturer.

Bradlaugh was also pursuing the more academic reaches of freethought, enlivening it with scathing comment on a rising evangelist of the period, the Baptist hot gospeller Charles Haddon Spurgeon. Iconoclast's youthful engagement with the Bible persisted as a labour of love-hate, but it had impersonal significance too. Great progress had been made in Germany in biblical, or anti-biblical, scholarship, but the English-speaking world had yet [47] to produce *Essays and Reviews* and Colenso on the Pentateuch. Though scepticism was growing quickly in intellectual circles, most savants had made little study of what they instinctively rejected, while millions of ordinary people still believed every comma in King James's Bible was divinely inspired. Now the Bible, like every other document of similar evolution, was more than just a textbook of the hereafter. It abounded in utterances of political, social and scientific moment, and was being used as a pin to knit the fracturing class structure of society. Until it had been discredited as an infallible reference book it stood solidly in the way of progress. Then there was God. This was another concept that university freethinkers were inclined to dismiss as a silly but harmless eccentricity. To Bradlaugh it had wider implications. The prophets of God sat in the House of Lords as a tight bloc vote, often crucial, against reform. Acting in the name of the Established Church, ministers of God at the local level dominated the parish council, the cultural and social life of the village, the guardians and overseers of the poor, the churchyard and most other burial grounds, the ancient charities and whatever schools there were, usually putting the interests of the Church before the needs of the people. The pastors of other churches were little better but had less power. Civil registrars for births, marriages and deaths had come in after 1836, but facilities were extremely limited in the smaller centres of population. Here the vicar was the only registrar. God was invoked to justify wars, just and unjust, canonize the vagaries of social convention as if they were immutable laws, and suppress free speech as an impiety on inconvenient occasions. Finally, [48] as a Victorian *autodidacte* Bradlaugh prized knowledge for its own sake as a pearl of great price, and wished to cleanse the mind of superstitious error as devotedly as any Christian minister wished to cleanse it of sin.

In whatever spare moments he had, he read everything that came his way. He was a fast reader and a lightning processor, and if he seldom read a book right through—a pardonable omission in confrontation with the average nineteenth-century tome—he rarely missed its essential features. In few fields did he claim expertise, but there were fewer fields in which he was quite ignorant. Philosophy he found interesting, but he believed with Marx that it is more important to change than understand the world. On basic points he thought out his position clearly, devised the shortest and clearest explanation he could, and avoided difficulties by thereafter adhering closely to this formula. Quite early in his career, for example, he developed his standard definition of atheism:

> 'I do not deny "God", because that word conveys to me no idea, and I cannot deny that which presents to me no distinct affirmation, and of which the would-be affirmer has no conception. I cannot war with a nonentity. If, however, God is affirmed to represent an existence which is distinct from the existence of which I am a mode, and which it is alleged is not the noumenon of which the word "I" represents only a speciality of phenomena, then I deny "God", and affirm that it is impossible "God" can be.' [49]

Whether or not this was sound philosophy [50] it was much less dogmatic or crude than Bradlaugh's detractors gave him credit for.

Most of the halls he spoke in at that time were tiny and have long since vanished. He did not care. Wherever two or three were gathered together in the name of truth he was always happy to expound. A hot ambition [51] blazed inside him, he felt destined for great things, but he took little interest in the jockeying for position that took place around him. The work of the moment was sufficient. If he were offered office, he accepted it gratefully. He gave scant attention to place-seeking or intrigues. His contemporaries were, on the other hand, as fractious as ever. After Southwell's emigration to Australia in 1855, the radical freethought movement was completely dominated by what one wealthy supporter described as 'Holyoakism'. [52] George Jacob Holyoake was now president of the London Secular Society and of a board of directors trying to form a national movement, and also the director of the Fleet Street House. Austin Holyake, who was known inside the movement as 'Jacob's ladder', was the House's company secretary and general manager. If any litigation occurred he, or one of his brother's religious employees, went to court and took the oath, which the older man always proclaimed he was too honourable to take. [53]

Never receiving its promised £1,000, the business was in financial difficulties. It was divided into quasi-agencies, which Holyoake later described as a profit-sharing arrangement. Actually they gave him a good return and powers of dismissal when things were going well, while minimizing his responsibilities, financial and prestigious, when they were not. In charge of the printing was John Watts. He was the son of a Wesleyan local preacher in Bristol and had himself been a Sunday school teacher. Largely responsible for bringing him into the secular movement was his younger brother Charles, who had come to London, met Southwell, and heard Holyoake and Robert Cooper. At first the Fleet Street shop was managed by Frederic Young, a former Unitarian, who Holyoake claimed was a Wesleyan [54] he had charitably employed. Then alleging the man had 'borrowed' some cash, he dismissed but did not prosecute him. Young's real misdemeanour was, it seems, his endorsement of Robert Cooper's allegation that Holyoake was suppressing Cooper's writings. As a result, the Manchester free-thinker supplanted Holyoake in the Fletcher will. Meanwhile Icono-clast peacefully continued his writing and lecturing, merely func-tioning 'by direction of the Committee of the London Secular Society during the absence of Mr Austin Holyoake Corresponding Secretary'. [55]

Though technically unqualified at law, Bradlaugh had been allowed to conduct cases in various London police courts on behalf of Rogers, and in January 1856 made some stir while acting as pro-secuting counsel in Manchester. One of his firm's clients was the Diadem Life Insurance Company, which was faced with a suspicious claim for £300. Bradlaugh was sent to investigate, personally arrested two men implicated in the affair, established that the will was a posthumous forgery, directed an exhumation operation involving dozens of bodies in an attempt to find the deceased and confirm poisoning, and, despite protests from defence counsel, conducted the prosecution himself. With these multifarious activities he had little time for personal affairs, but a daughter, whom they called Alice, was born to the Bradlaughs on 13 April. His lecturing continued unabated, as did his loyalty to Holyoake. Not that they agreed on vital matters of policy. The older man insisted that secularism was simply a movement to promote morality, science, reason and free discussion in 'this life' and had no comments to make on any other. Bradlaugh asserted that the churches made claims in these fields which could be answered effectively only by denying the theistic basis on which they rested.

More damaging charges and debts were growing against Holyoake. 'Occasionally we learn that some allege that works cannot be obtained through the Fleet Street House—that the business arrangements are not efficient.' [56] He tried to undercut the opposition by publishing *The History of the Fleet Street House. A Report of Sixteen Years.* Like the citizens of Rome after Julius Caesar's death, the freethinkers of Britain discovered to their astonishment that they were heirs. What had begun as an ordinary commercial concern when the prospects looked rosy had now become 'Property to be held on Trust, and when cleared to be Enrolled and placed under legally responsible management'.[57] The Director did not claim profits (which were non-existent) but a salary of £200 per annum. At the time, Bradlaugh was busily writing the first of fortnightly *Half-hours with Freethinkers*, devoted to Descartes. Collaborators in this project were John Watts and the emergent 'Anthony Collins'.[58] This was William Harral Johnson, an able but unstable man of obscure Huddersfield origin, whose multiple activities in the law, business and journalism were similar to Bradlaugh's but whose character was very different. About this time he amused himself by announcing his death and sending funeral cards, and writing 'Christian recantations to the *Bible Defender*, and Atheistical protestations to the *Investigator* by the same post'.[59] A worthier advent was that of the pioneering National Association for the Promotion of Social Science, in whose proceedings Bradlaugh showed the keenest interest down the years.

Despite its vicissitudes Holyoake & Co. remained publishers of the *London Investigator* until the end of 1856, when Truelove took over. Fletcher had died that May, with Robert Cooper still residuary legatee. Only a fraction of the £30,000 came his way. Shortly before his death Fletcher had invested £19,000 in government annuities and sold his business to his manager on an instalment basis. After settling duties and debts on the estate, and other legacies, Cooper had little for himself. But there was enough for a man who had been in bad health for a long time to retire and hand over his paper to 'Anthony Collins', [60] who had begun as confidant to Holyoake but turned critic. Indeed at this time it was probably true, as Johnson later [61] asserted, that the father of secularism had only two faithful sons, John Maughan, vice-president of the London Secular Society, and Iconoclast. In 1857 Holyoake decided to stand for parliament and chose Tower Hamlets as a constituency. Bradlaugh's house became his campaign headquarters. Thanks to his agent's hard work in the East London Secular Society, based on the Philpot Street hall, there were plenty of supporters for a largely secularist election platform, though few of them actually had the franchise. John Stuart Mill sent £10 but, probably realizing the bid was a forlorn hope, Holyoake allowed himself to be persuaded to withdraw so as not to split the vote for the official Liberal candidate Acton Smee Ayrton.

By this time Bradlaugh was ready to publish what evolved into his *magnum opus*, [62] *The Bible, What it is!*, in serial form. Holyoake & Co. undertook publication 'in the ordinary manner, without risk or cost to themselves, and at the full publishing profit'.[63] After the third number Holyoake declined further publication, though he made the author 'pay full publisher's profit for each copy which has been sold',[64] even after Bradlaugh became his own publisher. The House's Christian promoters [65] may have grown alarmed at this devastating biblical criticism, secularism's 'strongest and most impregnable position',[66] but the reasons for suspension given by the Director involved propriety. In the third number Bradlaugh had mentioned what was then a novel theory, that the Garden of Eden story was probably a sexual allegory. He also quoted extensively, and Genesis 19 and the depraved inhabitants of Sodom and Gomorrah were just around the corner. An anonymous reviewer of the series in the *Investigator*, probably Johnson, saluted 'one of the few young men who is rising in popularity as an author and lecturer, on our side, to replace those which our former lethargy and indifference have made aliens to our cause'.[67]

Almost simultaneously, sex raised its head in a yet more controversial way. In 1854 there was first published a book which was to pursue Bradlaugh almost to the grave. This 'Bible of the Brothel'[68] was George Drysdale's *The Elements of Social Science; or, Physical, Sexual and Natural Religion: containing an exposition of the true*

50

cause and only cure of the three Primary Social Evils—Poverty, Prostitution, and Celibacy. The identity of its author, described at first as 'a Student in Medicine' and later as 'a Graduate of Medicine', 'a Doctor of Medicine' and 'G.R.', was a closely kept secret. [69] Sections 1 and 3, with their censure of 'spiritualism' (religion) and their advocacy of birth control, were bad enough in an age that held Christianity aloft and kept sex under the blankets, but the second section was an outrage to the Victorian conscience. Intrepid readers came upon such advice as:

> 'The custom, moreover, of selecting one sole object of love ... has a narrowing effect on our capacity for affection ... Marriage diverts our attention from the real sexual duties, and this is one of its worst effects. Every individual man or woman is bound to exercise fully his sexual organs ... deem it perfectly honourable and justifiable to form a temporary connection ... Prostitution ... should be regarded as a valuable temporary substitute for a better state of things. It is greatly preferable to no sexual intercourse at all ... Chastity or sexual abstinence causes more real disease and misery in one year, I believe, in this country, than sexual excesses in a century.'

It was bad taste for egghead bohemians like George Eliot and George Henry Lewes[70] to put this into practice in St John's Wood, but to dispense such teachings to the masses at two shillings a head was criminal. In the spring in 1857 Truelove brought out a second edition of the book. The *Reasoner* [71] mixed high commendation with vague warnings, but 'Anthony Collins', while believing 'the work would be more appreciated and more useful' if the second section were separate, declared his 'conviction that this is one of the most useful books ever published', and his 'greatest hope is that it may get into families where the principles will be inculcated by a parent'. [72] Iconoclast took silent notice and continued to lecture on theology, challenging Holyoake's view of the implications of secularism, on his home ground, East London. 'I have vanity enough', he wrote to a supporter, 'to believe that when once my work is well-known it will force its own way.' [73]

In September the Bradlaughs moved to 3 Hedger's Terrace,[74] Cassland Road, Hackney, imitating the older generation's migration eastwards. Charles's attention, however, was soon brought back from domesticity to the freethought movement. Probably as a means of raising some ready cash, Holyoake had proposed a direct sale of his

51

agencies to the 'servants' of the House, whose position before had been imprecise. One of these was Thomas Wilks, who was responsible for the provincial news agency. After Holyoake had taken a deposit from Wilks he found a richer buyer, who was to pay a premium to be shared equally between the two secularists. This premium was never paid. Holyoake dismissed Wilks and concluded the sale to the other purchaser. As surety for his share of the premium, when he left Wilks took with him the agency account books. Believing that the arrangement between Wilks and Holyoake was a partnership, William Shaen, the latter's solicitor, prevented a simple action for recovery of the books. Instead the firm issued a writ for £146. It would seem that there was a credit arrangement whereby Holyoake supplied his publications for the provincial agency to Wilks, who was responsible for any failures to remit monies to Holyoake & Co. The figure cited in the writ represented sums owing but not overdue. Wilks had worked for Hetherington and himself suffered imprisonment, but he was, as Bradlaugh recognized, 'an uneducated man, and scarcely fitted to cope in a trial of wit with a man of calm reflection and cautious action'. [75] Knowing the claim was unjustified he ignored it, and Holyoake got an *ex parte* judgment. Both unwilling and unable to pay, Wilks was arrested and thrown into a debtor's prison. His wife and five children were left without support.

This was too much for Bradlaugh. He had tried to keep on filial terms with the father of secularism, even after his disappointment over *The Bible, What it is!* [76] Since his youthful obsession with his own wrongs at the hands of Packer and his riding master, he had come to react more sharply to injustices to others than to himself. He went to Shaen and offered to finance arbitration by a master of the Court of Exchequer. [77] This was refused unless Wilks would admit some element of fraud. Then Bradlaugh himself applied to Baron Watson to set aside the judgment. This was granted on condition that Wilks find security for the sum claimed. As this was unobtainable at short notice, appeal had to be made to the Court for the Relief of Insolvent Debtors. Against Bradlaugh's advice, Wilks's solicitors drew up a schedule on the basis that if Holyoake was claiming Wilks as his debtor for outstanding money, the provincial agents who owed it must be debtors to Wilks. In fact the money was payable to Messrs Holyoake & Co.; so Chief Commissioner Law, while declaring that 'Wilks did not appear to owe anything, and ought not to be a prisoner at all', gave Holyoake a perfect quotation for the *Reasoner* [78] with his observation that 'a more false and fraudulent schedule had never been brought before the court'. The case was remanded so the schedule could be amended. Holyoake quietly allowed proceedings to lapse. While thus claiming magnanimity, he left for Wilks 'a tendency to damage his character without giving him an opportunity of clearing it up'.[79] Meanwhile, he dismissed another agent who had lent Wilks money to support his family.

Holyoake's actions were probably motivated by resentment as his empire, such as it was, had begun to crumble. J.P. Adams had walked out to form a Society for the Promotion of Materialism. Holyoake's last disciple Maughan joined the doubters and began making enquiries into the numerous rumours. Some of Holyoake's enemies were clandestinely accusing him of downright fraud. Nobody was planning a *coup d'état*, most discounted the wildest stories, but everyone was discontented. The secular movement was making no progress. Indeed it was tending to regress. Holyoake blamed the presence of two papers, not on the best of terms, in a movement not large enough to support them. His opponents blamed his concern for his own reputation and financial interest at the expense of the cause. He alone was responsible for undertaking the ostentatious Fleet Street House. All the appeals of the movement were channelled into its support although nobody now believed in its efficiency or impartiality, and yet he remained accountable to none. As Cooper put it,

> 'The Fleet Street House in future must be considered either the property of Mr Holyoake individually, or of the promoters collectively. If the former, that gentleman ought to be allowed to manage it as he likes with such resources as he can command, *in his own name, and at his own risk*; and not with the funds of a party: if the latter, the promoters ought to have joint management, Mr Holyoake submitting his books and effects to them.'[80]

Still 'independent of all parties concerned',[81] in late November 1857 Maughan called a private and a public meeting of the promoters, subscribers and debenture holders of the House, attended by Bradlaugh, to consider the position. They asked Holyoake to take full responsibility and drop his assertion that the premises belonged to the movement. He refused to publish Maughan's report of the meetings in the *Reasoner,* so it appeared in the *Investigator.*[82] Simultaneously he issued two 'Institute Papers'[83] announcing that the House was to become the British Secular Institute for secularists and non-secularists to pursue 'Free-Truth' now that 'the darkness of past times' had vanished.

Calling *The Bible, What it is!* 'an obscene book', Holyoake refused even to advertise it, and Bradlaugh was 'compelled to appeal to the English body of freethinkers'. [84] Johnson joined in against the 'Atheistic Pope' with malicious enjoyment. Holyoake took advantage of the order of the Insolvent Debtors' Court, obliging Wilks to return the company's books, to make a portmanteau attack on his critics. He accused Bradlaugh of being the errant man's 'active legal adviser' [85] and Maughan of aiding and abetting him. Then the balloon went up. The whole saga of the Wilks affair came out in the open and the *Saturday Review* commented on the dispute. While deploring these 'Party Criticisms', Holyoake made a further attack on critics whose only excuse was they were 'inexperienced' and, apart from Maughan, 'young'. [86] Robert Cooper was now attacked, and replied with an accusation that the Director had 'usurped, by a *coup d'état*, a Secular despotism'. [87] Finally, Holyoake produced a *'soi-disant* propagandist balance-sheet' [88] whereby 'from being a recipient of public subscriptions as a help and gratuity, Mr H. ends by becoming a *creditor of the party, and claims £1,523 as his due'.* [89] By this time thoroughly roused and having, on rare occasions, 'something of Cromwell's Berserker temper', [90] Bradlaugh commented in characteristic manner. He gave little thought to meandering factionalism and the subtleties of slow character assassination—there were more important things to do—and his explosions left nothing to the imagination. Holyoake of course refused to publish this salvo, which appeared in the *Investigator:*

> 'You have made your statement and report in the *Reasoner,* and have put forward your balance sheet. I have read the whole with much pain, and I charge you with misrepresentation of actual facts; with wilful falsehood; with concealment, and over-statement, as it best suited your purpose. I deny that your balance sheet contains a proper account of receipts and expenditure; I deny that the auditors were appointed by the promoters; I deny the charge of avoiding "pecuniary responsibility". I challenge you to discuss the case on any public platform, and I offer to prove the main facts of the *Investigator* case, and to disprove the main case made out by you in reply.' [91]

Country secularists who knew little about Holyoake save by repute, which he sedulously cultivated himself, [92] affirmed, like Arthur Trevelyan, a member of the famous literary and political family, 'a thorough belief in your integrity and judgment'.[93] This opinion was far from universal.

In the middle of this row a fresh dispute with wider ramifications broke out. On 14 January 1858 a Roman patriot Felice Orsini, long simmering against the support given to the ancient regimes of the Italian city-states by the French Emperor Napoleon III, made an unsuccessful attempt on his life. Orsini had been in England in 1856 lecturing on 'Austrian and Papal Tyranny in Italy' and probably met Bradlaugh. As the Bonapartes were personal friends of the Queen and Napoleon had been invested with the Garter on his State visit to England three years before, the loyal British press denounced the Orsini outrage. This wave of righteousness infuriated a young republican, William Edwin Adams, who had helped Linton to print his *English Republic* and was then in an organization formed to propagate the teachings of Mazzini. So he dashed off a sympathetic pamphlet *Tyrannicide: A Justification* and took it along to Holyoake & Co. as the best-known publishers of 'advanced' literature. When he called back Holyoake declined[94] to publish on the grounds that he was negotiating with Mazzini for a similar pamphlet. Adams was glad to defer to Mazzini but when no news came of the other document he went to Truelove, whom Bradlaugh was finding helpful with *The Bible, What it is!* Truelove suggested changing the title to *Tyrannicide: is it Justifiable?* and using a *nom de guerre*. The title was changed but Adams insisted on his own name.[95] A few days after publication in February Truelove was arrested. No attempt was made to find the author, as it was assumed the unfamiliar name concealed a French exile.

A cry for press freedom at once arose, and a Truelove Defence Committee and Fund were started with Bradlaugh as secretary and Watson as treasurer. Support came from Mill, Trevelyan and Harriet Martineau. They were joined by Francis William Newman, a freethinking brother of the future cardinal; William Johnson Fox, the radical minister of South Place Chapel, Finsbury; Peter Taylor, a former chairman at South Place; and Joseph Cowen Junior, who had sponsored a Republican Brotherhood before forming the influential Northern Reform Union. This brought Bradlaugh into contact with the republican set. Soon he met Linton, the French *émigré* physician Simon Bernard, and the radical businessman Thomas Allsop. Allsop had in fact arranged for the manufacture in Birmingham of prototype bombs, which Holyoake secretly tested during his country tours, and had to flee to Santa Fe with a price of £200 on his head.

In France Orsini was executed. At the instigation of Count Walewski, the French Ambassador to Britain, Bernard was arrested. As both Truelove and Bernard had Montague Richard Leverson as their solicitor and Edwin James as their counsel, Bradlaugh became closely connected with the defence of Bernard. Also at Walewski's bidding Palmerston prosecuted a Polish refugee publisher, whom the Truelove Defence Committee defended as well, and brought in a Conspiracy to Murder Bill on 18 February.[96] Palmerston was defeated on a censure motion the following day and his government resigned. For the issue had become one of national dignity and brought out all the latent anti-gallicism in the English. Derby's government inherited the prosecutions. At public rallies Holyoake and Bradlaugh used the popular feeling to stir up hatred against the imperialist, pro-Vatican Napoleon. Fearing that attempts would be made to smuggle Bernard out of gaol for delivery to the French, volunteers kept a round-the-clock watch, and Bradlaugh organized a system of communications to keep in constant touch with the prisoner. Victor Hugo sent him a message of support for the London refugees from the land of 'Napoleon le Petit'.[97] Wherever Iconoclast went French spies tried to follow. On 31 March, after a lecture on Orsini, he amused himself leading his trailers on a wild goose chase and arrived home to find his second daughter had just been born. She was called Hypatia, after the Alexandrian freethought martyr rather than the youthful heart-throb.

At last Bernard came up for trial. It was the custom[98] then to starve juries into early decision; so to keep up the morale of a friendly juror Bradlaugh had his pockets well filled with sandwiches. The precaution was needless. So successfully did James play on the national sentiment that the jury brought in 'not guilty' in just over an hour. Still the attention of the French spies continued. On one occasion Bradlaugh literally smoked one out when, in a restaurant with Bernard and an old friend, Sparkhall, who helped to form an English legion the following year to support Garibaldi, he recognized a man pretending to be asleep at the next table and held a lighted spill under his nose. A few months later Truelove came up for trial for his 'libel' on Napoleon. But James, who had 'political ambitions',[99] privately arranged that the defence would withdraw the book. The Attorney-General withdrew the indictment and, much to the disgust of both Truelove and Bradlaugh, Lord Chief Justice Campbell dismissed the case.

Iconoclast had already distinguished himself among radical freethinkers as an able writer and lecturer. The Orsini affair displayed other qualities: that he was not only a fearless, but a disciplined and indefatigable agitator. From the respected Allsop, quietly allowed to return to England in September, he earned the label which literally followed him to the grave, 'Thorough'. In an age of developing admass he became almost over-night something of a national figure. It was a grim foreboding for Holyoake when, at the end of March, the London Secular Society moved out of the room it rented in the Fleet Street House. Publicly the secularists said that they were tired of the Director's autocracy. This was true; though there were signs of this quality in all potential rivals, especially Bradlaugh. But the authoritarianism would have been forgiven had Holyoake delivered the goods. What the secularists wanted was a leader, someone who would weld a national movement out of the heap of radicals and sceptics thrown up in all social classes by the technological explosion. Intellect and shrewdness were not enough. They were tired of shambling equivocations and genteel protests. Holyoake led a Walter Mitty life of hidden drama which, as he was not without courage, occasionally erupted into reality. But for the most part his propaganda reflected his person and his 'thin, tin-kettle voice'.[100] Bradlaugh was great in body and mind, in voice and charisma. On 18 April 1858 the tenth half-yearly meeting of the London Secular Society was held. Holyoake was in the chair. The report was read. It stated that he had not kept the promises made the previous November and regretted 'that any cause for distrust should have arisen'.[101] Vacating the chair he 'assumed a somewhat defiant tone but entered into no satisfactory explanations; announced his resignation as president, and deprecated the adoption of the report'. Iconoclast was elected in his place. The walls of great temples of church and state stood in his path, but the idol of freethought had, at least for the moment, toppled.

'Louis Blanc, Ledru Rollin, Victor Hugo ... were writers, talkers, and poets; good men to ride on the stream, or to drown in honest protest, but lacking force to swim against, or turn back, the tide by the might of their will.' — *The Autobiography of C. Bradlaugh.*

Iconoclast's first job was to lose his Cockney image. Ashamed of his forlorn appearance when first as a youth he mounted a soap-box, and obliged to dress soberly in his professional life, he began to cultivate an extreme formality[1] of dress on the platform in or out of doors: dark grey or black broadcloth, matching waistcoat, starched collar, black neckcloth. Indeed he was often mistaken for a Nonconformist minister, or even a Roman Catholic priest. He looked to his voice, naturally strong and musical,[2] he took special pains with intonation and the aspirate.[3] While remaining loyal to his East End friends he made more frequent visits westwards. Nine days after Holyoake's mantle had descended on him he addressed a meeting of the West London Secular Society at Hope Temperance Hall, Bell Street, whither Cardinal Wiseman, declaring that 'the open advocacy of atheism, by propagandists, among the lower orders, was becoming matter for serious concern', sent along an observer. Decades later she recalled a wandering 'h', 'evidences of insufficient education, an illiterate mind and a vulgar intonation', 'form of face and features unquestionably peculiar, decidedly the reverse of handsome, though indicative of intelligence and shrewdness' and occasionally becoming 'distorted with a revengeful and fiendish expression'.[4] Much of this caricature sprang from sectarian malice, but there was a groundwork of truth. He had then had little time to work on his voice to produce a classless and regionless production for national audiences. His youthful photographs show features, notably a long, overhanging upper lip obscenely out of control, that were far from handsome but of the type that took on impressiveness as he grew older, sterner and stouter. But, as with most great orators,[5] the most striking things about him were the eyes: 'large, protuberant, of that grey-blue colour which is most expressive, and they had depths of brilliancy, of passion, of menace that were calculated to somehow or other make you feel as if they could freeze your blood with terror'.[6] It was the fire within him coming out, the emotion otherwise under cast-iron control.

He had a vision of the New Jerusalem, where kings and priests, wars and famines, envy and hate were no more, where men were juster, wiser, kinder, better. In his later years especially, his audiences came from all classes and literally included poets and peasants, princes and proletarians, although mostly they were workers and tradesmen. We now know that he was little more successful than the churches in reaching the really 'submerged tenth', who have continued submerged. But to the artisan and trade unionist, the small businessman and self-employed craftsman, those whose formal education and earnings did not match their abilities, who were coming to demand that stake in the riches of the empire and the industrial revolution they had done so much to bring about, his was a message of high hope. By reason and common sense, by burning the old shibboleths and the tattered conventions, by self-education and self-help they would win through to the Promised Land. At the end of a hard day or a heavy week they would shuffle into some dingy hall, thick with smoke and gas fumes. At the appointed moment Charlie would stride purposefully in, arrange his books[7] on the lectern—in later years not waiting for the chairman if he had not arrived—and begin. He began tentatively, searching for truth[8] with his audience, finding an idea here and a quotation there, putting them together with quiet logic. Suddenly they fitted into place, they made a picture. He held it up for them to see, flourished it so high that the man and his image seemed to rise to the very ceiling, seared the description of it on their minds and exhorted them when they left never to forget it. As he sat down at the end of an hour they cheered and stamped and waved in a catharsis of delight, and there was a spring in their step as they faced the world anew.

From the metropolis he turned to the provinces. Owen and his disciples, Southwell, Holyoake and Robert Cooper, had evangelized the industrial towns of the North and large centres in the West Country. Iconoclast retrod the old paths. Then to the gasps of squire and parson he launched himself into new areas like East Anglia, into timeless market towns and clannish mining villages that had never in their entire history seen a freethought lecturer and rarely a radical politician, where supporters were as thin as spring ice and sometimes non-existent. They closed their halls to him and he spoke in the open air. They stoned him and he carried on unvanquished. They shrieked abuse and his stentorian voice rose above them all. The worse the opposition the shorter the interval before he returned. And gradually, on the second, or third, or fourth visit, things began to change. The squirearchy continued to rage together, the local newspaper to declaim, the odd heckler to cause a scene; but a hall, theatre or tavern opened its doors, the stoning and the threats of murder stopped, reasonable order prevailed as he spoke. Since his previous visit some village Hampden had defied the local tyrant, some mute inglorious Milton found a voice, some Cromwell proclaimed the commonwealth of man. Honourable Christians had expressed their disgust at their co-religionists' behaviour, and secret heretics suggested that there might, after all, be something in what he said.

All this took time, but he was prepared to wait. It also took money: the hire of halls, billposting, travel and hotel expenses, sometimes litigation. He neither charged a fee for his services nor gave free[9] lectures. He simply took whatever profit remained after all the expenses had been paid. For many years this was a negative sum. In his autobiography he recounted, 'for the encouragement of young propagandists',[10] his early experiences. One harsh midwinter evening he had lectured to a small audience at Edinburgh, and was to speak at Bolton the following night. After paying his bill at the Temperance Hotel he had only a few shillings more than the fare. To make his connection he had to rise at 5 a.m., missing breakfast. His train was delayed by a snow-storm and he missed the parliamentary train at Carlisle. The fast train was more expensive and he could book only to Preston, with fourpence halfpenny over for a mug of tea and a tiny pie. At Preston the Bolton train had gone and he had to borrow a ticket to browbeat the stationmaster into putting on an extra train. Once this was arranged he had the mortification of admitting to the guard he had no ticket and leaving his bag as security. There was just enough time at Bolton for him to run to his lodgings, wash and change before appearing in an unheated, candle-lit and foggy Unitarian chapel. In the discussion after the lecture an opponent upbraided him with the life of luxury he was leading as a paid propagandist against the Lord.

Bradlaugh had appeared as the main opposing speaker from the body of the hall after addresses by Holyoake on the implications of secularism and by Thomas Cooper, who had turned Baptist. But a new career for him as a formal debater began in June 1858 in Sheffield, an old-established freethought centre, with Brewin Grant, then minister of the local Lee Croft Chapel. He described Grant as 'a man of some ability if he could have forgotten his aptitudes as a circus jester',[11] but he was finally so stirred by his opponent's 'bounce and slander, misrepresentation and impudence'[12] that he exploded. Bradlaugh was accustomed to call every debater, in the legal manner, 'my friend', but after Grant's gibes at this courtesy and vilifications of freethinkers living and dead, he retorted:

> 'The habit, like a garment, fits me, and I have in this discussion used the phrase "my friend"; but believe me I did not mean it. Friendship with you would be a sore disgrace, and little honour'.[13]

From that time debates were sprinkled among Bradlaugh's provincial and London lectures, and were usually more lucrative. Sheffield organized a testimonial and he felt able to employ[14] a maid Kate, who stayed with the family till the disaster of 1870. On 16 May 1858 his reformist lineage was ceremonially displayed at the John Street Institution, when Robert Cooper fell ill in the middle of reading Robert Owen's annual address—a traditional occasion—and Iconoclast finished it. A month later the famous hall closed down. At its last meeting Bradlaugh gave 'a forcible and dashing speech, in which he compared himself to a young standard-bearer rushing forward into the fight, ready for any service in the good cause'.[15] Expressing pride in his distinguished companions he 'upbraided the working classes for their apathy to their best interests' in allowing the institution to close before a successor was built. In November the final accolade of the agitator came his way when 'Anthony Collins' resigned for undisclosed reasons and he became editor of the *Investigator*.

Gratifying as his propagandist work was, on balance it was costing rather more than it was bringing in. With family responsibilities at home and increasing responsibilities at the office, he had written to Rogers early in the year asking to be articled. 'I have my way in life to make—yours to a great extent is smooth and easy.'[16] The step would entail an advance of £80 stamp duty, which the young man could not afford. Rogers declined this proposal, but on 16 November Bradlaugh found a more accommodating solicitor in Thomas Harvey of 36 Moorgate (Street). Harvey had been a parliamentary agent, changed his address frequently, and had never been a member of any law association.[17] Whether or not Bradlaugh felt any misgivings, he appeared to embark on his other activities with a greater sense of confidence. He announced that the *Investigator* would not be 'the organ of one man' but 'in our pages we shall court the expression of opinion of every man, so he but express himself plainly and truly. We desire free thought and free speech, not for ourselves alone.'[18] In the middle of November he was one of the speakers, who included the radical cabinet-maker, Benjamin Lucraft, Ernest Jones and Digby Seymour, the Recorder of Newcastle, at a meeting of the Political Reform League recently inaugurated by a conference of delegates from all parts of Britain 'to form an union of the Middle and Working Classes'.[19] It sought modified Chartist demands: manhood suffrage, vote by ballot, equal electoral divisions and triennial parliaments. At the same time Bradlaugh heard of, if he did not meet, Christopher Charles Cattell, a former Christian who had become a tireless radical and a supporter, using his first names, of the Birmingham Secular Society. Thomson, with whom Bradlaugh had kept in correspondence, began contributing to the *Investigator* as 'B.V.',[20] opening with 'Notes on Emerson'. Then W.E. Adams, with whom he was now on friendly terms, became a contributor. By the end of the year Maughan, who had become financial manager of the *Investigator* in March and helped to make it a fortnightly, gave way to Iconoclast. With complete control of the paper, Bradlaugh hoped to make it a weekly like the *Reasoner*.

In January 1859 he paid his first recorded visit to Northampton, whose later association with him was to become an enduring part of British constitutional history. It was at the invitation of two local secularists, John Shipman and Joseph Gurney, the genial secretary of the Northampton Town and County Benefit Building Society,[21] popularly called the Freehold Land Society. This was formed in 1848 not only to provide homes for thrifty workers but 'to improve the Social, promote the Moral and exalt the Political condition of the unenfranchized millions'.[22] They had heard Bradlaugh speak at the John Street Institution, been impressed by his strength and sincerity, and invited him to address meetings at the Woolpack Inn, Kingswell (Street), Northampton, which were both crowded and orderly.

Back in London he threw himself into the growing demands for popular franchise and in March, as 'a young man well-known in the democratic circles', Bradlaugh gained his first report in the 'old thunderer', the *Times*. It was at a Hyde Park demonstration against 'the so-called Government Reform Bill', where he declared that 'all those who acted fairly and honestly in the sphere of life in which they were placed were as well worthy of their political rights as the greatest lords in the land'.[23] At a meeting in the Guildhall the following Friday the speakers included Lionel Nathan de Rothschild, a Jew recently allowed, after an eleven year wait, to take his seat for the

City in the House of Commons, the wealthy Congregationalist Samuel Morley, and Taylor; but when the cry arose for 'Bradlaugh' the Lord Mayor hastily closed the meeting and Iconoclast was dragged from the platform he had mounted in response. Cowen declared him 'altogether a likely man to go ahead if he has any backing'.[24] At the same time his close friendship with Bernard led to his meeting Mazzini and the French revolutionary socialists Louis Blanc and Ledru Rollin. His addresses on the French and Italian questions continued, provoking assaults from Catholic opponents and the banning of a meeting at St Martin's Hall by the direct intervention of Count Walewski. Bradlaugh was about to take legal action when the proprietor, indemnified by the government, volunteered damages. Bernard also introduced him to Continental freemasonry. He was admitted to the Loge des Philadelphes, founded in London in 1850 by *émigrés* who were members of recognized foreign orders as 'an institution essentially philanthropical, philosophical, and progressive. It has for its object the amelioration of mankind without any distinction of class, colour, or opinion, either philosophical, political, or religious; for its unchangeable motto: Liberty, Equality, Fraternity'.[25] Among its members were Mazzini, Garibaldi, Blanc and Rollin.

The excitement of these activities exhausted as it stimulated. There were also worries and disappointments. It had not been possible for the *Investigator* to become a weekly as Bradlaugh had sung in his first aria of editorship, and by April 1859 he had to say frankly, 'If our issue is to continue we must have sufficient support to protect us from debt and its accompanying annoyances.'[26] Debt and its accompanying annoyances were also stalking the offices of Harvey. It is questionable whether he ever paid the £80 stamp duty on Bradlaugh's behalf, though it would have been possible at the time for the clerk to have gained 'subsequent enrolment by a Judge's order, after the duty and "penalty" had been paid'.[27] Three decades later a libeller likened the situation to 'the general arrangement made between a clever attorney's clerk and a solicitor without practice', whereby the clerk could be said 'to employ the master, and not the master the clerk'.[28] The truth would seem to be that Harvey had little solid law practice and so was 'largely concerned in the promotion of joint-stock companies, and ... subsequently came to grief'.[29] The propagandist shield of Iconoclast had long since shattered to reveal the aspiring lawyer, Charles Bradlaugh, behind it, and his notoriety in both politics and heresy was not likely to commend him to the average respectable Victorian solicitor. A radical clerk was one thing; a radical partner was another. Bradlaugh's nose for talent was infinitely greater than his nose for character. He preferred to take people on trust, and, like many other young men, was to find snags hidden by pools of generosity. Harvey's readiness to provide what Rogers would not needed closer scrutiny. But for the moment he carried on in the hope that things would right themselves, and was able to assist Truelove legally in his forlorn[30] application to the Justice Room, St Martin's Lane, against the Clement Danes Church rate.

Soon accumulated overwork and strain took their toll. Bradlaugh went down with rheumatic fever. His recovery was slow. He was too weak and dispirited to play any part in the prosecution of Andrew Hepburn, 'who described himself as a public lecturer against infidelity and Mormonism'[31] and was paid by the rector of Whitechapel and other Christians to oppose Holyoake and 'Iconoclast—whom he described as the prince of infidels'. Hepburn also interpreted his instructions to include provoking a riot at the Philpot Street hall. At this time Bradlaugh was feeling like the prince without Elsinore and, already saddled with a printing debt of £60, gave his sad 'Last Words' in his dying paper:

> 'The *Investigator,* supported only by a small section of the Secular party, never met its expenses, and I am unable to meet the deficiency ... I war because I have no choice—I must either fight or die ... Farewell. I may never perchance address you again, for life is subject to innumerable contingencies. With these last words I say, "Unite!" and let us not be a divided and scattered flock wandering through life without leader or object.' [32]

At the beginning of September 1859 the family was ready for another move. With the growing overcrowding of the East End, those who could afford to were moving still further away. At first it was to the east. Then a new fashion developed. With the coming of the railways and a belief that the high ground of North London was a protection from cholera and other scourges of the metropolis, the migration moved noth. The more prosperous Jewish businessmen led the way to Stamford Hill, then swung west to Golders Green. Others continued north along the Lea. For Bradlaugh this was particularly convenient. The river's lower reaches were now polluted, but the angling fame of its Tottenham reach was as old as Izaak Walton.[33] In this newly opened suburb ribbon development had lined its main roads; trapping farms and fields in their meshes. The Bradlaughs moved into a seven-roomed, semi-detached house, Elysium Villa, whose rateable value was £25, [34] on the south side of (Northumberland) Park (Road). At the eastern end of the road was Park Station on the Great Eastern Railway from the City, then the electric telegraph, the marshes and the river. Two or three miles away to the west, reached by a still rustic Lordship Lane, was Woodgreen Station on the Great Northern Railway. When he went north lecturing, Kate carried his box of books to the station the evening before, or he took them in the morning, as there was no public transport and a carriage was out of the question financially. At the bottom of their long garden was a bridle-path communicating with Northumberland Grove, and here from time to time British or Continental spies kept watch. In this pleasant suburban villa, on 14 September, a lively son was born. He was called Charles.

Bradlaugh had great recuperative powers and by the following month was quite recovered in body and spirit. At a lecture in Halifax a local Baptist pastor, the Rev. T. D. Matthias, grew so excited that he rose to advance upon the infidel. His friends tried to hold him back but he shouted, 'Unhand me, gentlemen. By heaven, I'll make a ghost of him who lets me.' Bradlaugh rose to the literary occasion: 'Lay on, Macduff, and damn'd be he who first cries, Hold, enough.' [35] At the end of the month a formal debate between the two was held. This was his first courteous platform confrontation with a cleric but it did not end his problems as a lecturer. At Glasgow he was told the Chief Constable had taken out a warrant for his arrest at a lecture that night. He went straight to police headquarters: 'I understand you have a warrant for my arrest. I am the person to whom the warrant refers: if you will be kind enough to arrange a time convenient for myself I will be there.' [36] The Chief Constable denied this and the lecture proceeded without incident. But his most extraordinary encounter was with a Jewish rabbi about to enter the Church of England and put forward to show Bradlaugh's lack of Old Testament scholarship. In the greatest epic of religious evidence since the miracle-mongering of St Peter and Simon Magus, Iconoclast and the Rev. Dr Mensor spent four nights scrawling Hebrew characters on a blackboard 'to the delight and mystification of the audience'. [37] Brewin Grant came up again in May, this time at Bradford, with his customary 'outrage upon the ordinary proprieties and decencies of life'. [38] where rodomontade was interspersed with tongue-poking. But even the local papers and his friends expressed their disapproval.

On returning to London Bradlaugh narrowly escaped death when his train overran at King's Cross.

The following month, in Oldham, Iconoclast first met in debate another man who regarded the pursuit of the infidel as his peculiar vocation. This was Dr. John Brindley, whose apologetics he had answered as a youth. Brindley, an ex-schoolmaster, was a volatile Birmingham evangelist with a dubious doctorate and a long history of bankruptcy and alcoholism. But it was not only polemical clowns who debated with the young atheist, for shortly afterwards he had an important three nights' discussion at Liverpool on 'God, Man, and the Bible' with the Rev. Dr Joseph Baylee, principal of St Aidan's Theological College, Birkenhead.

As often as she could Susannah Bradlaugh plunged into the provinces with her husband. In London she attended his meetings and, as his daughter was to recall, 'shone at her best in entertaining my father's political friends'.[39] Almost as tall as he, strikingly brunette, gay, generous, she entertained more lavishly than their small means allowed in a childlike desire to please him and his associates. For she was conscious of her sad inability to provide him with the intellectual stimulus he enjoyed and, underrating his inner resources, she felt he needed. Their friends reciprocated her kindness, and kept her gay, offering her drinks which she never liked to decline. As a temperance lecturer who had remained teetotal, Charles noted this with some misgiving. But he was still deeply in love and wrote in her 'Punch's Pocket Book' for 1860 a poem including:

'You and I, my dear wife,
Must ne'er part while we've life:
Together we are bound
For life's uncertain round.
Let us each live and love
And true affection prove
For our babes and ourselves
Till death our bodies shelves.'[40]

His greatest early successes as a lecturer and debater were in Yorkshire, especially at Sheffield, and his friends there wished to set him up with a paper more soundly backed than the *Investigator*. For his part, he knew that no propagandist or would-be leader of a movement, however brilliant his writings or indulgent his editors, could succeed without a regular personal organ. All the heroic figures of his youth had had them, and when they lost them their influence declined or disappeared. The popular mood was apathetic. After the

Great Exhibition of 1851 and the India Act of 1858 trade and imperial riches flowed freely, and enough trickled into the pockets of the British working masses to damp down the worst discontent. The Chartist papers had all collapsed. So had the republican. Some semblance of decent relations had been patched up between Bradlaugh and Holyoake, now 'growing so respectable that I suspect myself', and the younger man supported testimonials to the older in 1858 and 1860.[41] The need for these emphasized the shakiness of the *Reasoner*'s position. Nevertheless, among the more articulate of the workers a new political and social awareness was breaking the soil. The London Trades Council with its co-ordinating Junta was about to sprout. In the emerging technological world there was no Garden of Eden and no place for God, no Fall and no Redemption, no Passover and no Pentecost. The new artisans wanted a philosophy of life to go with their politics and practical realism to go with academic freethinking. Iconoclast and his backers believed he could give it to them.

In February 1860 the Reformer Newspaper Co. Ltd., with a capital of 2,000 ten-shilling shares, was announced:

'The present platform of political views will be mainly that advocated by the Northern Reform Union, but every phase of the political question shall have free and unreserved treatment, and the most partial Tory will be allowed to answer the views of the Editor, as well as the most extreme Republican... On social science, the promoters intend specially to watch the conduct of the Social Science League... The newspaper will contain full reports of co-operative news, meetings and proceedings of trade societies, and... the important ground recognised under the title of Political Economy.[42] The present platform, of theological advocacy, will be that of antagonism to every known religious system... The Editor for the first six months will be Iconoclast, who will be continued in that office if satisfaction be given to the committee of management.'[43]

At this juncture a 'human weather cock'[44] returned from America. Joseph Barker was brought up in Yorkshire and became successively a minister of the Methodist Old Connexion, New Connexion, Barkerites (autonomous) and Unitarians. He was also a strong opponent of Owenism. Then he emigrated. In the New World he abandoned all his old positions and became a prominent infidel. Despite his public relations machine, reports had from time to time washed over the Atlantic that he had slipped back into theism, but Holyoake was able to assure the infidels these rumours were unfounded. At the whirl of functions organized in welcome, Barker proclaimed that his secularism was stronger than ever and he was planning to establish a weekly at the earliest opportunity. Anxious for a united movement Bradlaugh persuaded the committee to admit Barker as co-editor.

When the paper, its title expanded to *The National Reformer,* was launched on 14 April, Barker edited (and wrote most of) the first half and Iconoclast, with £26 in debts[45] still left over from the *Investigator,* the second. Though most of the reports appeared in his section he found space for distinguished outside contributors. Adams wrote on politics as W.E.A., then 'Caractacus'.[46] G.L.R.[47] aired 'The Population Doctrines':

> 'It is very remarkable that at a time, when the inestimable advantages of open discussion are so well known, and when almost every shade of opinion has its public organ and its party of zealous supporters, there should be one great set of principles which has not a single advocate or representative in the periodical press of this country, and which has no organised party. I refer to the Malthusian theory of population; and the other leading principles of political economy and social science.' [48]

Bradlaugh himself pilloried the last 'tax on knowledge'[49] together with the House of Lords:

> 'The Lords have thrown out the Paper Duty Bill. The Lords intend to reject the Church-rate Bill. The Lords would like to destroy the Reform Bill. Who are the Lords? If we answer honestly, the reply must be that the Lords are, in chief, the outgrowths of ages of ignorance, crime, and folly, scarcely in any sense redeemed by the few who are on the other side, who have deserved the peerage by their nobility in thought and conduct ... We decline to do anything today merely because we did it yesterday. We decline still more to let the Lords stand in the way of the people because they have repeatedly done so. The Lords are not necessary to the welfare of the state.' [50]

Radical secular campaigns continued by word and deed. In June 1860, Truelove formed a Ratepayers' Protection Society against church rates. This was the time of Garibaldi's sweep across Sicily with his famous 1,000 Redshirts, and Bradlaugh addressed a rash of public meetings in support. At one of these in Northampton his chairman was Thomas Adams, a much respected local Baptist. His anti-clerical lectures continued, the proceeds to go to Garibaldi, for whom he collected 100 guineas. But prejudice against the Iconoclast was still strong. At Norwich he received in lieu of money 'yells, hisses, abuse, a little mud, and a few stones'.[51] At the village of Shaw he was refused all halls and, having retired to a field, defied the local police sergeant and percussion band who tried to drive him off. At Wigan, egged on by a clergyman, there was a riot among the crowd unable to gain admittance to the lecture hall, and the address was punctuated by the tinkle of breaking glass, the swallow dive of the rector's secretary through one window, a shower of limestone through another, a spray of water down the ventilators, and an arm through a hole in the roof attributed to the devil.

Meanwhile there were rumblings in the *National Reformer*. On 1 September some surplus paragraphs from Bradlaugh's section were transferred by the printers to a space in Barker's. Barker protested. His critique of the items was quite sound but there was, of course, more behind it. It was not only the clash of personalities, professional jealousy, or basic ideology.[52] Barker was a prude who grew numb or emotive at the name of Malthus and kindred subjects. In a serious answer to what suggests a spoof letter from a coal-miner he declared:

> 'Circumcision is not making a mark on the forehead. It is a very unnatural and wicked thing and fit only for very religious people either to practise or to talk about ... We belong to a higher dispensation.' [53]

Bradlaugh must have given a wry grin. He himself was conservative and conventional in many things. 'He clung to old friends, to old habits, and to precedent.' [54] Both his daughter and his grandson have described him as puritanical, and there are quotations from his writings that will confirm this. Speaking of secularist organizations he decreed:

> 'Let no man remain a member who is habitually a drunkard, or who ill-treats his wife or neglects his children, or who is guilty of immorality.' [55]

'Immorality' he never defined. Personally he was abstemious. He had strong views on many 'with-it' fads, but these opinions were rarely known outside his family circle. He disliked bands and banners at public demonstrations, believing that less gaudy protest betokened greater moral earnestness and brought out demonstrators for the right reasons. He did not think the music hall was quite nice, and regretted that at halls of science in his later years smoking concerts and a 'club' atmosphere were tending to displace the choral madrigals and hymns of freethought and Chartism of his youth. But he accepted that other people had different tastes. It was the same with sexual matters. Naturally he was in some ways a creature or a prisoner of his time. Apart from family planning he rarely wrote or spoke about sex. But he was more liberal, more ready to accept a permissive society than his family realized. To him this was not a society of unbridled licence, but a society that left as much as possible to the individual conscience. There was only one thing he felt really strongly about, a by-product of his formula, *dictum meum pactum,* and this was the marriage vow. He believed it meant what it said: 'Forsaking all other, keep thee only unto her (him), so long as ye both shall live'. Even after divorce, a necessary institution where living together had become intolerable, he disapproved of remarriage while the former spouse was alive. For those who were not married, and for the patterns of sexuality by consent within marriage, he gave nudging hints of tolerance. In the books he reviewed or advertised, in the kite-flying answers to correspondents, he seemed to be peeping out of the hothouse window of Victorian conventionality towards the sun. With Barker's shrewdness, developed over a life of continual vacillation, and his personality, typical of the rowdy youth who had once found Jesus, he perceived his colleague's liberalism and shivered. The two editors began exchanging notes, but so far only privately.

The whirl of provincial meetings continued. In December 1860, suffering from neuralgia, Bradlaugh arrived for a week of lectures at Plymouth. One of them was to be given in Devonport Park, but the superintendent of police arrived just as he was to start, announced that he had orders from the Town Council to protect a place of recreation from propaganda, and threatened to arrest him. Bradlaugh pointed out that temperance advocates used the park. The superintendent was adamant and, as he did not really know the byelaws, Bradlaugh 'submitted, but with a determination to do better at some future time'.[56] In February 1861 he returned to Wigan to debate with a local Nonconformist sub-editor, W. Hutchings. Considerable goodwill among the inhabitants had grown up in the interim, and trouble began only after the event. A reporter, Stephenson Struthers, had sold the transcript of the debate to both parties, and Bradlaugh refused to pay the price he had contracted for an exclusive copy.

Struthers brought an action before the Wigan County Court. Counsel for the plaintiff asked Bradlaugh if he believed 'in the religious obligations of an oath', as soon as he entered the witness-box. Since 1854 affirmation in civil cases had been open to witnesses who declared 'that the taking of any oath is, according to my religious belief, unlawful'.[57] But not according to irreligious belief Bradlaugh began the sparring with counsel and the judiciary for which he was to become famous. He objected to answering any questions until he had been sworn. This was overruled. Bradlaugh persisted.

> Judge: You won't answer the question?
>
> Bradlaugh: I object that I am not bound to answer any question that will criminate myself.
>
> Judge: You will not answer my question. Do you believe in the existence of a supreme God?
>
> Bradlaugh: I object that the answer, if in the negative, would subject me to a criminal prosecution.
>
> Judge: Do you believe in a state of future rewards and punishments?
>
> Bradlaugh: I object that—
>
> Judge: Then I shall not permit you to give evidence at all; and I think you escape very well in not being sent to gaol.[58]

Whereupon the judge declared the action 'undefended' and gave judgment for the plaintiff. After the case a member of Hutchings's organizing committee wrote to Bradlaugh denying a vital part of Struthers's evidence, and Hutchings himself promised support for Sir John Trelawny's Affirmation Bill to extend the right to affirm to all witnesses.

At the end of February Iconoclast went to Guernsey by request. As the champion of self-help he felt a special warmth for Stephen Bendall, a local man who had been bound over for distributing infidel tracts, some of them by Bradlaugh himself. The *Guernsey Mail* refused advertisements of his visit but gave him free, if hostile, publicity. This he eked out by the distribution of handbills throwing down the gauntlet to Bendall's prosecutors, 'to M. le Procureur, to the Clergy (especially of the Methodist New Connexion),' and to the general public. One wealthy, orthodox old lady responded by financing a welcome with rotten eggs, and Bendall met Bradlaugh on the quayside with some trepidation. There were no eggs but 'greater curiosity could scarcely have been evinced had I been a red-buttoned mandarin or a tritailed Pasha'.[59] His booking of the Assembly Rooms was cancelled, the town crier would make no announcement of his meetings and no one would print bills. Providently he had brought along his own, and a new room was found. As there was a bill-stickers' embargo, Bradlaugh and Bendall put posters up themselves, though many were torn down. With only one helper it was impossible to take money at the door when, after pious hesitation, the crowd swept in. Lecturing was also impossible above the bombardment of stones against the walls by boys egged on by the bourgeoisie. Ignoring all advice Bradlaugh went outside to quell them. The mob retreated as he advanced. When he returned it was a little quieter, but he was followed to his hotel by a crowd screaming 'Kill the infidel!' The next day excitement had risen. Soldiers were given leave and alcohol was freely distributed. In the middle of a well-received lecture a drunken mob burst through the plate-glass doors. The ringleaders were with difficulty expelled, though an attempt was made to turn out the gas and many chairs and forms were damaged. Again Bradlaugh sought to go outside and command silence, but the proprietress of his hotel pretended to show him a short way out and locked him in a back room for his own protection. A day or two later, as he approached the boat to return home, suppressed hisses simmered along his route. They boiled up into a cauldron of furious shrieks when the boat had safely cast off.

In March Bradlaugh fulfilled his promise to return to Devonport. He set aside a fortnight. Trouble began the first day. The Plymouth and Devonport Secular Society had hired Parson's Field, next to the park, from a private owner, but the police arrived when Bradlaugh came to deliver his lecture. Superintendent Edwards forbade him to proceed. Saying he was the lawful tenant Bradlaugh took no notice. 'Friends, I am about to address you on the Bible—'. Whereupon he was seized by six constables, one of them half-choking him. He shook the offender off while the others, assisted by the superintendent and an inspector, dragged him away. With great difficulty he restrained his friends from rescuing him by force. At the police station he was charged with inciting a breach of the peace, refused bail and thrust into an underground cell without heat, light or furniture save a straw palliasse. Later in the evening he was removed to a corridor with a fire. The following morning there was a further charge of assaulting Edwards. So much excitement flared among those wanting to attend the court hearing, it was transferred to the large hall at the Guildhall. Many local Nonconformists, including a Unitarian, the Rev. W. Sharman, attended to see fair play, and confounded the authorities, who believed Bradlaugh's witnesses would

72

be atheists who could be set aside as incapable of either oath or affirmation, by coming forward to give evidence on his behalf. The case against him was dismissed, though a supporter was fined five shillings. On the following Sunday he spoke indoors but announced that the Sunday after he would lecture 'very near the park'. The town was flushed with posters:

> 'In consequence of advice received, Iconoclast will deliver an open-air address on Sunday forenoon, and will be present near the Devonport Park Lodge about half-past ten in order to vindicate the right of free speech.'[60]

The atmosphere was electric. A War Office directive had come through against the use of the park. Was Bradlaugh to lead an insurrection at the heart of British naval power? Most of the curiosity was blown or swept away on the day by a violent storm but a considerable crowd, followed by a large police contingent and angry representatives of the Watch Committee and the YMCA, accompanied Bradlaugh as he set out for the park. The mayor was ready with the Riot Act and soldiers were on call nearby. When he reached the Devonport Park Lodge he turned down to Stonehouse Creek, stepped into a boat and was rowed to a larger craft moored a few feet out. The lecture began: 'Pocket your Riot Act, friend Mayor. Right about, hence to Barracks, ye Military. Home, home, and gnash your teeth in seemly privacy, ye Young Christian Men.'[61] One of Bradlaugh's supporters, Captain R.W. Trenaman, had 'engaged the boat the Wednesday previous at the Admiral's Hard, Stonehouse, . . . got a platform made with hand rail breast high which we carried out on the Sunday morning, fitted up and rowed to the Devonport side of the lake'.[62] The jurisdiction of the Devonport police stopped at the water's edge, and Edwards was unable to intercept the lecturer, who soon stopped because of the weather, or to proceed against anyone else. Being thus made to look ridiculous he was not in a conciliatory mood when Bradlaugh demanded a published apology for his recent arrest, the defence witnesses' expenses and £20 for specified charities. So the matter was put in the hands of Leverson, who had acted so well for Truelove and Bernard, and proceedings began for assault and wrongful imprisonment. Edwards was supported by the Watch Committee and the YMCA, and the case came on before Baron Channell and a special jury at the Devon Lammas Assizes at Exeter. Bradlaugh wanted to plead the case himself, but was persuaded that a hearing of such interest should have qualified counsel. A QC and MP, Robert Collier, was briefed. Unfortunately he was 'far more anxious to assert his own orthodoxy than his client's rights'.[63] For the defence, Montagu Smith QC tried to cross-examine Iconoclast on his religious beliefs, but he successfully claimed exemption. Everyone, including the judge, so slated these in addressing the jury that though Bradlaugh won the case he was allowed only a farthing damages. He was refused costs, which amounted to several hundred pounds. Even the Catholic *Tablet* called the whole thing a 'frightful persecution'.[64] The following November he moved for a new trial before Lord Chief Justice Sir William Erle and Justices Williams, Byles and Keating in the Court of Common Pleas, Westminster. This was refused on the grounds that his pernicious opinions 'might be a matter he might afterwards deeply regret', so that arrest and imprisonment 'was an act which in its real substantial result was beneficial to the plaintiff'.[65] His appeal was heard by the same judges, who upheld their earlier decision.

Apart from his biblical researches, Bradlaugh rarely wrote for the joy of scholarship. His interest in the population question, for instance, was one of harsh practicality. He saw the population explosion in individual and family rather than demographic terms: overcrowded homes, high infant mortality, women old before their time, precautionary late marriages and prostitution. One of the most graphic books on this subject was the *Elements of Social Science*. He did not try for Johnson's lyricism in its praise, and was later to mention 'some points of ethics from which I expressly and strongly dissent'.[66] He had advertised it without comment in his *Investigator* and was to do so again in the *Reformer*. In the meantime he wrote a pamphlet *Jesus, Shelley, and Malthus; or Pious Poverty and Heterodox Happiness*, specially recommending the *Elements*, to show evolving in human history 'the spirit of religious submission, the spirit of humanitarian revolt, and the spirit of science'.[67] This he used as a peg to propose a Malthusian League 'to promote the discussion and recognition of the Malthusian doctrines'.[68] Two weeks later he received enthusiastic support from Dr. John Cookson for 'the most important subject in the world'. Cookson added:

> 'At present a large number are turned into mere breeding animals; and as for the rest, to quote the noble author of the *Elements of Social Science*, "their lives are shadowed in the gloom of celibacy, or quenched in the mire of prostitution". This work should be very extensively advertised, and every effort should be made to diffuse a knowledge of the population doctrines, and of their immense influence over the

happiness of the human race.'[69]

This tribute did not succeed in getting the Malthusian League off the ground but it certainly raised a hornet's nest. Having seen the proof, Barker blew up his usual notice 'END OF MR BARKER'S ARTICLES'. A fortnight later, in June 1861, he told a correspondent: 'We repeat; the two halves of the *National Reformer* are, in effect, TWO PAPERS. We have no control over the second half and are not answerable for anything that appears in its columns.'[70] Close observers had noted a widening gap for a very long time. About the only thing the two co-editors agreed on, in opposition to Holyoake, was that atheists could honourably take an oath (if they were allowed to) so long as the statutes did not admit affirmation. On other questions Barker seemed to delight in opposing the views of Bradlaugh. Dramatically he announced that he was a theist, believing religion 'necessary to the virtue and happiness of mankind'.[71] Nor did he share his colleague's low opinion of Louis Napoleon, or wish to separate church and state, or support manhood suffrage, or attempt to 'bring all Secularists into *one* organization'.[72] All of Bradlaugh's contributors were attacked for one reason or another: Drysdale for advocating population control, 'Caractacus' for supporting the anti-slavery states in the American Civil War and Garibaldi in Italy. Iconoclast could see that the journal, divided against itself, was likely to fall. Subscribers were already forsaking this babel of conflicting voices. Many who remained urged a definite policy. Loyalty could not be relied on. The *Reasoner* had just collapsed after fifteen years. So he sent out a private circular to subscribers suggesting that both editors tender their resignation and a single man be appointed.

Barker published the circular and attempted to answer Bradlaugh's charges. He gave most attention to his most telling argument with an audience unduly sensitive about their moral, if not their theological, orthodoxy: 'Certain persons . . . have been set astride the *National Reformer,* with their saddle bags so full of follies, indecencies, immoralities, and crimes, that the wonder is, not that the good-natured creature has slightly slackened her pace, but that she has not given up the ghost in disgust.'[73] He decided to review the *Elements*, whose author 'lacks the sense of decency and propriety with regard to sexual matters. Hence he recommends the most dangerous, wicked, and debasing practices.'[74] Nothing 'should induce an editor to puff an indecent and demoralising work'. Bradlaugh named certain distinguished men who shared his views. The following week Barker asserted he was 'terribly mistaken if he supposes, that he can either drag down Buckle, Mill, and Darwin, or Malthus and McCulloch, into the filthy slough in which he is wallowing, or raise himself from his horrid position by an abuse of their honourable names'.[75] Speaking personally, 'My reputation is of more importance to me than a dozen newspapers'.[76] 'Eternity would not be long enough to restore my peace or influence if I were to connive at vice and villainy.'

This swashbuckling campaign was not without effect in mid-Victorian England. Maughan, who had become the secretary of the Secular Benevolent Society and who Bradlaugh hoped would become corresponding secretary of the national body Holyoake and he were jointly trying to establish, declined his invitation: 'The mode in which Malthusianism has been advocated in the columns of the *Reformer*, and the unconditional approval and recommendation of a certain work by yourself, has placed the Secular party in the unfortunate position of being supposed to coincide in, and approve of such teachings, while the fact is there are few who can approve of all that is recommended in them'.[77] So Maughan formed a breakaway General Secular Reformers' Society. A meeting of National Reformer shareholders convened in Sheffield on 4 August 1861 was technically illegal, so a new one was called for the 26th. Barker made a further attempt to influence the debate by asserting that he had not resigned and might demand a year's notice unless the copyright were sold. He turned up with a solicitor and strong support from Leeds. But Bradlaugh rarely moved on shaky ground. He was the largest shareholder and had the majority of proxies in his pocket; but promised not to use them and to buy up the shares of all dissidents. By a vote of 113 to 64 it was decided to continue the company with Iconoclast as sole editor. James Dodworth of Sheffield, president of the company, observed: 'All the committee were very much in favour of Mr Barker eight weeks ago. The majority changed their opinions of him through his own revelations since that time.'[78] Bradlaugh's final assessment was: 'He came to me originally at Sheffield, pretending to be an Atheist and a Republican, and soon after pretended to be a Christian, and spoke in favour of slavery . . . If he had had the slightest thoroughness in his character, he would have been a great man; as it is, he is only a great turn-coat.'[79] Perhaps the best independent view was that of Dr P.W. Perfitt, conductor of *The Pathfinder, A Journal of Independent Religious Reform*. He detected a body of freethinkers wholeheartedly with Barker, another with Bradlaugh, and a deciding balance who were angry 'that a Secularist denied his brother'.[80] They were unhappy about the *Elements*, probably about the whole idea of Malthusianism but they valued conscientiousness, avoidance of personalities, and loyalty.

Barker went on to found *Barker's Review* to shame the 'Unbounded Licence Party' and 'oppose all vice, assail all forms of vulgar Atheistic fanaticism'.[81] In August Holyoake had established a monthly *Counsellor*. Before it finished in December he was projecting a weekly *Secular World*, but his health was bad and his influence uncertain. Austin had taken over the business of Holyoake & Co. John Watts was dismissed. Bradlaugh and his Sheffield friends had quite forgotten the little local difficulty with Holyoake in 1857-8. So, it seemed, had Holyoake. With the *Westminster Review* now eloquent on the disunity of secularists, negotiations took place and Holyoake triumphantly proclaimed 'One Paper and One Party'.[82] He was to become the *Reformer's* chief contributor, supplying original and other material for three pages, receiving two guineas out of Bradlaugh's weekly five pounds. John Watts, who had shared the printing with Barker Brothers, was now to become sub-editor. John Crawford, chairman of the Garibaldi Fund Committee, communicated his misgivings to Holyoake. Maybe friends cautioned Bradlaugh.

The prospects of journalistic peace enabled Bradlaugh to concentrate his energies on his other activities. It is not quite certain when his connection with Harvey terminated, but it was not long after being articled. Harvey seems to have been chiefly interested in company promotion and mining speculation.[83] His articled clerk had assisted him in these undertakings and gained some interest in speculation on his own account. Harvey was too ambitious and eventually burnt his fingers badly. He was lodged in a debtors' prison.[84] Believing that Bradlaugh was one of the detaining creditors or had influence with those who were, Harvey's son went to Tottenham to plead his cause. There was nothing the clerk, 'who found himself also involved in considerable pecuniary liabilities',[85] could do. These debts he gradually met from lecturing and journalistic income. The progress was by no means unimpeded. Apart from notable liabilities like his litigation after Devonport and repair of damage after Guernsey, he lost money in thirty-one freethought lectures in the first half of 1861. But overall he was beginning to show a profit. There was his *National Reformer* salary, out of which he insisted on paying contributors. And sometimes his investments were profitable. At the same time he was hopeful of returning to the law. Though

their judicial outcome had been unsatisfactory, his court performances in 1861 demonstrated a talent approaching genius for both
cross-examination of lying witnesses in lower courts and pleading
sophisticated points of law with the highest judges in the land. This
had not escaped the notice of Leverson, and in the latter part of
1861 he became his managing and confidential clerk.

After liberating Sicily, Garibaldi had captured Naples in
September 1860. Though the most obvious outcome of the
risorgimento was political, it had important cultural and economic
implications. Undeveloped mineral resources in southern Italy were
found by the more progressive and industrialized forces of the north.
In July 1861 a mining concession was granted to Count Luigi
Franchi and the Italian Coal and Iron Co. Ltd. formed in London to
exploit it. It was registered[86] on 6 November with a nominal capital
of 1,500 £10 shares. Montague Leverson was its first secretary and
his brother George, another radical, had 50 shares. Most of those
taken up[87] were owned by members of the Hyam family. In connection with this business Bradlaugh was sent to Italy and on the
29th negotiated two memoranda of agreement with citizens of Lecce
and Naples. Being extremely busy and well-organized, he always
linked projects when he had to spend time travelling, and on this and
many subsequent visits to Italy acted as contact man and letter-
bearer between republicans in Italy, Holyoake and Mazzini, then
living in Onslow Terrace as Signor Ernesti. The French spies had not
however watched Bradlaugh in vain, and news of his movements was
conveyed to Italy.

On this first visit he noticed that his hotel room in Naples had
been carefully ransacked in his absence. A few days after Bomba's
fall he received a packet of political letters in his room without any
accompanying conversation, and so took no special precautions on
his voyage home. When the boat, flying the flag of the Two Sicilies,
put into Cività Vecchia, the port of Rome, the papal police boarded
it and asked Bradlaugh to accompany them to the British consul.
Suspecting a trap and fearing for his safety if he set foot on papal
territory, he declined and went down to his cabin to guard his portmanteau. The police followed and demanded to search his luggage.
At this he drew a heavy naval revolver and promised death to anyone
who advanced. Some police officers were, however, behind him and
his position was precarious until an American passenger grabbed a
chair and shouted 'I guess I'll see fair play. You look after those in
front, I'll attend to those behind!'[88] At this the police returned to

78

shore to seek further instructions and Bradlaugh persuaded the captain to sail before their return. On another occasion he was travelling by stage-coach in Italy when the police at Montalbano discovered his revolver and tried to confiscate it, as carrying weapons was against the law. He snatched it back. Reinforcements came and seized him but he was released, with the revolver, when he explained that his policy with the Sovereign and Midland Assurance Companies required him to protect his life in every possible way. By this mixture of guile and courage Bradlaugh brought vital information for *Pensiero ed Azione*, established in 1858 in London by Mazzini, so that 'isolated though he was, it is surprising what political insight this magazine sometimes revealed and how often he knew diplomatic secrets long before others did'.[89]

In Iconoclast's absence on this first visit Holyoake looked after the *Reformer*. At the same time an interesting and perhaps decisive event occurred at Northampton. The Rev. Sydney Gedge, vicar of All Saints, the civic church, zealously 'levied distresses on the goods of Dissenters and others in his parish who refused to pay the Vicar's Rate'.[90] Eventually he brought a libel action against one of his foremost victims and opponents, John Bates,[91] a secularist bookseller in the Drapery. Naturally Bradlaugh had joined the fray against 'a good and faithful shepherd, doubtless, but you have more regard for the wool than for the sheep, and have an open eye to the shearing'.[92] While the case was pending Gedge attacked the defendant in the *English Churchman*. Bates's counsel, Sergeant Parry, successfully pleaded that Gedge had thus sought his own remedies by a counter-libel. The case was dismissed and the vicar had to pay the costs of both sides. This affair brought home to the Nonconformists of Northampton their community of interest with the secularists, and Bates is said to have been the first man to suggest that Bradlaugh should run for the constituency.

By virtue of his transactions in Italy, Bradlaugh was 'entitled to certain rights and benefits under or a certain interest in a certain Contract or certain Contracts which have been entered into or are about to be entered into with the Italian Government or some person or persons on their behalf for the supply of Rifles Guns and Small Arms'.[93] As he was a servant of Leverson's at the time, a memorandum was drawn up between them on 11 January 1862 equally sharing the proceeds. Since Bradlaugh had had to guarantee capital in London to work his mining concessions, in February David Hyam bought into the Leverson-Bradlaugh partnership, each of them now getting one third. On 17 January Leverson granted Bradlaugh a legal apprenticeship. By the articles of agreement[94] the solicitor was to forgo his premium, pay all expenses, including the stamp duty, and offer a partnership as soon as Bradlaugh was admitted as attorney. Meanwhile the clerk's salary was to be £150 for the first three years and £200 for the other two. While all this was proceeding, from December to March, he lectured three times a week, went six times to the Continent, and managed Leverson's business. Not surprisingly, there was no leisure for him to draw up a final agreement between Holyoake and himself in connection with the *National Reformer*—an oversight which was afterwards branded as a calculation. He had drawn up a draft on the eve of one departure for Italy. After discussions on his return he did a new draft, whose fate was uncertain.[95] In these circumstances, and with such a history of personal relations, it was a very short time before the two fell out. Just when he seemed to have attained a settled place in life, Bradlaugh was thus plunged into another row.

This was more unpleasant than the two secularists' earlier encounter, though it was decorously more private. Holyoake asserted that the arrangement was that 'he should have control of three pages, and a right of protest against the re-appearance in the *National Reformer* of that class of subjects and treatment which so lately brought discord and discredit into the Secular ranks'.[96] Bradlaugh's version was that Holyoake had only the status of chief contributor, supplying at least two columns of original material. 'Mr Holyoake having requested that I should ignore *The Elements of Social Science*—I declined to do that but volunteered not to put forward the views coming under the heads of Sexual Religion and Moral Physiology, stating that I had never yet done so but reserved to myself entire right of discussing the population question as advocated by the Malthusian School and as put forward by myself in the pamphlet *Jesus, Shelley and Malthus*.'[97] Bradlaugh continued however to advertise the *Elements*, and further annoyed Holyoake by announcing 'Editorially the *National Reformer*, as to religious questions, is, and always has been, as far as we are concerned, the advocate of Atheism'. So the 'chief contributor' tried to insert, in the Barker manner, 'for what follows the Editor alone is responsible'. Bradlaugh struck this out. For various reasons he believed 'that Holyoake was intriguing against me to get the editorship';[98] and when the directors instructed Austin to change the size of the paper to one which George had asked for, Bradlaugh decided to force an

80

issue. Simultaneously he sent his resignation to the board and a note to Holyoake saying that this decision would mean terminating their arrangement after the issue of 12 April 1861.

Dodworth asked Bradlaugh what alternative there was as editor and he privately suggested Holyoake. The directors asked Holyoake, who agreed.[99] Then Bradlaugh announced that the shareholders should decide. A meeting was called for 23 March, at which he proposed to withdraw his resignation. Holyoake reminded him of their year's agreement, so he offered to pay the two guineas, as promised, for just one original article of two columns.[100] At the special general meeting John Child of Leeds, who had led the Barker battalions, now captained the Holyoake cohorts. Again Bradlaugh had in his pocket a majority of formal votes — proxies and fifty personal votes — but he was also confirmed in office 18:9 on a show of hands. The directors resigned. Holyoake was informed his connection was 'now that of contributor only'.[101] Whereupon he withdrew his copy for the ensuing week. Joseph Jagger, his employee at the sinking Fleet Street House and secretary of the newly-formed National Secular Association,[102] called on Bradlaugh to represent the editor's action as an insult to Holyoake and assert that one of Bradlaugh's letters contained an offer to pay the 'two guineas a week for nothing'. Iconoclast exploded: 'If I were fool enough to offer it, he would have been a scoundrel and a swindler to have taken it.'[103] If Holyoake accepted the new conditions 'he would deserve kicking'. Bradlaugh was by this time contemptuous of his colleague in a way he had never been before, partly because he had learned from John Watts that Watts had never received monies recorded in the final *Reasoner* accounts as having been paid to him. Hardly conciliated by the report of this encounter, Holyoake published an edited version of his correspondence with Bradlaugh. Iconoclast proposed arbitration. At the end of April Holyoake put the matter in the hands of his new solicitor, W.H. Ashurst Junior, treasurer of the Garibaldi Fund Committee.[104] At the same time, Austin Holyoake left the House and spent the rest of his life working in intimate association with Bradlaugh. But the *National Reformer* still had problems. In May W.H. Smith & Son officially refused to handle it on their bookstalls.

A prolonged and stinging bee-dance between the two agitators took place. On 23 July articles of agreement were drawn up, naming Linton and Crawford as arbitrators acting for Bradlaugh and Holyoake respectively. On the face of it the choice was good: two impartial men of high reputation and radical devotion, while as theists outside any secular factionalism. Holyoake was angry however at the choice of Linton, though Bradlaugh probably knew more about their original collaboration on a Chartist paper than their later animosity. On the other side Crawford showed no great love of Iconoclast. If the arbitrators could not agree, the evidence was to be submitted to Shaen, Holyoake's solicitor in the Wilks days, for an award by November. The accusations began to flow: that Bradlaugh had 'let in the Sexual book which he had given his word of honour should not come in',[105] that Holyoake had broken his pledge not to publicize the affair till the award had been reached. The plaintiff's case was that Bradlaugh had breached the contract by resigning and then proposing new terms; the defendant's, that Holyoake was responsible for the breach through his willingness to accept the editorship and withdrawing his copy. Originally Holyoake's claim was for £81 18s compensation, i.e. 2 guineas per week for the rest of the year, and £100 damages, including a year's wages for Jagger[106] and 'losses, labours and annoyance' through scrapping his *Secular World* project. Since he had meanwhile started it, this portion of the claim was so preposterous even Crawford had to disallow it.

The wrangling dragged on. Bradlaugh said he had not demeaned a 'man of honour' as Holyoake had no honour to lose. Under his cross-examination the plaintiff became almost incoherent with confusion and rage. Numerous court orders were granted to extend the time. Bradlaugh suggested Holyoake bring in Ashurst and he Leverson, and Linton hinted that the prompt refusal sprang from Holyoake's desire to avoid embarrassment before his old friend. Crawford retorted that the suggestion violated the original agreement, that Leverson was anyhow persona non grata, and that Bradlaugh's frequent postponement of meetings was suspicious. At length everyone recognized what should have been clear from the start: the two arbitrators could not agree. Crawford seemed unhappy about a full settlement but declined to capitulate completely. Linton would not accept any liability at all. The matter was referred to Shaen, who on 27 July 1863 granted everything to Holyoake. Shock and shortage of cash did not expedite Bradlaugh's payment and on 9 December he had to be subpoenaed to explain the delay. Crawford's final comment on his labours was: 'Of course I grudge the time: however the case is a moral one and it is interesting to watch what great lengths the two long-range-guns of Modern Atheism go in ascribing base motives and conduct to each other. I am pulling choice sample fruit grown in this *New* Moral World and presented by its most advanced minds.'[107] He appears to have seen little of Holyoake thereafter. Five years later Linton went to America, where he remained. After Bradlaugh's death he recalled the arbitration: 'The one impact which such connection as I had with him has left is that of a man, whom, whatever and however wide the differences of opinion, I could but thoroughly respect for the honesty of his nature.'[108]

Bradlaugh's difficulty in attending arbitration meetings reflected the complexity of his legal, business and propagandist life. When his articles with Leverson were safely stamped on 25 June 1862 he arranged to move from Tottenham and live over the office at 12 St Helen's Place,[109] off Bishopsgate (Street). This soon became a mecca for political and other refugees. At a time when he was 'seeking some "brother man" who would "give me leave to toil" ', and a free breakfast 'was a matter of some consequence',[110] W.E. Adams and his wife were regular guests. At the end of October James Thomson was courtmartialled for being with a party of schoolmasters, one of whom swam in a forbidden pond at Aldershot, and discharged from the army. He took up residence with the Bradlaughs. There was now little time for Iconoclast's freethought lectures in the provinces save at weekends. The opposition had dwindled from being a hazard to a nuisance. Thinking of Barker and Holyoake, Bradlaugh wrote at this time:

> 'We honestly affirm that we have had opposition more severe and unkind offered to our approval of the opinion of Malthus than to our most extreme heterodoxy in theology.'[111]

Soon after this the National Reformer Co. was wound up.[112] Bradlaugh was appointed liquidator and thus became sole proprietor and copyright owner.

The popular cause was steadily expanding in 1862. The London trades' unions formed the Manhood Suffrage and Vote by Ballot Association, and the Working Men's Club and Institute Union began. Renewed demonstrations were held in support of Garibaldi, who had been prevented by Victor Emmanuel II, the nominal King of Italy since the previous year, from invading Venice and Rome. On 28 September a great crowd swamped Hyde Park to protest against the protective occupation of Rome by French troops. Bradlaugh was asked to speak. Among the radicals who came from all parts of London and met him on that occasion was a young freethinker Robert Forder. Also in the crowd were a number of Irish Catholic toughs singing 'God and Rome' and secretly armed with bludgeons and other weapons. Though John Watts was the secretary of the Garibaldi Demonstration Committee, the meeting was not properly organized and speaking began on mounds of earth and gravel. Suddenly the Catholic 'lambs'[113] charged with shillelaghs swinging and 'an attempt was made to stab Mr Bradlaugh'.[114] A number of Grenadier Guardsmen who supported Garibaldi linked their canes in the van of a counter-assault which retook the mound. Bradlaugh never confused courage and foolhardiness and later said: 'We have no wish for immediate martyrdom, and considerably abbreviated our speech when we found that knives were used as arguments.'[115] Towards the end of the year the death of Bernard was the occasion of a great international rally at the graveside. Italy, Germany, Poland, Hungary and France were represented. Among the Russian *émigrés* were the republican intellectual Alexander Herzen and the militant anarchist Michael Bakunin, who had just reached London after an epic flight across Siberia to Japan and America. Holyoake and Bradlaugh both made speeches. Their dispute was trifling beside the in-fighting of the Continental revolutionaries, but on this occasion fraternal solidarity prevailed on all sides.

Throughout the winter Bradlaugh was busy in two related causes. The American Civil War had cut off the main source of cotton and thrown thousands of English textile workers into unemployment and squalor. So to his advocacy of the Northern cause in the war he added appeals for victims of the Cotton Famine. Apart from the General Relief Committee, a Lancashire Secular Union Special Distress Fund was established, for many charities would offer aid only as a *quid pro quo* for church attendance. At the same time the Irish Church and land questions made one of their periodic surfacings from the bogs of apathy, and, with the help of Peter Fox André, Iconoclast went to work on the Anglo-Saxon conscience. But the great issue of 1863 was Poland. Russia had been in occupation of Poland since the Congress of Vienna, and there were sporadic insurrections. Refugees had established a Polish Democratic Committee in Britain in 1831, but only a few radicals and other *émigrés* paid much attention. Then, during the night of 15 January 1863, on the pretext of ordinary conscription, Russian police seized all their known opponents. A major uprising broke out whose shock waves spread over Europe. Palmerston, now back in power, expressed 'the deepest sympathy' but could not see how Britain might intervene. Others called for joint action by the Vienna powers. With the help of Bradlaugh a Polish Committee of support was established under the chairmanship of Taylor and secretaryship of W.E. Adams. Before long, Bradlaugh's commendation and eloquent testimony from his own *Reformer* pieces secured for Adams an appointment as leader writer on Cowen's *Newcastle Chronicle*. Thomson then took over the secretaryship. The poet had perhaps always been unstable and melancholy, and the collapse of his career did not help. He fell into periodic drinking bouts, when he walked out on friends and responsibilities and took to the streets. Eventually someone would find him and bring him home a wreck. In May he walked out on the Polish Committee, leaving its affairs in disorder.

These multifarious worries and activities sapped Iconoclast's great strength, always more muscular and psychological than organic, and 'his health broke down'.[116] He decided to hand over the editorship of the paper to John Watts. In his farewell message he revealed more than ill health. First, he was concerned to answer the perennial rebuke to freethinkers, that it is easy enough to pull down religion but what are you going to put in its place?

> 'Tell the backwoodsman, who, with axe in hand, hews at the trunks of sturdy trees, that his is destructive work, and he will answer: "I clear the ground, that plough and reaping-hook may be used by and by." And I answer that in many men—and women too, alas!—thought is prison-bound, with massive chains of old church welding; that human capacity for progress is hindered, grated in by prison bars, priest-wrought and law-protected; that the good wide field of common humanity is over-crowded with the trunks of vast creed frauds, the outgrowth of ancient mythologies . . . Atheist, without God, I look to humankind for sympathy, for love, for hope, for effort, for aid.'[117]

To this humanist message he linked gratitude to his enemies.

> 'I pray the opposing forces to continue their attacks, that by teaching me my weakness they may make me strong.'

But these comforts were intellectual, abstract. The jeers of Christian scholars and pseudo-scholars had left their mark.

> 'I am an Infidel, a rough, self-taught Infidel. What honour shall I win if I grow grey in this career?'

None, certainly, from fashionable society. For this he cared nothing. But was he valued by the masses for whom he worked unsparingly? Or even by his colleagues?

The row with Holyoake was snarling to its close, and deeply troubling him. It was always assumed that because he had an aggressive manner and cross-examining virtuosity that he was quarrelsome, litigious, insensitive. Few people really knew him. He had a small circle of intimates and was too busy to cultivate wider friendships. Even in the secular movement his actions were misrepresented. Why did those who cheered the words of goodwill and co-operation so loudly in halls of science, who mouthed them so eloquently themselves, slide so quickly into slander when they moved outside?

'Your duty lies not in petty personal strife, but in the diffusion of the great and mighty truths for which our predecessors have risked stake and dungeon. Your duty is not to take part in disputes whether John or Thomas is the better leader, but rather so to live as to need no leaders. A public man's life is composed of strange phases. If successful, he wins his success with hard struggling. As he struggles the little great ones before him, who envy his hope, block up his path. His ignorance is exposed, his incapability made manifest; and then when he has won the victory, and made a place for standing, each envious cowardly caviller, who dares not meet him face to face, stabs him with base innuendo in the back. I do not envy any statesman's character in the hands of his political antagonists, still less do I envy when I hear him dissected behind his back by his pseudo-friends.'

Was it all worthwhile? He cared little for himself, but he had a growing family. The past as always had lessons. Carlile had died poor and neglected in Central London, his family unprovided for. Southwell had died poor, and even more neglected, in New Zealand. When he could afford to, Robert Cooper pulled out. The faithful Adams was about to leap. Thomson would not, but Thomson could not. Holyoake was keeping an eye, and often two, on the main chance. He had effectively wandered off into other fields, merely keeping a stake in his old territory, with the *Secular World*, in case someone else struck a rich vein. Bradlaugh was now in his thirtieth year.[118] He really ought to give more time to his profession, or to making his pile. Then he could return to a life of propaganda with security and independence.

CHAPTER FIVE — ON THE THRESHOLD

'I am in favour of the establishment of a National party which shall destroy the system of government by aristocratic families, and give the members of the community born poorest fair play in their endeavour to become statesmen and leaders, if they have genius and honesty enough to entitle them to a foremost place.' — 1868 *Election Address.*

Bradlaugh's legal career, as orthodoxly understood, did not last long. Like Harvey, Leverson had grown more and more interested in the world of finance and in 1860 was solicitor to several companies.[1] He was also a patent agent and member of the Metropolitan and Provincial Law Association. By 1861 these companies had gone and by 1863 his association membership had 'lapsed'. In September of that year the Italian Coal and Iron Co. Ltd moved their registered office from under his wing to Windsor Chambers, Great St Helens, a maze[2] of passages just south of St Helen's Place and Church. Some little time after this his articled clerk joined the general exodus. It was just in time. The City's fraud investigators were interested. Two years later a warrant was issued and Leverson hastily left the jurisdiction.[3] Bradlaugh appears to have made no further attempt to embrace the law. His age was now against him and his notoriety growing; two unfortunate legal associations were little recommendation. The Bar, where his talents really lay, was prohibitively expensive and even more clannish, establishmentarian and class-dominated. As he had picked up a lot of financial expertise and had a quick mind and plenty of push, he decided to devote himself to business. Setting up an office[4] at 23 Great St Helens, whither the Italian Coal and Iron Co. moved at the same time, he took on a number of roles: company promoter[5] and secretary; agent for provincial insurance companies; loan broker for Italian municipalities; general financier.

When he left Leverson he returned to a suburban life at Tottenham in Sunderland Villa, a semi-detached house next door to Elysium. Thomson continued to live with him, and family lame ducks—his sister Harriet and brother William, and one or two of his wife's relatives—came for short or long stays. Visitors were prolific. Bradlaugh was unable to drop his public life like a dripping greatcoat, and Blanc, Herzen, the revolutionary barrister, Alfred Talandier, the communist geographer, Elisée Reclus, the poet, Alphonse Esquiros, and other Continental refugees dropped in. His house was an island of cosmopolitan freethought and revolution in a sea of suburban respectability. Yet he was not without local contacts. His children went to a nearby school taught by two maiden ladies. The young Bradlaughs were generally popular, though eyebrows were raised at their being withdrawn from religious instruction.[6] Regularly commuting with City gents, he was invited to join the Tottenham High Cross Lodge No. 754 (after his anti-theological views[7] had been discussed and dismissed). After a year he ceased to subscribe when it changed its locale, and he ostentatiously returned his certificate when the Prince of Wales became Past Grand Master of the United Grand Lodge in 1869. He also figured for about a year on the local vestry. His first recorded attendance was in May 1864, when he gave notice for the next meeting 'to consider the state of an open ditch at the bottom of Park Lane',[8] the street some distance to the back of his house. On the vestry he was caught up with other interests of the time: the cost of draining the Burial Ground, the accounts of Mary Overend's Charity, accommodation for the vestry officers, and the supply of fresh water. Bradlaugh was appointed secretary of a committee to investigate the last problem, and wrote to the Tottenham Local Board of Health asking for the right to inspect reservoirs, water-mains and service arrangements, but not wishing 'to act in a litigious spirit towards the Board'.[9] These important public health matters were apparently disposed of satisfactorily by the summer of 1865. The vestry's solid work continued in more modest fields, but Bradlaugh moved on to other spheres worthier of his epic talents.

His provincial forays were now confined to the weekend, with a Sunday morning, afternoon and evening lecture. The morning one was political, the evening theological, the afternoon optional, but increasingly political. The Polish and Lancashire crises continued and engaged most of his attention. In April 1864 Garibaldi came to London and caused such excitement that Gladstone, then Chancellor of the Exchequer, successfully hinted that the Italian revolutionary should abandon his provincial tour 'in the interest of his health'.[10] The National Reform Union was founded in Manchester and the International Working Men's Association (First International)[11] in London, but Bradlaugh played no part. The following year the American Civil War ended with a victory for the Union and William Lloyd Garrison came to Britain to thank John Bright, Bradlaugh and other radicals who had supported it. Around this time the National

Reform League was founded in London. A Christian radical and barrister, Edmond Beales, was its president. Its secretary was George Howell,[12] then a sceptic, a bricklayer and a council member of the International. Bradlaugh was a vice-president from the start. Among his colleagues were George Odger,[13] a freethinking official of the ladies' shoemakers and secretary of the London Trades Council, who became president of the International; William Randal Cremer,[14] general secretary of the International; Lucraft,[15] who had joined the council of the International; and William Bonner, a clergyman and lecturer for Pease's Peace Society. Not only were there these diverse ideological and class interests among the reformers, there was considerable dispute among advanced thinkers over how far the franchise might reasonably be extended, or whether the whole structure of government should be changed instead.

Thomas Carlyle was ridiculing the parliamentary system as a 'national palaver' and yearning for some unspecified 'hero' who would lead the nation with distinction and disinterest. Opponents denounced this as reactionism but were uncertain how to advance. If everyone had the vote, said many liberals, not only would working-class representatives be in the majority but they would constitute the entire Commons, as there was no constituency where Burke's 'swinish multitude'[16] did not outnumber the other classes. Surely this would lead to a dictatorship of the proletariat in very earnest, and deprive many reformers of proven intellect and dedication of their seats. So alternative proposals were made. The most obvious was simply to lower the property qualification slightly.[17] This principle was the basis of Bills by John Bright[18] and Edward Baines. Believing it to be unacceptable, Earl Grey proposed a system of apartheid whereby the poorest classes would be put on a separate register for a national constituency to elect a certain number of representatives. F.W. Newman[19] declared it was more important to promote temperance than to extend the franchise. Mill[20] advocated universal suffrage, but got cold feet and suggested a plurality of votes for the wealthier classes. Charles Buxton elaborated this plan. Holyoake toyed with the Grey and Buxton proposals and then suggested an 'Intelligence Franchise' as 'he is not a democrat, but an anarchist, who insists that the vote of the most ignorant shall count for as much as that of the most highly educated class in the community'.[21] Still retaining his confidence in the people, Bradlaugh urged 'that every sane human being unconvicted of crime should have the means of exercising, through the electoral suffrage, an influence on the management of the public affairs of the state in which he or she is resident'.[22] Anxious that minorities should be represented and votes should not be wasted, he supported Thomas Hare's proposals for proportional representation and preference voting.[23] Then he turned to tactics. Popular agitation had in the past led to 'state prosecutions for treason and misdemeanours', but without it the workers were 'upbraided for their apathy' and 'little concession has been obtained by the people from their rulers from a sense of justice'.[24] Bradlaugh was to play a key role in the league in urging the committee to maximize their demands and demonstrations.

His other interests continued. There were provincial lectures and debates. William Bendall was unable to renew the lease of the City Road Hall of Science, and a Hall of Science Co. Ltd was formed with Bradlaugh's aid to provide new premises. At a soirée and ball for foreign delegates to the International, he took Ernest Jones's place in seconding Cremer's address to the 'great Republic'.[25] At home he had dependants to be helped. He found his brother William a job as a book-keeper and manager to a freethinking tailor and furnisher. After forming the Caerhun Slate Co. Ltd,[26] he got Thomson the post of secretary. This was more an act of kindness than prudence, for Thomson was as unstable as ever. But Bradlaugh was prospering[27] and 'B.V.' was valuable in other ways. He provided intellectual conversation of an evening in the den, and devotedly took the children on rambles and told them stories.[28] They idolized their father, whose stern rebuke—he did not believe in corporal punishment—was more effective than their mother's beatings, but, apart from some fishing expeditions to Carthagena Weir up the Lea on Lord Salisbury's Hatfield estate, his life left little time to devote to them. In February 1866 his career as a capitalist reached its high point with the formation of the Naples Colour Co. Ltd,[29] principally to manufacture bright corrosion-resisting paints and steel from the ferruginous sands near Naples. It had a nominal capital of 5,000 £10 shares, of which only seven were issued. Bradlaugh himself had one; so had his clerk James Potterton,[30] Thomson, a well-to-do secularist James Hillel, whose affairs Bradlaugh managed, and three other associates.

Then disaster struck. In the heyday of *laissez faire* there were many operators as impatient of moral as of governmental restraint. On one occasion Bradlaugh was negotiating a loan of £750,000 for the city of Pisa. 'His percentage, small in name, was to be considerable in total.'[31] As soon as the deal was arranged, the London financier who was backing it sent his clerk to Pisa to offer slightly better terms in return for the commission. Bradlaugh thwarted him by going to Rothschild, but lost the commission. In May 1866 he went to Portugal to negotiate the supply of horses. Business was proceeding smoothly. Though interest rates in Britain had been high and some country banks and a speculative railway company had collapsed earlier in the year, he had no anxieties about the situation at home when, on the 10th, a telegram summoned him back. The great discount house of Overend and Gurney, with £19 million commitments, had collapsed. The following day, 'Black Friday', saw a panic. Within a week numerous banks and credit companies went bust and the bank rate rose to 10%. Once a decade something similar had happened, but this was the worst crash to date. Bradlaugh's was not the only company undercapitalized and dangerously dependent on credit. 'The new system of limited liability had tempted large numbers of small and inexperienced capitalists to invest their money in speculative undertakings. As they were for the most part liable to calls on a large proportion of their shares, painful experience taught them that the limitation of their responsibility was little more than nominal.'[32] The crisis 'was the inevitable reaction from the speculative mania and inflated commercial transactions of the preceding year, which had launched so many shallow and fallacious schemes upon the world, seducing thousands of unwary persons into liabilities utterly beyond their power to meet.'[33]

Bradlaugh was not ruined, but dangerously embarrassed. In London, as the bank rate gradually drifted back to normal, and in Italy, he was able to raise enough capital to develop what were basically sound schemes. Factories were built at Granili, Naples, and Hatcham New Town, London, and products of fine quality emerged. But general confidence was a long time returning and he was dangerously stretched. He could easily, like W.S. Gilbert's financier,[34] have gone bankrupt, paid what he had, and started again under a new name. Instead, he reduced his overheads, worked harder and battled on, buying up shares and paying off debts when he could.[35] One liability vanished when 'B.V.' moved into lodgings in Pimlico.

Throughout Bradlaugh's life triumphs and disasters, dangers and difficulties, flowed together. Just before the crash two unexpected problems welled up. John Watts, only 32, was suffering from tuberculosis. In April he fell seriously ill[36] and had to relinquish the *Reformer*. Busy as he was with business matters, Bradlaugh decided to resume the editorship and Charles Watts became sub-editor.[37]

John had been able but had lacked Iconoclast's dynamism. The paper's circulation had gradually sunk to an all-time low. Life had to be transfused. Bradlaugh had no sooner begun the daunting task than the most distressing libel of his career occurred. At the top of his street[38] lived a chemist, W.J. Wall, who was a friend of Dickens. He attended All Hallows, the ancient parish church near Bruce Castle, and knew of the rivalry between its Anglo-Catholic vicar, the Rev. John Hale,[39] and the militantly Low Church vicar of St Paul's in Park Lane, the Rev. Hugh McSorley.[40] Using material supplied by Wall, Dickens published a skit in the magazine he was conducting at the time, *All the Year Round*,[41] and this 'very unadvised lampoon',[42] entitled 'Our Suburban Residence', was reproduced in the local *Tottenham and Edmonton Weekly Herald*. There was a bantering reference to churchgoing: 'Sunday is truly a day of rest in our suburban village. We lie late in bed, and breakfast just in time to go to church, which we all do.' McSorley was referred to as McSnorter and the author was identified as living in Park Road. The vicar at once jumped to the conclusion that his notorious parishioner Bradlaugh was responsible, and published an 'Appendix' in the issue of 28 April. Most of it was mere vulgar abuse of 'Swear'em Charley', but it included the following:

> 'The house he lives in is a sort of "Voltaire Villa". The man and his "squaw" occupy it, united by a bond unblessed by priest or parson. But that has an advantage; it will enable him to turn his squaw out to grass, like his friend Charles Dickens, when he feels tired of her, unawed by either the ghost or the successor of Sir Creswell Creswell.'

McSorley might just have got away with this if Iconoclast had been married in a register office, but as he had been married in an Anglican church the statement was defamatory *per se*. Both writer and paper published profuse apologies and the former contributed £100 to local charities. He also expressed gratitude that Bradlaugh allowed him to remain anonymous (so as not to ruin his prospects in the Church), but continued to attack the infidel in ultra-Protestant publications.

At a great demonstration for Reform on Primrose Hill in May, Bradlaugh 'awakened in the wind-chilled throng a faint thrill of something like enthusiasm', especially when he declared, of the House of Lords, 'he would like to see that wretched institution that battened upon the life-blood of the English people swept away for ever'.[43] Some eighteen years later he amplified and moderated this bald statement:

> 'If the spiritual peers will retire from the House, and if the hereditary privilege be gracefully abandoned, then the question is purely one of reform, and to win that reform the present holders of power by privilege should even be met in a liberal and generous spirit.'[44]

The demonstration launched a new Reform movement and a cry to 'mend or end' the obstructive Lords. If they would not consent to reform however, it was unlikely they would ratify a Commons Bill for abolition. The alternative was revolution, and he desired 'to avoid encouragement of revolution in this country'. Some peers were happily 'disposed to regard reform of their House as necessary, and with a strong popular movement many more peers might not only be brought to regard such reform as inevitable, but the legislative proposal for such reform might come from the peers themselves'. Even in April 1866 he was still prepared to accept a slice instead of the full loaf, agreeing with 'Caractacus' that while Earl Russell's Reform Bill was 'not a measure about which a Radical, a Chartist, a Republican can be expected to go into ecstasies . . . reform makes reform more easy'.[45]

In June Russell resigned after the defeat of his Bill. Derby came to power to 'stem the tide of democracy'. The country was in turmoil. A protest rally in Trafalgar Square was organized by the National Reform League on 2 July. Mayne banned it, then changed his mind. 'The mass soon commenced clamouring'[46] for Bradlaugh. Three weeks later he was a leading spirit in a demonstration at Hyde Park. Some days in advance Mayne announced that the gates would be closed. Two days before, the council of the league met to decide a course of action. Cremer wanted to call the protest off. Bradlaugh urged it should proceed but not use force. This view prevailed. Thousands marched to the gates. Beales, Bradlaugh and other leading leaguers demanded admission. With flourished truncheons and bustling horses the police refused the demand. The procession then divided and marched off to Trafalgar Square for the speeches. Bradlaugh led a contingent down Park Lane. Suddenly a breakaway section tore up the railings to take the park by storm. Iconoclast tried to prevent them, was mistaken by some as a government spy and knocked down. But soon he rallied the errant and the army of the unenfranchised moved peacefully to the square.

In the middle of these excitements Bradlaugh put out a new feeler for what had always been a cherished project. The *Reformer* called for plans 'to place the Secularists of Great Britain, who, during the last few years, have enormously increased in numerical strength, in more intimate communication with each other'.[47] A few weeks later 'a National Secular Society, having its headquarters and office-bearers either in London or Lancashire, and having branches in all the provincial towns'[48] was formally proposed. Because of the density of secular societies it was 'suggested that Lancashire or Yorkshire would be the most fitting centre for the commencement of such an organization'.[49] By September a programme was drawn up: (1) to form a mutual help association (2) to conduct a more vigorous freethought propaganda (3) to expand the General Secular Benevolent Society for the aged and distressed (4) to remove disabilities on religious opinions (5) to establish secular schools and adult instruction classes. The first principle was 'that the promotion of human happiness is the highest duty'.[50] Four candidates were given for president: Robert Cooper; Bradlaugh; John Watts, already at death's door; Harriet Law, 'not what would be called a woman of culture' but with 'a great deal of natural ability'.[51] Sometimes with her husband Edward, sometimes alone, she fearlessly trod the lecture halls, defying groans and stones, in support of freethought and feminism. This, too, was now gaining national status since the presentation of Mill's petition for women's suffrage of 7 June 1866.

The issue of the presidency was never in doubt. Iconoclast was chosen. Charles Watts became secretary. Largely for their convenience, the society was based on London, not the North. With his barnstorming provincial tours and rapidly growing prestige as a popular leader of national status, Bradlaugh gradually got all but four[52] of the local societies throughout the country to join the National Secular Society. In his hands it became not only a sounding board for the great intellectual issues of the day, which he and his colleagues did much to popularize—biblical criticism, Darwinism, comparative religion, the rise of sociological, anthropological and archaeological studies—but also a sensitive instrument for political performance. A signal would suddenly go out from the society's general council or officers, often from Bradlaugh personally, and in all major and many minor centres of population throughout the country indoor and outdoor meetings would be held, leaflets distributed, petitions signed and MPs lobbied.

With the equally indefatigable Beales, he tramped the country selling Reform. Always the people welcomed him. Sometimes the moderate Liberals looked askance. At Northampton they felt the

Corn Exchange and Mechanics' Institute were suitable venues, but the Town Hall[53] was a different matter. Many of them were as disturbed as the Tories at the rising popular enthusiasm, and wondered how big a bank of reform would be needed to stem the flood. Every effort was made to damage the livelier reformers, and through them the league itself. Bradlaugh was an obvious target. Enemies were able to take out of context sentences of impassioned oratory which could readily be construed into threats of revolution. And they tried to smear the league with his heretical views. He was, as it happened, scrupulous about the segregation of opinion in his campaigning. While it was common for orthodox reformers to begin, 'Speaking as a Christian', he never at political meetings claimed to be 'speaking as an atheist'. The most that could honestly be said was that when he went alone on a Sunday lecturing programme, his placards would list the three subjects for the day and 'Reform' might lie side by side with 'The Twelve Apostles'. While the title was unsensational enough, as his titles always tended to be, his attitude to these biblical personalities was by this time a matter of common notoriety.

On one such occasion, at Huddersfield in November 1866, the local freethought society had booked the Philosophical Hall, paid a deposit and moved in a harmonium. On the Saturday night the proprietor was persuaded to cancel his contract, and Bradlaugh found on the Sunday morning that the doors were locked and barred. As the harmonium constituted legal possession he decided to force his way in. Smaller alternative accommodation was available, but he did not wish to disappoint friends who had come from miles around to hear him—or, indeed, to give a triumph to the orthodox of Huddersfield. Secular friends, including the brothers-in-law of the future trade union leader Sir Ben Turner,[54] brought along a crowbar, and Iconoclast was himself twisting it out of shape when he was arrested. It was all he could do to stop them from rescuing him. Two supporters went off by cab to find a liberal magistrate who would go bail, but before they returned successful, Bradlaugh had talked his own way out. Wonder and joy, as when Peter was miraculously delivered by the angel, spread through the city and the lecture on Reform had an apostolic audience. The following Tuesday he appeared before the magistrates charged with damaging the hall door and committing a breach of the peace. Prosecuting counsel insisted that both charges be heard together. Bradlaugh persuaded the court it had no jurisdiction on the first count and, to the rage of the prosecutor, the second count lapsed with it.

At the quarterly elections of the league in December Bradlaugh was returned to the executive. But enemies were looking for a chance to discredit him. Week by week they watched the *Reformer* for something incriminating. Their temperature rose when the Rev. Charles Voysey, vicar of Healaugh, Yorkshire, began contributing letters. One of these promised to work 'with all my heart to remove the stigma which attaches to my order through its blind and senseless bigotry'.[55] In a private note he gratefully accepted Bradlaugh's offer of complimentary copies of the paper, adding, 'The fact of your being "self-taught" adds much to the feeling of respect with which I regard both yourself and your work'.[56] In June he contributed further letters, suggesting the term 'God of the Bible' 'ought then to be abandoned as useless and misleading'.[57] Voysey was now a marked man and two years later was convicted of heresy in the Chancery Court of York. In February 1867, still dominant in the league, Bradlaugh appeared in a new role at a Trafalgar Square rally. As a mounted deputy-marshal, he impressed bystanders by showing more control over the crowd than a contingent of police and even pursued a stone-throwing youth up the steps of the National Gallery. But a few days later, 'for many reasons'[58], he resigned from the executive of the league. On this occasion Howell persuaded him to change his mind. Immediately afterwards J.P. Adams reproduced in the *Reformer* a German anti-Trinitarian fable, translated by Southwell and entitled 'Fanatical Monkeys'. On 9 March the *Saturday Review* published an article 'Who are the Leaguers?' citing Bradlaugh as the source of the offending fable. Two days later the *Standard* gave the story wider circulation, and it stayed with him all his life. Such lurid publicity distressed Beales and 'injured the League with many in a moral and pecuniary point of view', but did not outweigh the secularist's 'oratorical power and talent'.[59]

On 18 March Disraeli, the government leader in the Commons, introduced a Reform Bill. Led by Gladstone for the Opposition, a prolonged wrangle to liberalize it ensued. The league gave outside backing. Though he had declared his intention of opposing any government ban on public demonstrations, Bradlaugh was re-elected to the executive. A great Hyde Park rally was called for 6 May. The second reading of a Parks Bill was announced for the 2nd. If it went through the demonstration would be illegal. That morning Bradlaugh went to Beales with a petition asking to be allowed to speak against the Bill at the Bar of the House, and sought his advice on who should present it. Bradlaugh mentioned Bright, but 'as the papers were then linking together Bright, Beales and Bradlaugh we passed Mr Bright's name'.[60] Beales suggested Mill, but they agreed on Gladstone. In the course of conversation with the 'People's William', Bradlaugh expressed his firm view that the rally was legal and would proceed whatever the government attempted, and Gladstone sent him with a message urging moderation on the Home Secretary, Spencer Horatio Walpole.

On the morning of the rally Thomas Hughes, the Christian Socialist who had become a radical member for Lambeth, heard some lobby gossip alleging that Iconoclast, after being the first to urge resistance, had gone to the House to see Gladstone and Disraeli and put himself in the clear in the event of a major collision. Hughes urged that the whole thing be called off, but Beales, Bradlaugh and a majority of the league's executive stood firm. The *Times* had just expressed the view of the Law Officers of the Crown that intervention would be illegal, but in the afternoon Derby sent a message to the league's office at 8 Adelphi Terrace announcing he had invoked park regulations to intervene.

That evening the Royal Horse Guards and 4,500 soldiers assembled. The league's supporters advanced, its militant Holborn and Clerkenwell branch turning up with a red flag and red cap of liberty on a red pole, playing the *Marseillaise*. Republicanism was ready to emerge. Among the leaders of the demonstration were the O'Donoghue, a prominent Irish MP, Hughes, Taylor, Beales and Bradlaugh, than whom, said Fleet Street, 'perhaps no man connected with the Reform League has laid himself open to more harshness of censure, for violent speech'.[61] But when 300 leaguers marched up to a bench seeking to commandeer it for his address and three men on it declined to budge, Bradlaugh said they were entitled to it and went off elsewhere. Derby changed his mind once more, the troops took no action and the meeting came to a 'quiet conclusion'. By this time, however, so much controversy was associated with his name that Iconoclast thought it right to tender his resignation from the league executive again. Because of the 'many, very many sneers and innuendoes', Howell felt unable to press him to reconsider as he did before, and simply thanked him for the 'utmost kindness, and ... very able support'.[62] Beales expressed his 'great pain' and 'very sincere regard'.[63] The Reform Bill came before the Lords in June as Derby's 'leap in the dark'. Ratepayers and £10 lodgers in boroughs were admitted—more than the Whigs[64] had originally offered. A million new voters appeared. But millions were still unenfranchised.

Just before the introduction of the Reform Bill, Sunderland Villa had many Irish visitors. Bradlaugh was one of the few Englishmen who really knew or cared much about Ireland. Her plight had improved little since the fifties, and Irish patriots were only awaiting suitable opportunities to rebel. Many of them had gone to the United States, where John O'Mahony founded the Irish Revolutionary (later Republican) Brotherhood. At Chicago in 1862, this brotherhood, now known as Fenians (dwellers in Ireland), proclaimed their intention of establishing Irish independence by armed force. The end of the Civil War in 1865 found many of them armed and jobless. They split into two forces, one which invaded Canada, the other which returned to Ireland. The following year the British Government panicked and introduced a Coercion Bill suspending Habeas Corpus in Ireland. In the early months of 1867 various Irish Land Bills were introduced but lapsed. Habeas Corpus was again suspended.

It was at this stage that General Cluseret and Colonel Kelly called on Bradlaugh with a draft Proclamation. It 'proclaimed the Irish Republic, and appealed to the religious and Catholic feelings and the sentiment of race that animate the Irish people'.[65] They wanted his reaction as a liberal Englishman, and his legal advice. He was in a difficult position. Both his sympathy for Ireland and his republican views were well-known. At the same time he was 'against any separation of Ireland from England. I am against it as an Englishman. England is not strong enough to do without Ireland, and I do not believe, on the life of me, I do not believe that Ireland is strong enough to do without England. You are not as you were, nor are we. You are married to us, and we are married to you.'[66] What he wanted for the British Isles was a federal system of government, with separate parliaments for Ireland, Wales and Scotland. He was also opposed to any appeal to religious bigotry. And he was against needless violence: 'I do not ask you to present your cheek to be smitten; but I do entreat you not to be the first to raise your hand to strike.'[67] Bradlaugh got to work on the draft. He recalled the appeal 'in vain to the reason and sense of justice of the dominant powers . . . against the aristocratic leeches who drain alike our blood and theirs . . . Remember the past, look well to the future, and avenge yourselves by giving liberty to your children in the coming struggle for human freedom'.[68] It is debatable how much Bradlaughisms interleave with Fenianisms. Certainly he managed to remove Celtic racialism and Catholicism: 'We declare also in favour of absolute liberty of conscience, and the complete separation of Church and State.' Kelly apparently made some final revisions before, as a compositor, he set the text up himself overnight. One of these additions was the climactic 'Herewith we proclaim the Irish Republic'.

Very soon sporadic uprisings occurred in England and Ireland. Kelly and Captain Deasy were arrested in Manchester in September. Thirty friends ambushed the police van carrying them. Their guard, Sergeant Brett, refused to open the door. They shot at the lock and accidentally killed Brett behind it. Many of these 'Manchester Martyrs' were tried for murder. Three of them were hanged, despite the plea of their counsel, Ernest Jones. While they were under sentence of death in November Bradlaugh addressed a great but fruitless rally for reprieve at Clerkenwell Green, supported by the 'poor man's lawyer' William Prowting Roberts. But when, the following month, some Fenians blew up Clerkenwell Prison to rescue General Burke, killed twelve and wounded 120 local residents, Bradlaugh denounced this 'Clerkenwell outrage'.[69] In January 1868 he produced a pamphlet on Ireland urging a Commission of Inquiry into Irish grievances. Gladstone declared: 'With many important parts of it I cordially agree.'[70] Ireland was now the pivot of Bradlaugh's political addresses, but the Quakers declined his services when they learned of his atheist identity. The following month an Ireland Society was formed with his aid to disestablish the Church of Ireland, settle the land question and promote education and Irish industries. He crossed the sea to speak for the Irish Reform League, and earned the gratitude of most Irish Catholics. In England his meetings competed with William Murphy's violent No Popery Campaign, and Orangemen burst angrily in.

His private worries continued. In January 1867, despite pleading that won high praise from Vice-Chancellor Wood,[71] he failed to win £12,350 owing to him as commission on a transaction for the English Joint Stock Bank Ltd. In May there began the voluntary winding up of the St Nazaire Co. Ltd in which he was interested. The Naples Colour Co. Ltd was forced to borrow money[72] from Baron Geraldo Ferreira dos Santos e Silva, secretary of the Portuguese Legation first in London and then in Vatican City. In August Bradlaugh had to take action in the Court of Commons Pleas against a debtor.[73] A similar but much more famous case in the same court took place four months later. *Bradlaugh v. De Rin* involved the realization of bills of exchange. It was heard before Mr Justice Montagu Smith, his old rival from the Devonport days, and a common jury. While saying that he had 'never seen any conduct on his part unbecoming a gentleman',[74] counsel for the defence objected to the swearing of Bradlaugh as he was an atheist. Privately believing that such objections should be waived, Montagu Smith said he would allow affirmation. This too was objected to. Then the facts of the case were agreed and a rule *nisi* was granted to the plaintiff pending solution of the legal conundrum whether the law of France, where the bills were last endorsed, or the law of England operated. The following July the Court of Common Pleas granted a rule absolute reversing the former decision. Bradlaugh appealed to the Court of Appeal. Bail had to be given for costs and Austin Holyoake was tendered; but he too was unable to be sworn. Agitation was fomented throughout the country by the National Secular Society and led to the passing in August 1869 of the Evidence Further Amendment Act. This was not just an act of common justice to Bradlaugh. Orthodox jurists were able to point out that an important felony prosecution might depend upon the testimony of an atheist, who could be objected to as the law stood. By gradual evolution one class of citizens after another had been made eligible to affirm. 'The discovery of truth in courts of justice has been signally promoted by the removal of restrictions on the admissibility of witnesses, and it is expedient to amend the law of evidence with the object of still further promoting such discovery.'[75]

Meanwhile the Court of Appeal had found that there was a question of fact to be decided: were the bills posted to Bradlaugh in England or handed to him in France? A Q.C., S. Prentice, was nominated to ascertain this simple fact. Again objection was taken to evidence from Bradlaugh as a man who did not believe in 'any being independent of the universe, governing or ruling it' or 'a future state of rewards and punishments'. Everyone believed there was now the alternative of affirmation, but Prentice disallowed this and Justice Brett upheld his decision. Bradlaugh appealed to the full Court of Common Pleas. Lord Chief Justice Bovill and Justices Keating, Brett and Montagu Smith said he could not proceed without an affidavit. He would have to swear that he was incompetent to swear. Though sarcastic at the time Bradlaugh, who throughout his life believed that the law of England was a perfect substitute for the law of God, doggedly proceeded. He was allowed to swear the affidavit, but the court decided it had no power to instruct an arbitrator. Then he appealed on an overriding point of law to the Court of Exchequer Chamber, sitting in Error. The new Lord Chief Justice, Sir Alexander

Cockburn, Lord Chief Baron Kelly, three justices and two barons unanimously decided that he was entitled to sue and awarded him the verdict. It was a great victory for Bradlaugh, for freethought, for British justice; but it cost him more than £1,100 to get it. Not even the original debt of £360 was recovered. De Rin promptly went bankrupt. The plaintiff had no complaint against the courts. The High Court judges of England were very different from petulant country magistrates. Even Prentice was right. Though originally drawn up by a sympathetic and able lawyer, J. Denman, who was himself to become a justice, the 1869 Act applied only to a 'court of justice' and a 'presiding judge'.[76] Technically an arbitrator came outside this purview. As a result of more secularist activity Denman's new Evidence Amendment Act 1870 defined these terms 'to include any person or persons having by law authority to administer an oath for the taking of evidence'.[77] Jurymen, affidavits, and Scottish courts were still excluded. It was uncertain what was the position of members of parliament.

In the middle of the De Rin struggle a more vexatious, equally triumphant, somewhat less prolonged piece of litigation occurred. On 3 May 1868 the *Reformer* announced itself 'Published in Defiance of Her Majesty's Government, and of the 60 Geo. III cap. 9'.[78] This was the first of three 'Security Laws' directed against 'Pamphlets and printed Papers containing Observations upon public Events and Occurrences, tending to excite Hatred and Contempt of the Government and Constitution of these Realms as by Law established, and also vilifying our holy Religion'. It defined a 'newspaper' as a publication more frequent than every twenty-six days, not more than two sheets of newsprint in size, and costing less than sixpence. The proprietor was required to give a recognizance of £300 and two or three sufficient sureties 'in a like sum in the whole' against the appearance of 'blasphemous and seditious Libels'. These sums were increased to £400 by an Act[79] ten years later. Penalties for non-compliance were £50 for every day of publication and £20 for every copy sold. On every issue of the *Reformer* since 1860 this would amount to something like £70 million, but the Treasury Solicitor was good enough to reduce this by many millions through confining himself to two issues. After a period of phoney war the fight was on. A Defence Fund was opened and supported by Mill, Austin Holyoake, Watson, Truelove, Ayrton, Milner Gibson, MP, and Collet Dobson Collet, secretary of the Association for Promoting the Repeal of the Taxes on Knowledge. Gladstone had tried unsuccessfully to name the

Security Laws in his reforming measure of 1855, which abolished the kindred newspaper stamp. So had Ayrton in 1857. Then, in the absence of prosecutions, concern had dwindled. The fact was that since the demise of Holyoake's *Reasoner* no popular heretical paper had been stable enough to excite establishmentarian alarm.

As soon as Iconoclast resumed the *Reformer* and began to build it up in 1866, the English Church Union started gunning for it. Its editor had since become a political force to reckon with, and more influential figures joined the attack. In this new defence he played the usual game of attrition, having Informations set aside as defective or demonstrating procedural errors by the Law Officers of the Crown. The case was to be heard before Baron Martin in the Court of Exchequer on 13 June 1868. The prosecution was led by the Attorney-General and Solicitor-General. Bradlaugh defended himself. In their excitement his friends in court bubbled like new wine. Suddenly they went flat. Only ten jurors turned up and the case lapsed. At the end of the year the Liberals under Gladstone were returned. To everyone's amazement, on 16 January 1869 he took up the Tory gauntlet. A new set of Law Officers went through their paces before Baron Bramwell. Chivalrously the Attorney-General offered to renounce the penalty if Bradlaugh would comply with the law. But the editor had no intention of yielding, 'even if we could find friends insane enough to enter into recognizances'[80] whose doom was sealed by almost every issue. The Crown gained a verdict but seven points were reserved. On 8 April the government brought in a Bill to repeal the Security Laws, but the case went on, Bradlaugh arguing before Kelly, Bramwell and Baron Cleasby that his periodical was not technically a 'newspaper'. By the end of the month the prosecution was called off after what Collet called 'the most valuable personal contribution ever made to the liberty of the Press'.[81] But 'not one paper has said a word in our favour, or congratulated us on the battle we have had to fight'.[82] Most of them felt they had nothing to fear. They took a different line however in 1872 when the Postmaster General threatened to withdraw the *Reformer's* registration for overseas transmission. As this was a universal weapon, the journal was widely backed and the threat withdrawn.

There was one accolade still to fall to Iconoclast: parliamentary honours. In days before MPs in lobbies had 'to leave that brain outside and vote just as their leaders tell 'em to',[83] to become a member was the ultimate achievement. Especially was this true of men of humble origin, who looked towards the legislature as a mystical presence in the way mediaeval lepers gazed through the squint of the parish church at the altar and the elevated host. Party machines[84] were still unpatented. It was not until the Unitarian Joseph Chamberlain, the new radical member for Birmingham, formed the energetic National Federation of Liberal Associations (the 'Birmingham caucus') in 1877 that modern politics came alive. Even then there was no national party manifesto, though the address to his electors from each party leader in the Commons had a quasi-official status. After the passing of the 1867 Representation of the People Act, Iconoclast looked increasingly towards parliament. He was now a national figure, known and loved by thousands, perhaps millions. In any system of proportional representation his election would not have been in doubt. But he had to find a single constituency that would return him, and this was a very different matter.

Some effort had been made in the recent Reform Act[85] to correct the gross under-representation of his home territory, with the division of the old borough of Tower Hamlets into Tower Hamlets and Hackney, including Bethnal Green and Shoreditch, each with two members. The problem was, however, more sociological. Though Bethnal Green was friendlier and more stable than other parts of the East End, there was generally a 'lack of neighbourliness and co-operation among working class Londoners' and 'it was common for a third of the population in working class districts to move during each year'.[86] Lodger voters had to be resident for a year, and re-registered every year, before they became eligible. With so much mobility this was difficult. Poverty intervened to bring apathy, and in the absence of local officials or, very often, party workers, many voters never troubled to get registered at all. In the original industries of the district, workers tended to live over or near their places of work and be peculiarly subject, before the advent of the ballot, to influence from their employers. Conversely, artisans in the newer industries often walked long distances from their homes and had trouble getting to the polling booths in opening hours. Though there were many devoted secularists, with or without the vote, in the East End, there were also many devout Jews, Catholics and members of other immigrant religions. In reaction partly to this 'invasion' and partly to their poverty, many Anglicans and Nonconformists clung to their religion with a sharp possessiveness that made their resentment of Charlie's atheism particularly deep and bitter. It was one thing to be cheered in the Philpot Street hall or chaired on Clerkenwell Green; it was quite another to get enough local voters to turn out and name him as their man. As for bourgeois Tottenham . . .

So he turned his back on London and offered himself for North-ampton. The borough had a notable radical history[87] dating from the Domesday Book. Becket was tried at Northampton Castle in the twelfth century, and the town supported the barons and de Montfort in the thirteenth. At this time there was a short-lived local university. Great councils and parliaments frequently met at the castle or priory from the twelfth to the fourteenth centuries. In the latter part of this period Northampton, being near the village of Lutterworth, where Wycliffe was rector, was influenced by Lollardism. During the Wars of the Roses the Battle of Northampton was won by the House of York. Robert Browne, founder of the Independents, spent most of his life here, and one of the Martin Marprelate Tracts was published locally. It thus had 'the reputation of being one of the most puritan towns in England'.[88] Throughout the Civil War it kept Cromwell's army well-shod, and it gladly provisioned him for his crucial victory at nearby Naseby. When Charles I surrendered to the Scots and was handed over to the English, he was held for a time at a neighbouring manor. In the early eighteenth century the borough, inspired by the Congregationalist divine Dr Doddridge, supported the Whig succes-sion against the Pretenders, but then it declined in size and influence. It gained a lurid notoriety in 1812 when one of its MPs, Spencer Perceval, became the only British Prime Minister to be assassinated in office. As the nineteenth century advanced and its population and living standards rose, the boot and shoe industry had a renaissance, especially after the introduction of machinery.[89] By 1868, however, this had extended only to rough work, and skilled operations were still done by outworkers at home. The worst rigours of the 'dark Satanic Mills'[90] that blighted the industrial areas further north with slums and resentment never reached Northampton. By the time the shoe industry was fully mechanized, improved labour relations, trade union bargaining and some social conscience were nationwide.

When Bradlaugh began campaigning, 38 per cent[91] of all house-holders were engaged in the boot and shoe trade. 'Shoemakers were ever philosophers and thinkers . . . They lived a full life, based on their own resources, and so built up a sturdy independence on the social and intellectual side, as well as in industry.'[92] They were used to working in isolation and with concentration, but they had great community spirit and periodically erupted with ideas and actions on the social scene. Down the years they have had something of a repub-lican reputation, contributing English radicals like Thomas Cooper,

Allen Davenport, George Odger and the Paineite Thomas Hardy, and being named as instigators of the Paris Commune in 1871. 'There has always been a curious kind of affinity between shoemaking and free-thinking.'[93] This should not be interpreted too narrowly. The 'infidel Crispinites' were to become notorious in Victorian England, but 'as a matter of fact there were fewer Freethinkers in Northampton for the population than in any town of its size'.[94] The many nineteenth-century churches and chapels—a lot of the latter redeployed today—bear testimony to a surging religious spirit in the town throughout the Bradlaugh period. But it was a Nonconformity with noncon-formism, a Christianity without christology, a baptism in the fire of politics and the water of religion, sects without sectarianism. There 'everyone is more or less a politician'[95] and 'the mildest Liberal in Northampton would be termed a Radical elsewhere'.[96] In short, Iconoclast 'showed great skill in selecting Northampton as his con-stituency'.[97]

Gurney and Thomas Adams nominated him, in his absence, in February and supporters began to subscribe towards his expenses, but it was not until June, the time of the first Trades Union Con-gress, that he published his acceptance and election address *To the present and future electors of the borough of Northampton*. It was a highly personal amplification of the Gladstonian formula, 'peace, retrenchment and reform'. He called for (1) compulsory national education (2) land law reform (3) purging the public sector of ex-pensive aristocratic drones (4) wealth and land taxes (5) equality of capital and labour before the law and the provision of industrial courts of arbitration (6) disestablishment (7) representation of minorities in parliament (8) the abolition of penalties on opinion (9) all new peers to be life peers for national services, habitually absent peers to be deprived of legislative privileges, and voting by proxy in the Lords to be abolished (10) the replacement of the Whigs by a truly National party.

One of the most characteristic of advanced radical proposals of the period was (2): land law reform. Bradlaugh therein named 'abolition of the laws of primogeniture and entail; diminishing the enormous legal expenses attending the transfer of land, and giving greater security to the actual cultivator of the soil for improvements made upon it'.[98] The strength of the English barons *vis à vis* the monarchy, which was always the envy of their Continental peers, stemmed from the English system of inheritance. This was directed towards the maintenance of the big estates by ensuring unbroken succession through the eldest son or nearest male relative, without division among younger brothers or the possibility of sale. This had a number of consequences. There was no great incentive for an indolent heir to develop the property efficiently; a lot of land was kept permanently off the market, thus raising the price of what did change hands; there was always a swarm of impecunious younger brothers for whom sinecures had to be found at court, in the army, civil or colonial service, government (backed by safe parliamentary seats) and the like.

Not only was this a grave injustice but, to a practical man like Bradlaugh, a sad waste of scarce resources and a means of keeping abler men out of office. Most of the cultivated land on these large estates was not worked by the owner himself but was rented to tenants who had no security of tenure. If they improved it they ran the risk of being charged a higher rent for what was now a more valuable property and, if they refused to pay, of being displaced by someone more co-operative. If they did not improve it agricultural wages remained low and food prices for city workers high. The population explosion of nineteenth-century England introduced another element in the 'tight little isle'. As Bradlaugh put it some years later,

> 'In a country like our own the ownership of property has surely its duties as well as its rights. The labourer able to work who will not work is prosecuted and punished as a rogue and a vagabond. It is a misdemeanour for a labourer to suddenly transfer his labour from what has been his domicile in order to avoid the maintenance of his family. He is indictable at common law, and printed rewards may be seen on most workhouse gates for the apprehension of labourers who have absconded, leaving to the community unfair burdens. Unoccupied and unused land near great towns escapes the local rating, whilst its value for building purposes is often enormously increased by the mere augmentation of population. Why should the owner of this land escape its proper burden any more than the labourer, who is punished if he tries to escape?'[99]

This situation lent colour to the orthodox views of an influential Manchester School economist Stanley Jevons. But Marx and Engels described as 'vulgar Economy'[100] the belief that rent, like cost, depended on supply and demand. The Marxists believed that rent was 'the payment of the English capitalist farmer to his landlord'[101] and that cost depended on labour value. They saw the landlord as a more or less passive instrument who benefited incidentally from the machinations of capitalists.[102] Indeed Alfred Russel Wallace said that a freer trade in land would not open it up to the people but, as in Ireland, to 'capitalist English manufacturers and speculators'[103] who could afford the price. To individualist reformers like Bradlaugh, on the other hand, the capitalist seemed to be a man of initiative whose enterprise put a premium on available land and lined the pockets of parasitic landlords. Many radicals who were shocked by demands for full nationalization of the means of production, distribution and exchange, did call for the nationalization of land. Bradlaugh seldom, however, pursued abstruse theory except in matters thrust upon him and never demanded outright nationalization of all land, though his ideas on land, whose primacy he recognized, evolved throughout his life. Always he advanced reform against revolution. His 1868 proposals were substantially those of Maccall, who had unsuccessfully advocated a National Land League in the *Reformer* a few years before.[104] His basic intention was to abolish 'laws which make pheasants more valuable than peasants'.[105]

The campaign in Northampton was one of the liveliest in England. Friend and foe vied to publicize it. The radical women of the borough met to choose Bradlaugh's election colours and settled on green, white and mauve.[106] Leading members of the National Reform League supported him. So he wrote to a local Liberal: 'May I hope to have your valuable co-operation? Mr Beales and the League support me in my candidature.'[107] When this assertion was publicly challenged, he asked Howell to put the matter on the executive's agenda so that he would 'be able to state officially that I have the support of the Council of the Reform League'.[108] The executive sent Odger to investigate Bradlaugh's prospects and, on receiving a favourable report, endorsed his candidature. In elections of the day it was customary for supporters, no longer bribed on the spacious eighteenth-century formula,[109] to run up the maximum of expenses against their candidate. The remarkable thing in Bradlaugh's case was the modesty of his budget, the proud determination of his poorest campaign worker to charge nothing for his own expenses and if possible contribute to the candidate's rail and hotel bills. For it was soon apparent that the existing Liberal organization in the town, the 'Bundle of Sticks', would not endorse him. Their candidates were the sitting members, Lord Henley, nephew of Sir Robert Peel and a conscientious Whig, 'still clinging to State Churchism and all that it implied, for instance, in National Education',[110] and Charles Gilpin, a liberal Quaker. Bradlaugh contended that the 1867 franchise had doubled the electorate,[111] that Henley was no longer representative of Liberal opinion in the borough, and that the fairest thing would be to have a 'primary' contest, as Ernest Jones had had in Manchester, between himself and Henley. The Liberals would not agree. Many, like Gurney, walked out to support Bradlaugh. Bates was his election agent. Odger, Austin Holyoake, Truelove and Charles Watts came up from London to speak on his platform. Hostile cartoonists got to work representing Iconoclast struggling along on an 'old donkey Secularism' as his opponents galloped past on more respectable mounts.

The secularists were soon joined. The Rev. James Applebee, minister of Stoke Newington Green Unitarian Chapel in London, 'at once packed my gripsack and travelled down to Northampton, with the view of doing what I could to aid'.[112] His local colleagues more discreetly lent their help. To those already 'on the slippery slope to atheism', Bradlaugh's heresy was of little moment. Not so in the shrines of orthodoxy. Unavailingly did Bradlaugh cease all secularist lectures in the town as a token of his complete political impartiality, and call attention to his long record of public service without—for his part—ever quoting a theological quibble. His notoriety was enough. But even in 1868 there were rays of that liberal Nonconformism that was later to shine so brightly upon him. The first breakthrough came when Councillor Thomas Purser, deacon of Princess Street Baptist Chapel, threw in his lot with the atheist reformer. Gradually the feeling grew that 'the Market Square stump orator',[113] as the Whig *Mercury* described him, was not offering himself as a candidate for local preaching but for the national legislature.

With certain exceptions, sectarian support for Bradlaugh divided on class lines. In Victorian England, as in modern America, this was one function of denominationalism. Well-heeled Anglicanism was Tory. Prosperous Congregationalism and Wesleyanism were Tory or Whig. Presbyterianism, with its Scottish associations, was Whig or Liberal if only from hostility to the English Tory Establishment. Poorer Primitive Methodism, 'pre-eminently the religion of the industrial north and midlands',[114] and most Baptists were Liberal or Radical. In 1868 there were some 1,000 Catholics in Northampton, many of them Irish who had come originally to carve the railways through the midlands. Though their main church had had cathedral status since 1864, they were not at this time very active in the local community. Since pogroms in the thirteenth century there had been few Jews in the town.

Bradlaugh's campaign soon escalated to national proportions. Even a National Party was formed with some of his demands for its platform, but stipulating that electoral divisions ought to be equal in 'area of land' and 'the rights and privileges of the Sovereign in no way to be disturbed, but to be energetically upheld'.[115] The *Daily Telegraph*, then under Liberal Jewish control, deplored the 'outrage on good taste' committed by a man who encouraged Englishmen to 'revile the sublime moralities of the New Testament'[116] while standing for parliament. In reply Bradlaugh condemned the editor's 'want of good taste or good feeling'[117] in this witch-hunting. Kite-flying letters were written to national figures and the replies published. Bright did 'not think you can improve the Representation of your Borough by changing your Members'[118] and Gladstone considered 'both these gentlemen entitled to respect and confidence'.[119] The Working Men's Lord's Day Rest Association posted the town with warnings of what would happen to its Sunday rest if the atheist were returned. And Charles Capper, MP, sought to father on him a 'watch story' that refuses to die.[120] It originated in America[121] and was even imposed on women freethought lecturers like Harriet Law. Bradlaugh inherited it in 1867 through the Tory journal *British Monarchy*. The infidel was supposed to have taken a watch from his pocket and given the Almighty five minutes—in different versions the time ranged from one to fifteen—to prove His existence by striking him dead. Capper impudently claimed to have got the story from Gilpin and refused to apologize when this was indignantly denied. Bradlaugh brought an action against him but he died before it could be heard.

A more serious libel appeared in an obscure rag[122] *The Razor*. It sought to connect Bradlaugh with the frauds of Leverson and with William Broadhead of the 'Sheffield outrages'. These were acts of violence, including a gunpowder plot, against Sheffield non-unionists in 1866, followed by the appointment of a Royal Commission of Inquiry into Trades Unions and a special Commission, which in turn stimulated the formation of the TUC. Bradlaugh began proceedings against the publication when a promised apology did not appear. In the hearing before Justice Blackburn and a common jury at the Guildhall, counsel for the defence attempted no justification of the libel but ladled up the religious issue, garnished with Southwell's 'Fanatical Monkeys'. When Bradlaugh refused to answer his questions he then told the jury 'it is fair to assume that he has no character which can be injured by such a criticism as this'.[123] Despite censure of these tactics by the judge, the jury, obliged to find for the plaintiff as the defence had called no witnesses, awarded him a farthing damages. Bitterly he posed the question, 'Outlaw or citizen? Which am I?':

> 'If when I am libelled I take no notice, the world believes the libel. If I sue, I have to pay about one hundred pounds costs for the privilege, and gain the smallest coin the country knows as a recompense. Duelling is forbidden alike by my code of morals and the law of the country. If I horsewhip[124] the libeller, I am punishable for assault.'[125]

Naturally he pursued the matter. The High Court granted a rule for a new trial. In November 1869, before it could take place, a full apology was published. The proprietor was now in financial difficulties and soon ceased publication. Bradlaugh never collected his costs, which totalled £200.

If there were frustrations in his election campaign there were also satisfactions. Believing Bradlaugh to be 'a man of ability, and . . . the reverse of a demagogue, by placing himself in strong opposition to the prevailing opinion of the democratic party on two such important subjects as Malthusianism and Personal Representation',[126] Mill sent £10 towards his election expenses. Whereupon, despite his liberal theology, Dean Stanley urged Liberals in Westminster, Mill's own constituency, not to vote for him. Edward Keevil, vice-president of the Irish Reform League, 'gladly and heartily' recommended Bradlaugh 'to the Irishmen and friends of Ireland in Northampton',[127] and earned the displeasure of the Irish priesthood. As the weeks proceeded the zeal of his supporters, who in later years called themselves the 'Old Guard' in distinction to the bandwagon-jumpers, mounted. A young shoemaker, James Wilson, wrote 'Bradlaugh for Northampton', set to music by John Lowry, which was to ring through the borough streets for a generation and with a devotion out of all proportion to its literary excellence:

> We'll toil, we'll toil in freedom's cause,
> Nor rest content with vain applause,
> But fight determined for just laws,
> And make our member, Bradlaugh.[128]

Another shoemaker, Robert Hill, 'Bradlaugh's Lieutenant', canvassed all day and made his shoes at night. His home in the Mayor Hold was the campaign headquarters. On one occasion he entered to tell the candidate he had found fifty votes available for a sovereign. 'Hill', said Bradlaugh, 'if I could have every vote on the register for five shillings I would not pay it.'[129] Canvassing had been forced on him, much to his—and Gilpin's—displeasure,[130] by a precedent set by a rival candidate. As if two Tories and two official Liberals were not enough, he had to contend with the intervention of another radical, the temperance advocate, Dr Frederick Lees, who paraded 'a public life of thirty-five years, devoted to the spread of Education, morals, and religion'.[131] As his irritation with Lees increased, Bradlaugh disputed this pious claim. Election posters and speeches embarrassingly proclaimed 'Gilpin and Lees' and 'Lees and Bradlaugh', though Gilpin was pledged to Henley and both Bradlaugh and Lees to Gilpin. Wilson's muse was answered by siren voices from the Whigs:

We will NOT have him—cannot let
Northampton sink so low,
Our standard shall be right with might,
No, BRADLAUGH, no!—you go.[132]

Some were a good deal less polite. 'Bradlor's Friend' depicted the typical Bradlaughite as a chap 'so drunk, he scarce could stand'. A cartoon 'BOMBASTES BRAGLAW, HIS PROCESSION' featured him as a man crying 'Hurrah! No work and all Bull's Eyes'. The local clergy leapt to arms. Lees's was a banner the most radical could decently rally round. The Rev. Thomas Arnold, the town's leading Congregationalist, urged Nonconformists not to vote for ' "the fool" who "has said in his heart there is no God" '; and that became the slogan of St Giles's Evangelical Anglican church, which has persisted to today. Bradlaugh's old enemy Gedge dispensed his hostility from All Saints. It became pointless to pretend any longer that Iconoclast and Charles Bradlaugh were two separate people, so he dropped the *nom de guerre* for good. On 17 November the candidates appeared on the hustings. Gurney, now a councillor, nominated Bradlaugh. At the last moment Lees withdrew, after wasting almost 500 radical votes. Bradlaugh's speech got the greatest applause, but, apart from Lees, he got the fewest votes: just over 1,000.[133] Gilpin and Henley came in first. Both the mayor and Gilpin paid tribute to Bradlaugh's compaigning, and Gilpin contributed £10 to his election expenses. Mill lost at Westminster.

A year later there was a vacancy at Southwark and Bradlaugh's was one of six names put forward. Gibson and Odger were two others. At a meeting of working-class electors to which Odger was unable to come, Bradlaugh was overwhelmingly selected to stand on their behalf. Admiring Odger, grateful for his support in Northampton and, despite subscriptions, burdened with debt from that election and vexatious litigation, he declared he would not stand in opposition to the 'inspired shoemaker'. Odger, who had recently withdrawn from Chelsea and Stafford, decided to offer himself to the newly formed Labour Representation League and Bradlaugh called on his friends to support him. Though Odger was unsuccessful, he did considerably better than the official Liberal, Sir Sydney Waterlow.

Bradlaugh was unable to relax after the excitement of the Northampton election, for personal and professional problems were piling upon outstanding litigation. For the campaign he had had to borrow £600 from an acquaintance, Javal, offering the machinery of the Naples Colour Co. as security. Javal in turn raised money from the Advana Co. In January 1869 Bradlaugh moved his office to 15 Palmerston Buildings, 34 Old Broad Street,[134] whither the Naples Colour Co. and Caerhun Slate followed him. The Italian Coal and Iron Co. moved to the neighbouring office, No. 16. At the same time his brother William nearly bled to death from acute haemorrhage of the gums and 'recruited my strength at my brother's house at Tottenham'[135] till he returned home in June to get married. Haemorrhage was not William's only disability; like Thomson he was subject to periodic binges. Susannah Bradlaugh's condition had also deteriorated. Though she bravely managed to hide the fact in public, as when she visited Northampton during her husband's campaigning, she was by now a chronic alcoholic. Expensive hydropathic treatment was tried, but in vain.

Bradlaugh's other activities threaded through his life. The National Secular Society began to assume some elements of a church when Watts introduced a secular Sunday school and a ceremony for the naming of infants as recruits 'to fight against the evils and wrongs which will confront . . . in the stern battle of life'.[136] Later Austin Holyoake devised a marriage, and a burial service: 'We this day consign to the earth the body of our departed friend . . . He derived his being from the bountiful mother of all; he returns to her capacious bosom to again mingle with the elements. He basked in life's sunshine for his allotted time . . . He fought the good fight of Free Inquiry, and triumphed over prejudice and the results of misdirected education . . . He had long been free from the fears and misgivings of superstitious belief . . . The atoms of this earth once were living man, and, in dying, we do but return to our kindred who have existed through myriads of generations.'[137]

112

In 1869 all the recognized intellectuals of the country came together in the Metaphysical Society. Very soon this was mirrored by a poor man's version, the London Dialectical Society, which met at 1 Adam Street, the home of the Social Science Association. Bradlaugh was a leading member from the start and joined its committee investigating spiritualism. With his iron grip upon the leading charlatans of the day, rapping tables were choked in their cadenzas and D.D. Home obstinately refused to levitate. Academic colleagues on the committee, like Professor Wallace, were more favourably impressed by the alleged phenomena. These diversions lasted several months. Spiritualism was then a leading topic of the *salons* and the academies, even of some secular societies, and the ghost had to be displayed or laid.

Returning to more serious themes, Bradlaugh nursed along the popular movement. In December 1868 he was re-elected to the executive of the Reform League, but the tale of 1833 was to be retold and the following March the league dissolved with the resignations of Beales and Howell. On behalf of the millions still unenfranchised, two months later the Working Men's National Reform League, followed by the Poor People's Union, came into being. At the same time Bradlaugh assisted Mill and Taylor's wife 'in extending the operations of the Women's Suffrage Society in new directions'.[138] His demand for state education gained powerful augmentation from a National Education League. Among its supporters were Chamberlain, Mill, Henry Fawcett, the Cambridge economist, radical member for Brighton and 'member for India', and Sir Charles Dilke, 'a metropolitan *rentier*'[139] and new member for Chelsea. When an International Republican Association was mooted in July 1869, Bradlaugh was invited to participate, but it came to nothing.

His lecturing continued unabated. At Blyth the Bedlington Secular Society was unable to find a hall, and a chapel was provided for his lecture on the bible. Afterwards he found there were no trains or cabs available and no hotel would provide hospitality. A then unknown miners' official, Thomas Burt, caused a 'flutter' in his Primitive Methodist 'dovecot'[140] by inviting the notorious atheist home to supper. Later in the year, when Seghill Colliery Schoolroom was refused him, Father O'Dwyer offered him his Catholic chapel. He now had a secure forum in London. In 1868 he had raised £1,298 for Robert Owen Smith to build a New Hall of Science in Finsbury at 142 Old Street,[141] between a coffee room and an appraiser's. Just behind was an asylum for the homeless poor, and not far away, on the other side of the street, were St Luke's Church and—a godsend for Spurgeon and other clerical wits—St Luke's Hospital for Lunatics. As its name suggests, Old Street was one of the oldest streets in Britain, part of the military way to Colchester. For many centuries the area was noted for its salubrious climate, rose gardens and orchards, but by Bradlaugh's time its best days were past. The new secularist headquarters was a corrugated iron building including a large hall which would seat 1,200 and pack in 500 more, a minor hall accommodating 200, and rooms for a library, classes, refreshments and committees. Friend and foe alike fell short of adulation. It was variously described as a 'usually sepulchral building'[142] and 'that badly-lit squalid hall in a squalid and prosaic region of London'.[143] But such as it was it belonged to the movement. When other doors were shut upon him Bradlaugh was sure of a 'pulpit' here, and he 'rendered it famous over the English-speaking world'.[144] At different periods Moncure Conway, the new minister of South Place Chapel, Turner, Carlyle, George Bernard Shaw, Charles Stewart Parnell, Professor John Blackie, Lord Snell, Ramsay MacDonald, Prince Kropotkin, George Lansbury, Prince Jérome Napoleon and Olive Schreiner joined the regulars at Bradlaugh's feet, and only the last confessed disappointment. George Meredith probably began this pilgrimage when he wrote to John Morley, then the editor of the rationalist *Fortnightly Review*, 'The man is neither to be laughed nor sneered down, nor trampled'.[145] Far from laughing, in 1870 the churches established the Bible Defence Association and the Christian Evidence Society. In February of that year the Quaker William Edward Forster introduced an Education Bill. A month later at the Finsbury hall Holyoake and Bradlaugh acrimoniously debated 'Secularism, Scepticism, and Atheism'. Confusing secularity and secularism Holyoake censured Bradlaugh for jeopardizing secular education at that vital moment by advocating atheism as a tenet of secularism. It was too bad, especially when Bradlaugh came 'into the field' only 'at the eleventh hour'.[146]

Allsop told Bradlaugh: 'You are doing *too much* and thinking that you are *bound* to do it and thus risquing your future usefulness'.[147] But he took no notice. He joined the council of the Land and Labour League, and just lost the presidency to Patrick Hennessey. With its slogan of 'The Land for the People', it combined the Chartist proposals with the advocacy of free, secular and compulsory education, the nationalization of land and banking, the abolition of a standing army, 'home colonization' (settling unemployed workers on the land)

114

and a single tax on property (presumably a state rent if the land were nationalized). At the same time Bradlaugh helped to launch at Clerkenwell an influential Patriotic Society with similar aims.

As his theological and political notoriety grew, respectable trades-men thought twice about dealing with companies under such pro-prietorship. In March 1870 an extraordinary general meeting was held and the Caerhun Slate Co. voluntarily wound up. Dos Santos arranged to take over the Naples Colour Co. 'While prejudice and clamour bring ruin to me as a business man', Bradlaugh said, 'they can do me no injury as a lecturer and a journalist.'[148] He made a final decision:

> 'As after five years' severe struggle—so severe indeed as to repeatedly endanger my health—I find it is utterly impossible to remain in business in the City in the face of the strong pressure excited against me on political and religious grounds, I have determined to entirely give up all business and to devote myself solely to the movement.'[149]

The bailiffs moved into Sunderland Villa. On 26 May the household furniture was sold up 'without reserve'. Bradlaugh persuaded his creditors not to take bankruptcy proceedings, which could yield them only a fraction of what was owing, but to give him time and he would pay off all his debts. In the meantime he would reduce his living expenses to a minimum. They agreed.

The family was split up. Little Charley had already left the local school and gone for tuition under John Grant of the 2nd battalion Grenadier Guards, where he was to stay. Susannah Bradlaugh and the two girls went to live with Hooper, now in retirement at Cocking, a village outside Midhurst in the misty downs of north-west Sussex. Bradlaugh agreed to pay £3 per week for their keep. He himself took the two ground-floor rooms of a poky four-storeyed terrace house at 29 Turner Street, [150] Stepney, on the London Hospital Estate. His landlady was a widow who had known the family for many years. At 3s 6d a week the rent was not enough to qualify him for the lodger franchise he had done so much to secure. He filled the rooms with the girls' bed, nursery washstand, chest of drawers, writing table and half a dozen wooden chairs—the least saleable of the Tottenham furniture—and his beloved books. With these to hand he could shut his windows and defy all the drunken brawls and smells outside. And so his life proceeded. Indeed, from the public record there is little to indicate the private tragedy.

In a way, it was less tragic for him than it would have been for

115

others. He had a great head for business, it is true, but he lacked the heart, or, rather, had too much. Not for him that single-minded dedication to the pursuit of wealth and worldly success which distinguishes the real businessman. Certainly he was persecuted by small tradesmen, just as he was ostracized by the baker's wife in his youth, but the world of industry and high finance cares little for speculative opinions. A large measure of Bradlaugh's failure must be attributed to his own lack of concentration. No one was more 'thorough' in what interested him. His real interests were elsewhere. As he himself once admitted, 'I have great faculties for making money; and great faculties for losing it.'[151] In 1870 he was not alone. 'The continued commercial depression was to be attributed partly to the discredit which had attached to joint-stock enterprises since the discovery that liability on shares of which only a small part was called up might be practically unlimited. And other causes were to be found in the ruinous litigation entailed by the power of winding-up companies, and the series of criminal prosecutions of directors for alleged misrepresentation, which, whether right or wrong in themselves, had necessarily rendered men of commercial experience and reputation cautious in undertaking a hazardous office.'[152]

Though essential in themselves, the family's economies served a second purpose. They were an excuse to separate a couple who had other difficulties. In the depths of the country there was some chance of braking the wife's free fall into alcoholism and overspending. Try as he would, and never losing a real affection, Bradlaugh found love and respect draining away. Though not now teetotal he had not lost his emotional reaction to intemperance. It was a sharp irony that his brother and his wife, her brother Edwin and his own soul-mate Thomson all became alcoholics. It is probable he had ceased cohabiting and that this distressed her. As the children grew older and more observant, their parents' strained relations embarrassed everyone. It is also probable that Bradlaugh had little need of physical sex. He was aware of a dictator's character, which he rigorously mastered, and dictators not infrequently sublimate their *libido*. The separation occurred with regret, but without rancour; the children remained devoted to both parents. A month later Charley fell ill with scarlatina[153] and was belatedly sent home. Bradlaugh came down to see him, then returned to London for another court case. Javal had been unable to repay all his loan to the Advana Co., which had bypassed him and seized the machinery of the Naples Colour Co., which Bradlaugh was about to sell to dos

116

Santos. He won the case but in his absence the boy died of kidney disease. His heart cracked. Yet he gave twenty-six lectures that month. As the years passed the girls came periodically to London, usually in alternate months, to give him secretarial help. The Bradlaughs and Thomson all kept up an affectionate correspondence. It was about trivia. Sensibly so. How could anything great flow from two rooms in Turner Street? Nonetheless Lincoln had come from a log cabin to the Presidency.

CHAPTER SIX – LONG LIVE THE REPUBLIC

'During the storm-strife provoked by Charles Stuart's arrogant imbecility, Cromwell had taken the helm of the State ship, and had navigated her, roughly but safely, through tempest, fury, and dangerous passages.' – *Cromwell and Washington: A Contrast* (1875).

On 1 September 1870 an anonymous penny paper appeared. It was called *The Republican: A Monthly Advocate and Record of Republican and Democratic Principles and Movements.* Its slogan began as 'Labour is Prayer' and evolved into 'Labour, the source of all Wealth: of the Food, Clothing and Lodging of the Nation: of the Rents of the Landlord: of the Interest of the Monied-Lord, and of the claims of the Tax-gatherer'. Its opening address set its preoccupations: 'The mission of Republicanism and Democracy is work - and for that work to be complete, we include the evolution of thought or ideas . . . We shall endeavour in our experiment to make the "REPUBLICAN" the "Irreconcilable" to wrong, fraud, oppression, and crime, and fearlessly to speak the truth in preference to saying what is merely agreeable. The press is falling more and more into the hands of the capitalists, and threatens to become their monopoly . . . Whatever may be the wrongs of the governing or capitalist classes, we cannot accept that they should be, as individuals, despoiled and vituperated.' Maccall, that most devoted staple of struggling papers, urged morality on politicians, and an editorial on 'The War' (the Franco-Prussian War, then six weeks old) named war as the 'horrible offspring of Royalty and Imperialism'. A long piece on the Land and Labour League followed. Later issues dealt with the Representation of Labour League, 'an abortive thing, with so long a name',[1] the First International, the French Commune and the English republican movement. There were, as could be expected, harsh words on monarchy, which was indicted for dishonesty, robbery, pauperism and 'wholesale murder'.[2] The economic argument against it was made precise: in the last 32 years the monarchy had cost Britain £12,320,000 while the presidency had only cost the United States £160,000. Now the monarchy was running at £1 million a year and idling on 10 million acres of waste land that could produce £100 million a year. But when the paper turned to how the English constitution could be scrapped and what should replace it, the republican skies clouded over. This was no new experience.[3]

Bradlaugh closely studied the history of any movement he was interested in. What lessons could be learnt from the tortuous path of republicanism? Primarily, that inspired journalism was not enough. People's enthusiasm must be anchored in firm organization or it floated off and was lost. Large programmes were useless. They might be passed at conferences with acclamation, but their supporters could neither digest them intellectually nor hope to tackle the whole gamut of national vested interests at once. Psychological appeals were important. The fostering of idealism tended to divert men from action, but without it they concentrated on self-interest. Not only was this unworthy, it was self-defeating, as their interests were so disparate. Was the main enemy the monarch, Lords, landed gentry, capitalists, priests? Was the goal co-operatives, socialism, communism? How could freedom in ideas, initiative and personal action be made compatible with the suppression of go-getting, either first-generation or hereditary? Bradlaugh came from the workers and identified with them. But he hated the idea of class struggle. He always preferred 'popular' to 'working-class' movements, on the grounds that the latter really fossilized class divisions. His socialist critics attributed this to snobbery, and he did perhaps take a certain satisfaction in aristocratic friends. But, unlike Holyoake, he did not go out of his way to cultivate them, and he used them to advance causes and not personal interests. He realised that the 'social contract' was a sham if it were not signed by all classes. It was easy enough to start class war, but not so easy to end it, with or without the dialectic. Before the upper class hegemony in Britain had ended, angry young men were turning on the bourgeoisie with a special red republican malevolence. He knew its faults well enough. He also knew its virtues. For many years he had commuted with its members without feeling of them or against them. At least they took risks and contributed more to the gross national product than did the landed gentry. And already he could hear the managerial revolution bubbling beneath the lid of tycoonery.

In France the revolutionary situation was, as ever, more dramatic than in England. If he was repelled by the violence of French politics and its guillotine alarums, he was also fascinated. Equally he was impressed by and reactive 'against Bismarck and his blood-and-iron theory'.[4] From his Orsini days he had nursed an almost irrational hatred of Louis Napoleon. Yet, insofar as he cared much for culture, he loved French literature and life. He was fluent in French with an Albion accent, and had often passed through the country on his way to Italy or on Belgian business. Never rushing to oratory for its own sake unless he were himself explosively convinced by his message, he stayed silent when the Franco-Prussian War broke out on 19 July 1870. Then, on 4 September, yet another revolution in France deposed the captured Napoleon and proclaimed the Third Republic. At last he felt able to 'throw in my lot with France − Republican France'.[5] Three days after this proclamation appeared in the *Reformer,* the ragged dwellers of Turner Street, Stepney, were surprised to see a *grande dame* enter No. 29. It was Nina, Vicomtesse de Brimont Brassac. She had come to urge Bradlaugh to stir up British public opinion for the cause of the new republic. Earl Granville, the Foreign Secretary, was, she said, planning to restore Napoleon. She had been well briefed, though her visit was superfluous. Her appeal was simple and direct. There was no sex, and no money involved. A cause in which he believed was its own incentive.

The following day Charles Tissot, the French Chargé d'Affaires, wrote him a briefing letter, suggesting that the Eastern Question[6] was exacerbated by the weakness of France. 'There is there, I believe, a theme to develop and treated with your talent it could produce an immense impression.'[7] On the morrow Bradlaugh moved into action. Ill, bereaved, in debt, he began a new barnstorming tour. At a rally in St. James's Hall, co-sponsored by the positivists, the gas failed and a stampede was averted only by fifteen minutes of his ad libbed reassurances. At the Grosvenor Hotel, where the vicomtesse was staying, he met Prince Jérome Napoleon, a cousin of Louis's who was to become head of the family after the emperor's death. Jérome, or 'Plon Plon', had been notorious in France as a playboy, and only three years before had set up the British floosy 'Cora Pearl'[8] in an £80,000 mansion in the Rue de Chaillot. Events had in the meantime damped his ardour. After the outbreak of the war he returned to Paris from Norway and was given command of the troops in Denmark, which were to attack Prussia in the rear. Because of a dispute over strategy he relinquished this post and went instead on a special mission to Italy. When his cousin was overthrown he wrote to him from Florence, quixotically offering to join him in captivity as 'all defence of our country is impossible for me after the events in Paris'.[9] Napoleon graciously declined. 'Plon Plon' went to Switzerland and then to England. 'The Empire is lost', he told Bradlaugh; 'but there is yet time to save France.'[10] The prince's co-operation was not, however, very welcome to the Government of National Defence, whose Foreign Minister Jules Favre accused him of having provoked the war and then evaded his duty in Denmark. Bradlaugh and the playboy prince took to each other at once, and the Englishman believed that, whatever his past, the Frenchman was now a sincere republican.

A conference of the Land and Labour League demanded recognition of the French Republic. Gladstone invited its representatives to come to Britain. The Provisional Government itself assured Bradlaugh of their gratitude for the 'noble help which you bring to the cause of France and of Europe'.[11] Tissot wrote to Favre that 'M. Bradlaugh has put himself at my entire disposal, and I do not doubt that his help should be fully accepted at any moment it might be necessary to exert new pressure on public opinion'.[12] The moment came within a month, as the French delegates had not created a very favourable impression on Gladstone. On returning from Scotland Bradlaugh undertook 'a new campaign at Leeds, at Liverpool and in the hostile industrial areas where Prussian agents have conducted a counter-propaganda more actively favoured elsewhere by those material interests which a certain number of very important firms attach to Germany'.[13] The war and the pro-Gallic campaign dragged into 1871. There was another great rally at St James's Hall, with Bradlaugh, Odger, Howell, the positivists Professor Edward Spencer Beesly and Frederic Harrison, and the republican Captain (later Admiral) Maxse. It was held to urge the conference of European Plenipotentiaries in London to consider securing peace between Prussia and France without too much loss of French territory, but Favre was unable to get to London. At this time Bradlaugh complained of the snooping activities of Reitlinger, Favre's private secretary. Tissot assured him that the secretary's 'folly' and 'clumsiness'[14] did not surprise him and that France 'will never forget' his contribution to her cause. It is quite likely however that word of Bradlaugh's friendship with 'Plon Plon' had reached France and was being investigated. Understandably, the French were less ready than the Englishman to take their playboy prince's reformation at its face value, and wondered what game he and his associates were playing.

As in the earlier years, so in 1870, the formation of the French Republic recharged a British movement whose batteries, though drawing current from the recent Reform agitation, were pretty flat. Towards the end of the year, as an offshoot to his Radical Club, Fawcett formed at Cambridge a republican club whose secretary was the young mathematics don, William Kingdon Clifford. It defined republicanism as 'hostility to the hereditary principle as exemplified in monarchical and aristocratic institutions, and to all social and political privileges dependent upon difference of sex'. Happily Victoria could sleep soundly in her bed, as the club was 'purely private in its nature, and was scarcely more than a sociable meeting of a set of friends who amused themselves, after the fashion of young men at the University, by taking the title most significant of thoroughgoing opinions'.[15] By the end of the year, however, the papers got on to the story and made it sound far from sociable. At his annual report to his Brighton electors in January, where a hostile vote was pending, Fawcett 'disclaimed all disloyal feeling, and said (what was scarcely necessary to say) that no one would be more opposed than he and his friends to any revolutionary movement'. Nevertheless, the following month, with Taylor and Dilke, he voted against a dowry to Princess Louise.

In Birmingham Cattell 'consulted no one' before he 'initiated the Republican movement';[16] i.e. founded a local club which became a prototype throughout the country. London followed three months later, with Bradlaugh as president, Charles Watts as vice-president and George William Foote as secretary. Foote was only twenty-one but already a rising sun in the secular firmament. He was brought up in Plymouth by his widowed mother, a Wesleyan who allowed him to go to Anglican services, 'found the Lord'[17] at a prayer meeting when ten, lost him when fifteen to the Unitarians, and on coming to London as an eighteen-year-old heard Harriet Law and 'kept himself warm with applauding'[18] Bradlaugh at Cleveland Hall.[19] Shaking hands with the great man 'was the proudest moment of my young life'.[20] Very soon he was writing for the *Reformer* and doing secular youth work. At the inaugural meeting of the London Republican Club on 12 May, Bradlaugh set the tone of the new movement. There were in the country 'evils which it is impossible to fairly remedy while the present system of government endures', which demand a 'social revolution . . . gradual, peaceful, and enduring, rather than sudden, bloody and uncertain'. The Royal Family was 'remarkable neither for virtue, intelligence, decision of character, nor devotion to national interests', and the Lords were 'mischievous'. In the last 144 years the National Budget had risen from £4 million to £70 million and the National Debt from £52 million to £800 million, while fewer than two hundred families owned half of England and Ireland and three-quarters of Scotland. As a result, natural resources were wasted. Some 600,000 able-bodied paupers were without work and eleven million acres of cultivable land uncultivated. Republicanism was concerned with liberty and did 'not attack any Churches except State Churches'. Since the death of Albert in 1861, Victoria had abstained 'almost entirely from any part in public affairs'. This inertia and the vices of the Heir Apparent justified 'the repeal of the Act of Settlement under which alone the Brunswick family have the right to sit'. Yet 'a true Republic cannot exist until the majority of the citizens are both desirous and worthy of political life'. To liberty and fraternity he added equality, 'no dead-level equality of either property or person' but the right 'to climb to be the highest'.[21]

Bradlaugh felt no personal grievance, real or fictitious, against Victoria. But the monarchy was the pivot of a system he detested. If certain legislative and state functions were to be hereditary, what was wrong in making them all? If the Sovereign's privileges went unchallenged, who could object to general class privilege? The monarch was the fount of the law, consecrated by the Archbishop of Canterbury, head of the Church of England, granter of styles and titles, dissolver and opener of parliaments, signer of Bills before they became law, summoner of prime ministers, shibboleth of patriotic songs and the wars they jollied along. It was all very well to say the British monarch was constitutional and her powers mere pomp. Under her were the House of Lords, the Established Church, and the noble families who ruled the army and the constituency parties, sat on benches of magistrates and boards of charities, and pocketed perpetual pensions while the destitute old toiled in workhouses. These powers and privileges were real enough.

The London Republican Club was slow off the mark because Bradlaugh had been busy with France and distressed by the recent death of his mother.[22] Much had been happening across the Channel. On 29 January 1871 a Franco-Prussian armistice was signed and the 132-day siege of Paris lifted. Formal peace was to be made by a re-elected French Assembly, and Bradlaugh was even put forward as a candidate for Paris at the February elections. These returned a government, recognized by Britain, under Adolphe Thiers, a survivor of the revolutions of 1830 and 1848. Essentially he was conservative, republican in name but suspected of betraying the cause before. Many of his new deputies were Legitimist or Orleanist, in favour of restoring the Bourbons. When he agreed to the Prussian demand for a three-day victory occupation of Paris, the National Guard rebelled and entrenched themselves on Montmartre. The people joined them and the Commune was declared on 28 March. Thiers's government retired to Versailles, where—as 'the Prussians of Versaillles'—they organized a second siege of Paris at which the foreign invaders looked on. Inside the capital the red flag was raised, the standing army abolished, the guillotine burnt, prostitution and gambling forbidden, the Jesuits outlawed, the poor protected from landlords and usurers, and free, secular and compulsory education introduced. Bradlaugh had somewhat mixed views about this mixed programme. Many of these measures he had long advocated himself, but there was a fanaticism about some of the *communards* which presaged excesses; while as a civil libertarian he could not agree with the outlawing of the Jesuits. So he stayed silent, 'unable to approve, but refusing to condemn'.[23] To his great pleasure, towards the end of April he was asked to sue for peace between the 'white terror' of Versailles and the 'red terror' of Paris. The terms he proposed were (1) clear national acceptance of republicanism (2) political amnesty for all (3) election of the Chief Executive by the people. He did not unfortunately get past Calais and Boulogne. Under instruction from Favre, the police, asserting that he was a member of the International and an organizer of Hyde Park rallies in favour of the Commune, packed him off home. The following month, tragic and savage in its death throes, the Commune was crushed. Bradlaugh left it to Foote to censure both sides for the final bloodbath and deplore 'the lamentable characteristics of French socialists who seem ever to confound political and social questions, and to have no scruple in resorting to "political and violent remedies for profound social disorders".' Yet he believed that 'the principles which the Commune—though often in error—sought to embody must live and flourish'.[24]

Marx, even better informed in international affairs than Bradlaugh and not squeamish about revolution, submitted to the International a draft *Address on the Civil War in France*, which they accepted for publication. It described Thiers as a 'monstrous gnome', Favre as a forger and Jules Ferry as a once penniless mayor of Paris who had turned blackmarketeer. From this moment Bradlaugh came into conflict with the International, and the beginning of its own disintegration can be traced. Odger and Lucraft, who were absent from the meeting which endorsed the *Address*, withdrew from the organization. While recognizing 'a master pen', Bradlaugh condemned the document's 'coarse and useless personalities'. 'That Jules Ferry was "penniless" ', he said, rather missing the point, 'is surely an objection coming with ill grace from any writer on the popular side'.[25] Then he turned to 'another phase of this sad story' and advertised a fund for refugees from Paris, organised by P.A.V. Le Lubez, who was an auditor of the National Secular Society. In this way he could support the men but not the malice. His general outlook was expressed in social rather than political terms:

> 'We do not want a Commune in England, but we do want that the poor shall not increase in misery, while a very few increase in wealth. Believing that in England a Republic will be possible in a few years, the *National Reformer* desires to train men gradually to take part in it.'[26]

When the refugees arrived, he gave benefit lectures on their behalf. 'The madness of cruelty had been great on both sides,' he asserted; 'the criminality was the greatest on the part of the strongest.' The opponents of republicanism in England alleged that it had been tried in France and found wanting. On the contrary, in France it had 'never been tried at all'. There the middle classes wielded power just as the aristocracy did in England. But the Commune did not recognize the rights of labour in the case of the agricultural labourer. He believed that government belonged 'to all classes equally'. In England 'he desired a Republic, and would work for it, but if he could picture, as the only possibility, the walking to its achievement with bloody hands, fire and smoke, and grim visage, he would turn away now, ere it was too late. Republicanism in France would have enough difficulty without class war'.[27]

Adolphe Headingley Smith, who was later to write an enthusiastic biography of Bradlaugh, intervened to support the Commune. As an English republican and linguist, he had held a commission in Paris in command of ten ambulance men, and exonerated the Commune leadership of any responsibility for the terminal killings. Whereupon Bradlaugh trenchantly attacked it. He had information that the *communards* could have defeated Thiers had they marched on Versailles in March. 'They were fools not to have done so. That, in itself, was a lesson to the people not to put their trust in leaders who were not able to lead them to victory.'[28] Fresh from its first victory over the 'subversive' anarchist Alliance founded by Bakunin, the International found this a suitable opportunity to turn its attack on Bradlaugh. A report by its new general secretary, John Hales, published in the Hackney *Eastern Post*, asserted that the refugees were so indignant at the secularist's criticisms that they resolved not to accept financial aid 'from a man who had traduced and insulted them'.[29]

Though it is unlikely that any refugees present at the meeting and able to understand Bradlaugh's fluent English, would have been particularly pleased by his observations, he was able to demonstrate that the report was 'absolutely untrue'. The official body of *émigrés*, La Fraternelle, had accepted his help gratefully. Wrongly assuming that Marx was the instigator of this attack, he concluded:

> 'I feel indebted to Karl Marx for his enmity. If I were one of his own countrymen he might betray me to his government, here he can only calumniate.'[30]

Marx retorted that, on the contrary, since the *Address on the Civil War* Bradlaugh, 'that huge self-idolater', had 'chimed in with the world-wide chorus of slander against the "International" and myself'[31] by first suggesting that the German was a Bonapartist and now a spy for Bismarck. He challenged the Englishman, a dupe of 'the infamous Émile de Girardin and his *clique*', to express himself more openly so that he could be challenged in an English court. In the same paper Hales denounced 'dirty tools' used for 'dirty work' in 'the recent Bonapartist intrigues'. Le Lubez, who had chaired Bradlaugh's meeting on behalf of the French refugees, came to his defence. He declared that the language used by Marx and Hales against Bradlaugh, a man who 'criticizes fairly, openly, and in decent language', was 'a disgrace to any cause', and pointed out how often the secularist leader had 'paid money out of his pocket'[32] to support deserving causes.

In the meantime, another report of the International sought to discredit Bradlaugh among the popular party by quoting a tribute to him from the French Right-Wing paper *Le Soir*;

> 'Mr Bradlaugh has never been present at a meeting of the International. Mr Bradlaugh has never exchanged a single word with M. Karl Marx. Mr Bradlaugh is a sensible constitutional (governmental) Republican, and has no taste whatever for the demagogical intrigues with which he is being mixed up.'[33]

An anonymous letter[34] in the *Eastern Post* dissociated Marx from the International reports, while Hales denounced Bradlaugh as 'this pretended Republican egotist'.[35] In repudiating 'all sort of connection with the political tendencies of *Le Soir*, the 'egotist' emphasized that, in talking about the Commune, 'I never mentioned or alluded to the International, I made no attack upon it'.[36] Marx declared that Bradlaugh's imputation that he had 'given information to his own Government' was a 'calumny, as ridiculous as it is infamous'[37] and called for facts. His opponent suggested arbitration by a Council of Honour. Of this proposal, stemming from what he called 'the low cunning of a solicitor's clerk', Marx was contemptuous:

> 'Does he really fancy that a Bradlaugh ... have only to slander me, in order to make me amenable to clear my public character, and even to do so before a "Council of Honour", of which the friends of those "honourable" gentlemen must form part? I have done with Mr Charles Bradlaugh and leave him to all the comforts he may derive from the quiet contemplation of his own self.'[38]

In the ensuing months Marx was to be busy inside the International, getting rid of Hales for what Friedrich Engels and he called 'his own personal intrigues',[39] and finally outflanking the anarchist Alliance at the Hague Congress by shunting the International off to New York, before returning to his writing. It is unlikely that Marx and Bradlaugh would ever have been able to find a joint programme for the English republic, but their public wrangle, together with the disintegration of the International, was not auspicious for republican prospects. This was realized by Bradlaugh and some supporters of the International, who tried to patch things up.

While the London republicans were jockeying for position, the cause was advancing throughout the country. In April 1871 the students of Wadham College, Oxford, formed a republican club, and a three-night conference was held at the Eleusis Club, Chelsea, to inaugurate a Universal Republican League. Towards the end of the year it announced that its 'programme has been accepted by a large number of the Democratic party in the country'[40] and called for support in securing a Central Republican Hall in London. It does not seem that this was ever found, but the Old Street Hall of Science served pretty well the same function. As republican clubs were bursting out across the country the *Republican* called for 'a better means of intercommunication'.[41] By August it announced a republican campaign. Courtesy titles for the children of the aristocracy should be attacked, the *'long credit system'* which allowed the nobility to be in debt to tradesmen for years should be abolished, and 'a very large reduction of Royal allowances'[42] should be demanded.

Early in the year Bradlaugh had written *The Land, the People and the Coming Struggle*, which attracted some notoriety. Soon he produced a more famous manifesto. Many of his pamphlets began life as pungent 'open letters', articles in the *Reformer*, or debates.

The Impeachment of the House of Brunswick was born as a series of lectures, which raised storms throughout the country. It was to go into several editions and be the most famous of all his publications. When the Northampton Town Hall was booked for this indictment, only the casting vote of the mayor, Pickering Phipps Perry, confirmed the booking, thus enabling the iconoclast 'to insult the Royal family at a given time and place'.[43] More subtle insults were on the way in parliament itself. In July Gladstone announced a £15,000 settlement for Prince Arthur on his coming of age. Taylor moved its rejection and got eleven votes; George Dixon, the chairman of the National Education League, moved its reduction to £10,000 and got 53. In his speech 'Dixon indicated that he was forced to demand a reduction of the vote by his constituents, among whom Republicanism, he said, was spreading, because they considered it cheap'.[44] To point this statement, Odger organized a protest meeting in Hyde Park. The government tried to ban it. When, however, Bradlaugh advised that the ban was illegal, it was raised at the last moment.

In the autumn a 'nine hours movement'[45] gained strength in Newcastle and support from the Universal Republican League. At an agricultural meeting on his home soil at Hughenden, Disraeli admitted that Victoria, then suffering from a sore throat and glands, was 'physically and morally incapacitated from performing her duties'.[46] Bradlaugh took this as a text for a London lecture, giving it a somewhat different gloss. Then he turned to the Prince of Wales:

> 'My opinion is that if four or five years of political education are allowed to continue in this land, that worthy representative of an unworthy race will never be king of England . . . I trust that he may never either sit in the throne or lounge under its shadow.'[47]

At the King's Nympton Farmers' Club in November Earl Fortescue interpreted this as an 'impudent and disloyal announcement that he and a certain number of his friends would take care that the Prince should never come to the throne'.[48] Many journals called for his prosecution.

Bradlaugh attached more than propagandist importance to Disraeli's observations. At the annual conference of the National Secular Society in September 1871 he declared:

> 'The illness of the Queen—which was of a more serious nature than officially stated—if it did not end in death, would probably end in a regency. It was advisable that they should consider

the question so that they might be prepared for any event'.[49] Declining to accept nomination for the ensuing year he moved the election of Arthur Trevelyan as president. With obvious regret this was agreed to. Bradlaugh was heavily committed with his journalism and lecturing, and was toying with the idea of standing at the next suitable by-election. But his decision to relinquish the presidency was probably determined mainly by a wish to be officially uncommitted to a particular party if the chance of a republic should soon occur.

The speculation was not entirely idle. Lacking popular devotion the Queen had attracted little active hatred. It was certain that as long as she was alive and chose not to abdicate the monarchy was secure. But if her health were indeed so precarious that she might imminently disappear from the scene, the political situation would be highly unstable. Thanks largely to the exertions of Bradlaugh himself, the Prince of Wales was a figure of active antipathy. The prospect of his becoming Head of State might well precipitate a constitutional crisis. Waiting in the wings were the republican contenders. One of them might be called on. Bradlaugh looked round at his rivals. There were, as he said at the time in the *Reformer*, grave doubts about the decisiveness of established public figures like Mill and Bright. Dilke had a *coterie* of personal friends and was becoming known throughout the country, but in many ways lacked the common touch. Odger was a great favourite with the workers, but they were largely unorganized. Within the International Hales and Marx were the leading figures. It was, however, riddled with factionalism and had never had a solid English base outside London. Though not lacking in ambition Hales was a political lightweight. Even if he had had ambitions in the presidential direction Marx was as an alien and a supporter of 'red revolution' out of the running. His image was too un-English, insofar as he had an image at all in the country at large. But in the secular movement and its satellites Bradlaugh had a nationwide sounding-board, guaranteeing him a platform, an audience, and devoted literature sellers and other helpers wherever he went. Because of his heresy he might have more enemies than his rivals. He also had more friends. With his combined East End and legal background he had a suitably classless image. Though no one more stirred the masses, no one could cite seditious utterances against him. And, if the crunch came, he could claim many friends in the army. Meanwhile he carried on much as before.

The tide seemed to be moving in his favour. At the Dialectical Society Austin Holyoake advocated abolition of the monarchy but not of a second chamber. In the ensuing debate the only dissent was on the latter issue. But consternation really stirred the nation when pillars of respectability quivered on their axes. Most notable of these was Gladstone himself when he praised the 'good sense' of a parody of the National Anthem, 'And Save Yourselves'. Even worse than its content was its source: Austin Holyoake and Charles Watts's *Secularist's Manual of Songs and Ceremonies*. At the same time George Otto Trevelyan, who had been Civil Lord of the Admiralty until his resignation over the increased grant to denominational schools in the Forster Education Bill, wrote an anonymous pamphlet *What does She do with it?* Victoria had been living in retirement for ten years, though the Civil List, which envisaged an active royal life with much official entertaining, was as high as ever. Additionally, she demanded marriage settlements and coming-of-age handouts for the numerous brood that was now nearing maturity. Apart from these, monarchy, with all of its adjuncts, was costing the country £1 million annually at a time when the entire National Budget was little more than £70 million. And the Queen had a vast undisclosed personal fortune. The pamphlet itself had however nothing like the political effect of a speech referring to it.

This was given by Dilke at Newcastle in November, with Cowen in the chair. After setting out the direct costs of the monarchy, Dilke pointed out that 'the Royal Family are the only persons in the kingdom who pay no taxes' and that the 'ridiculous sinecures' about the Court set a tone which 'does much towards continuing the political demoralization in high places which all of us deplore'. In view of the reduction of what 'used to be spent on tradesmen's bills', 'has there not been a diversion of public moneys, for which the advisers of the Crown are responsible, almost amounting to a malversation?' Then he turned to the principal function of royalty, the granting of the Royal Assent to parliamentary measures and other official documents. Either the Queen is so flexible in 'political conscience' she approves of everything submitted to her, or nothing is submitted to her of which she is likely to disapprove. In Britain he detected 'republican virtues' like 'public spirit', the practice of self-government and general education:

> 'Well, if you can show me a fair chance that a republic here will be free from the political corruption that hangs about the monarchy, I say, for my part—and I believe that the middle classes in general will say—let it come.'[50]

Now, all this was mild enough when compared with what Bradlaugh was saying, but he was not speaking on behalf of the middle classes. Dilke could even claim to come from the *petite aristocratie*, however *parvenu*. Indeed, as the 1871 *Annual Register* ironically observed, 'the Dilke baronetcy was generally supposed to have been created for his father as a reward for assiduous and obsequious attendance on the Prince Consort'.[51] Three days after this speech was reported locally, the *Times* took it up. Chamberlain sent his congratulations: 'The Republic must come, and at the rate at which we are moving it will come in our generation'.[52] But the middle classes did not rise in a body in Dilke's support. All the press abandoned the Tichborne trial to denounce his treason, and the 'storm of indignation... was louder and more general than the most loyal could have anticipated'. In some places even the lower classes 'took up the cause of royalty with such violence that the police were called in to protect the Republicans in the free utterance of their subversive sentiments'.[53] In one riot a supporter lost his life, and in another Odger barely escaped.

These happenings neither stimulated nor deterred Bradlaugh, who continued his campaigning at his own pace. Up and down the country he took his *Impeachment*:

'I loathe these small German breast-bestarred wanderers, whose only merit is their loving hatred of one another. In their own land they vegetate and wither unnoticed; here we pay them highly to marry and perpetuate a pauper prince-race. If they do nothing they are "good". If they do ill loyalty gilds the vice till it looks like virtue.'[54]

With characteristic thoroughness, he gave more economic arguments for republicanism than anyone else and highlighted the Queen's inactivity:

'Parliament is usually opened and closed by commission—a robe on an empty throne, and a speech read by a deputy, satisfying the Sovereign's loyal subjects.'[55]

And there was no dearth of royal tittle-tattle for the groundlings, especially from 'the wretched reign of George IV'. So rich was this in scabrous doings that 'George, Prince of Wales'[56] blossomed into a lecture on its own account. This was to occasion alarm at Sowerby Bridge in early December. Posters for this address had been put up wrongly proclaiming, 'Albert Edward, Prince of Wales', about whom equally lubricious stories could be told. The timing also seemed insensitive, as only three weeks before the prince had gone down with typhoid, thus prompting the *New York Herald* to suggest that

Bradlaugh had poisoned him. A hugh police force and a government reporter turned up for this latest outrage on good taste and loyalty, but the occasion passed off quietly when the speaker explained the mistake. As the prince's condition deteriorated, 'the nation seemed to gather round the throne with a single heart and a single prayer'.[57] Throughout the empire prayers were offered up, and 'even the Republican societies had sent addresses of sympathy to the Sovereign'.[58] When he recovered, London was 'wild with Thanksgiving Day',[59] 27 February 1872. The more cynical republicans were wild with other feelings, and anonymous pamphlets declared that this royal saga was a diplomatic invention. There is little doubt the sickness was genuine, but its timing was ideally suited to the interests of monarchism. Bradlaugh, who had remained decently quiet while the prince was ill, organized a meeting at the Hall of Science to protest against the exaggerated public sentiment on his recovery. Two days later Victoria gained further sympathy when she was physically threatened by Arthur O'Connor, the unstable nephew of Feargus.

Early in 1872 Odger had wanted to stage a march of 'the Democrats of London' to Hyde Park 'from all parts of London', but Bradlaugh apologetically advised against it because of insufficient organization. Odger concurred: 'No man has a greater right than yourself to advise in all democratic movements.'[60] The secularist leader was not, however, so popular in other republican circles. On 1 February 1872 there appeared the last traceable number of the *Republican*.[61] No hint of demise came with it. On the contrary, it published its thanks to Dilke for taking out an order. This issue was also noteworthy for a swingeing attack on 'Bradlaugh and Atheism':

> 'Bradlaugh, the self-worshipper, not only condemns himself by his gross quackery, but succeeds in bringing unmerited obloquy upon persons and organizations which have neither fellowship nor sympathy with his arrogant and despicable teachings . . . If Mr Bradlaugh chooses to rank himself no higher than the brute, let him do so. We compliment him upon his discernment . . . Our watchword is "Progress", and we believe in unceasing progress. How limited must be the aims and aspirations of those who believe that by the death of the body we are annihilated!'

The religious was but one of the rifts within the republican lute in the paper's short history. On the evils of an absolute monarchy all its contributors were agreed, but their harmony was broken when they turned to positive policies. Following a proposal to unite the British Empire and the United States, traditionally the paradise of republicans, there came a warning that in America 'the public lands are going into the possession of the corporations and monopolizing railroad companies'.[62] One correspondent even pointed out the advantages of a 'limited monarchy'. What had influenced him was the state of the Latin American republics, 'continually engaged in intestine commotion and civil war'.[63] A far cry from the enthusiasm with which they had been welcomed half a century before in Carlile's *Republican*. There were frequent approving snippets about the International. But trades unionism was also to be censured as 'selfishness and despotism' and the middle classes hailed as 'politically omnipotent' and 'part of the great industrial army which has contributed so efficiently to the making of this the most wealthy country in the world'.[64] The editor abhorred 'the obnoxious Socialistic doctrine of Communism',[65] while most of his contributors hated capitalism. The unity of the republican cause was, therefore, little impaired when the *Republican* disappeared.

In the following month a new journal took its place. William Harrison Riley's *International Herald* was established to promote the International and by the sixth number had became 'the Official Organ of the British Section'.[66] Despite the uneasy relations that had existed since the Commune, it began with a warm tribute to Bradlaugh's paper, which, however fashions might change and periodicals come and go within the popular movement, went from strength to strength:

> 'The *National Reformer* is a formidable opponent to all mere superstitious and traditional theology; it is as hearty a hater of kingcraft as it is of priestcraft, and very effectually exposes some of the great social and political usages inflicted upon the people.'[67]

Bradlaugh warmly reciprocated. To which Riley genially responded:

> 'The *National Reformer* persists in recommending this paper. This sort of thing may be all right once in a while, but let the conductor of that disloyal journal beware! There is such a word as retaliation! None of the readers of this "meek and mild" publication should ever read the *National Reformer* unless they are prepared to risk all the thunderbolts of orthodox beadledom and bumbledom.'[68]

Other tributes showered upon the atheist republican. Maxse toured the country lecturing on 'The Causes of Social Revolt' and 'defended most warmly Mr Bradlaugh and other popular advocates'.[69] The great American lawyer and orator, Col. Robert Ingersoll, wrote: 'All Americans who are in the least in love with real freedom associate your name with the great cause of Progress in England.'[70] It seemed that at last republicans of all classes and outlooks were uniting.

Within the secularist movement Bradlaugh was now, despite relinquishing the presidency, its unrivalled leader. In the world outside, G.J. Holyoake wrote the encyclopaedia articles on 'Secularism', but as a living force it had quite adopted the intensity and direction Bradlaugh gave it. When a *Secular Chronicle* was started in Birmingham by George Reddalls Junior, Bradlaugh was hailed as 'so long the leading spirit of the movement'[71] that strangers must think him an old man. In the new spirit of harmony social events became more prominent. A Hall of Science Club and Institute were formed, and gave intimate musical and dramatic evenings free from 'the blackguardism of a London music hall'.[72] The main performers were Austin Holyoake's wife and Charles and Kate Watts. Kate was his second wife, young, attractive, vivacious and the daughter of leading Nottingham freethinkers. With Susannah Bradlaugh out of circulation, she became the chief hostess for secular occasions. And, when he could spare the time, Bradlaugh himself recited and acted.

This tranquillity in republican circles was not to endure. In July 1872 John De Morgan turned up in Middlesbrough-on-Tees, and declared himself a champion of the popular cause. A few years later a clerical supporter was to describe him as a man with 'not only a handsome body, but a beautiful mind and soul'.[73] He produced a lecturing programme that bore a striking resemblance to Bradlaugh's own, and claimed on one occasion to have addressed an audience covering 55 acres. This programme he sent to London for insertion in the *National Reformer*. Now, it was tacitly assumed that such insertions bore some measure of endorsement, so Bradlaugh wrote off asking for personal details. He had to be careful. Police spies were not uncommon. Neither, now that secularism was becoming established, were religious infiltrators. And the progressive movement, ever anxious to extend aid to a brother in distress, was particularly prone to welcome—and then be discredited by—unscrupulous adventurers with a plausible hard luck story and a pleasant manner. At the same time, remembering the hardships of his own youth, he did not wish to exclude young talent.

In his reply De Morgan said he recognized the necessity 'to keep the Platform of both the Secular and Republican Societies as pure as possible, and therefore, I was not surprised or offended at the questions you asked'. He then gave a potted biography. At the age of ten he became a preacher, but for the last five years he had been a 'sceptic', having no knowledge of any God or the existence of a future state. Till recently he had been a teacher of elocution, oratory and advanced English in Cork, but when he declared himself a republican and member of the International the local clergy denounced him as the 'spawn of hell', and he was 'literally starved out of Cork'.[74] Bradlaugh responded: 'Thanks for your frank letter. If you are loyal, you may count on my aid to push you on.'[75] And De Morgan's lectures were advertised in the *Reformer*. It was not long, however, before rumours flowed into the office to make the editor wonder if he had made the right decision.

Even without the acquisition of De Morgan, the paper was able to cause consternation in many quarters. Madame de Brimont had persuaded Bradlaugh to let Hypatia and Alice go to school in Paris, where she looked after them at the weekend. Personally the headmistress regarded their lack of religion as a convenience rather than an embarrassment, and allowed them to receive the *Reformer*. With his usual objectivity, Bradlaugh told them that she was nevertheless 'quite right . . . to require you not to shew it' to the other girls, 'and you will of course take care in no respect to infringe her injunctions'.[76] When he came to fetch them at Christmas they noticed his abstraction. On reaching Midhurst he announced, 'Well, Bob's in prison'. His brother, William Robert, had embezzled £30 from his employer and been remanded in custody. Charles was supporting his wife and family and retaining a solicitor. 'Knowing well the acute pain the publicity of my case must have caused you',[77] William was both grateful and apologetic. Though he declared he could establish his innocence, he was convicted at Middlesex Sessions and sentenced to six months' imprisonment with hard labour. While his brother continued to support his family, he avowed remorse for his 'misconduct' and a 'determination to obtain an honest living after my release'.[78] Years later, after his conversion by Moody and Sankey, he asserted that he had been exploited and framed by his atheist employer and abandoned by his atheist brother in his hour of persecution. Bradlaugh's other lame duck was still unsettled. He had got Thomson a job as secretary of the Champion Gold and Silver Mines Co. of Colorado, but the poet was inefficient and returned to England in early 1873. Ideally, 'B.V.' said, he would have been happy to 'emigrate and become a citizen of the free and enlightened

Republic. But for mere clerks and accountants and *sick,* they have more out there than they want.'[79]

These domestic distractions vied with Bradlaugh's republican labours. Though open hostility to the Royal Family had passed its prime, growing numbers were becoming aware of the irrelevance of the monarchy to the nation's real problems. Republican and radical clubs were flourishing. Taylor founded an Anti-Game Law League, which had at least symbolic value. There was hope of a republican break-through if, as Lenin was to say, popular agitation coincided with a sudden worsening of social conditions and a failure of nerve in the ruling classes. At this time the balance of power was precarious and the moral authority of the establishment weak. Under 'some monstrous and ridiculous regulations invented by Mr Ayrton',[80] who had become the Commissioner of Works, Odger and some friends were prosecuted for staging a meeting at Hyde Park in support of certain Fenian prisoners. Bradlaugh held what was becoming his speciality, a huge peaceful protest rally. As a result the prosecution was abandoned and the regulations were annulled the following parliamentary session. A few days after this rally, Bradlaugh figured at an important meeting in Exeter Hall. This was for the launching of Joseph Arch's National Agricultural Labourers' Union. Arch was a Primitive Methodist lay preacher who had recently organized farm workers in Warwickshire. In the chair was Samuel Morley; Cardinal Manning was among the notables present. He moved the first resolution, couched in words of statesmanlike vagueness. Consternation seized the organizers when Bradlaugh insisted on moving an addendum:

> 'And there can be no permanent improvement in the condition of the agricultural labourer until such vital change be effected in the land laws now in force in this country as shall break down the land monopolies at present existing, and restore to the people their rightful part in the land.'[81]

Manning left the hall. The amendment was carried by a big majority.

By this time, December 1872, Bradlaugh's *Impeachment* was creating such a stir that the influential *Gentleman's Magazine* had found it desirable to commission a reply. In a masterly critique, John Baker Hopkins described the author as 'the brains and soul of English republicanism'. He then passed into his arguments. There were a number of debating points and an attempt to demonstrate how democratic British society and government had become under the monarchy. More damaging was his charge that, while the book asserted that the case for republicanism was independent of the character of kings, most of it simply retailed 'scandalous stories'. But he found his best means of answering a constitutionalist like Bradlaugh was to argue that 'unless Queen Victoria assented to a Bill for the repeal of the Act of Settlement, that Act could not be repealed by the constitutional authority of Parliament'.[82] To the horror of the orthodox, the editor allowed Bradlaugh a reply. In carefully moderate language he easily answered the secondary points and tried to settle the primary issue with an assertion 'that the British Parliament can prevent the succession of the "lawful heir to the throne" is certain'. Of thirty three sovereigns since William the Conqueror, only thirteen had ascended the throne by 'divine hereditary right'. He ended on a modest, even a querulous, note:

> 'I am not the chief of the English Republicans. I am only a plain, poor-born man, with the odium of heresy resting on me and the weight of an unequal struggle in life burdening me as I move on. I have, I may boast, won the love and affection of many of the people; that is the whole of my chieftainship. I can affirm that I never flattered the masses I address. That I have ambition to rise in the political strife around me, until I play some small part in the legislative assembly of my country, is true. If I live, I will; but I desire to climb step by step, resting the ladder by whose rounds I ascend firmly on Parliament-made laws, and avoiding those appeals to force of arms which make victory bloody and disastrous.'[83]

Hopkins was given the last word. It was certain, he said, that whatever irregularities there were in the British succession resulted from civil wars and like upheavals. 'What is done in a period of revolution is not a precedent to be followed in a time of settled government.'[84]

The defensive tone of Bradlaugh's contribution to the *Gentleman's Magazine* was no doubt evoked by his recent republican experiences. In these De Morgan played a leading role. He had contrived to become secretary of a committee set up by a meeting of South Yorkshire republican clubs at Mexborough to call a National Republican Conference. A circular was then sent to all the clubs in the country. By this time Bradlaugh knew quite a lot about De Morgan's real history and had heard even more 'rumours'. Letters were privately sent 'warning clubs that "mischief" would be done'[85] if they supported this conference. On behalf of the London Republican Club, Foote replied most diplomatically to the Yorkshire invitation:

'We cannot but think that in this case sufficient precautions have not been taken to render the Conference nationally representative. The proper mode of convening such a Conference as we would wish to see would seem to be to consult the whole of the clubs and associations throughout the country . . . and also to seek the advice and co-operation of such men as Professor Beesly, Frederic Harrison, Mr Bradlaugh, Mr Cattell, Sir C. Dilke, Auberon Herbert, Peter Taylor, Professor Herbert, etc, not indeed as men without whom no work can be done, but as men whose public services and outspoken attachment to democratic principles entitle them to an indubitable right to share in the deliberations . . . Certainly the country at large could not be held in any way bound by decisions made upon such slender and unstable foundations.'[86]

Leading radicals, including most of those named by Foote, were invited to the conference, but declined. Sir Wilfrid Lawson, afterwards head of the temperance United Kingdom Alliance, said bluntly: 'I have no intention of attending it.' [87]

It was held in Sheffield on the first two days of December 1872. Twenty-two clubs were announced as having sent delegates or signed voting papers, and another twelve as committing themselves in advance to what might be passed. Among the resolutions was the adoption of a tricolour based on that selected some twenty years before by Linton for his stillborn republican organization. Its green, white and blue represented, respectively, fertility, purity and the sky 'beneath which all men are equal'.[88] A number of revolutionary speeches were made, and a National Republican Brotherhood was set up. De Morgan was one of two nominated for the position of secretary, and among those nominated for the council were Bradlaugh, Watts, Cattell, Reddalls and Riley.

In the *Reformer* Bradlaugh gave his immediate response to the conference and the rabble-rousing of some of its organizers:

> 'As the Association, the establishment of which was voted last Sunday at Sheffield, is at present in the nature of a treasonable conspiracy; as language involving a threat of ridiculous physical force was used by Mr Morgan, calling himself *de* Morgan; and as there is evidently at present no sufficient guarantee for Mr Morgan's stability and discretion in the movement he has so recently entered, I earnestly entreat our friends throughout the country to abstain from joining the so-called "Brotherhood" until a fully representative conference can be called.'[89]

On behalf of the London Republican Club, Foote wrote to the Sheffield Conference declining to join the Brotherhood on the grounds that it was an 'illegal association' and 'Mr "de" Morgan is yet too little known to be trusted in such a position as that which he aspires to'.[90] This resolution was circulated round the clubs. Not surprisingly, the Sheffield Republican Club, which had done much to organize the conference, declared the London resolution 'out of place and uncalled for and we hereby express our confidence in John de Morgan'.[91] In publishing this retort from Sheffield, Bradlaugh appended a note: 'I insert this in justice to those who moved the resolution, and regret that the Stockton riots have already justified my fears.' A fortnight later he was forced to admit that 'the meeting at Stockton was not convened by Mr Morgan, and that that person's discourse on that occasion was most temperate'. Continuing, he made it clear that Foote was guilty of euphemism when he said the objection to De Morgan was that he was 'too little known to be trusted'. By this time he was too well-known:

> 'In consequence of the extremely unsatisfactory information in our hands as to the personal conduct of Mr Morgan, we shall insert no further reports containing his name . . . If Mr Morgan chooses to give an exact account of his last six years' life, we are willing to insert it as he sends it.'[92]

The republican elocutionist deemed 'it right to say a few words in my defence' in the *International Herald*. He asserted that he had accepted Bradlaugh's invitation 'on condition that he would enter into a bond to the value of £50 that he would insert all I sent'. To this the editor of the *Reformer* retorted:

> 'Your proposition is an absurd one, and I refuse it. You mistake your position in the tone you adopt to me. With so many instances of *persons employed by the Police to entrap poor men in political movements*, I must regard with suspicion one who, like yourself, wilfully suppressed the truth, when, in thorough honesty, I wrote for some account of yourself. At present, I regard you as more foolish than traitorous, but am not sure of my opinion being well founded.'

De Morgan was then asked to submit his private and public life to an arbitrator. While agreeing he asked Bradlaugh when he became a dictator and would he submit his own life and 'French experiences' to the same arbitrator. Bradlaugh consented, adding a wish to meet De Morgan 'face to face'. To this correspondence the secretary of the Brotherhood added his gloss on both the secular leader and himself:

'Mr Bradlaugh then came out in a new character—he became a GOVERNMENT INFORMER, kindly inventing the falsehood that the "Brotherhood" was *a treasonable conspiracy*, that I used threats of physical force, and that my language was prosecutable. Very kind, to put me—a fellow Republican—out for prosecution . . . The flag adopted by the Conference was declared to be illegal, Mr Bradlaugh showing his knowledge of the law by naming a few exceptional cases . . . I am now well known throughout England, and I ask, what have the old questions connected with my private life five or six years ago to do with my advocacy of Republicanism? If there are youthful mistakes, have I not atoned for them? Is Mr Bradlaugh without sin? Has not Sir C. Dilke entrapped poor men into riot at Leeds, Bolton and Derby—is he a police spy? The Clubs can best judge who is right. I aspire to no leadership, because I believe leaders are a curse, and I for one, could never believe a movement could succeed if led by any Dictator.'[93]

The most substantial of the republican clubs were in no doubt whose side to take in any conflict between a man whose prudence and probity in the popular cause had been demonstrated continuously from 1855 and one whose credentials and behaviour were alike histrionic and whose history before the previous July was, to say the least, obscure. As Bradlaugh did not make allegations lightly, there was some curiosity over the 'extremely unsatisfactory information' about De Morgan that had come his way. So private letters were exchanged. The London leader advised the Bristol Republican Club that his rival was 'an adventurer without a character',[94] and the readers of the *Herald* that his real name was John F. Morgan and there were 'facts in his career occurring more than once and of an extremely grave nature'.[95] This only heightened the curiosity. Bradlaugh suggested that Riley might preside at a confrontation between himself and De Morgan; but the *Herald* editor felt unable to act without Brotherhood backing, while De Morgan pleaded that he was 'too poor to visit London, unless my lecturing engagements call me there'.[96] And he further copied his rival's tactics by suggesting a 'council of honour' to investigate their private and public character, and that of Watts.

At the beginning of 1873 the election results for the executive of the Brotherhood were announced. De Morgan was confirmed as secretary and Watts, Riley, Bradlaugh, Reddalls and Cattell were elected to the council. Only Riley agreed to serve. Cattell declared bluntly: 'Another Secretary will have to be elected as I cannot work with the one elected.'[97] In April 'A Republican' wrote to the *Birmingham Morning News* suggesting that the secularists wished 'to split up the party for the selfish ambition of a few', though he admitted that, as the majority on the Brotherhood council, they 'could have moulded the work as they liked'. Their hostility was attributed to the policy of the Brotherhood to 'embrace Christians as well as Atheists, but that will not suit Iconoclast.'[98] This allegation was equally unfounded. In his political life it was always Bradlaugh's enemies, never himself, who obtruded his atheistic views. He was always happy to work with Christians unless they played ecclesiastical politics. Foote came to the defence:

> 'Who mixes his Atheist up with his Republicanism? Nobody in this country that I know of; and surely nobody will have the arrogance to ordain that a Republican may not be an Atheist if he choose . . . If you want men in whom you can confide, you have them. Mr Bradlaugh and Mr Odger are the chief representatives of Republicanism in this country, and they have for years, in spite of all obstacles, bravely and consistently advocated your cause.'[99]

Bradlaugh himself was in a difficult position. The republican movement was passing through a delicate phase. If he said what he knew about De Morgan, there could be unfortunate personal and public consequences. First of all, the possibility that the refugee from Cork might bring an expensive and vexatious libel action. If he lost he would, as a man of straw, simply go bankrupt. But, with his plausible manner and flair for rousing prejudice, he might even win. Win or lose, he would represent himself as a martyr, and a certain number of provincial republican clubs would rush to his support. From the late eighteenth century, when London began to assume its dominating position in the popular movement—despite reversals in the heyday of Owenism and the co-operative movement—appreciable jealousy and hostility built up in the provinces. Mostly it was latent, but malcontents could, in suitable circumstances, activate it. Bradlaugh had, moreover, a distaste for personalities and an awareness of how they had bedevilled Chartism and recently disrupted and castrated the International. Yet this allegation against him was potentially damaging, and there was a good chance that De Morgan could do more harm if allowed to live truculently under a cloud than if he were drenched by a downpour of truth. So Bradlaugh opened the flood-gates. 'One objection to Morgan is,' he said in the *Reformer*, 'that he absconded in 1870 with the funds of a Manchester Temperance Society, and took a false name to hide his theft, this not being the only case of dishonesty against him. As a politician his conduct is monstrous; at Kettering he pretended to be connected with an association having 250,000 armed men in England ready to rise at a moment's notice; and he also stated to a Hinckley friend that Mr George Odger was sold to Samuel Morley.'[100] With sublime faith the Sheffield Republican Club declared 'that the said charges are entirely false, and J. De Morgan is worthy of the fullest confidence of all *true* republicans'. [101]

A few weeks later, in one of his replies to correspondents in the *Reformer*, Bradlaugh supplied some more lowdown:

> 'The person who signs the article is really not worth contradicting; he is only a disreputable swindler. We regret that the journal you send should insert his falsehoods, but we have done our duty long since in cautioning the public, and he must now find his own level. We have written him down a thief. If not one, he could have appealed to the public or to the law; as he has not done either, our only duty is to treat him with utter contempt. He recently misappropriated £1, obtained from a Midland County Magistrate.'[102]

De Morgan rose to the bait. In identifying himself as the person referred to, he pleaded that he took no action because 'the poor man can scarcely ever obtain justice'. Bradlaugh was, he said, a friend of the 'lazy, licentious Prince Napoleon (Plon-Plon) the patron of Cora Pearl, etc., etc. It is only Conservatives that can ride first class, stay at head hotels, play billiards and drink claret till early morning.' And he raised the religious issue again:

> 'I know many earnest strict Catholics, who are social Republicans. Do not let us sow discord by talking about these speculative subjects in connection with Republicanism. One great misfortune has been, that the leaders of the atheistic party have been so prominently connected with the advanced political party.'[103]

Bradlaugh wrote to the publisher of the *Herald*, a former secularist who had been Wilks's old colleague and supporter at the Fleet Street House:

> 'In the event of the *International Herald* continuing further libel on me, I must proceed against you as its publisher'. [104]

De Morgan was, however, allowed a last fling:

'My victory is yours. Tricksters, Friends of Princes, and Sham Republicans must be exposed.'[105]

Soon after this the paper became the *Republican Herald*.

One of the reasons why De Morgan's colleagues gave him his head was that the Brotherhood now had competition and was anxious to demonstrate to the world its rival attractions. Though he had shown little piety before, in December 1872 Riley embraced a caption in the Mazzini-Linton manner: 'We should yield only to the laws of God and the voice of the People.'[106] Four months later he formally committed himself to Communism as the last stage in the evolution of society. Then there would be 'no buying, no selling, and no money to waste time over'. At this time he was wasting a lot of time finding money to keep his paper going, and his communism was of no utopian kind:

> 'If any man supposes that the change from one of these systems to another can be fully accomplished without physical force, he has not studied the past, seen the present, or foreseen the future. After the people have succeeded in disarming the usurers throughout the world then all succeeding changes from system to system may occur without the aid of physical violence; but so long as the usurer classes insist upon retaining armies of hireling fighters—soldiers or police—they will compel the Individualists to submit or to fight—and they will fight.'[107]

A fortnight later, in asking for affiliations to the Brotherhood, the *Herald* urged:

> 'Do not regard such a matter as a question of following John De Morgan or Charles Bradlaugh, but of platform and principle. The National Republican Brotherhood is striving for a Social Republic. It will not be long before a second Conference is held, meantime let all Social and Democratic Republicans co-operate in preparing to make it a success. We shall be all the stronger for the separation, as in France, of the conservative from the Social Republicans.'[108]

It was a separation that, on every count, Bradlaugh was more than willing to promote. His energies were now directed towards the organization of those clubs—the majority—which supported him. At the beginning of the year a circular was sent out by the London Patriotic Society, the West Central Democratic Society and the London Republican Club calling for a conference to establish a National Republican Association with 'none of those vexed

143

economical or purely social questions which so greatly divide even avowed Republicans'.[109] Bradlaugh urged support. And he dealt with the allegation of conservatism:

'The editor of the *International Herald*—and we believe he writes honestly and earnestly—suggests that we are so Conservative that Messrs Thiers Bright, Gladstone, and Rothschild might attend the Conference . . . While it would be well for us if we could win such men as Bright and Gladstone, no one can pretend that, to gain them, there has been any sort of truckling in our propaganda. We have persisted in a movement which for years has been allowed to die away. We have put the Government at defiance, and yet have offered no menace from which we have had to recoil, and we have, so far as we are concerned, guarded the movement free from turmoil or disaster . . . At least the editor of the *International Herald* might remember that we were sufficiently free to be the first to speak a word of welcome and encouragement to him, and that, but for our 15 months' fight with the Government in 1869, he would have been liable to legislative restrictions, which might have prevented the printing of a single copy of his journal.'

He was feeling tired, dejected and old before his time.

'We apologize to our general readers for even this semblance of a plea to the *International Herald* for friendlier treatment, but when every Whig, Tory, and Religious journal in England attacks us without truce or mercy for going too far, it is sometimes a little wearisome to read writers, whose pens might lighten our labours, adding to the difficulties in our way. For ourselves personally we care not, it is twenty-five years too late. For the movement we care much.'[110]

Foote became secretary to the provisional committee, which included Bradlaugh, Odger, and the treasurer of the National Secular Society, a big manufacturer R.A. Cooper of Norwich. It was in this capacity that Foote defended Bradlaugh from the charges of 'A Republican' in the *Birmingham Morning News*. They appeared in this paper because Birmingham was the city chosen for the conference. All the republican clubs and radical organizations were invited. What survived in London of the International declined on the grounds that 'all important questions of a true social character' were excluded from the programme. To which Foote replied that no programme then existed and 'the Republican delegates may themselves constitute one'.[111] When the conference took place in the Birmingham Town Hall on 11 and 12 May 1873, there were delegates from the London Republican Club, Universal Republican League, Eleusis Club, Land and Labour League, suburban secular or radical societies and forty provincial republican clubs. Cattell wrote to Bright for a message. He carefully replied: 'I have no public sympathy with the object which gives its name to your club'.[112] Though most of the conveners were Christians, it is probable that most delegates were not; R.A. Cooper took the chair.

The first title proposed for a new national body was 'Universal Federal Republican League'. Since, however, as a Brotherhood critic put it, 'English Republicanism must have nothing to do with the Republicanism of other lands',[113] this title was abandoned in favour of 'National Republican League'. Whereupon it was resolved that 'the objects of the League be furthered by purely legal and moral means'. This, wrote Watts, fully answered Bright's statement that he wanted political reform 'by a less hazardous method' than republicanism. All republicans wanted was 'a government that shall have the unfettered will of the people as its foundation, such government to be chosen by national consent independent of class distinctions and birth influence'.[114] But the Brotherhood critic asked, 'Is it more immoral to employ force in defence of liberty, of justice, than to employ it in defence of tyranny?' Resolutions were then passed in favour of disestablishment and disendowment of the Church of England, abolition of the House of Lords and standing armies, the 'establishment of a national system of compulsory, gratuitous, secular and industrial education', equal electoral divisions, the extension of local self-government, and the election of popular representatives. There was also a mini-manifesto:

> 'This Conference declares the Republican form of government to be the only form worthy of the support of a civilized people, meaning by a Republic a Commonwealth, a State, or a Unity of States, which guarantees the fullest individual liberty compatible with the general security, in which the sovereign power resides in deputies elected by the people according to equitable principles of representation, to the complete exclusion of all hereditary or class privileges which are absolutely contradictory to every principle of justice and of reason.'[115]

Such a programme was, claimed the Brotherhood, 'no better than constitutional monarchy'. Later they alleged that the majority of republican clubs were unrepresented at the conference, where ' "delegates" were received but . . . the *Clubs* did not exist'.[116] This reaction was to be expected. From the general press, however, came such favourable comment as an *Examiner* leader:

'The Conference of Republicans held at Birmingham on Sunday and Monday last far exceeded in numbers, importance, as well as in the intelligence displayed by its members, anything of a similar name or nature that has been held since the present movement was first originated . . . the Conference will go far towards . . . reassuring the timorous. But it must be admitted that a party that can afford to speak in the moderate but decisive tones adopted by most of the speakers, convinces us, and, we would fain believe, all thinking persons far more of its reality and permanence, than had it indulged in the most savage braggadocio or bombast.'[117]

For five years a civil war had sputtered in Spain, originally over the succession to the throne. By 1873 it had become a struggle between the royalist Carlists and the republicans, who took Madrid and established a provisional government just before the Birmingham conference. So the English republicans unanimously passed a resolution in support of their Spanish colleagues, and called on the British Government to recognize them. Foote, who had been declared secretary of the league, copied out in a fair hand a message from R. A. Cooper to Emilio Castelar, the new Spanish Foreign Minister. This was to be conveyed by Bradlaugh, as the moving spirit and brains behind the league. Immediately the conference was over he set out. Just inside the Spanish frontier his train stopped. Carlists were still in possession of Basque territory, and the journey had to be continued by coach. Once it was attacked by bandits, twice by Carlists. On one of these occasions Bradlaugh's luggage was carefully gone through and the address to Castelar discovered, but the soldier was illiterate and was thus persuaded the document was an English passport. After delivering it to Castelar, Bradlaugh went on to Lisbon[118] to learn what had happened to dos Santos, who had endorsed a £300 bill that had not been honoured. In fact the baron died there in 1870.

Back in Spain, Bradlaugh was given an official address in reply to R.A. Cooper's, and a banquet by the civic authorities of Madrid. Here he expressed 'little doubt that, within twenty years or less, we shall have the Republic in England'.[119] Bands played, speeches were made, Bradlaugh and Castelar exchanged visits. Bradlaugh, who was

146

reporting his Spanish visit for the New York *World*, was able to record a most enthusiastic welcome everywhere and apparent friendship from the Foreign Minister. After Bradlaugh's death Castelar asserted that he 'sent a message by a trusty emissary requesting him not on any account to call on me at the Foreign Office, but to come to see me at my house, alone, at an early hour of the morning, rarely chosen for visits in Madrid, where few people are early risers'.[120] Castelar's original notes [121] belie the time, but Bradlaugh's visits were certainly to his home. The Foreign Minister was indeed playing a double game. He wanted to secure his guest's goodwill, for Bradlaugh's influence on public opinion in Britain had been clearly demonstrated over France, so he allowed the address from the English republicans to be delivered at and replied to by the Foreign Ministry. On the other hand, he had been privately warned by the British Government, to whom he was making direct overtures, that official recognition of the English republican would be taken as an affront to HMG; and leading members of the Spanish Government were notably absent from the civic galas. Nevertheless, the Spaniard impressed Bradlaugh as 'one of the most honest, thorough and loyal republicans in Europe',[122] even after he had become president and then declared himself dictator. For his part Bradlaugh impressed his host as 'a very tall man, of stentorian voice and of Herculean appearance', with 'a delicate white complexion, long chestnut hair, and the manners of a timid sacristan'. The Saxon further contrasted with the Latin in the rather disappointing realism of a speech he was later reported to have made at a celebration banquet in Madrid: 'I am a Republican, but my countrymen are not Republicans. And as they are not Republicans, it is impossible to force them violently to declare themselves in favour of a Republic. As our Monarchy opposes no progress, gainsays no liberty, and does not endeavour to exalt itself above Parliament, no one in England, as far as I know, thinks seriously of overthrowing it. I am a Republican and a young one, but I do not expect however long I may live, that England will become a Republic in my lifetime. We are preparing the way, but we shall retain the existing institutions. In future times the generations to come will have to decide for themselves what is best.'[123]

At the same time the impermanence of republican triumph was demonstrated to them both when Thiers fell in France.

Despite his admiration for Castelar, Bradlaugh recognized that what Spain needed was 'a Cromwell with the purity of a Washington ... Senor Castelar feels too deeply.'[124] During his visit his military eye noted bad discipline among the republican forces. But when he offered 'to ride with fifty dragoons and shoot'[125] a rebellious general, there were no takers. He also disapproved of Carlist prisoners being sent to fight in Cuba. Republican Spain was thus to be for him, like France, a bitter disappointment. When he came to return home he heard that Carlists were on the watch for him. As in Hyde Park before unequal odds, he had 'no ambition to be a martyr'.[126] So he went by train to Santander in the north and by ship to Bordeaux. The voyage was delayed and a report was put out that he had been killed. On his arrival home another report said the Carlists had paid him.

His Spanish visit suggested to him another way of helping Thomson. Using his influence with Pierre Girard of the New York *World*, he got the poet the post of correspondent in Spain. It proved another disaster of intemperance and incompetence, and the engagement was soon terminated. Bradlaugh himself had to think of new ways of paying off his debts. It was all very gratifying to have the unique position which he described at this time in a short autobiography:

> 'It is, as far as I am aware, the first time any English citizen has, without tumult or disorder, and in buildings belonging to various Municipalities, directly challenged the hereditary right of the reigning family.'[127]

In Britain, and especially overseas, many thought he might at any moment become the president of a British republic, though he himself gave no countenance to these speculations. Many more spread stories that he was already living in luxurious presidential style. In reality he was, as he confided to a friend from whom he borrowed on and off over a period of fourteen years, 'miserably short of money'.[128] So he decided to go to the United States on what was then, as now, a profitable venture for celebrities, a lecture tour. Invitations had often come from the 'Great Republic' but been sadly declined because of his English commitments. Even now it was only a desire to amass money quickly that tempted him away. Probably he would not have gone at all had there been any dramatic prospects on the political scene. But, as he was shrewd enough to see, despite the apparently flourishing National Republican League and the continuously noisy National Republican Brotherhood, the republican kettle was already going off the boil. After his recovery the Prince of Wales had been assiduous in performing many of the State functions neglected by his mother; and when she herself went to the opening of Victoria Park in the East End of London, the enthusiastic reception she found demonstrated how conservative, except in times of crisis, the English working classes really were.

In the spring of 1874 a new general election was expected. Before his departure the previous September Bradlaugh issued his election address. Tower Hamlets Radical Electoral Committee invited him to stand there, but he thought it better loyally to nurse one constituency, Northampton. Holyoake had stood for Tower Hamlets in 1857, Birmingham in 1868, and was to try Leicester in 1884. The result was that he succeeded in none. Bradlaugh was still able, in 1873, to begin:

> I shall regard the measures under discussion, and not the men who propagate them, and shall not consider myself bound to follow the "Liberal whip" into the lobby of the House except to support Radical measures.'[129]

His platform was similar to that of 1868, but with a new proposal to make 'the veto of the House of Lords a suspensive veto only, capable of being overruled in the same session by a sufficient vote of the House of Commons'. Immediately after issuing this address he dashed to Liverpool to join his ship.

The Cooper Institute which arranged his tour had done its work well, and he stepped ashore in New York on a carpet of ballyhoo. Not only was he a personality in his own right, but the American people had never entirely forgotten their War of Independence and took to their hearts anyone who twitched the British lion by its tail. Pressmen clustered round him and the *New York Herald* proclaimed: 'CHARLES BRADLAUGH. The Future President of England at the Fifth Avenue Hotel.'[130] Unfortunately he also stepped into the middle of a financial panic. At first there was little evidence of depression among his hosts. Dinners and receptions at the Lotos Club abounded. Here he met other overseas celebrities like Ludwig Büchner and Wilkie Collins, and pillars of the WASP (White Anglo-Saxon Protestant) and freethinking establishment such as Francis Bret Harte.

Bradlaugh's first lecture was at the Steinway Hall on 'The Republican Movement in England'. The audience included[131] Colonel Henry Steele Olcott, Colonel John Hay, the writer who had been Abraham Lincoln's private secretary and was to become Secretary of State, and Stephen Pearl Andrews, one of the founders of the Republican Party. It was one of the most formidable audiences New York could assemble and, as with an opening night on Broadway today, the success of the rest of the tour depended on their reception. It was rapturous. The papers placed him among 'the greatest of living orators'. During question time Bradlaugh was perhaps astonished when his old opponent Dr Brindley, who had followed him to America 'to hunt up and show up and finally shut up the six-foot leader of the English radicals', [132] leapt to his feet. At once his lather of abuse was washed by a shower of hisses and protests from an indignant audience. Then Bradlaugh rose to Brindley's defence. His two-edged plea to 'let the gentleman who represents the aristocracy and the Church of England go on'[133] turned anger into delight. Four days later Brindley began a rival campaign. But his money and his health soon broke down and he died in poverty in Chicago within a month. Bradlaugh had now gone on to Boston.

In the great heartland of WASP intellectuals, where Irish labourers were known as 'white niggers', Bradlaugh was even more fêted. At his first lecture Wendell Phillips, the valiant opponent of slavery and champion of the rights of workers and Indians, took the chair. On the platform beside him were Holyoake's old foe, Garrison, and (the chairman of the Senate Committee on Foreign Relations) Senator Charles Sumner, who had been viciously assaulted by a Southern Representative[134] for his advocacy of abolition. Phillips introduced Bradlaugh as 'the Samuel Adams of 1873'[135] and 'a man who, Sir Charles Dilke says, does the thinking for more minds, has more influence, than any other man in England'.[136] As Bradlaugh spoke Garrison reverberated with enthusiasm. At the close of the lecture Sumner told Phillips, 'This is, I think, the most eloquent speech I have heard for some years.'[137] This commendation ensured the lecturer's success in New England.

The following day Bradlaugh was shown round Boston by Phillips and Harney. Harney had emigrated[138] to America and become a clerk in the Massachusetts State House and Boston correspondent of W.E. Adams's *Newcastle Weekly Chronicle*. Particularly moving for the visitor was his discussion with the widow of Theodore Parker, for many years the doyen of American Unitarians and also a great abolitionist. At a dinner to Sumner given soon afterwards by Dr George Loring, President of the Massachusetts Senate, Bradlaugh met Joshua B. Smith and Henry Wilson. Smith was a freed slave who had become a senator. Wilson, the Vice-President of the United States, invited the English republican to Washington. During the rest of his time in Boston there were more meetings and lectures, autographs to be sold at the Theodore Parker Fraternity fair, and enthusiastic reports and receptions. Then he went into the 'provinces', beginning with New England. Here he stumbled upon difficulties. In the smaller towns lectures had to be cancelled because of the financial distress which had not hitherto had much impact on the prosperous *literati* of New York and Boston. But he had triumphs too. At Cambridge, just outside Boston, he greatly impressed Henry James, a graduate of Harvard Law School who was beginning to make his name in literature. Then on into the Bible Belt, where press censure of his atheism was far more damaging than in the East Coast cities. Nevertheless, in Cincinnati the Roman Catholic archbishop attended his lecture. While in Kansas he slipped on the December ice and badly gashed his right palm and wrist. The wounds were slow in healing, but the relentless programme of talk and travel allowed for no convalescence. In Chicago there was a sentimental encounter. Outside the lecture hall he was accosted by a woman whose face was faintly familiar. It was Theophila Carlile Campbell. She had married an early free-thought colleague of Bradlaugh's and was quite prosperous, but she looked lonely and isolated. Hypatia Carlile Cooke had married another old colleague and lived nearby. Theophila did not see her much. Cooke was in poor health, and poor. No doubt Bradlaugh thought of his own daughters and the rewards of a reformer's life.

At Kalamazoo he heard of the death of his lecture agent and had to dash back to New York. When matters were resolved he again went to Boston. At a society party he was delighted to meet the man whose writings had inspired him as a youth with 'Self-reliance'. Emerson, 'the sage of Concord', reminded him of Robert Owen as he gently recited his new poem 'The Tea-party Centennial'. Bradlaugh was then called on to speak. Using Emerson's verse as a peg he sounded a 'kindly, courteous, but frank rebuke of the spirit of the age'.[139] Bradlaugh's comments on America were always kindly and courteous.[140] It would have been churlish to be otherwise. Everyone he met was so kind, so anxious to please, so proud of the past, so confident of the future, so liberal to the underdog—so long as local slum-dwellers stayed quietly downtown and the taxes did not go up. But what had this endless whirl of parties for the affluent to do with the republic? What did these genial suburban intellectuals really know of the people? 'Hardly a day passed on which he was not asked to aid some English emigrant who had landed at Montreal, New York, or Boston—emigrants who had lost all hope, who were broken down with despair; strangers in a strange land to which they had not been able to adapt themselves.'[141] On this occasion there was a lively, but equally kindly and courteous, debate in reply, with eloquent contributions from Phillips and Wilson. Soon afterwards Loring invited Bradlaugh to Salem. The Rev. Dr A. A. Miner, who two years before had been one of the vice-presidents of a National Association calling for a 'Christian Amendment to the United States Constitution',[142] invited him to Tuft's College. By the middle of January 1874 the lecturer was homesick, though there were still some 20,000 miles of barn to storm.

At home Gladstone, troubled by criticism of his Ashanti War policy and by a heavy cold, suddenly called for the dissolution of parliament. A telegram from Austin Holyoake reached Bradlaugh on his way to Washington, and he sped to New York for the first ship home. In Northampton Gurney acted as his election agent and Watts and Foote held nightly meetings. G.J. Holyoake's offer of help was politely declined. At Chelsea Dilke assured a supporter that he had 'always declined to take part in a republican agitation',[143] and came in at the head of the poll. Most Liberals were not so fortunate, though Burt at Morpeth and Alexander Macdonald at Stafford became the first working-class MPs. Gladstone said that, as temperance advocates, his party colleagues were 'borne down in a torrent of gin and beer', and in Northampton Gilpin was certainly forced into second place by a Tory brewer Pickering Phipps.[144] But the real reasons for the Liberal defeat were Nonconformist and Catholic dissatisfaction with the government's partiality to Anglican schools, Gladstone's irresponsible attempt to bribe the taxpayers, and the superior organization of the Conservatives under Disraeli. Gilpin and Henley were both 300 down on their former vote. With 1,653, Bradlaugh was 600 votes up, just 143 below Henley. Three days after the election the republican candidate reached home to face defeat and a large indemnity bill, met by a loan from 'Plon Plon', for his cancelled American lectures.

Two months after Bradlaugh's return the faithful Austin Holyoake died and Watts assumed full sub-editorial responsibilities on the *Reformer*. Sporadic assistance came from Thomson, for whom a niche was found on the paper, which had just begun the serialization of his black epic 'The City of Dreadful Night'. At Holyoake's death-bed Bradlaugh promised to raise £650 to buy the dying man's printing and publishing business for the benefit of his family. Most of this sum was collected by subscription. £100 was to come from a legacy, but the trustee absconded and, by instalments, Bradlaugh made up the deficiency himself. Largely because Kate Watts's ability matched her appearance, Bradlaugh handed over Holyoake's old business to Watts on behalf of the secular movement.

Difficulties also pursued the republican movement outside and inside Britain. Louis Napoleon had died at Chislehurst in 1873, throwing the imperialist party into confusion. A codicil to his will disinherited 'Plon Plon', now allowed back into France, in favour of Prince Victor. Madame de Brimont described Prince Napoleon as 'agitated, perplexed and undecided'[145] what to do now that his son had supplanted him in the imperial will but not in the family responsibilities. Thereafter he borrowed from Bradlaugh as often as he lent. The vicomtesse continued that the French Minister of the Interior, 'Gambetta is annoyed and worried at the disturbance which is made around my prince and he would like to find a pretext to expel him from France'. By April 1874 'Plon Plon' himself felt it necessary to assure Bradlaugh, who remembered that the prince's cousin had become president in troubled times and soon afterwards made himself emperor, 'You know my politics, which do not change.'[146] During this period there was as much disturbance in Spain as in France, and the following month Castelar fell.

Republicanism in Britain was equally languishing. Just before going to America, Bradlaugh had dashed off for the 1874 *National Secular Almanack*:

'The Republicans are in no hurry, but they will not wait unless some progress be made to a better state of things. Turn the Bishops out of the House of Lords in 1874, and Republicans will hope and wait. Give agricultural labourers the vote in 1874, and Republicans will hope and wait. Abolish the Game Laws in 1874, and Republicans will hope and wait. Make some progress to reduce the National Expenditure in 1874, and Republicans will hope and wait. Take up the Land Question seriously in 1874, and plan some fashion of letting some portion of the land be owned by those who till it, and then Republicans will hope and wait. In a word, show real intent for real reform, and we prefer slow progress to sudden revolution. But we refuse to stand still; the stream has been dammed too long, the floodgates are bulging, a little more pressure, and the flood will sweep all before it. There is yet time to prevent the disastrous flood, but it must be done not by strengthening the weirs, but by lifting the gates—not by still further penning back the waters, but by cutting fresh channels for its peaceful onflow.'[147]

It was heady stuff, splendid New Year reading. But, as the year advanced, the vapours dissolved and sobriety returned. The Tories were now in power and showed no desire to grant what the Whigs had withheld. Neither did they make any strenuous effort to strengthen the weirs, or worry unduly about bulging floodgates. For the fact was that they had ceased to bulge. By one of those strange cycles of history the flood-waters were already subsiding.

In various parts of the country, especially in the north, republican clubs continued to flourish. From their inception there were critics who said that they were simply secular societies under other names. Though there was initially little evidence [148] for this assertion, it was certainly true that Bradlaugh's influence was keeping the republican torch burning longer in his sphere than elsewhere. Whatever the strength of some local clubs, in 1874 all pretence of national organization was dropped and the League and the Brotherhood quietly disappeared. [149] Their departure was symptomatic. In the *Republican Herald* can be traced some of the embarrassments of the movement. At one stage Riley lost control of his paper because he was 'so destitute of money that I have not sufficient to pay for one week's rent of the three rooms I hire for my family to dwell in'. [150] Naturally, this position strengthened his belief in communism, where 'all, except those who *would not* work, should have an abundance of these necessities', [151] and his hostility to money, 'the gold medals of the usurers'. [152] He began to hanker after more inspiring organizations than the Working Men's Parliamentary Association, which came to occupy the secretarial energies of De Morgan when the Brotherhood folded. Beginning with plans for a co-operative village, he proceeded to a more grandiose project:

> 'Within twelve months of the first establishment of the Mutual Help Association every original member will, if living and "in health", be employed by the Association . . . I have arrived at a method of organization such as never has yet been published. By means of this method we can do all I have stated, and can, also, so extend our powers as to gain at least half the capital in England for our Association, in less than ten years. And the Parliament of England may, by the same means, become exclusively ours (the Mutual Help Association's) ere ten years from this date. Of course I am called a "visionary" and I hope and believe I am one.' [153]

A month later he announced branch secretaries *pro tem* of the new association, and the ubiquitous Maccall wrote: 'The idea and design of your Mutual Help Association are excellent. That God may bless your labours is my hearty prayer.'[154] The prospect of a mammoth venture of this sort ruled by Riley—with, perhaps, De Morgan looking after the accounts—was not, however, generally appealing. There were many radicals who still remembered the dubious O'Connor land scheme which did so much to wreck Chartism, and Riley's association never seems to have been other than a talking-shop more or less confined to London. That one wing of the movement should be harking after these visionary schemes did little to enhance the overall credibility of republicanism in the nation at large. It also involved the certainty of disputes among established advocates, even those formerly connected with the International. And religion continued to cause dissension. When 'Mr Freedom' claimed that 'the poor and working classes . . . are tricked out of their money' by paid preachers, a 'Christian Republican' declared that 'there is much more in religion than he seems to think'.[155] By this time De Morgan had quite thrown off his secularist pretensions and was lecturing on 'Christ the Great Reformer'. But piety was still atypical in a movement which had been closely associated with free-thought from at least the time of Carlile. Critics pointed to this as one of its difficulties. Andrew Boa, president of the Scottish Trades Council, observed that English republicanism 'is identified with a religious difficulty, inasmuch as its most prominent advocates, Charles Bradlaugh, and Holyoake and Watts, are Secularists'.[156] He added that Scottish trades unionists 'look on Queen Victoria as an exceptionally good monarch'. A similar religious point was made in an anonymous satire, *The Fall of Prince Florestan of Monaco*, which came out in March 1874:

> 'No system of government can be permanent which has for its opponents all the women in the country, and for supporters only half the men; and any party will have for opponents all the women which couples the religious question with the political and the social, and raises the flag of materialism.'[157]

When it was revealed that Dilke was the author he was accepted back into fashionable society.

By this time nearly all middle-class practical politicians had leapt from the republican bandwagon. The motto of the movement was 'Ballots, not Bullets', but the votes were not coming in too briskly, even after the introduction of secret ballots in 1872. Bradlaugh was defeated in Northampton. So was Odger at Southwark. Fawcett lost his seat at Brighton, though Dilke soon got him in again at Hackney.

The British electorate has always been suspicious of parties, especially parties of change, that seem to be torn by internal dissensions; while parties of change have tended to be those most torn in this way. However diverse the personal interests within the British ruling classes, in moments of stress or in the face of a common foe they stick together. The working classes, on the other hand, have never been able to resist the luxury of histrionic in-fighting. Though bourgeois radicals have liked to be thought of as men of the people, and have been happy to support unpopular 'popular causes' if they think these have prospects, they do not go in for quixotic gestures on behalf of shrinking movements. Publicly Bradlaugh kept the flag flying:

> 'Monarchy has been truly described as a government for children: Republicanism is for men.'[158]

Privately he despaired of the nation's capacity for growing up. But in July 1874 a neatly written letter came from a lady in Norwood asking if it were necessary to be an atheist to join the National Secular Society, and a new interest came into his life.

CHAPTER SEVEN — THE FEMME FATALE

'I love her very dearly and esteem her very highly, and hope the day may yet come when I may have the right to share with her my home and give her the protection of my arm.' — Letter to Kate Watts, 9 March 1877.

Annie Wood was born in 1847 into a poor branch of the Wood family. Lord Chancellor Hatherley was her second cousin; Sir Matthew Wood, Bart., her grand-uncle. Other relatives[1] were Field Marshal Sir Evelyn Wood and Kitty O'Shea of Parnellite fame. She was brought up in Low Church austerity by her widowed mother and Ellen Marryat, a sister of the novelist captain. In 1867, while she was staying with Roberts and his family during the Fenian upheaval, she first met radicalism and discovered her power to pacify an angry crowd. At the end of the year she married the Rev. Frank Besant, a brother of the novelist Sir Walter. Her husband was a missioner who had introduced her to the seductions of Anglo-Catholicism the year before. Miss Marryat had been an excellent teacher, liberally including a mini-Grand Tour for the cultivation of French and German, but sex was not on the curriculum and Annie got a rude shock on her wedding night. If such there were, her husband was the typical Victorian clergyman: formal, unimaginative, humourless, conscientious, zealous for his rights, marital and otherwise, unlovely, unloving and unloved. Annie was desperately unhappy. She sought comfort in religion, but her gospel studies revealed the inconsistencies found by Bradlaugh. She wrote short stories. She lost herself in her son Digby and her daughter Mabel, but they caught whooping cough in 1871 and Mabel almost died. Prostrated with worry and the exhaustion of constant nursing she sought final release in suicide. As her attempt failed a voice said, 'O coward, coward, who used to dream of martyrdom, and yet cannot bear a few short years of pain'?[2] At that time her family's influence secured for Besant a living in Sibsey, Lincolnshire, thereby increasing his resentment and her isolation. In 1872 she heard Voysey at St George's Hall, and was introduced by him to Thomas Scott and his circle of rationalist writers. The following year she wrote for Scott two sceptical pamphlets, *On the Deity of Jesus of Nazareth* and *The Gospel according to St. John*, 'by the wife of a

Beneficed Clergyman'. Just before their appearance a furious Besant was told by mutual friends who the author was.

One day she walked into Sibsey Church. 'Locked alone in the great, silent church, whither I had gone to practise some organ exercises, I ascended the pulpit steps and delivered my first lecture on the Inspiration of the Bible. I shall never forget the feeling of power and delight—but especially of power—that came upon me as I sent my voice ringing down the aisles ... All I wanted then was to see the church full of upturned faces, alive with throbbing sympathy, instead of the dreary emptiness of silent pews ... As the sentences flowed unbidden from my lips and my own tones echoed back to me from the pillars of the ancient church, I knew of a verity that the gift of speech was mine, and that ... if ever the chance came to me of public work, this power of melodious utterance should at least win hearing for any message I had to bring.'[3] The opportunity was very near. Annie's visits to church conspicuously avoided the communion rails. Her husband cared for his creeds, but he cared for the conventions even more. In August 1873 he told her she might believe what she liked but unless she turned up at communion and went through the motions she could get out. She got out. Her brother[4] arranged a legal separation with a settlement of £110 per annum, she to keep Mabel, he to keep Digby, and both children to have annual stays with the other parent. Digby's visits soon stopped because 'both my parents agreed that my grief at the inevitable parting was too much for me'.[5] Coming to London with her daughter, Annie Besant found sanctuary with the Conways, who ran an ever open hospital for wounded spirits, 'until she could make satisfactory plans'.[6] They found her odd translating jobs but she felt she was imposing and moved to Colby Road, Upper Norwood, close to Scott, for whom she began more pamphlets. Conway's wife Ellen Davis, 'one of the sweetest and steadiest natures whom it has been my lot to meet',[7] advised her to go along to the Hall of Science and hear Bradlaugh, 'the finest speaker of Saxon-English that I have ever heard, except, perhaps, John Bright, and his power over a crowd is something marvellous'.[8] First she went to Truelove's shop, now at 256 High Holborn, and bought herself a copy of the *Reformer* for 19 July 1874. Then she wrote her query on atheism. Bradlaugh replied:

'To be a member of the National Secular Society it is only necessary to be able honestly to accept the four principles, as given in the *National Reformer* of June 14th. This any person may do without being required to avow himself an Atheist. Candidly, we can see no logical resting-place between the entire acceptance of authority, as in the Roman Catholic Church, and the most extreme Rationalism.' [9]

She applied. On 2 August she went to Old Street to collect her certificate after the lecture. It was only a small group and Bradlaugh had no difficulty identifying the trim, elegant figure, about five foot five, in a dark silk dress edged with white, her soft oval face lit by piercing grey-blue eyes and framed by dark brown hair swept into plaits tied at the back. He gazed at her quizzically, kindly. 'Mrs Besant?' She gazed back. He stood like a sculpted pharaoh. Though his life was turbulent, he had found intellectual peace; though it was uprooted, it was not rootless. She was desperately adrift and her 'quick, impulsive nature found in him the restful strength it needed'.[10] 'Yes' she said in a low clear voice. He made a few general remarks to the group. She left. But they knew they would meet again. At the bookstall in the Hall of Science she acquired his *Plea for Atheism* and *Is there a God?* Two days later she turned up at his study with a discussion paper 'On the Nature and Existence of God', in which he was delighted to find that she had 'thought herself into Atheism without knowing it'. The truth was that she had a chameleon's mind and a genius for rapid study. She invited him to Norwood. He declined. She tried again by letter. He went. She was taken on as a regular contributor to the *Reformer* at a guinea a week (what Watts was then getting as sub-editor) doing reviews and a regular column as 'Ajax'. The pseudonym was adopted to protect Scott, not her husband. At the same time she took to the lecture platform on 'The Political Status of Women', which Bradlaugh rated the best speech by a woman he had ever heard, at a Co-operative Institute, and 'Civil and Religious Liberty' at Conway's chapel. At first she strained and sounded 'harsh and disagreeable',[11] but soon she found a bell-like voice that filled and thrilled the largest halls.

Though Bradlaugh's judgment of character was often to let him down, he had an unerring nose for talent. In Mrs Besant he at once recognized a major acquisition for the causes of freethought and radical reform. Writing to his daughters in French—a language they and Thomson often employed in personal correspondence—he enthused:

'Mrs Besant is a very intelligent woman whom I hope to see on our platform in the future. She is one of the writers for

Thomas Scott's series. Well-educated and sufficiently robust, capable of making a great sensation as writer and orator. She is Ajax but this is very confidential.'[12]

He ended in English: 'If she stays with us poor Mrs Law may say her prayers.' Naturally he thought they might like to meet 'the wonderful Ajax'. They would indeed, and were 'eager with delighted anticipation' and 'ready to be impressed and to be pleased'. Or so Hypatia long afterwards recalled. But they were also eighteen and sixteen years old, conventionally educated, and painfully aware that a married lady separated from her husband had thrust herself into the life of their father, who was living away from their mother. At any rate, one day when Alice and Hypatia were both in London they were taken to meet Ajax in a sitting room at the Midland Hotel, St Pancras. To their discomfort she greeted them 'in a perfunctory manner' and sat them on the sofa while she had a whispered *tête-à-tête* with their father at a table. Vainly he tried to bring them into the conversation. As they left he asked them gaily, 'Well, how do you like Mrs Besant?' Though younger, Hypatia 'was usually the quickest to speak, but this time my sister forestalled me, and promptly answered "I do not like her at all!" This was our introduction, and this first impression then made upon us never changed, although in course of time we became on an outwardly friendly footing. The surface however was thin, and it did not take much to break through it.'

In the first week of September 1874 Gilpin died. Bradlaugh's supporters saw the by-election as a splendid chance, especially as Gilpin had advised his own agent to vote for the London radical. Though Bradlaugh had undertaken to honour his broken engagements in America throughout the autumn, he decided to wait for the hustings. C.G. Merewether again stood for the Tories. Henley stood down. But the Moderate Liberals would not follow Gilpin's advice. Chamberlain, Peter Rylands, Jacob Bright (John's brother), Arthur Arnold and Bernal Osborne were approached to stand, but they declined. At last William Fowler, a Quaker barrister and banker, accepted the official Liberal ticket. At the Lord Palmerston Inn, beside the Tory *Herald* office, he set up his headquarters and made such a bad speech that a prominent Unitarian Frederick Covington declared for Bradlaugh. Bates established the *Radical* (not to be confused with the later paper of the same name), where Odger championed Bradlaugh. Maxse subscribed to his fund. Foote, Watts and Odgers came up for the campaign, Annie Besant was the *Reformer*'s political correspondent, and the Agricultural Labourers and

Northumberland and Durham Miners sent their best wishes. Fowler pulled out all the stops. The clergy, notably the Princess Street Baptist, J. T. Brown, and the Independent, Thomas Arnold, rallied to his support. That was not enough. New tactics were tried. Previously the Crispinites had been vilified as drunkards. Now cartoons canonized them as innocent dupes toiling and subscribing for Bradlaugh and his party

> 'To fill my stomach at the George,
> And line my belt with gold.'[13]

The watch story was elaborated, Bradlaugh was declared to be unmarried and his daughters illegitimate, his dead mother was said to be on parish relief. After repeatedly challenging Fowler to meet him face to face in debate on his 'vilely untrue' charges, he called the man 'a liar and a coward'[14] and was himself denounced for 'foul-mouthed' language. At last on 6 October the poll was declared. Merewether won and Bradlaugh, albeit with 113 more votes than before, was third. His supporters went berserk. They had taken the day off and were already drunk. The shopkeepers closed their shops by 5 p.m. and put up their shutters. Now the crowd's full fury was unleashed. Merewether was left in comparative peace but assault parties charged Fowler's hotel and the Liberal *Mercury*. Bradlaugh rushed out to stop them. Sullenly they gave way and it seemed that peace would win. But Bradlaugh left at 9 p.m. to catch his ship for America. When he had gone rioting broke out with fresh vigour. The police charged and were dispersed. Special constables under Perry, President of the Liberal Association, fared no better. Mayor Richard Turner read the Riot Act and the local artillery were brought out. High school boys joined in, 'armed with pebbles and doing damage to their heart's content',[15] knowing that the shoemakers would get the blame. The Riot Act was read a second time and the army at Weedon alerted. But exhaustion had come and the 'Bradlaugh riots' ended. The local Liberals had however learnt their lesson. A Tory poster was soon proclaiming 'The Rev. Gooderidge will Publish the Banns of Marriage between the LATE CENTRAL LIBERAL ASSOCIATION (alias Fowler and Christianity) and RADICALISM (alias Bradlaugh and Infidelity)'.[16]

After an unpleasant voyage the disappointed politician reached New York. Bradlaugh's brother, William, had tried to go with him, hoping to be palmed off as a young man he knew and could recommend. But Charles's patience was at an end. In America Sumner had died but his words of praise had echoed round the country and produced invitations to the lecturer from many clerics to address their congregations. All his old friends gathered round with speeches and presentations, but he had more time to investigate social conditions. There were many hard luck stories and people borrowed money from him.[17] Watts, anxious to please, wrote to say how well the *Reformer* was doing, asking Bradlaugh had he 'no word of praise to say for this?' and to let him know what Mrs Besant, who 'is exceedingly good altogether',[18] thought of his last debate. When Bradlaugh turned west he ran into the worst winter in living memory. At Chicago he called on Hypatia Carlile Cooke and her family, saying he 'had very good offers for next season and . . . should like to bring his family out with him'.[19] The tour glaciered on. Watts was looking for 'sensations' to boost circulation, and Thomson, now forty and frustrated, complained of being 'crowded out of late' though this saved him 'from writing nonsense'.[20] At Bangor Bradlaugh was eagerly heard by the Chief Justice of the Supreme Court of Maine, and in every respect the tour went better than he had dared to hope at the outset. At the end of February he was able to return to England with his former liabilities cleared and £1,000 off his English debts.

On his return he raised £284 10s as part of a testimonial to Holyoake, then seriously ill. Two new associates appeared who were to support him loyally to the end. The Rev. Stewart Headlam, a Christian Socialist assistant curate of St Matthew's, Bethnal Green, went to the Hall of Science and heard first Harriet Law and then Bradlaugh on American slavery. After the lecture he went to the platform and caused 'terrific excitement'[21] by saying he often read the *Reformer*. Bradlaugh mistook him for his rector, the Rev. Septimus Hansard, praised his work in the East End and wondered what his bishop would say. George Standring, a studious nineteen-year-old printer, was not an entire stranger. Originally a chorister in a Ritualist church, he had embraced secularism two years before and become the National Secular Society's corresponding member for Hackney district. At the society's 1875 conference he was appointed national corresponding secretary. Watts grew from secretary to general secretary. Just before this event Standring launched a new magazine. He had occasionally contributed to the *International Herald* and the *Herald and Helpmate* of the Mutual Help Association, whose members 'consider themselves to be Republicans of the most advanced kind'.[22] Though these had folded through lack of funds, he opened *The Republican Chronicle* as a penny monthly in April 1875.

It was Bradlaughite in its moral force appeal, non-theological, and took as its motto, ' "Republic" should be the name to cover the whole ground of Political and Social Reform'. This *dictum* came from Cattell, who contributed the first article. He appealed for 'one powerful organization' to assume all reformist work. The chief function of republican clubs was 'still education in liberty, intelligence, and truth'.

Bradlaugh himself delighted Maxse by breaking ground at Oxford, 'seat of Toryism and Clericalism—the nursery of English priests—and withal "learned" '.[23] Those students who imported the techniques of rugby scrums and Union debating got more than they bargained for, and the visit was a great success. His host was a sympathetic undergraduate, A. R. Cluer, in whose rooms he had a sparkling conversation with a lively young don, Herbert Asquith. Back in London he had his last marathon charade with Brewin Grant, in South Place Chapel. Things were far from smooth closer home. By July Thomson was 'quite off' the *Reformer*, 'Bradlaugh having taken the first opportunity of terminating our connection'.[24] Foote and Holyoake hoped 'to start a good Secular weekly, price 2d,' for those old secularists 'who don't like B's hammer-and-tongs style'.[25] The Hall of Science Club and Institute, where Bradlaugh warned that smoking would exude 'an air of loose manners', was officially opened, Mrs Besant being one of the gracious hostesses. She had just announced a new *Secular Song and Hymn Book*. That by Watts and Austin Holyoake was still in print and another was already being prepared by Reddalls for Manchester. At the last secularist conference, within months of her joining the society, Annie Besant had become a vice-president. The following winter a 'monster petition' against further Royal Grants was to be promoted and 'Mrs Besant has kindly undertaken this very necessary labour'.[26] The executive of the society was never large, but now increasingly, for added efficiency, sub-committees were set up. The key sub-committees consisted of Mr Bradlaugh and Mrs Besant.[27] In July Mabel stayed her usual month with her father. After she told him her mother told her not to say her prayers, he refused to send her back. When Annie and Charles paid a personal visit, he was ejected by a constable. His solicitors Lewis and Lewis threatened proceedings and Mabel was returned. By the time Bradlaugh left for his third trip to America in September, he was the subject of gossip in more than the Royal Palmerston.

Unlike the last occasion the voyage this time augured well and Bradlaugh and Dr Fessenden N. Otis were deputed to sign a passengers' resolution of thanks to the captain. In America there was the familiar jamboree, enlivened by a Republican rally at Faneuil Hall, 'cradle of liberty', in Boston. But Phillips and Bradlaugh had different views on the contemporary currency issue and their relations were less friendly. So were those with Bradlaugh's old religious friends, apart from Miner, for a pirated version of the infidel's more lurid writings had been sedulously circulated. At home, Watts, editing the *Reformer*, reported that Foote had issued the third circular for his proposed *Secularist* and 'is not *with* nor *for* us. Mrs Besant is well and exceedingly active in the movement . . . She is very good and kind to me as a co-worker, does anything most willingly that I ask her.'[28] One of the new young writers whose contributions had been endorsed by Bradlaugh in advance before he left was William Stewart Ross ('Saladin'). He had abandoned his studies for the ministry in Scotland to become a rationalist publisher trading as W. Stewart & Co., 41 Farringdon Street, London. Impressed, as he claimed in an obituary, by 'the splendid qualities of the demigod',[29] he sang a canticle:

> 'And, Theists, if you'll have a god,
> Hail one where Bradlaugh stands.'[30]

Whatever his motives, religious opponents found this supposed demonstration of the essential devotionalism of mankind a useful weapon.

In America, though feeling unwell, Bradlaugh tramped the circuit, addressed women's suffrage meetings and attended masonic functions. There were, on the whole, fewer big names[31] in attendance. No doubt news of the declining prospects of English republicanism had drifted across to the land where, pre-eminently, nothing succeeds like success. Bradlaugh thus had a little more time for his economic and social enquiries, aided by the Bureau of Statistics of Labour at Boston.[32] Suddenly in Washington, where Wilson was on his deathbed and unable to meet visitors, Bradlaugh himself felt gravely ill. Returning to New York, he consulted Otis, who eventually diagnosed pleurisy and typhoid and put him into St Luke's Hospital. Close to death, he took special pains that his nurses and callers should record that he showed no sign of fear or recantation, but the assiduity of the Rev. Moncure Conway, who was also visiting America and from whom he borrowed some ready cash, was mischievously misinterpreted. On recovery, he was advised to abandon the rest of his tour and so returned to England poorer than when he left. But with his 'nice ideas of honour'[33] the first thing he did was to repay Conway's

The Young 'Iconoclast'

Annie Besant

wife.

Still weak and short of breath, on his return Bradlaugh plunged into a fresh political row. While he had been away Disraeli had earned high praise for statesmanship when, for £4 million, he bought 176,602 non-voting shares in the Suez Canal from the bankrupt Khedive of Egypt. The French Ambassador 'expressed some fear, or at any rate thought that some would be felt, that the Khedive might be unable to pay his promised £200,000 a year' and that Britain 'would use some means to coerce him'.[34] Bradlaugh agreed with His Excellency and went about the country saying the purchase 'would be the commencement of complications which might land Egypt in the most serious difficulties'.[35] The £200,000 was not dividend, which the Khedive had already disposed of, but interest to Rothschild on a bridging loan. With neither dividend nor votes the shares were, declared Bradlaugh, unsaleable and had only political currency, as Disraeli was well aware.

There were new rows in the secular movement. On New Year's Day 1876 Holyoake and Foote launched the long-awaited *Secularist*, 'A Liberal Weekly Review', in an atmosphere of diplomacy and decorum. But in the sixth number there was an article on 'Destructive and Constructive Freethought' by Foote. It was, he said, 'an unwise and a disastrous policy to go on exposing orthodox errors week after week to people who have for years discarded them . . . Bradlaugh's utterances, alternately violent and entreating, are painfully feverish in their extravagance. Wild talk about traitors, as if we were a great secular Society, whose existence depended on the scrupulous reticence of every member, or as if nobody could be loyal to Secularism without servile devotion to one man.'[36] Holyoake issued a private circular complaining that his 'abridged eyesight' made it necessary for Foote to handle all insertions and that from the fifth number his colleague thus 'had the opportunity of preventing some of mine (which I deemed important) from appearing'.[37] Moreover, 'before the end of January he received one of Mr Bradlaugh's stiff legal notes—generally the shadows of coming lawsuits—asking for a meeting with "the editors of the *Secularist*" so that he could fix their "joint responsibility" for something which Mr Foote was reported to have said'.[38] This was that he had convicted Bradlaugh of a lie at the last secularist conference. So Holyoake announced that the 'Joint Editorship into which I entered involves me in far more anxiety, personal correspondence and responsibility than editing it alone'.[39] He offered to take the paper over or leave it with Foote. Foote chose to keep it. Bradlaugh offered Holyoake a regular platform in the *Reformer*, which he relinquished in May to establish a *Secular Review*. This finally appeared on 6 August as 'A Journal of Daily Life': 'We conceal nothing, we have nothing to conceal. We maintain that the secular is sacred, as that which affords self-guidance and self-trust alone is ... separateness of instruction; in theology, neutrality; in religion, reasonableness and duty.'

Foote continued his hostile campaign. In the spring Bradlaugh brought out Part I of *The Freethinker's Text-Book*. Part II was to come from Annie Besant. In view of the great intellectual ferment and conflicting theories of the period it appears in retrospect a remarkable work of syncretism in biblical criticism, anthropology and philosophy, an ingenious navigation of what has proved to be the mainstream in the eddying currents of nineteenth-century thought. It is also clearly and concisely written. But, like so much of Bradlaugh's writing, it lacks a story-line, passing inconsequentially from one slab of quotation to the next without sign-posts of chapter or sub-headings. Though of immense value to the converted, it lacks the sort of sparkle or inspiration demanded by the uninitiated. This Foote seized on with precision and malicious delight. 'B.V.' was brought in to the attack, declaring that Bradlaugh's 'old courage seems to have evaporated in immeasurable boasting, bullying, and bunkum, while as to the clash of intellect for which he was wont to profess such eagerness, he appears to have at length grown marvellously aware that he has no intellect available for the clash'.[40] Too deeply wounded for recriminations, Thomson's old friend and host declined to discuss him, tried to forget he had ever lived. Out of loyalty to their father Hypatia and Alice looked away at any secular function where Thomson was present. As their eyes sneaked back they saw his sad poetic face straining forward in silent appeal. His *City of Dreadful Night* had become a minor *salon* success, and he was now in correspondence with William Michael Rossetti, the critic brother of Dante Gabriel. Yet even as he professed to scorn the *Reformer* path by which he had risen, when his demon was quiet he recalled real friendship.

Bradlaugh's brother, William, had found 'another berth'[41] with the *Christian Herald* and just opened up a mission school in Clerkenwell, where his animosity against Charles was further nurtured. The story of the latter's abandonment of his mother to the parish gained a sequel involving his children. Edmund Yates, the publisher of the English *World*, 'unreservedly' withdrew this accusation and contributed to the Masonic Boys' School, but an Oxford grocer and town councillor refused to apologize. At a *nisi prius* hearing Justice Field warned the jury against religious prejudice and Bradlaugh was awarded £40. Because of such prejudice, rumour at this time had it that his name had been struck off the speakers' list for a conference and rally on county franchise, but Cowen, Fawcett and Anthony John Mundella, MP, assured him he had never been proposed. Among the freethought leaders he was no more popular. For a long time Foote had made vague allegations, the disclosure of which Bradlaugh forced at the 1876 secularist conference in Leeds. Even Holyoake declared that 'a more limp, flabby, boneless, confused, or (as I thought) impertinent story was never told by a pretentious accuser'.[42] Unashamed, Foote bounced back: 'The greatest blow I can strike against you is to strive to make our party too powerful and proud to submit to your tyranny'.[43] But when Bradlaugh and Mrs Besant threatened to resign, he was dropped from the vice-presidency. Undercurrents flowed round the conference. Harriet Law declined the vice-presidency and Watts handed over his secretarial functions to Standring. Assiduously taking notes, eagerly planning future triumphs for the movement, Annie Besant from time to time glanced round the hall with a sad, puzzled frown, innocently wondering what was the real cause of the carps and quibbles directed against their beloved and indefatigable president.

To be nearer the *Reformer* office she had moved to a house at 19 Westbourne Park Terrace, Bayswater, which she shared with two lady friends. From time to time Bradlaugh took tea with her and once his daughters came along. Emerging radiant as ever, he asked rhetorically: 'What does one say when one likes being in a place?' Alice was equally rhetorical. 'What does one say when one does *not* like it?'[44] In June 1876 Annie took and furnished 'Oatlands', 17 Mortimer Crescent (Road), St John's Wood, where she kept two servants. Her clothes were quiet, but a three-quarter length black silk coat cost her fifteen guineas. 'It was a constant puzzle' to the girls how Mrs Besant, 'who we had been told was extremely poor',[45] was able to live in this style. When the gossips heard of her transfer to St John's Wood they nodded knowingly and said 'How appropriate'.[46] They were not thinking of the original Knights Hospitallers. Before Cora Pearl graduated to the Rue de Chaillot she had operated among the 'yellow-chignoned denizens of St John's Wood'.[47] It was also where George Eliot and George Henry Lewes were living in sin. To the gentry of St Marylebone it was decidedly on the 'wrong side of the park',[48] a place where you kept women but not company. For any separated lady to chose to live there seemed a deliberate flouting of the conventions. At this time an anonymous pamphlet *Wife or Mistress?* was published. Of course, said society, she had written it herself. Annie Besant was far from unwilling to flout conventions if they struck her as unjust or repressive, but most of the time she was quite unaware of the byproducts of her actions. Too busy herself to trouble about people's private lives, she imagined that the concerns of others would be similarly impersonal. St John's Wood was, as she saw it, the ideal spot to be. It was quite near Central London when she was at home, and quite near the mainline stations when she had to travel north. Regent's Park was handy to exercise her dogs and her pony, while houses there were still relatively inexpensive. Though there were naughty associations there was also the aura flowing from intellectuals like Thomas Huxley and freethinking writers, musicians and artists, of whom the most fashionable was Sir Lawrence Alma-Tadema. Indeed it was Sir Edwin Landseer who had pioneered the Wood's intensive settlement. And it was where she had been brought up.

Apart from servants and employees,[49] with whom she had—in contrast with Bradlaugh—something of the imperious manners of the class she came from, Annie tried very hard to please everyone but was always misinterpreted. The Bradlaugh girls resented her affluence, asking themselves 'when had she the money to pay cab fares apart from her earnings due to our father's influence'[50] forgetting that 'the men she charmed ... were not few' and her powers of concentration and hard work unrivalled.

Bradlaugh himself frequently stated that he had 'no means whatever except what I earn from day to day with my tongue and pen',[51] and he lived as if this were literally true. But it was a picturesque hyperbole. In 1876, after much forbearance, he took legal action against Brewin Grant and the reverend gentleman demanded security for costs. In respondent affidavits[52] Bradlaugh showed that, apart from the copyright of the *Reformer* and other publications, he had 'Stock in the Grand Book of the Kingdom of Italy, of the value of at least £6,000' and 'investments made by me in stock' producing 'an annual income of £100'. From time to time he was left money, though often in trust for others or for the secular movement, and his regular earnings as a writer and lecturer were in excess of £1,000 annually.

What even his own family sometimes failed to appreciate was that in the name of great issues of freedom and freethought he carried on a style of litigation normally pursued only by the wealthiest in the land, that his other public work was a source of loss and not of profit, that the debts from his commercial days ran into thousands. His Italian stock was probably of doubtful negotiability, but, without the buoyancy of some sort of floating capital, he would soon have sunk without trace in a sea churned up by enemies anxious to torpedo him with sudden litigation and seize the *Reformer*, or make him bankrupt and imperil his political career. If regular public subscriptions to the cause were withdrawn he would soon be finished. Annie was fast becoming second to Bradlaugh in popularity as a lecturer and writer within the secularist movement, and had many journalistic contacts, his and hers, in Britain and America. Her income must have been several hundreds and she had no public liabilities or responsibilities. But his daughters resented the gross disparity in the two homes; especially when, one hot summer's evening as his windows were shut against the smells, Conway called to accompany Bradlaugh to a working men's club in the East End and, with dubious tact, observed that Turner Street was 'just the right place for my father to live in'.[53] About this time a party including the Bradlaughs and Annie, all now in 'a sort of neutrality', went to the theatre. Suddenly Mrs Besant leaned across to Bradlaugh and in a loud voice said 'Charlie'. The two girls 'felt turned to stone'.[54] Only their grandfather and their mother addressed him thus. Hypatia believed that Mrs Besant was 'absolutely insensitive to the feelings of others', but on this occasion she noted their looks and they 'never again heard Mrs Besant call him by his name'.[55] Instead she adopted the title first given to him by John Lees, an Edinburgh twine manufacturer, 'Chief'. This became Bradlaugh's badge in the secularist movement till his death.

With Alice and Hypatia, Annie could do no right. 'She tried now and again to interest herself in us and did us many kindnesses, but we never felt that it was spontaneous on her part, we always had the impression that it was done to please my father, and was probably prompted by him. That indeed would have been quite natural for she had little in common with us, or we with her, apart from him.'[56] For their part, they kept up a brave public front and even allowed him to take up their complaints about Mrs Besant's forgotten borrowings or indiscreet correspondence with the inner circle of thick-and-thin Bradlaughites, in full knowledge that nothing more would be heard of the matter. Whatever she said or did he never criticized her, and he tried to curb the criticisms of others, even of his daughters. To external 'worries which all the world might know of' there was added this new domestic upheaval, a psychological *ménage à trois*. Bradlaugh 'had a pretty hard time between us, i.e. between Alice and me on the one hand, and Mrs Besant on the other'.[57] Soon Annie and Charles took to going round the country speaking on alternate nights and chairing each other's meetings. At Congleton there was a renewal of the stone-throwing that had tried to maim other days, and crowds followed them to the brave home of freethinkers who put them up. Now the faithful had new slogans to shout, for to their Anti-Christ had come the Scarlet Woman. But the two had moments away from the hard suspecting eyes of London on safari where companionship, cheers and crisis royally paved the path of duty. With Mrs Besant's admiring eyes upon him Bradlaugh rose to new feats of crowd defiance, and personally ejected prize matmen from his lecturing arenas. But at Midhurst his wife's condition required a nurse and, Hypatia thought, a new home. He thus had to remind his family to avoid 'quarrelling or disagreement' so as not to worry him. Despite appearances, his own health, 'on which everybody's means of existence depend',[58] was uncertain.

On 29 October 1876 the *Secular Review* referred to H. Cook as 'an enterprising bookseller of Bristol'. By 21 January 1877 Henry Cook was described by a correspondent in the *Secular Chronicle*, now edited by Harriet Law, as 'a low, pitiful, black blackguard, of whom I know so much, that I should be exceedingly sorry if anyone reckoned him as a Freethinker'. In between, there had been a display of Cook's enterprise that set up an explosion which split the secularist movement in two before rippling around the world. In 1832 a Massachusetts doctor Charles Knowlton had published a sixpenny booklet *The Fruits of Philosophy; or the Private Companion of Young Married Couples*. Essentially it was a contraceptive manual, giving wrong information about physiology and the 'safe period', and right information about simple physical and chemical preventives, together with nineteenth-century absurdities on masturbation, aphrodisiacs and 'cooling' diets and profundities on political economy. On the whole, it decided, sex was a good thing:

> 'It is a fact universally admitted, that unmarried females do not enjoy so much good health and attain to so great an age as the married; notwithstanding that the latter are subject to the diseases and pains incident to child-bearing. A temperate gratification promotes the secretions, and the appetite for

food; calms the restless passions; induces pleasant sleep; awakens social feeling, and adds a zest to life which makes one conscious that life is worth preserving.'[59]

Stereos of the *Fruits* were part of the job-lot that passed from Watson to Watts via George Jacob and Austin Holyoake. Watts once asked Bradlaugh about it, but the Chief was in a hurry and merely said: 'O yes, it's indictable; I'll speak to you again about it';[60] but both of them forgot. Throughout the years it had enjoyed a steady, unspectacular sale. Watts handled about 1,000 copies a year. Cook sold secularist literature from time to time, but his main trade was in another kind of material, for which he had already done two years hard. For a while he retailed odd copies of the Watts edition of the *Fruits*, then decided his profits could be greater if he issued it with his own title page, added two interesting illustrations and charged one and eight instead of sixpence.

On 8 December 1876 the Bristol police showed interest. Cook was summonsed on the grounds that he 'unlawfully wilfully maliciously and scandalously did publish a certain indecent wicked scandalous and obscene book . . .'[61] Without mentioning the changes he had made Cook wrote to Watts, enclosing his summons and seeking advice and money. Watts replied: 'The book is *certainly defensible* and were I summoned I should defend it . . . Fear not, nothing can come of it.'[62] Touzeau Parris, the *Reformer* agent in the Bristol suburb of Clifton, also wrote to Watts about the proceedings. As Bradlaugh was out of London Watts handed a copy to Annie Besant for her opinion. She was on the point of leaving herself but read it on the train and telegraphed back: 'Book defensible as medical work.' Early in her freethought career she had had the 'Secularists' Bible' (*The Elements of Social Science*) metaphorically flung at her by a heckler, and replied quite honestly that she knew nothing about that or similar books. On returning home she read it, got interested in Malthusianism and had thought of writing about it in her section of the *Freethinker's Text-Book*.

Back in London Bradlaugh confirmed that Watts should go to Bristol to defend the *Fruits*, but was too busy to give the matter much attention. The Eastern Question was posing itself again, with Bradlaugh citing the 'Bulgarian atrocities' of the Turks against the Christian Balkans to quell the Jingoist[63] demand for a military alliance with Turkey against Russia, without supporting Gladstone's incitement of a crusade against the Turks. Meanwhile, reassured by his colleagues, Watts confirmed with Cook that he would, 'you may depend, be present myself upon that day, and will assume all responsibility for the book'[64] The City of London Police were asked to send a dozen copies to Bristol for the trial. They approached Watts and got the usual baker's dozen. The thirteenth copy was retained in London. At Bristol Watts got a shock to discover the real set-up, but gave neutral evidence about 'not a very profitable book'.[65] As soon as Cook was convicted and sentenced to two years, Watts telegraphed to London to suspend sales. He was just moving into new premises, 84 Fleet Street, with their echoes of Carlile. New type had been brought and 'National Reformer' proudly etched his shop-window. Though noses might be put out of joint among the inner circle of secularists, the Bradlaugh-Besant partnership was proving a winner in the country. Petitions and publications were flowing as never before. Despite the array of rivals the *Reformer* circulation had reached a new peak. At the next conference the National Secular Society was to be reorganized on an integrated branch structure. Watts did not want trouble from an unprofitable contraceptive tract.

The extra copy of the *Fruits* had however been lodged with the City authorities and on 8 January Watts was arrested. In his usual masterful way Bradlaugh told him not to worry and instructed his own solicitor, George Lewis[66] of Lewis & Lewis, to defend him. In Lewis Bradlaugh had found someone who, while of the highest repute, had Leverson's readiness to tackle the toughest cases and was a specialist in torts. The following day, accompanied by Truelove, the three men entered the Guildhall. Sergeant Green gave evidence for the prosecution, asserting that Watts had promised to stop all sales and destroy all plates. Surprised, Lewis asked Bradlaugh for advice but was told to take his instructions from Watts. The case was adjourned and then remitted to the Central Criminal Court. Watts was frantic, changing his mind every day. He had spent most of his life publishing, writing on and debating the heroic deeds of past freethinkers. Here was a chance to fall in among them. Bradlaugh asked him how he could plead guilty to publishing a book the movement had issued for years under the imprint of its most respected figures and, if the plea were justified, with something like criminal negligence. The Chief's great sense of tradition, his craving for cultural freedom, shone like a fiery beacon. Yet he too was unhappy. At Johnson's Court after the Guildhall hearing he said to Kate Watts, 'The case is looking rather serious, but we must face it. I would the prosecution had been against any other book, for this one places me in a very awkward position.'[67] The book was neither theological nor political. It was on a subject which he himself deemed important but over which there had already been savage recriminations, by an author unknown in Britain and forgotten in America, in a style which he did not himself like, and quoting physiology overtaken by many decades of medical advance. He admitted frankly that if the manuscript had been submitted to him he would have rejected it. Now that it was published and had attracted the notice of the Vice Society it was a matter of principle, but he did not see how he could appeal to the movement to help in its defence. Mrs Watts was surprised at his strength of feeling against the book and said that if she had known she 'would soon have stopped' its publication. He tried to reassure her with the hope that he could obtain a grand jury hearing on a technicality and have 'no bill' returned without the issue itself being tried. Then he went off to see Mrs Besant.

Not appeal to the movement? Annie's golden words flowed out in one of her richest orations. Did they not come of a tradition that embraced Robert Dale Owen, Mill, Place, Drysdale, even that noble martyr Richard Carlile? And, as a tear appeared in Bradlaugh's eye, she pointed to those nameless millions struggling in penury or waiting to be born to yet greater misery, beggars crying out for material and intellectual sustenance. The *Fruits* might be bruised, but it was all they had. There the thirsty could find sap. Next time they would plant better. An urgent message was sent round to the Wattses. When they arrived Annie gave an encore, perhaps more eloquent. In a heaven of massed secular choirs Watts saw himself joining the immortals before the throne of truth, crowned in honour of a race well run, a fight well fought. Even Kate glowed in the effulgence. Annie drew out a draft appeal to the movement which she had prepared in advance, got their agreement, posted if off to Truelove for instant printing, then dashed off to a lecturing engagement in Plymouth where she would baptize the campaign. Away from the heady air of Oatlands Kate Watts took a copy of the book home for her Saturday reading. She was not at all pleased with it *'in its entirety'*. Or with her sober reflections. She could imagine the faces of the jury, middle-aged, middle-class and middle-brow, especially when the prosecutor sneaked in the Cook saga. Some faces in the movement would be no brighter. And the outcome? The Chief and his lady dashing round the country on whistle-stop tours, vindicating the unsullied cause of freedom, while her husband and breadwinner moped in gaol branded as a dirty bookseller. She had a word with Watts.

Bradlaugh received a note appreciating 'the kindness of Mrs Besant and yourself last night' but wishing 'to change, if possible, the plan of defence'.[68] The Wattses were summoned to Turner Street, where Bradlaugh confronted Watts: 'You coward, you had better make up your accounts on Tuesday morning, and let us separate.' On the Monday Lewis advised that the appeal circular could honourably be sent out only if the case were to be fought. Annie returned from Plymouth flushed for the fray and with £8 already collected. The quartet had another meeting. Annie urged Watts not to 'disgrace and ruin himself'. They parted in both sorrow and anger. The issues were weighty and the men had had a long if shallow relationship. But Kate Watts's passions were monumental as the two secular Valkyries, like two puppet-mistresses, fought for domination. In her limited world Kate had always got her own way. But she had never come up against an Annie Besant. Three days later Bradlaugh wrote to Watts instantly dismissing him as *Reformer* sub-editor, with ten weeks' salary, after which he would also cease to be the Chief's printer and publisher. Almost immediately, to republish the *Fruits* and their other works, Annie and Charles formed a partnership as the Freethought Publishing Company, making no allowance for copyrights except £1,000 for the *Reformer*, which would revert to him on dissolution or to her on his death. She took over Watts's place on the editorial staff and soon became co-editor. In February they acquired for £60 a year ramshackle premises at 28 Stonecutter Street,[69] near Ludgate Circus, and put in as manager William James Ramsey, who ran the bookstall at the Hall of Science.

The movement's leaders at once took sides. Foote's hostility was predictable. After repeatedly refusing executive demands that he come to explain himself he had sent in his resignation from the National Secular Society. Instead of accepting it the committee expelled him. His pointed comment on the *Fruits* was that the contraceptive question 'should be calmly considered in the privacy of the closet, or gravely discussed by persons without interests involved in any solution of it'.[70] J.P. Adams, now living in Northumberland Park, urged freethinkers to 'purge our literature of a work which never ought to have been mixed up with it'.[71] Holyoake agreed that 'freethought literature should be kept free from the suspicion of immorality'.[72] The *Secular Review* was proving no more popular than his other publications and he was glad to sell it to Watts. At first Watts had tried to get Annie to intercede for him with Bradlaugh, saying he was in financial difficulties and a son was dying; then he raged and swore to have nothing to do with the tyrant again. A defence committee with W. F. Bull as secretary began to issue tendentious circulars, some of them being sent out by Watts with the *Reformer*. One of the committee members, a promising new lecturer M.C. MacHugh O'Byrne, wrote privately to Bradlaugh dissociating himself from the attacks on the Chief while abominating the booklet. He was on Watts's staff but received a week's notice when this letter came to light. Against Standring's wishes Bull was expelled from the council of the National Secular Society for personal abuse of Mrs Besant. Kate Watts made her debut as a pamphleteer in her husband's cause.

As the protagonists stomped the country, their bewildered audiences were given personalized accounts of proceedings and snap votes of support or censure were taken. Watts was particularly pathetic. An able lecturer and writer and, according to all accounts, a distinguished debater, he lacked real fibre. When things went wrong he went to pieces. He won considerable support with his basic claim that Bradlaugh had taken advantage of his vulnerable position—without a contract, for he had never anticipated difficulties—to try to impose a course of action he deemed both foolish and dangerous, and had turned nasty when disobeyed; but lost it again by intemperate abuse and patently false statements. As he squirmed and struggled, Bradlaugh quietly pushed him back. His argument was that a colleague who could not be trusted in a tight spot could not be trusted at all. Soon after seeking Mrs Besant's intercession Watts told her 'in future to abstain from interfering between us. Remember, Madam, I won my position in our movement years before the Secular party heard of you.'[73] Privately Hypatia made the same assessment:

> 'It was over the Knowlton Prosecution that there came the final breach between my father and his old friends, dear, much loved James Thomson (B.V.), Mr and Mrs Charles Watts and some others. The disappointment as to the defence of the Knowlton pamphlet was really the last "straw" to a "fire" which had been smouldering for some time. No sooner was Mrs Besant assured of my father's loving friendship than she estranged him from his old friends, treating them carelessly and even contemptuously.'[74]

When Watts came before the Recorder in February he pleaded '*in point of law* guilty', was discharged on £500 recognizances and ultimately let off with £25 in costs. Soon the Freethought Publishing Co. edition of the *Fruits* was available. Watts pointed out self-righteously that it had a new sub-title, 'An Essay on the Population Question', a virtuous Preface, footnotes by 'G.R.' and alterations in the text. The last was a recension problem and quickly altered in a second edition. Hypatia was staying at Oatlands and at Annie's suggestion the two of them hid bundles of the booklet round the house and garden until Bradlaugh returned from the provinces and ordered exhumation. The two publishers delivered copies to the Chief Clerk of the Guildhall, the Detective Department and the City Solicitor and, named a day, Saturday 24 March, when they would sell the pamphlet in person. Plain clothes police joined the throng which gathered. They were readily identifiable. Not long before, a detective had called round at Turner Street to buy the apparently salacious first section of Bradlaugh's contribution to the *Freethinker's Text-Book*, 'Man: Whence and How?' To the chagrin of the authorities it turned out to be on Old Testament studies and anthropology. Another sale of the *Fruits* was held five days later, and shortly afterwards the publishers were arrested on a warrant, brought before Alderman Figgins and remanded to the Old Bailey. The indictment charged them with 'unlawfully and wickedly devising and contriving and intending, as much as in them lay, to vitiate and corrupt the morals as well of youth as of divers other liege subjects of our said Lady the Queen, and to incite and encourage the said liege subjects to indecent, obscene, unnatural, and immoral practices, and bring them to a state of wickedness, lewdness, and debauchery, therefore . . . unlawfully, wickedly, knowingly, wilfully, and designedly did print, publish, sell, and utter a certain indecent, lewd, filthy, bawdy, and obscene book . . . '[75] Whether or not they had actually read the book their friends were appalled by the terms of this indictment. 'Some of Mr Bradlaugh's best friends at Northampton warned him that unless he abandoned his action in the Knowlton case it would be impossible for him to obtain a seat for Northampton.'[76] The Conways 'entreated' Annie Besant to dissociate herself from the case 'because we foresaw that evil tongues would be busy with her reputation'.[77] But neither of them would be deterred. To both it was a sense of honour.

At this stage they had almost thrown discretion to the winds. In 1876 Bradlaugh received £2,500 through some horse-trading in the probate court over a disputed will—or rather wills—of Henry Turberville, a brother of the novelist Richard Doddridge Blackmore. This paid off most of his debts and allowed him to feel he could, by February 1877, honourably move to less depressing lodgings. But eyebrows were raised when he moved to the Wood, within walking distance of Oatlands. For £50 a year[78] he acquired the top floor, basement and first-floor bathroom of 10 Portland Place (later renamed 20 Circus Road) from George Rogers and Son, pianoforte and music sellers. It was a Norman Shaw-style end of terrace house on the corner of Kingsmill Terrace.[79] Most of the space was, as usual, taken up by his books. His own bedroom was nine by ten feet and he retained the girls' nursery bed. The only reception room was the study, the family eating in the basement. As there was much more room at Oatlands he did most of his editorial work, and now his legal researches, there. The housekeeper, Mrs Kenwood, and the parlour maid obliged as chaperons. Occasionally Charles and Annie would break off for a game of euchre or, more rarely, 'make holiday' in the country, but usually there was ceaseless toil from mid-morning to 10 p.m. Naturally the world wondered about the full extent of their philosophy and whether they were concerned to produce or prevent the fruits thereof. Tongues which had before wagged now began to oscillate. Far from trying to duck the controversy both publishers confronted it.

In March Bradlaugh wrote his last letter to Kate Watts:

'I am obliged to you for your present opinion of Mrs Besant, which contrasts strangely with what both yourself and Mr Watts wrote to me while I was in America . . . Does it not occur to you that if you try to make my love for her a weapon against me you must expect some indignant rebukes? . . . Do you think that we are simply to stand still and be struck just as you please? Knowing how thoroughly proud I am of a woman whose work for our movement is so great you, a woman too, are party to the paltriest insinuations. Never insinuate against us again—if you want to do your very worst say that I love her very dearly and esteem her very highly, and hope the day may yet come when I may have the right to share with her my home and give her the protection of my arm; but add to this that you have known it a long while, that you wrote to me in America knowing it, and that you have written to her pretending affection since you have known it.'[80]

Mrs Besant's response was more brutally frank. She wrote to a Leeds correspondent:

'It does not apparently strike you that to interfere in our private affairs is an impertinence. Mrs Watts has full liberty to

179

publish everywhere she likes Mr Bradlaugh's letter. Mr Bradlaugh and myself are engaged to be married, and Mr and Mrs Watts have known this for a *long time*; and, knowing it, have visited at my house, accepted my hospitality, and eaten my dinners. It is a pity that they never disapproved of it until they were excluded from my house. There is no secret as to the attachment between Mr Bradlaugh and myself; we are not ashamed of it; his daughters know it and are on terms of the closest friendship with me. Mr Watts spoke with deliberate untruth when he said that I caused the separation between Mr Bradlaugh and himself. I was away from London when Mr Watts' change made the first breach, and I had no communication with Mr Bradlaugh about it until Mr and Mrs Watts maliciously attacked me in public. I used all my influence with Mr Bradlaugh to soften him, not to harden him . . . I do not, however, wonder that Mr Watts, being publicly disgraced himself, strikes wildly about in the endeavour to justify himself; it is only by trying to injure us that he can hope to remove some of the discredit resting on himself.'[81]

In the event, Kate Watts did not publish Bradlaugh's letter. Copies of both letters were however passed around. A mutual friend George Stewart, a wholesale tea merchant in Edinburgh, asked the Bradlaugh girls if Mrs Besant's reference to them were correct. They complained bitterly to their father of being 'outraged' but 'replied briefly to Mr Stewart that Mrs Besant was mistaken'.[82] The following Sunday Annie came to dinner. When Bradlaugh left the table she remained behind, knelt by the girls and said that although the letter *'was not true now, she hoped it would be true!!'*.

Touzeau Parris came up from Bristol. As a former Unitarian minister and an 'able but not too exhilarating speaker',[83] he was to take Watts's place on the lecture platform. He became secretary of the Bradlaugh-Besant defence committee, which Holyoake declined to be associated with, and Bradlaugh's second in a long wrangle with Watts over publishing accounts, which ended in a writ from the Chief for £58. Thomson acted for Watts. The Parrises, whom Hypatia found 'most kindly, amiable people, for whom Alice and I had a great liking but small respect for their discretion',[84] joined the inner core of the secularist establishment. Bradlaugh tried to persuade his partner not to persist as a defendant, but she insisted on bearing her full responsibility. While he pursued the legal maze planted by the 1857 Obscene Publications Act and Lord Chief Justice Cockburn's definition of 'obscenity' (that 'tendency . . . to deprave and corrupt those whose minds are open to such immoral influences and into whose hands such a publication may fall'[85]), she researched the medical aspects. His application to Cockburn and Justice Mellor obtained a writ of *certiorari* removing the action to the Queen's Bench and a special jury, but he failed to persuade Justice Lush to reveal the name of the responsible prosecutor. There was no doubt that a raid on Truelove at this time for stocking two other contraceptive tracts, R.D. Owen's *Moral Physiology* and J. H. Palmer's *Individual, Family and National Poverty*, was prompted by the Vice Society, but Bradlaugh suspected the Christian Evidence Society in his case.

Mrs Besant and he offered their resignations to the National Secular Society's executive, which, despite eager responses from Watts and Holyoake, would not accept them. At the secularist conference in Nottingham in May there was an operation to abolish the offices of president and vice-president, but when this was defeated amid tumult the two publishers were re-elected. Parris gained office; Holyoake accepted it but later walked out; Harriet Law declined; Watts resigned. Almost immediately a circular was issued and a meeting held at Cleveland Hall, presided over by Holyoake, which proclaimed a British Secular Union with 'regular Secular Services'[86] in South Place Institute, the sponsorship of Holyoake, the Wattses, Foote, J.P. Adams and Cattell, and corresponding members in sixteen towns. On 9 June the *Secular Review and Secularist* merged, with Watts and Foote as joint editors.

The *Fruits* trial was to be before Cockburn, with the Solicitor-General Sir Hardinge Giffard prosecuting. Bradlaugh issued subpoenas. Fawcett indignantly rejected his and declared he would send his wife Millicent, the feminist leader, abroad before she should swim in such muddy water. Darwin pleaded he was 'much out of health'.[87] Headlam gladly testified. A few days later he founded his Christian Socialist Guild of St Matthew's,[88] but was thrown out of St Matthew's the following year when a rocket launched by Frank Besant's superior, the Bishop of Lincoln, struck home. Important evidence was given at the trial by Dr Charles Drysdale, younger brother of George, and a medical student Alice Vickery, who became his wife. The Court of Queen's Bench was then[89] situated in the south-east corner of Westminster Hall, where Alice and Hypatia, chastely excluded, paced and fretted. Joseph Biggar, the member for Cavan, spoke kindly to them; Bernard Shaw, still unknown, slipped past into the court. In describing the history of the *Fruits*, which

Watts had not done, Annie Besant mentioned that one of its publishers had been 'Mr George Jacob Holyoake, whose name is probably fairly well known to you'.[90] Two days later the *Times* contained Holyoake's protestations of utter ignorance of the thing's contents. The foreman of the jury was Arthur Walter, son of the paper's chief proprietor. After a sympathetic summing up by Cockburn came the verdict: 'We are unanimously of opinion that the book in question is calculated to deprave public morals, but at the same time we entirely exonerate the defendants from any corrupt motives in publishing it.'[91] The foreman accepted that this was a verdict for the Crown, though some jurors later asserted that his assent was contrary to their intentions. Sentence was deferred. Bradlaugh deputed Hypatia, the more practical of the daughters, as business manager of the company in the event of a prison sentence, telling her to pay Ramsey by cheque. But he went along to court with £250 in his pocket, expecting only a fine.

In the meantime Annie had spoken on the trial in the Hall of Science and was reported in the *Morning Advertiser* as saying the judge was opposed to the verdict. It was also asserted that the *Fruits* was on sale in the hall. Before an angry Cockburn the defendants denied the one allegation but admitted the other. The sentence was six months' gaol and a £200 fine for each. Bradlaugh asked for a stay of execution. 'Certainly not', barked Cockburn. The prisoners shuffled out of court under escort. Relenting, he called them back. On a pledge not to publish the book while the appeal was being heard he released them on £100 recognizances each. Eight months later Lords Justices Bramwell, Brett and Cotton in the Court of Error quashed the sentence. The indictment was faulty, having failed to set out specifically obscene words. Though a magistrate found against him Bradlaugh now persuaded Queen's Bench to return those volumes of the *Fruits* seized in Truelove's shop. Its proprietor was not so lucky. At a second trial he was convicted and sentenced to four months' gaol and a £50 fine.

In May 1877 Mrs Bradlaugh died of heart disease induced by alcoholism. To the end she retained 'the greatest affection'[92] for her husband. After a decent interval Mrs Besant told Alice and Hypatia she was thinking of moving to a larger house and took them to view a spacious villa and garden in Avenue Road. They thought it very nice but rather large for her small household. She then pointed out the rooms she had allotted to their father and themselves. Again the 'girls "froze", and would say nothing further, except to intimate that the

182

plan did not commend itself'.[93] When they told Bradlaugh they got 'the impression that he was not best pleased at Mrs Besant's odd attempt' to gain their endorsement.

Mrs Bradlaugh might be dead but the Rev. Frank Besant was militantly alive. The following January he announced Chancery proceedings to deprive his wife of Mabel, and action was commenced as Mrs Besant was nursing the girl through scarlet fever. Her writings, notably *The Gospel of Atheism*, her association with Bradlaugh—though Besant 'never once attempted to attack her in court'[94] on any personal relationship his detectives may have looked into—her publication of an 'indecent and obscene pamphlet', and the danger to Mabel's 'morals and happiness'—these were his complaints. The case was heard before the Master of the Rolls, Sir George Jessel, whom Bradlaugh had congratulated five years before on becoming the first Jewish judge. Accompanied by the Conways, the Bradlaugh girls and Annie Parris, Mrs Besant 'entered the court-room young and beautiful'. Frank Besant was there, striking her friends as 'mean and narrow-minded'. Jessel seemed 'brutally intolerant'.[95] Even worse than the *Fruits* in his eyes was her determination to 'educate the child as to prevent her having any religious opinions whatever until she attains a proper age'.[96] Mabel was handed over to her father and Annie 'came out old and hard'. She said to Conway, 'It is a pity there isn't a God; it would do one so much good to hate him.'[97] With Bradlaugh beside her that was not the end of the story. Litigation dragged on another year. Besant stopped his wife's settlement. Annie claimed it or restitution of conjugal rights. He tried to end the 1873 agreement. Jessel flushed her with new hope when he suggested a counter-claim for divorce—the Bradlaugh girls could have no objections then—but drained it away with his correction that only a divorce court hearing in 1873 could have helped her. In the end Mabel was lost and Frank remained legally appended.

When the print order of some 266,000 copies of the *Fruits* was nearing exhaustion, Annie wrote her own *Law of Population: its Consequences and its Bearing upon Human Conduct and Morals*, which enjoyed a huge sale throughout the English-speaking world. At the same time she challenged the orthodox with *Is the Bible Indictable?*, 'being an enquiry whether the bible comes within the ruling of the Lord Chief Justice as to obscene literature'. With the help of the Dialectical Society, the Malthusian League was reformed with Charles Drysdale as president, and A. Trevelyan, Parris, Talandier, Alice Vickery and J. Bryson, president of the Northumberland

Miners Association, among its vice-presidents. Bradlaugh and Annie Besant were at first on the council and later became vice-presidents. The *Fruits* trial was by no means the last attack on a contraceptive manual, but it was the last court spectacular. In 1877 it was touch and go which way public opinion would run. Whatever the logic of family planning it cut across bourgeois concepts of decency and working-class notions of virility, violating strong religious feelings that conception is a sub-section of the natural law, God's gift and not man's thrift. Even in freethought circles there were powerful figures urging reticence. On the edges of the British Secular Union, rasping voices, especially from undistinguished publishers envious at the success of the *Fruits* and the *Law of Population*, spoke of the National Secular Society as the 'sexual school of freethought', the 'dirtites', 'filthites' and 'Cat and Ladleites', and self-righteously wrote obscene doggerel against 'Brassy Cheek' and 'Breezy Bouncer'.[98] But Bradlaugh had not devoted a lifetime to popular education, personal projection and perfect frankness in vain. Whatever their private inhibitions, the great bulk of the secular movement and trade union and radical forces on its fringe put unquestioning faith in his judgment. If he declared himself there must be grounds at least for exploration; and when they explored, their conviction grew that he was right. From that date the large Victorian family began noticeably to dwindle.

What might be the reaction of the Nonconformist shoemakers of Northampton was more unpredictable. With ill-concealed satisfaction the *Mercury* declared that he was finished politically. Thomas Barber seized the opportunity of writing a sixpenny pamphlet 'hostile to this gentleman's candidature for Parliamentary honours in connection with the Borough of Northampton'.[99] But when Bradlaugh went there the month after his conviction, he received a tumultuous welcome. His general political work was quickly resumed. As a separate entity the republican movement had died on him. Holyoake was lecturing on 'Neglected Republican Agitation', though few had been more neglectful than he. In January 1878 the *Republican Chronicle* pointed out sadly there was no republican club in the country. In Disraeli's warm sun Victoria was blossoming anew; and English snobbery, compounded of a love of infinite social gradations and differentials, gladly drew nectar from its source. But Bradlaugh pursued republican policies tangentially. In *Taxation: How It Originated, How It Is Spent, and Who Bears It* (1877) he advocated graduated land and inheritance taxes. In December 1877 he presided at a meeting to form an International Labour Union. Annie Besant, Harriet Law and Headlam were on its council. Soon afterwards the curate was driven from St Matthew's and Bradlaugh organized a testimonial for him.

This was the time of Jingo militancy, with Disraeli urging support of Turkey in the Russo-Turkish War as a buffer for Britain's Middle East interests, notably the Suez Canal. Bradlaugh joined the Hon. Auberon Herbert to invite the workers of London to demonstrate for peace. His contingents wore his election colours, Herbert's a green favour. Because of recent violence the deputy marshals carried 'wands of office' like constables' truncheons. A square four-deep was formed round the Hyde Park platform, but no sooner had Herbert begun to speak than a Jingo mob, led by Tory medical students, broke through one side. In the ensuing chaos Bradlaugh dashed to rescue Herbert before putting a hasty resolution, which was breathlessly carried. A fortnight later he decided on a more satisfactory demonstration. His opponents added hired toughs to their stop-at-nothing volunteers and armed them with gas piping and sharpened iron. Just as the meeting was peacefully ending trouble broke out. In a skirmish Bradlaugh was momentarily knocked over and took on his arm a fusillade intended for his head. Up he leapt and with five blows filled five beds in St George's Hospital. His friends warded off an attack from the rear, but his old enemy erysipelas set in. Herbert wished 'the division of hard blows had been more equal . . . I am afraid you always draw the fire'.[100] Derby's resignation forced Disraeli to climb down. But no sooner was the Eastern Question temporarily resolved than Britain declared war on Afghanistan and Bradlaugh was involved in new peace demonstrations.

For all the wealth of freethought talent behind the British Secular Union, it remained largely a head without a body. As early as 1880[101] the *National Secular Society's Almanack* was able to announce meetings of the BSU Kingston-on-Thames branch, whose secretary was also the secretary of the union, with the dry comment 'No information to hand as to other branches'. Even before this, its leadership was drifting apart. Though sundry meaty issues were stewed up to make a nourishing broth alternative to Bradlaughite secularism, these were not what really held the chefs together. At other times of their lives or under pseudonymns most of them served up tarter blasphemies and spicier obscenities than Bradlaugh or Annie Besant ever dreamt of. All they really had in common was hatred and jealousy of the Chief and his partner. For their part the duo stated their case fully then let it drop, partly as a matter of tactics, mainly because creative work was what interested them. First of their opponents to see which side his bread was buttered and prise himself loose was Foote.

In February 1878 he walked out[102] of the *Secular Review and Secularist*, which soon reverted to the *Secular Review*. At the beginning of 1879 he founded the *Liberal* and by August, when that had folded, returned to the columns of the *Reformer*. Towards the end of the year he had a rupture with Thomson, who had formed with him something of the close relationship formerly existing with Bradlaugh. By 1881 he was suing for peace and learned 'through Mr Smith that you are willing to be reconciled with me and to let our past differences sink into practical oblivion'. He expressed willingness to re-apply for membership of the National Secular Society and 'terminate my connection with the British Secular Union which, after a fair trial, seems to give no promise of success'.[103] Bradlaugh gladly accepted the olive branch and Foote quickly regained his old position.

Matters did not end so tranquilly with other members of the union, though they had the grace to express sympathy for Mrs Besant in her battle over Mabel. Exhausted by this she succumbed to rheumatic fever in the summer of 1878 and was nursed by all the Bradlaughs, though she later recalled only Charles 'behaving more like a tender mother than a man friend'.[104] To recuperate she went with the girls to North Wales. At this time there was a drag ball in a hall at Leeds used by the Secularists and, though the organizers were apparently Christians,[105] enemies said that secular philosophy produced unnatural as well as natural fruits. At the end of the year Standring took over the failing *Secular Chronicle* and buried it three months later. Meanwhile he gave the *Republican Chronicle* more life as the *Republican*,[106] but the movement itself did not revive. A new comet entered the secular firmament. Edward Bibbins Aveling was the son of one Congregationalist minister and the brother of another, the Rev. Frederic Aveling of Northampton, a strong Bradlaugh supporter. After gaining a science doctorate he had taught young ladies biology. Lecturing at the City of London College he was introduced to Annie Besant through one of his students, J.H. Levy, a political economist and journalist. Under Bradlaugh's influence it had been decided that, with Hypatia, Mrs Besant should read for a degree in law at London University, newly open to women, but soon 'it was Science which attracted her, as exemplified in the person of Dr

186

Aveling'.[107] At the *Fruits* trial she had most creditably defended herself, but the medico-social aspects of the case really interested her more than the legal.

Alice and Hypatia 'never liked Dr Aveling' but admitted that he was 'a splendid teacher'. Partly it was an instinctive reaction, like that of Annie Besant's St Bernard dog, Lion, who growled the whole time the insinuating doctor was in the room; partly they were annoyed at his trying to 'pump' them over his chances of writing for the *Reformer*. Mrs Besant's reaction was very different. Bradlaugh had told Conway there was no emotion he could not crush in his palm like an egg, and she finally decided he would do nothing domestically to jeopardize his public career. Soon Aveling had a key to Oatlands and was not reluctant to use it. Hypatia recalled that her father's first disappointment in Annie was 'her intimacy with Dr Aveling . . . for this man had not in him a spark of loyalty for man or woman'.[108] He was taken on as a *Reformer* contributor, though, as he was one of the finest science writers of his day. Alice and Hypatia studied botany with him; Annie and Hypatia, Latin and chemistry. In the summer, under 'Credo ergo laborabo'[109] in the *Reformer*, he admitted to the world he was a freethinker and began lecturing at the Hall of Science. This, he said, lost him all his college classes; so he proposed to Bradlaugh the establishment of science classes in the minor hall at Old Street, with practical instruction at his private laboratory at 13 Newman Street. Beginning with chemistry and animal physiology, these classes were under the auspices of the Science and Art Department, South Kensington. Headlam became chairman of the committee so that it could get a government grant. Hypatia acted as secretary. Under Aveling's 'triple traversing'[110] system, with its banning of note-taking, brilliant results were achieved and soon mathematics, French and advanced science were added. The three women became teachers of the elementary classes. Much more publishing was now demanded, and when a legacy to the National Secular Society matured, the Freethought Publishing Company borrowed the bulk of it.[111]

In 1879 the 'Revolutionary Agitator and Labour Leader'[112] Michael Davitt, organizing secretary of the Fenian body for England and Scotland under the Supreme Council of the Irish Republican Brotherhood, rebroadcast the cry of 'the land for the people' with his Irish National Land League. Thus stimulated, in January 1880 Bradlaugh issued his programme for a Land Law Reform Convention, codifying all his former points. Compensation for compulsory purchase of uncultivated land was to equal twenty times the average annual value for the previous seven years. The meeting took place on 10 February at St James's Hall. Bradlaugh was elected chairman and proposed that Forder, who had been the paid secretary of the National Secular Society since 1877, be secretary. Papers were read by Arch, Burt, and J. Grout of the London Trades Council, who 'declared, amid loud and sustained applause, that that Organization was in favour of the nationalization of the Land'.[113] J.M. Ball of the National Agricultural Labourers' Union proposed the formation of a Land Law Reform League. This was agreed to. Bradlaugh became president, Forder secretary, Le Lubez treasurer, and the vice-presidents included Taylor, Burt, Macdonald, Arch, Ashton Dilke (a younger brother of Charles and an editor who had made the *Weekly Dispatch* into a great radical journal), Gurney, Aveling, Annie Besant and Headlam. William Reynolds, a vice-president of the secularists, proposed the adoption of Bradlaugh's programme. When an amendment was moved in favour of land nationalization Mrs Besant admitted 'the nationalization of the land was the true theory, supposing they had a new country in which to begin'.[114] Britain was different. Here confiscation was unreasonable and, with national rentals at £200 million annually, purchase would cost £4,000 million. Despite the earlier applause the amendment was lost. In the evening there was a public meeting chaired by Gurney. It began with the London Secular Choral Union singing Ernest Jones's 'Song of the Lower Classes', rose to the *Marseillaise* and thrilled to the speakers. Davitt declared that all landlordism was 'a conspiracy and a robbery' while Aveling, 'hitherto unknown in the front rank of advanced movements, startled and delighted the audience by his eloquence'.[115] Bradlaugh emerged with heightened stature to fight the impending election.

In 1879 Gladstone, after four years' virtual retirement, went on a great barnstorming tour against the Tories. Bradlaugh helped to launch this with his account of an interview with the Turkish Foreign Minister, who bitterly complained of being 'led into war'[116] with Russia by British promises of help. Waves of popular feeling were soon lashed up. They now frothed at specific issues and did not break against central pillars of the constitution as they had a few years before; so that an advertisement in the *Manchester Guardian*, in February 1880, proposing republican clubs received no replies. The next month a sudden dissolution was announced by Disraeli, now the Earl of Beaconsfield, to endorse his policy of coercion in Ireland.

188

The old wheeler-dealing broke out in Northampton.

A new association of moderate Liberals, the 'New Jerusa-lemites',[117] declined to treat with the Radical-Liberal union and put up Ayrton. When he had a riding accident they tried to interest Hughes, but he fell ill. In turn they next approached Herbert, a local wine merchant J.M. Vernon, a tramway proprietor Jabez Spencer Balfour, and Samuel Morley; but all of them declined. The other Liberals had more or less settled on Bradlaugh and Thomas Wright, a Northampton man practising as a solicitor in Leicester. In this state of flux a leading Liberal, Unitarian and shoe manufacturer of the borough, Philip Manfield, went down to London to ask the Liberal Whip W.P. Adam if he could team up with Bradlaugh a running-mate who might unite the town. Adam said he had just the man. Henry Labouchere was a tiny puckish figure who usually paid lip service to Christianity and the conventions but was 'a born *impie*'[118] and a casual shocker. Originally a diplomat, during the siege of Paris he was a correspondent for the *Daily News*, more as an interest than a profession, for he had just inherited a great fortune from his uncle Baron Taunton. He had represented Middlesex briefly and unspec-tacularly in the 1860s but gained political stature after 1877, when he founded *Truth*.

In Northampton 'Labby' struck just the right note of unity and common sense. He was the perfect complement to Bradlaugh, one a man of the world who was no stranger to ideals, the other a man of ideals and no stranger to the world. In later years he was able to record that 'never during all these years we had a shade of a dif-ference, and a better and truer colleague never lived'.[119] But satis-faction with this arrangement was not universal. In Midlothian, Gladstone's new constituency, and many other parts of the country, Adam's simple response to Manfield's request was represented as a sinister plot of the Liberal leaders to post Bradlaugh in a package deal to Westminster, where he would help Gladstone to disestablish the Church of Scotland, and probably the Church of England, as he had already despoiled the Church of Ireland. In Northampton Canon Robert Hull had inherited Gedge's incumbency, and with it his animosity to Bradlaugh; while the Rev. Henry Woffindin told his congregation at St Giles's that Christ would say 'Well done!' to all Liberals who voted against the infidel. The Rev. W. Ashworth added primitive prejudice on behalf of the Primitive Methodists. Francis Mulliner sent an open letter from Liverpool against a man 'who has made a trade of blasphemy'.[120] But the bigots had little time to get organized, and their efforts were outweighed by Samuel Morley's [121] influential advice to Nonconformists to vote for Bradlaugh. From 8,189 electors [122] Labouchere gained a record 4,518 votes to become the senior member. Bradlaugh was his junior with 3,827. The Conservatives Phipps and Merewether were some hundreds behind. For the first time in history an avowed atheist had won his place in the mother of parliaments, where his 'struggles against authority, penury and obloquy were now to be transferred to a more brightly-lighted stage'. [123]

'If I am not fit for my constituents, they shall dismiss me, but you never shall. The grave alone shall make me yield.' — *Hansard* CCLXVI (1882), 75.

The 1880 election was a major victory for the Liberals, whose absolute majority over the combined Conservatives and Home Rulers exceeded forty.[1] It was largely Gladstone's victory, but Victoria said 'she would sooner *abdicate* than send for or having anything to do with that *half-mad fire-brand*'?[2] He was not moreover the official leader of the Liberals. That was Earl Granville, who Gladstone thought should be approached. Beaconsfield suggested the Marquess of Hartington, but both Hartington and Granville told the Queen there was nothing for it but the 'People's William'. With this sop to the radicals in its leader, a cabinet 'loaded with Lords and weakened with Whigs'[3] was set up. It was hoped that Dilke might have joined it as Chancellor of the Duchy of Lancaster, but this post went to Bright. Only by repeating his dignified 1874 recantation of republicanism did Dilke become a minister at all, Under-Secretary at the Foreign Office. On being elevated to President of the Local Government Board, to the agitation of Victoria, two years later, he insisted that 'crude ideas'[4] more fittingly described his youthful republicanism than abandoned 'opinion'. The only really advanced politician in the cabinet was Chamberlain, President of the Board of Trade. From the start of Gladstone's Administration, therefore, the masses were disappointed. They were even more disappointed by its achievement. For some years before, times had been hard during poor harvests and Tory militarism, leading to increased national debts. The secret Treaty of Berlin in 1878 left 'embarrassment and complication'[5] overseas. With Parnell's fuel on it the Irish Question was still smouldering. Only the Liberals, it was stated, could clean up and start afresh. But Gladstone soon found he had little room for manoeuvre. For all his tree-felling, he lacked decisiveness with advancing years and was unable to fulfil most of his rash electoral promises of 'peace, retrenchment and reform'.[6] But apologists for Gladstone were later able to excuse his record by bemoaning the irruption of the 'Bradlaugh question'?

In sending Bradlaugh his congratulations, Ashton Dilke, newly elected as a member for Newcastle and as much an atheist as the notorious infidel, asked him 'whether you intend to take the oath, as I think that if any protest is entered it would come with more force if done by several members'[8] There were plenty of unbelieving members known to them both, but somehow the scheme petered out. In the end it was only Bradlaugh who, after consulting the Law Officers, advised the Speaker Henry Brand, a former Liberal Chief Whip and close personal friend of Gladstone, that he wished 'to affirm under the 29 and 30 Vict.,c.19,s.14, and 31 and 32 Vict.,c.72,s.11 as "a person for the time being permitted by law to make a solemn affirmation or declaration" and shall tender myself at the table to the proper officer, being entitled to affirm under the "Evidence Further Amendment Act" 1869,s.4.'[9] He sent a similar letter to Sir Thomas Erskine May, Clerk to the House of Commons and an outstanding constitutional lawyer. Brand believed it was 'obvious that this question is one for the judgment of the House, and that I must await for instructions from the House'[10] so he asked Bradlaugh to defer his presentation till 3 May when sufficient members would have been sworn in to adjudicate. After prayers on the agreed day the junior member for Northampton came to the table and gave May a paper:

> 'To the Right Honourable the Speaker of the House of Commons. I, the undersigned Charles Bradlaugh, beg respectfully to claim to be allowed to affirm as a person for the time being by law permitted to make a solemn Affirmation or Declaration instead of taking an Oath.'[11]

When May asked him his grounds he said 'by virtue of the Evidence Amendment Acts, 1869 and 1870', which he had done so much to bring into law. The House agreed to appoint a Select Committee to investigate. Sir Stafford Northcote, the old-world leader of the Conservatives in the Commons, told his diary: 'It seems strange to require an oath from a Christian and to dispense with it from an atheist. Would it not be better to do away with the members' oath altogether, and make the affirmation general?'[12] A cross-section of papers, including the *Baptist* and the *Times*, echoed this view. It was far from universal. After demanding a Burials Bill[13] for themselves, the Wesleyan Conference protested that atheists had no right to legislate. Some 198 petitions against Bradlaugh's taking his seat reached the House before he did. Sundry papers revived the old libels but apologized on confrontation. James Edgcombe,[14] the shady editor of the shaky *British Empire*, a weekly 'National Newspaper', refused to apologize for the watch story. Bradlaugh applied for a summons, making the matter a Crown prosecution and requiring counsel. Giffard appeared for the defence and successfully moved the hearing from Bow Street to the Queen's Bench. Faced with the impossible task of dealing with vague allegations involving six provincial towns and three halls in London over a period of twenty years, Bradlaugh demurred to the defendant's pleas. Eventually a motley crowd of expenses-paid layabouts was assembled to make specific charges, but when he heard that Bradlaugh had solid rebutting evidence from both secularists and Christians Edgcombe dropped the case. He also dropped the *British Empire*. Meanwhile the member for Northampton had more important litigation on his hands.

When the names of the Select Committee were announced, one of the Portsmouth members, Sir Henry Drummond Wolff, objected to the entire procedure, though Northcote had supported it. Soon Wolff was joined by Lord Randolph Churchill, who was the member for Woodstock, the pocket borough of his father, the seventh Duke of Marlborough, and angry at Bradlaugh's attack on perpetual pensions, through which his family benefited to the tune of £4,000 annually. Arthur James Balfour and John Gorst supported them. The four became known as the 'Fourth Party'. Apart from Churchill they had no personal hostility to Bradlaugh, but hoped to boost Tory morale by impeding government business and to embarrass Gladstone among his pious supporters throughout the country by associating him 'in the public mind with Mr Bradlaugh's atheism and *Fruits of Philosophy*'.[15] The Select Committee consisted of nineteen members under the chairmanship of Walpole, and included the top legal brass of both sides. Apart from Charles Henry Hopwood, a Liberal who voted against Bradlaugh's right to affirm under existing legislation but who wanted reform, the division was along party lines and the application was lost on the casting vote of the chairman. What was on the face of it the simplest matter proved on investigation to be highly complex, and the party vote was to some extent the last expedient of men utterly uncertain what the true legal position was. Bradlaugh himself distinguished four different types of oath: (1) promissory (loyalty-pledging) (2) purging oneself of some charge, as in an answer to a bill in chancery (3) for witnesses (assertory or testimony) (4) for a jury sworn to try an issue. For practical purposes only (1) and (3) needed distinction. Bradlaugh had already devoted much of his life to the reform of (3); he was now to devote much more to (1).

Before members of parliament could take their seats they had to comply with the provisions of the 1866 Parliamentary Oaths Act.[16] This decreed it 'expedient that one uniform Oath should be taken by Members of both Houses of Parliament' and abolished the earlier oaths.[17] There was a 'promise to maintain and support the Succession to the Crown, as the same stands limited and settled'. An affirmation was available for 'every Person of the Persuasion of the People called Quakers, and every other Person for the Time being by Law permitted to make a solemn Affirmation or Declaration instead of taking an Oath'. Two years later the Promissory Oaths Act reduced the form to 'I—do swear that I will be faithful and bear true Allegiance to Her Majesty Queen Victoria, Her Heirs and Successors, according to Law. So help me God.'[18]

Bradlaugh and his supporters claimed that it would be tautological if 'every other Person' in the 1866 Act did not have application to the legal system at large, or otherwise it would simply be saying that everyone allowed to affirm in parliament could affirm in parliament. They also claimed that 'for the Time being' meant any subsequent time when the Act was in force. The Evidence Amendment Acts of 1869 and 1870 extended the categories of affirmers, and these must now be declared within the scope of the Parliamentary Oaths Act. His opponents asserted that the 1866 Act might have been badly drafted but it could not be considered alone. To ascertain the intention of parliament the whole history of oaths and affirmations must be looked into. Then it would be seen that assertory and promissory oaths always ran independently, as the situation of Quakers clearly showed. Liberalization of procedures in law courts was in the interests of justice and the whole community, while promissory oaths and affirmations were to secure privileges for individuals. Though Bradlaugh was later to rebut these assertions with considerable eloquence, he did not regard them as utterly outrageous, and when on 20 May the Select Committee decided against him he cheerfully announced his readiness to take the oath. Papers that were later to say that if he had taken the oath quietly in the first place a lot of bother would have been saved, now accused him of hypocrisy. Holyoake seized the opportunity of reminding the world that he had never taken and never would take the oath. Bradlaugh cared little about empty forms but had sought to affirm when convinced he had the right, because it was 'more decorous'.[19] When denied this he had no objection to swearing, though most commentators to this day assert that the trouble which ensued arose from his refusal to take the oath. But where he blundered, probably for the only time in the whole long struggle, was in issuing a—for him—rather garrulous statement on his reasons. He would take the oath 'although to me including words of idle and meaningless character', although it was 'a form less solemn to me than the affirmation I would have reverently made' and couched in words which 'are to me sounds conveying no clear and definite meaning'. Then he would consider himself 'bound not by the letter of its words, but by the spirit which the affirmation would have conveyed'.[20] Not only did this seem the snub direct to the oath, it also acknowledged that the asseveration 'So help me God' was an essential part of it.

The day after the committee's report the leading Liberals met in the Speaker's library and decided to move 'previous question' if the Tories tried to prevent Bradlaugh's taking the oath. This Wolff, after consultation with Churchill and the lawyer William Grantham, MP, determined to do. Instead of getting back to square one and refusing any intervention between a member and his taking the oath—the usual procedure when he came forward in the prescribed manner, as Bradlaugh was careful to do—the Speaker, mindful of the recent debate over the atheist's right to affirm, felt obliged to allow comment on his proposed oath. In a temperate speech Wolff quoted the unfortunate wording of the 1869 Evidence Further Amendment Act giving a freethinker the right to affirm if 'the taking of an oath would have no binding effect on his conscience'.[21] He also quoted the *Impeachment of the House of Brunswick* as proof of Bradlaugh's inability to 'be faithful and bear true Allegiance to Her Majesty Queen Victoria, Her Heirs and Successors, according to law'. Waxing eloquent, Wolff continued: 'You know, Mr Speaker, we all of us believe in a God of some sort or another'—a quasi-blasphemy that 'lived in Mr Gladstone's memory to the end of his days'.[22] Alderman R.N. Fowler then pleaded on behalf of the City of London for the unsullied purity of parliament. Gladstone, who had just been warned by the Whips that there would be a revolt if he tried to force the oath through, moved for another Select Committee to consider it. Appalled by his 'known atheism' and 'other horrible principles', Victoria told him she deemed Bradlaugh a 'disgrace'[23] to the Commons. In the adjourned debate three days later, the Tories, who less than a month before had all joined in the jolly wrestle at the table of the House to grab one of the available testaments and had then merrily mumbled the ritual words after the Clerk or one of his assistants, now found the oath to be something of awful and holy solemnity. Churchill whipped them up with a philippic against 'an avowed Atheist and a professedly disloyal person'[24] while Baron Henry de Worms, a Jew who had found Christ, hoped the House would 'prevent an avowed Atheist from swearing a lie... on the holiest of books'.[25] Sir Henry Tyler, member for the rotten borough of Harwich and 'a gentleman who is a director of some fourteen public Companies, and who has great ability in making a large fortune, when the shareholders of the Companies are not always as successful',[26] proposed to deal with the writings of Bradlaugh, but these were declared irrelevant. The eloquence of Bright and other Liberals kept most of the government side loyal to Gladstone, and a second Select Committee, finally of twenty-three members, was set up.

It attracted a good deal more excitement, and its hearings were more protracted, than the first. Apart from the hysteria in the country and the House, the issue was novel. 'There is no precedent of any Member coming to the Table to take and subscribe the Oath, who has not been allowed to do so, nor of any Member coming to the Table and intimating expressly, or by necessary implication, that the oath would not, as an oath, be binding on his conscience. The present case is, therefore, one of first importance.'[27] Both Erskine May and Bradlaugh nonetheless amassed their 'precedents' and were closely cross-examined on them, while Bradlaugh tried to duck the essential difference between an oath and an affirmation (or oath without the words of asseveration) by saying that these words were not deemed essential to the oath in *Miller v. Salomons* and *Lancaster and Carlisle Railway Company v. Heaton*. He declined to answer questions as to his belief in God and tried to explain away indiscretions in his statement of 20 May. The issue to be determined by the committee was theological and legal, not political; but if pressed on the republican question Bradlaugh would have maintained that his loyalty to the House of Brunswick persisted while they reigned 'according to law'. The committee decided, however, as it might have done if such an inquisition had been conducted into the beliefs and writings of a good many members, that he was not entitled to take the oath but should be allowed to affirm.

The committee reported on 16 June and five days later Labby moved that his colleague be allowed to affirm. Fowler and Tyler performed again; Giffard joined in. When the motion was put after a two-day debate and defeated by 275 votes to 230, there was, said Northcote, 'shouting, cheering, clapping of hands, and other demonstrations, both louder and longer than any I have heard in my parliamentary life'.[28] The following day Bradlaugh made his maiden speech without notes at the Bar[29] of the House, standing there 'as no criminal' but 'as the chosen of a constituency of this country'. If they would not accept him he 'must appeal to a tribunal higher than yours—not to courts of law, for I hope the days of conflict between the assembly which makes the law and the tribunals which administer it are passed... But there is a court to which I shall appeal: the court of public opinion.'[30] Labby tried to rescind the earlier motion. The Speaker asked Bradlaugh to withdraw. He 'respectfully' refused. Gladstone declined to act to extract the House from an *impasse* of its own making. Northcote moved a formal motion that Bradlaugh withdraw, which was carried 326:38. Still Bradlaugh would not budge. Brand called for the Sergeant-at-Arms, elderly, diminutive Captain Ralph Gosset, to remove him. After what Gladstone hyperbolically called 'almost a corporal struggle with the sergeant',[31] the persistent atheist came back. Northcote then moved that he be 'taken into the custody of the Sergeant-at-Arms', and when this was carried 274:7 Bradlaugh suffered himself to be led away. He was imprisoned in a curious U-shaped room high in the Clock Tower and forming the first floor of its habitable chambers. Gosset was a most obliging gaoler and the atmosphere was almost festive as many visitors, including Parnell, came to express their sympathy. Headlam sent a telegram: 'I wish you good luck in the name of Jesus Christ, the Emancipator, whom so many of your opponents blaspheme.'[32] When this message got into the press his bishop wrote 'anxiously awaiting a denial'. Instead Headlam coolly retorted: 'I have always thought that it was a Christian duty to have sympathy with all "prisoners and captives".' It was only the intervention of Archbishop Tait's chaplain that saved Headlam on this occasion, but not for long. If Victoria felt peace of mind now that 'the most heavy desperate sort of character'[33] was safely locked up, it did not last long. Scarcely was the ink dry on Annie Besant's leaflet 'Law Makers and Law Breakers' when he was released. Beaconsfield advised Northcote that Bradlaugh, though comfortably provided for, could pose as a martyr so long as he was imprisoned, and the following afternoon Sir Stafford surprised the House by proposing an amnesty. This was agreed to. Bradlaugh emerged with another record: he was the last person ever to be imprisoned in the Clock Tower. The veteran agitator for merchant shipping regulations, Samuel Plimsoll, whose 'line' had been secured four years before, deplored the 'old spirit of domination and intolerance'[34] which was embittering true Christianity. At a mass meeting in Northampton, presided over by Purser, Bradlaugh paid tribute, climaxed by cheers, 'to the loyalty and bravery and the generosity and the intelligent service rendered to me by the colleague you have given me'.[35] Thomas Adams moved a vote of confidence in the junior member, which was carried unanimously. Even Watts said Bradlaugh should be supported, while adding the sanguine comment that if he had affirmed quietly in the first place no one would have challenged him.

On 1 July Gladstone moved that, 'subject to any liability by statute',[36] unbelievers be allowed to affirm. Gorst called the proposal 'disorderly'. Hearing that his Catholic followers were already being priest-ganged against him, Parnell gave an *apologia* for his forthcoming pro-Bradlaugh vote. That night the motion went through 303:249. The following afternoon the Speaker 'took the Chair' after prayers, at about 2.15 p.m. Waterlow took the oath and went through the formalities of admission. In a setting of noiseless, suppressed excitement Bradlaugh made the affirmation, signed the test roll, was 'introduced' to the Speaker, shook hands and took his seat. Charles Newdigate Newdegate, a North Warwickshire pillar of the establishment, both secular and ecclesiastical, who during his thirty-seven years in the House waged vendettas against all religious minorities, now presented a portfolio of petitions against the admission of atheists and the Sunday opening of museums. There were thirteen other matters of private business; the chairman of committees presented his report; a few minutes were given to noting the ratification of the disputed Thirsk election result; Lord Richard Grosvenor, the Chief Whip, moved that a writ be issued for a new election at Tewkesbury, whose recent results had been set aside by an election judge. After nine short speeches the house divided. As Bradlaugh was coming out of the Aye Lobby, Newdegate drew the attention of W. Gibbons, one of the division clerks, to the fact that Bradlaugh had voted, observing, 'This may become the subject of inquiry hereafter'[37] As soon as the doors were opened Newdegate collected his secretary and they took a cab to his solicitor, William George Stuart,[38] in Grays Inn. Then they went to the Temple chambers of Giffard's junior, Samuel Kydd. Presently Stuart's clerk, James John Stuart, joined them with a writ made out in the name of

'The Great Question of the Day. Can they get him out?'
From the cartoon in *Vanity Fair*

"KICKED OUT." (?)

Henry Lewis Clarke, described as a surveyor, claiming £500 from Bradlaugh for voting without taking the prescribed oath. Newdegate then returned to Westminster. The House adjourned at 6.50 p.m. and when Bradlaugh emerged ten minutes later the pious member personally thrust the writ into his hand. Perhaps the most celebrated of the lay lawyer's cases had commenced. A few days later Cecil Barbour[39] obtained a similar writ, which was shown but not served. As a precautionary measure Joannes Swaagman (Darwen), one of the secularist vice-presidents who lived nearby, began a friendly action claiming penalties for all of Bradlaugh's subsequent votes, ultimately amounting to £108,500.[40] But the Chief had faced larger paper tigers than this.

Next day Bradlaugh made his first non-personal speech in the House. Despite the bitter opposition of many Irish members he pleaded for more aid for Ireland: 'On behalf of an English constituency, which consisted of a very large number of English working men, he thought he should only be doing his duty in asking the Government to allow some of the loss to fall upon them.'[41] For their part his Northampton supporters rather enjoyed his notoriety. F.V. St Clair wrote a new song 'Bradlaugh', including:

> We know that he once sold a book, which caused a great
> sensation,
> For it told the people plainly how to stop the population;
> Some wise men got the needle, and they said it was too hot,
> But it proved that Mr Bradlaugh was the 'Daddy' of the lot.[42]

Bradlaugh had little leisure to be amused. He now had unpaid parliamentary duties and complex litigation to cope with in addition to his professional writing, lecturing and editing. The government assured the Tories it would not instruct its law officers to assist him in *Clarke v. Bradlaugh*, so he had to bear both the research and the financial burden. Hostile petitions, whose signatures were in many cases duplicated or demanded from Sunday school children, came flooding in. With monumental effort his supporters, mostly operating through branches of the National Secular Society, managed to do better in their tally for 1880. And when Sir J. Eardley Wilmot introduced a Bill to exclude all atheists from parliament, it was defeated.

Manning said significantly that 'there still stands on our Statute-book a law which says that to undermine the principles of moral obligation is punishable by forfeiture of all places of trust'.[43] He did not deign to mention by name 'one whose notoriety relieves me of an odious duty'. In March 1882 he returned to the attack. Bradlaugh riposted with *A Cardinal's Broken Oath*. Savagely he drew attention to Manning's broken Anglican vows in a pamphlet which was widely distributed in Rome by Manning's enemies and effectively ended any chance he might have had of becoming pope. This was perhaps the origin of the story, for which no real evidence seems to exist, that Bradlaugh was concerned in a plot to put a liberal pope in the chair of St Peter.

His brother William now formed an Anti-Infidel Tract Enterprise, to include a book depot and a monthly journal, in which he found the enhanced notoriety of his family name a source of profit. Charles found that although his celebrity added to the sales of the *Reformer* and attendances at the Hall of Science, it also saddled him with a huge correspondence from all over the world. Every morning he had to devote hours in his library to dealing with his numerous callers, sometimes psychiatric and even homicidal, who burdened him with their personal and legal problems. He was indeed a one-man Citizens' Advice Bureau. In the House he was no less active. He pressed the Attorney-General, Sir Henry James, to undertake criminal law codification, pleaded for Maoris detained without trial after an insurrection on the West Coast of New Zealand, and on 8 February 1881, when 'Parnell was somewhat mysteriously absent from the House',[44] he moved the rejection of the Coercion Bill brought in by Forster as Chief Secretary for Ireland. Fighting the Bill clause by clause he missed only one division, when he was in bed after an all-night sitting caused by Home Rule filibustering. In March the subject of army flogging came up. No less than in the bringing up of children he believed that in the services 'to use brutal and violent means is to brutalize and to degrade human nature'.[45] The numerous requests of soldiers were unnecessary to make him intervene, for he combined humanity with a realization that 'men who once felt the lash were not loyal to any command'.[46]

What seemed to the world like a final decision in *Clarke v. Bradlaugh* was looming. But new combat was in the air. The opening shot came the day after his anti-flogging speech. Henry Varley, a former butcher and cattle-dealer who had opened a Free Tabernacle about the size of the Hall of Science in St James's Square, Notting Hill, wrote the first of his notorious letters. This one was addressed to 'the electors of the Borough of Northampton'. The only way to get the Liberal Party off the hook in the Bradlaugh case, he said, was for Northampton to find another Liberal or vote Conservative. This might seem to be faithless to the party but '*the case is exceptional*'.

And he hacked out of context all the most hair-raising quotations from Bradlaugh, Annie Besant and the 'vile' *Fruits* and *Elements* to show how exceptional it was.

Clarke v. Bradlaugh had opened with a simple Statement of Claim, which needed to be amended. Three months later came Bradlaugh's Statement of Defence, asserting that he had duly affirmed and setting out why he was so entitled. In his reply the plaintiff protested that Bradlaugh was a person 'who by want of religious belief was not entitled to make and subscribe a solemn affirmation',[47] and joined and took issue on the reasons he had given. The court struck out the second paragraph. As a basic legal objection it should have taken the form of a demurrer. The first paragraph was not struck out, but Bradlaugh was allowed to demur to it on the grounds that the plaintiff was not entitled to make any assumptions in advance about his religious beliefs and their consequences. He then submitted a rejoinder and a demurrer to the plaintiff's reply to his statement of defence, while the plaintiff amended his reply and added his own demurrer. All this merely set out the issue to be tried. When it came up on 7 March before Justice Mathew, a new Roman Catholic judge, and Giffard was late, the hearing was delayed. Kydd awakened sympathy in court with his frank 'I do not feel able to argue this myself'.[48] And he was a professional lawyer.

Bradlaugh brought a new statute into his arguments: the Parliamentary Witnesses Oaths Act 1871,[49] which allowed the Commons to administer oaths to witnesses. This then put the Speaker, he argued, into the category of a 'presiding judge' in the Evidence Amendment Acts. When the case was adjourned, Giffard and Bradlaugh dashed from Queen's Bench to the Court of Exchequer Chamber for one of the *British Empire* libel hearings before Justices Grove and Lindley. When that was over Bradlaugh had to appear before Justice James Fitzjames Stephen, a brother of Sir Leslie, and a special jury in a claim by a solicitor for a debt discharged over thirteen years ago. It was dismissed. This was Bradlaugh's third complex court case on one day. Four days later Mathew gave his judgment in *Clarke v. Bradlaugh*. As a jury was to hear the issues of fact he granted the defendant's demurrer. More significantly, he also granted the plaintiff's demurrer against Bradlaugh's legal case, but with a stay of execution till the final verdict was reached. Both plaintiff and defendant were given leave to appeal.

As this judgment laid down that Bradlaugh was legally unable to affirm, Gorst at once sought to have his seat declared vacant.

Gladstone asked James's advice. This was to resist Gorst's motion as it would 'produce very inconvenient results'[50] if the member's appeal were successful. Bradlaugh advised his supporters, as he had already told Mathew in chambers, that when the issues of fact came up at *nisi prius* he had another card to play, 'that the nominal plaintiff, Henry Lewis Clarke, has no right, under the statute of 1866, to sue at all'.[51] If anyone, it should be the Attorney-General. Most of Bradlaugh's supporters made violent attacks on Mathew for popish prejudice. Under the guidance of Manning, Catholicism was becoming organized with an ultramontane bigotry at the same time as Anglicanism was presenting something of a Broad Church image, abandoning its heresy trials and certain of its privileges with more or less good grace. Rome was thus emerging as the new *bête noire* of secularism.

Bradlaugh never drew the line at censuring magistrates or judges and was on many occasions lucky not to have been committed for contempt of court. But he made no attack on Mathew, whose conduct was courteous enough and whose decision was at least reasonable. Justices Bramwell, Baggallay and Lush in the Court of Appeal thought so too. While paying tribute to Bradlaugh for having 'presented every argument that could be presented',[52] they dismissed his appeal and even upheld the plaintiff's subsidiary appeal with costs. Bradlaugh at once gave notice of appeal to the House of Lords. He agreed to bypass the central issue of whether or not he could legally affirm and concentrate on fringe grounds: (1) a common informer could not sue (2) if he could the statute gave him no right to a penalty (3) there was no cause of action at the time of issuing the writ. This last point was a technicality he had recently thought up, by which he asserted that, whatever the actual time of issue, a writ operates from the morning of the date it bears. As he had voted in the afternoon, the Clarke writ was in legal existence before the event it referred to occurred and was therefore invalid. He thus hoped to confound Newdegate's cleverness in taking out a writ before one of Bradlaugh's friends could bring a pre-emptive action. But Gladstone could not keep the wolves at bay till these complicated matters were tried, and Bradlaugh's seat was vacated.

There was a short, but not too sharp, by-election contest. The *Christian Globe, Daily Chronicle* and *Times* were among those papers that praised his parliamentary work. Even the cartoons were relatively genial. The most pointed was a design for a memorial window with 'sanctus' Bradlaugh holding the Bible, 'sanctissimus' Gladstone clutching Knowlton, and a caption 'By their *Fruits* ye shall know them'. In Northampton however there was the damaging Varley Address. Labby came up to help. The editor of *Truth* knew well how unsaleable was the unvarnished commodity. He described how Gladstone personally saw him off 'and, men of Northampton, that grand old man said to me, as he patted me on the shoulder, "Henry, my boy, bring him back—bring him back".'[53] Which on 9 April 1881 he did, with 3,437 votes to the Conservative Edward Corbett's 3,305.

Northcote informed Bradlaugh that he would again object to his taking the oath when he presented himself after the recess. By agreement this was extended to 26 April, after Beaconsfield's funeral. As soon as the infidel stepped forward Northcote intervened and the debate began. The most notable contribution was a blast against bigotry from Bright. Bradlaugh made his second speech[54] at the Bar. He denied that he had ever made 'an avowal of opinions to this House' or that the Liberal Party had ever 'aided me in any way to this House'. 'Do not mock at the constituencies. If you place yourselves above the law, you leave me no course save lawless agitation instead of reasonable pleading.' Notwithstanding, Northcote's motion was carried 208:175. As before, Bradlaugh refused to withdraw; but the House adjourned. The following day he turned up again, but was persuaded to leave by Gladstone's promise of an Affirmation Bill and his plea to be allowed to get on peacefully with his Irish Land Bill, incorporating the three Fs (fair rent, fixity of tenure and free sale). When the Attorney-General sought to introduce an Affirmation Bill on 2 May, Churchill, incensed at Bradlaugh's hotted-up campaign against perpetual pensions, especially the Marlborough one, led a filibuster against 'placing in the House of Commons brazen Atheism and rampant disloyalty'.[55] The obstruction continued, Balfour making his first—hostile—speech on the subject. In the *Reformer* Bradlaugh published an 'Appeal to the People of England'. He sent a copy to Gladstone with a covering note: 'John Wilkes had private fortune, he had rich and titled friends. I have no fortune and my friends are among the poor.'[56] On 10 May he again presented himself. Northcote moved: 'That the Sergeant-at-Arms do remove Mr Bradlaugh from the House, until he shall engage not further to disturb the proceedings of the House.'[57] This was agreed to without a division. Bradlaugh stayed away for the sake of the Irish Land Bill.

Outside, his poor friends mobilized to form a League for the Defence of Constitutional Rights. There was no president. The office was reserved for him but he felt obliged to decline it. Among the vice-presidents were Thomas Adams, Arch, Aveling, Annie Besant, Conway, Charles Drysdale, Foote, Gurney, Headlam, the Rev. M. Miall, Sharman, Standring and northern mining leaders. W. A. Casson was secretary. Enemies organized an Anti-Atheistic Committee of the Protestant Alliance, promoted by Earl Percy, Sir Bartle Frere and Varley. Frere was a 'prancing pro-consul' and 'hot annexationist'[58] whom Bradlaugh had often attacked for his rapacious imperialism in India and Africa and for fomenting the Zulu War three years before. They arranged a 'public' rally at Exeter Hall, with tickets, bruisers and a large police force to ensure that no hostile speaker got in. Bradlaugh was afraid of the 'prejudicial effect on public opinion in the provinces'[59] of any successful meeting and deputed Foote, who had just founded the *Freethinker* with his blessing, to move an amendment when the anti-Bradlaugh vote was put. Foote and his friends got tickets but still had to fight their way in. No amendment was accepted but the meeting was a fiasco.

Bradlaugh himself was busy with litigation. Before John Duke Coleridge, who had become Lord Chief Justice the year before, and Justice Bowen he raised the technicality about the writ. Clarke was again given leave to amend his statement so as to define the time of the Tewkesbury vote as 'before the issuing of the Writ in this Action'.[60] To the defendant was granted leave to demur. Bradlaugh was not altogether happy about the chances of his technicality over the writ. So he sent off a list of Interrogatories to the plaintiff to try to ascertain precise times on the day in question. The writ office closed at 4.0 p.m. and a lot had happened in the House that afternoon. Labby introduced a Bill to indemnify his colleague, which Newdegate had the coolness to block. Later in June Justices Denman and Watkin Williams presided over a particularly acrimonious exchange between Bradlaugh and Giffard. Though Denman intervened to back the defendant, he gave judgment for Clarke, observing that 'a legal fiction is for the purpose of doing justice, not for defeating it'.[61] His colleagues concurred. Bradlaugh announced another appeal.

Gladstone added to his disappointment by saying there would be no time for an Affirmation Bill before the recess. The resolution of exclusion was now looked at in the hope that it might in law amount to 'forcible removal', but Bradlaugh at that time believed 'the privileges of the House of Commons protect its Officer even in wrongful acts, if such acts are done in pursuance of the Order of the House'.[62] Ten days later, however, he decided on a confrontation,

206

and sent a circular letter to the officers of the House advising them that he would turn up on or before 3 August and if 'illegally' opposed 'resist such physical force, and shall endeavour to overcome the same'. On 19 July came the chance he was waiting for in *Clarke v. Bradlaugh*. Detailed evidence of the issue of the writ had to be given and Newdegate was to appear. Foote was at Bradlaugh's side and the versatile Aveling found a new role as a sparkling court reporter for the *Reformer*.

The afternoon of 19 July, before Justice Grove and a special jury, was hot and sultry. Giffard came in, cold, colourless, flecked with mint sauce. Newdegate was covered in snuff. Sobriety was not one of his many pieties and he was perhaps a little apprehensive about the coming encounter. Fortified too well over lunch, he hit his nose with the testament when kissing it for the oath. Giffard intervened to say that the witness wanted protection in giving evidence regarding the House of Commons. 'He wants my £500',[63] snapped Bradlaugh. Coming to details of events Newdegate said he always knew 'within two hours' when he left the House, and on the day in question it was 'between one and four'. At the absurd vagueness of this answer general laughter, in which Newdegate joined, swept over the court. Devastatingly Bradlaugh bellowed: 'It may be a very good joke for you, sir.' Finally Newdegate volunteered a time of about 3.45 p.m., thus giving himself ten minutes to reach his solicitor and a few minutes for the clerk to make the writ office in the nick of time. Bradlaugh asked him if he had taken a written minute. 'I expected —'. 'I don't want to know what you expected.' Then he took the befuddled man in detail through every item in the day's business, signposting appalling lapses of memory and finally getting him to agree the division must itself have been after 4.0 p.m.

The following day Bradlaugh explored the witness's connection with the case. Newdegate had frequently discussed the subject with Kydd 'as a friend' and was anxious to prevent a collusive action like *Miller v. Salomons*. How had he come to know Clarke? He saw him ordinarily as an accountant he employed. When he first knew him as a young man he was connected with the office of his solicitor's father. Bradlaugh's eyes lit up. The enigmatic Clarke, who had never appeared, figured in the record as a 'surveyor'. 'Have you found any funds for Mr Clarke in this matter?' Newdegate parried and grew flustered. Bradlaugh repeated the question. Newdegate tried anew to turn the tide. Again the question. In his agitation the witness 'smote a small boy below the witness-box severely on the head'. Grove sought to come to his rescue. It was of no avail. For a fourth time the awful question thundered out. Newdegate admitted that he had given Clarke £200 together with a bond undertaking to pay what he 'has incurred or will incur in costs and expenses', and Bradlaugh bent over to Foote and said 'I have him'.

That was not the end. The matter of Labby's blocked Bill of indemnity was raised. Newdegate admitted a parliamentary custom 'that no member shall take part in a matter in which he is personally interested'. That meant, interposed Grove, 'pecuniarily interested'. Just so. But what about the £500 spoils? Had Newdegate declared an interest to the House? The question of his connection with the case had not arisen, said the witness, and it would have been 'highly improper' for him to raise it. 'Why should it be improper that you should indemnify the common informer?' The House had referred the case to the courts. Had it referred the bond to the courts? Finally Bradlaugh raised the question of Newdegate's reported statement that the courts had ruled the atheist disqualified from sitting and voting in the House. The witness protested that these reports were no more untrue than the defendant's description of Newdegate carried out of the Commons drunk; when in fact he was ill and only 'insensible for a few minutes'. Staggering from the witness-box after his ordeal he certainly looked ill then.

Bradlaugh began on the clerk Stuart. The first surprising thing was that the disbursement book which he tendered in evidence showed the date of issue of the writ as the day before the vote. On his second day in the witness-box he changed the time of issue from 'almost four' to 'nearer 3.30 p.m.' The original time was fixed to fit in as closely as possible with Newdegate's movements, but Bradlaugh elicited that the evening before Stuart had been chatting with another witness and had discovered that about a dozen writs had been issued after his on the vital day. Grove's face darkened. Corroborative witnesses finished the case. Giffard pleaded with the jury not to find for Bradlaugh and so put a stain on the integrity of his client after a lifetime of public service. 'Rather too anxious to refrain from propaganda',[64] Bradlaugh confined himself to summarizing the findings. The jury disagreed. After one of the great cross-examinations of all time Bradlaugh looked gravely ill himself. But five days later he accompanied Lewis when unsuccessfully seeking a summons against Newdegate for maintenance.[65] The day after, he applied to Justices Grove and Lindley for a rule *nisi* for a new trial. In August this was granted. Meanwhile the most dramatic event of his parliamentary struggle had taken place.

When Bradlaugh was not crammed into tight London courts he swept through the halls and open spaces of the provinces. Great as had been his peak of oratory before, he found new heights now. Cut free from the biblical quotations and sheaves of statistics that usually roped him down, he winged off into the air of verbal magic where all could see and feel and identify. Wherever he went he reminded his supporters they were not alone: 'The men of the provinces are protesting, the miners are protesting in Northumberland . . . I represent the working men in every mill, in every mine, in every factory.'[66] He was speaking now for no sectional interest; not for atheism, or republicanism, or neo-Malthusianism, or radicalism, or Liberalism, not even, or not only, for Northampton, or the working class. He was speaking for the rights of the little man against authority, of the constituencies against big government, of the provinces against London, of justice against bureaucracy. Though he was too high-principled to play on or even to mention the sentiment precisely, he was able to touch off, where no spark of real sympathy glowed, the latent populism, poujardism and provincialism that every country incubates outside its metropolis. It was Us against Them, and those who had no sympathy with his politics or his philosophy found murmurs of assent leaping to their lips and their hands shooting up in support[67] as he raged and pleaded for their endorsement of his action. As the third of August drew near excitement in London crackled. The day before, his London regulars and platoons from all over the country, especially Northampton, gathered in Trafalgar Square. Cloth caps and top hats, cottons and satins mingled in a huge, peaceful, jolly demonstration.

The next morning most of them gathered in Parliament Square. Some hundreds came with petitions, pasted together into huge snaking scrolls, seven people to each. They were allowed to cross New Palace Yard, traverse Westminster Hall and present the documents to their MPs at the steps leading into St Stephen's Hall. Inspector Denning, in charge of the usual Commons police contingent, was joined by Superintendent Gernon of the local King Street station and 100 of his men, lurking in the Court of Queen's Bench. The Metropolitan Commissioner Sir E. Henderson paid periodic anxious visits. F.H. O'Donnell, most vicious of the Home Rulers, passed through into the members' entrance to loud groaning and cries of 'Pensioner'. At the head of the petitioners were the Bradlaugh girls and Annie Besant. Bradlaugh had briefed her in advance: 'The people know you better than they know anyone, save myself; whatever happens, mind, whatever happens, let them do no violence; I trust to you to keep them quiet.'[68] At 11.45 a.m. there was a great shouting in the street as Bradlaugh, immaculate in black frock coat and silk topper specially made by his secularist outfitters, arrived with Aveling in a hansom cab gay with his election colours. Denning joined them and together they went to the members' entrance. Bradlaugh went on alone to the members' lobby, nodding to his friends. As the Speaker processed into the chamber he stood tense and alone in the middle of the lobby, eyeing the door as a picador surveys the gate to the bullyard. Equally tense the deputy Sergeant-at-Arms, David Erskine, with four of his messengers, closed the door behind the procession and stared at the outcast.

At 12.09 p.m. the shout went round, 'Speaker in the chair'. Bradlaugh strode to the door. 'I have the instructions of the Speaker to prevent you from entering the precincts of the House', said Erskine. 'I am ready to obey any lawful orders of the House', was the retort, 'but I am here in obedience to the mandate of my constituents, and I will not yield to what is illegal.' 'My orders are imperative; and the authority of the House of Commons is sufficient for me.' Bradlaugh said he would enter at all hazards, and thrust aside the hand Erskine put out. At a signal one of the ushers seized him. Bradlaugh grabbed him by the throat. 'If anyone dares to hinder me—.' The others joined in. Bradlaugh thought Erskine 'glad of the opportunity',[69] though the official himself later said 'the removal of Mr Bradlaugh was the most painful duty that ever fell to my lot to perform'.[70] The huge man, still with his youthful strength and weighted with the fat of middle-aged inactivity, struggled to regain the door. Ten policemen were summoned to the fray, heaving and pushing their quarry across the lobby, down the members' stairs and into Westminster Hall halfway down the east wall. Like a dancing dervish, Fowler bounced up and down at his side shrieking 'Kick him out!' and the more daring of his Tory colleagues tried to do just that. Bradlaugh's glossy new hat rolled away; his clothes ripped from his back; his face, a strange sullen yellow, 'distorted with passion', his huge eyes seeming 'almost to start out of his head'.[71] As the tumbling group burst into Westminster Hall a great cry went up: 'They are killing him; they are killing him!' His supporters rushed towards St Stephen's Hall. Alice and Hypatia flung themselves against the door. Annie sprang in front of the surging crowd, her golden voice urging them to remember his wishes. It was not revolution[72] he sought but justice. They faltered and fell back, waging something of Bradlaugh's own inner struggle against a wild atavistic urge to sweep his army through the building and purge the nation's bowel of its pensioners and placemen, parasites and hypocrites. As he was flung into Palace Yard and crumpled into the arms of his friends, a louder shout went up.

Forgetting the recent years of difficulty 'B.V.' rushed at the police with a cry of dreadful night, but his colleagues pulled him back. In a scuffle Aveling's fountain-pen[73] was broken. Apologetically Denning brought a glass of water and a chair. As Bradlaugh collapsed into it he muttered, 'I shall come again with force enough to overcome.' The inspector asked when. 'Under a minute if I raise my hand.' Reporters heard 'minute' as 'million' and the evening papers conjured up pictures of 1789. Inside the House Labby raised the expulsion as an urgent question of parliamentary privilege. Ashton Dilke seconded the motion. Lawson proposed rescinding the resolutions of 26 April and 10 May. Cowen called on Gladstone to reintroduce his Parliamentary Oaths Bill. Bright declared that 'no scenes like that had ever been recorded in the annals of the British Parliament'. But on division Labouchere's motion was lost 191:7. As soon as this intelligence was brought outside, Denning agreed to stop Bradlaugh's entering the door to Westminster Hall so that he could proceed for assault. Then the member took a hansom cab to Westminster Police Court and applied for a summons. He was advised to research more facts about the exact 'precincts' of the House and jurisdiction of the court and submit an information to the senior magistrate D'Eyncourt. Despite his exertions, that evening he presented himself, bloody but unbowed, at the Hall of Science. A few days later he succumbed to erysipelas where the muscles of his arm had been torn, and agreed to take his first holiday—at Worthing.

With the aroma of 1789 in the air, Standring proposed a metropolitan republican club in September 1881. A provisional committee was set up, of which he became secretary, and by December he was hoping for a new Republican League. This got off the ground at the Patriotic Club's Clerkenwell headquarters the following July, with Standring optimistically surveying the 'Position of the Modern Republican Party'. The Rev. Frederick Verinder, secretary of the Guild of St Matthew and the English League for the Taxation of Land Values, declared himself a 'Christian Republican'. When Bradlaugh returned to London from Worthing, temporarily recovered, he presided at a new development on the radical front:-

the second congress of the International Federation of Freethinkers. This had been launched in Brussels the previous year. He had been unable to get away then and Britain had been represented by Hypatia, Annie, Le Lubez, Standring and Swaagman. At the same time as the 1881 freethought congress there was an English Church Congress, where the Bishop of Durham observed that past heresies had become present orthodoxies and men like Büchner, Ernst Haeckel and Bradlaugh were prophets of a new religion.

After this interlude the English prophet plunged back into *Clarke v. Bradlaugh*. First there was an appeal to Coleridge, Baggallay and Brett against the decision of Denman and Watkin Williams over the technicality of the writ. Bradlaugh asserted that as it was a 'penal action' he was entitled to latitude in interpreting a general rule of law. (Their lordships had said there were different sorts of writs and not all of them were 'judicial acts' operative from the morning of the date they bore.) Then he thought up a yet more abstruse point, 'that the clause enacting the oath has been repealed'.[74] This plea was based on the fact that the Statute Law Revision Act 1875 repealed the key section of the 1866 Act, which Bradlaugh said had already been replaced by the 1868 Act, so that a void remained. The appeal was lost. On the question of the actual time of issue of the writ he was on much stronger ground. Grove and Lindley granted a rule *nisi* for a new trial and Denman and Hawkins made it absolute. Affidavits from parliamentary reporters and others were called for.

Meanwhile Bradlaugh's enemies were working along other lines. Following Manning's hint they turned to the 1697 Blasphemy Act. Technically Bradlaugh was breaking it every other day. He had been brought up as a Christian and he wrote, printed, taught and spoke advisedly against the truth of Christianity and the Divine authority of the Holy Scriptures. But several of Manning's fellow-contributors to the *Nineteenth Century* did just that; review journalism in general abounded in heresy of all sorts; Coleridge's friend Matthew Arnold had spoken of the Trinity as 'three Lord Shaftesburys'; and in his biography of *Rousseau* [75] the fashionable John Morley wrote 'god' with a small 'g'. If however Bradlaugh could be caught out on something particularly lurid it would be more than a tactical advantage. On first conviction under the Act he would be unable to 'have or enjoy any office or employment, ecclesiastical, civil or military', which many thought hopefully, but wrongly, included a seat in parliament. On second conviction he would be 'disabled to sue, prosecute, plead, or use any action or information in any Court of law or equity'. This would certainly be his undoing. In January 1882, therefore, the epistolary Varley wrote to all MPs calling their attention to the 'horrible blasphemies' of the *Freethinker* issued from the same office as the *Reformer* and edited by 'one of Mr Bradlaugh's prominent supporters'.

Despite his former allegiance to the Holyoake line, Foote had now swung over to the opposite tack. From the beginning of his new paper he made whoopee with clerical absurdities in a regular column 'Acid drops', and in July introduced his first cartoon, 'Jonah and the Whale'. For the next eight years he scandalized Victorian England with some 300 'Comic Bible Sketches'.[76] As his parliamentary life and battle proceeded Bradlaugh was forced to devote more and more space in the *Reformer* to politics, and thus acquired a large circulation among people who had no interest in or sympathy with his other causes. He was therefore pleased to back Foote's scheme for a specifically freethought and—insofar as parliamentary debates and court transcripts seldom scintillate—livelier paper; and Annie Besant and he were the original publishers. The new journal was undoubtedly lively. At the beginning of 1882 Foote had to face a complaint 'that the style of the *Freethinker* offends Secularists, who therefore cease to buy it. Our answer is, first that our circulation increases every week.' True, but it left Bradlaugh vulnerable. By amicable agreement Ramsey took over as publisher. Foote still lacked the badge of freethought greatness and was aware of it. Nobody had dragged him in bellowing defiance before the courts. He tried an article on 'Was Jesus Insane?'[77] But there was 'no prosecution yet!'[78] By summer, as his hopes were fading, Mrs Grundy came to life and 'We are in for it at last'.[79]

D'Eyncourt had refused Bradlaugh's application for a summons against Denning, but the exclusion resolution was only a sessional order. On 7 February, at the beginning of the new session, he presented himself again, was challenged by Northcote and made his third speech[80] at the Bar. The Prince of Wales was in the gallery. Marx's *Das Kapital*, published fourteen years before in German, had only recently been translated into French and read by any significant number of educated Englishmen. This provided a new term of abuse to hurl at Bradlaugh. 'I am a red rag to a wild Conservative bull, and it must rush at me and call me Socialist.' In fact, he said, as an innocent harbinger of a new controversy that was in turn to split the freethought movement, British radicalism and the world down the middle, 'I happen to think that Socialists are the most unwise and illogical people you can happen to meet.' He turned to the disgraceful episode of his expulsion. Will the House 'substitute force for law? . . . If I am not fit for my constituents, they shall dismiss me, but you never shall.' At the vote he was defeated 286:228, but allowed to sit under the gallery, technically outside the House.

Evidence came to hand that neither oath nor affirmation was required of legislators in France, Germany, Rumania, Sweden and Wurtemberg; there was an option in the Netherlands, Switzerland and the United States; only an affirmation existed in Austria-Hungary; no asseveration was appended to the oath in Belgium, Italy and Spain. Yet Gladstone dodged further attempts to change the law in Britain. Parnellite obstruction was forcing him to seek powers of *clôture* (closure) and he was impatient of further controversy. Bradlaugh seemed to thrive on it. On 21 February a Joint Commission set up in 1875 reported on schemes for a Channel Tunnel, which, despite press opposition, he was to support as a means of fostering 'the peaceful co-operation of France and England'.[81] Meanwhile Labby proposed a new writ for Northampton. Churchill tried unsuccessfully to have the infidel declared 'disqualified by law from taking his seat in this House,' but Labby's motion also failed. Immediately Bradlaugh left his seat and strode up to the table. The benches quivered. What new devilry was afoot? He had been talking to Edward Waugh, a solicitor and member for Cockermouth, and got a new idea.

In front of the bewildered May he took a piece of paper and a testament from his pocket, read the words of the oath, kissed the book, signed the paper and handed it to the Clerk. 'I tender that as the oath which I have taken according to law.' The Speaker asked him to withdraw beyond the Bar. Almost too readily he obeyed, to double back and take a seat below the gangway. On further admonition he withdrew, 'having taken my seat according to law'. First to surface from the morass of 'order', 'oh', cheers and 'shame'[82] was Churchill, now anxious enough to have a new writ made out. The impious member for Northampton had 'deliberately, and almost, I may say, of malice aforethought, offered a wanton insult to the House of Commons'. This piece of paper! This book! Was it really a testament? 'We have not the slightest guarantee that it was not the *Fruits of Philosophy*.' Labby had a hasty word with Bradlaugh and said his colleague would be happy to accept Churchill's view that he had 'sat' during a debate after a disputed oath-taking. That might give something to take to the courts. Gladstone fumbled in his

214

'surprise' and shock but O'Donnell and Philip Callan, a quarrelsome, drunken Irish Catholic who first used the title 'Fourth Party', said they knew about the 'outrage' in advance. The House adjourned, still dazed by the pantomime. The following day Bradlaugh took a seat inside the chamber and on Northcote's motion was expelled by 297:80. He voted with the minority. Labouchere got a writ for a new election. The day after, Clarke successfully appealed to Lords Justices Brett, Cotton and Holker to reverse the order of Denman and Hawkins for a new trial. They thought the division had begun at 3.15 p.m. and that there was no clear evidence of perjury by the clerk Stuart. As with all the other unfavourable decisions, costs were awarded against the defendant but were yet to be paid.

The new election was a good deal nastier than the one before. For the Anti-Atheistic Committee, 'B.W.M.' asked *Shall Atheism Force on Us an Alteration of Our Laws?* Varley sought a wider audience in *An Appeal to the Men of England.* Bradlaugh, he claimed, supported a book [83] which made 'the position of the *wife* . . . worse than the position of the *prostitute'.* Samuel Morley now declared for Corbett 'as an act of allegiance to God'. [84] The Conservative candidate was described by Labby as 'a young man fond of shooting, hunting, cock-fighting'. [85] Though quiescent in the former contest, this time he led the pack against his rival. On the other side, Dr Robert William Dale of the Carrs Lane Congregationalists declared for Bradlaugh in Birmingham and a Stoke-on-Trent versifier sent his contribution. On 2 March, the day Roderick Maclean tried to assassinate the queen, Bradlaugh was returned 3,796:3,688. Corbett returned to his usual amusements with a petulant 'I shan't come back to this dirty town any more'. [86] At Westminster Northcote announced a new motion against accepting an oath from Bradlaugh, who wrote to him denouncing this 'conflict of which I am sure you must feel heartily ashamed'. [87] The Liberal Edward Majoribanks proposed an amendment in favour of an Affirmation Bill. It was narrowly defeated, 259:244, to scenes of jubilation. On promising not to pass the Bar, Bradlaugh was allowed to sit under the gallery. The following day in the Upper House the Earl of Redesdale introduced a Bill imposing a theistic test on all legislators as a gesture 'due to Almighty God', but later withdrew it in deference to 'what had fallen from the noble Marquess' [88] of Salisbury, Conservative leader in the Lords. Three months later the Liberal Duke of Argyll, who was, like the queen, Anglican south of the border and Presbyterian north of it, introduced an Affirmation Bill, but an abnormally large house turned it out 138:63.

Interest was equally great outside Westminster. As 'Ion', Holy-oake[89] published his own cartoons and recent anonymous ballads from the *Evening News* and *Whitehall Review* in a pamphlet larded with quotations from Bradlaugh and Shakespeare. These *Blasts from Bradlaugh's Own Trumpet* also saluted 'Queen B.' Annie Besant as she held up the tablets of a 'revised Decalogue' with the first and fourth commandments crossed out. There was the suspicion that Holyoake meant the first and seventh. To the tune of 'The Village Blacksmith' was:

> 'Tap-room of Science' is his Haul,
> Where many a simple boor
> Pays pence to swig seditious swipes,
> Served out by B. the brewer;
> And though he takes a pile each night,
> They seem to think he's poor.[90]

Holyoake was glad enough to lecture there whenever he was invited. And there was 'The Vicar of Bray', of whom the veteran 'agitator' was particularly well-qualified to write:

> In good Victoria's palmy days
> When Chartism was prating,
> I joined the Democratic craze,
> And practised stump orating.
> To teach my mob I never missed
> That king-made law is bad law,
> And damn'd be all who dare resist
> The rise of righteous Bradlaugh.
>
> But finding Atheists weak and thin,
> I sought a higher mission,
> And found much greater profit in
> The vending of sedition.[91]

Gurney brought an action against Bradlaugh on 21 March, using friendly solicitors Harper and Battcock.[92] A charade of Statement of Claim, Statement of Defence, Plaintiff's Reply and Defendant's Demurrer was gone through. This made the issue one of law to be tried by judges without an unpredictable jury. Gurney asserted that Bradlaugh had voted in February without taking the oath; the defendant triumphantly showed that neither the 1866 and 1868 Acts nor the parliamentary standing orders laid down that the oath must be administered by the Clerk. Alderman Gurney, JP, was by this time no nonentity. And when the case came up before Justices Watkin Williams and Manisty in May on demurrer, they gave it a jaundiced look and refused to treat it as a matter of law on the grounds that not all the facts had been disclosed and it was a friendly suit weighted in favour of the defence. Bradlaugh then reclothed it as an issue of fact, but Mathew, on similar grounds, would not allow it to go before the jury. The *Law Times* commented: 'We regard the action of the judge as very questionable on constitutional grounds, and as being an arbitrary interference with a suitor's right to the verdict of a jury.'[93] Gurney was dragged in only because the government themselves would not bring the issue to court. This case of Bradlaugh's dovetailed with another. Brought against Erskine in May for assault during the famous expulsion, it was heard in December *in banco* before Field, with the Attorney-General deputed by the House to defend its deputy Sergeant-at-Arms.

This was the most interesting and technical of all the Bradlaugh cases. It proceeded in the way the member preferred: Statement of Claim, traversing Statement of Defence, Demurrer to the defence statement. The plaintiff alleged that he proceeded peacefully to the outer door of the chamber, where men acting under the defendant's orders 'assaulted and beat' him 'whereby he became sick and ill and suffered great pain for a long time and incurred expenses in medical and surgical attendance',[94] for which he claimed £2,000 damages. On the contrary, alleged the defence, it was the defendant who was assaulted as he was trying to prevent 'noise and disturbance at the door' of the House in the execution of his duty 'to obey and carry out the lawful orders of the said House'.[95] Bradlaugh demurred that these grounds were bad in law. At the trial he raised a number of fringe issues: that the exclusion order of 10 May 1881 might not be valid beyond the day of ratification; that he could not 'disturb the proceedings of the House' while he was outside it, and it was probable he could not 'engage' not to do so without a personal appearance; that the order gave no powers to the defendant to 'assault' him outside the House. But, as Field pointed out, the real issue was not whether Erskine's actions were justifiable but whether the order was valid. This raised the central constitutional question of the powers of the legislature, or part thereof, *vis à vis* the judiciary. Over this the plaintiff, Attorney-General and judge soared into a rarefied air of legal abstraction in which two of the men seemed to forget how much their political metabolism depended on the out-

217

come. Bradlaugh contended that he was elected to 'serve' his constituents and could do this only if he were allowed to take his seat. The legislature was supreme only in the combined power of all the estates of the realm to pass statutes, for example, a Bill of Indemnity protecting Erskine. By itself the House of Commons was not immune from the surveillance of the courts. If a return was challenged an election judge decided the issue. The House was supreme only in its power to commit for contempt and imprison till the end of the session, suspend for a defined period, or expel and order a new election. It had no right to exclude a lawfully elected member by a simple resolution. Otherwise, as soon as a quorum of members had been sworn in at the beginning of a parliament they could 'resolve' to exclude all the other members. Nothing comparable had happened since Pride's Purge and the courts would surely intervene if it did. As a trump among his precedents Bradlaugh cited *Clarke v. Bradlaugh*, tried in that very court, where it was ruled that a Commons order preventing him from taking the oath did not set aside his statutory duty to take it before voting. At great length James pleaded that the order sprang 'from the constitution of the Houses of Parliament as the highest Court of the realm'.[96] Field reserved his decision till January 1883, when—somewhat reluctantly, it would seem—he ruled that the order was, after all, a matter of parliamentary privilege. At this stage Bradlaugh had so much litigation on his hands he decided not to appeal.

When Clarke belatedly applied to Grove and Baron Huddleston in March 1882 for judgment following Bradlaugh's failure to get a new trial, counsel demanded costs as well. Kydd angered Grove by claiming he had already applied for these and as Bradlaugh had not then challenged the application it was too late now. In fact, said his lordship, no such application had been made. The defendant argued that even if a common informer had the right to a penalty he had no right to costs. In Clarke's case this was no hardship as he was indemnified by Newdegate. Huddleston then mentioned the maintenance action against the Tory member. As soon as Bradlaugh said that this had been dismissed by the magistrate on the grounds that the operative law was obsolete, Grove interposed: 'But it is by no means obsolete. I set aside an agreement for maintenance only a little while ago.'[97] Bradlaugh's eyes flashed. The bibulous Newdegate would yet repent. Grove and Huddleston had to award judgment to Clarke, but costs were reserved till the Lords' hearing of his right to sue. Three appeal courts had however awarded costs against him and, though execution had been stayed, Bradlaugh decided to apply in May to Lords Justices Brett and Cotton for leave to appeal on this point. For part of the object of Newdegate's legal exercise was to unseat him for bankruptcy. But Bradlaugh's application was dismissed pending the main Lords appeal.

About this time Tyler and Tim Healy, the noisy member for Cork City, sought to prosecute the *National Reformer* but were advised against it. Tyler's armoury was far from exhausted. On 8 July his solicitors wrote to Bradlaugh and asked him to sell them a copy of the *Freethinker*. He sent back a polite note enclosing a catalogue of his publications. The *Freethinker* was not among them. Tyler was not discouraged. Hoping to exploit the Ramsey link between the Freethought Publishing Co. and the paper, three days later he began a prosecution for blasphemy against Foote, Ramsey and their printer E.W. Whittle before Lord Mayor Sir John Ellis at the Mansion House. At the hearing counsel applied to have the directors of the original publishing company, Bradlaugh and Annie Besant, added as defendants, even though the issues cited as blasphemous came out between March and June 1882, after they had ceased to be publishers. Kydd kept a watching, and hopeful, brief for Newdegate. The case was adjourned so that the application against Bradlaugh could be heard privately. Later the reason for this secrecy became apparent when his St John's Wood bank manager[98] and personal and company accounts turned up in court under subpoena and warrant, though the jurisdiction of the Lord Mayor did not extend beyond the City walls. Ostensibly this investigation was to try to establish a link between Bradlaugh and the *Freethinker*, but Tyler hoped he might gain leads for other proceedings.

Busy defending a Maidstone freethinker similarly charged, Bradlaugh applied to have his case taken separately, and tried to confound the prosecution with technicalities over whether the action should or could proceed by common law or statute. Apart from the notorious 1697 Act specifically so-called, blasphemy figured in the 1547 Sacrament Act, the 1548 and 1558-9 Act of Uniformity and the 1819 Criminal Libel Act.[99] But these statutes had become archaic and nobody could recall that a prosecution had ever in fact taken place under the 1697 Act. It had become the norm to bring charges under the common law. This has always been nugatory, especially as the three-tiered universe of the classical theologians has faded and left not a wrack behind. To lawyers blasphemous libels have been attacks on the Queen's peace and those supernal sanctions purportedly uniting an otherwise fissiparous society. To the lay believer they are something in the nature of personal defamations of the Deity. In the reign of Henry VI it was decided that 'upon the Holy Scriptures are grounded the laws of every kind', but the chief precedent has been the decision of Lord Chief Justice Sir Matthew Hale in *King v. Taylor* (1676): 'Such kind of wicked blasphemous words were not only an offence to God and religion, but a crime against the laws, state, and government, and therefore punishable in this court. For to say, Religion is a cheat, is to dissolve all those obligations whereby civil societies are preserved, and that Christianity is parcel of the laws of England; and therefore to reproach the Christian religion, is to speak in subversion of the law.'[100] With the question of the indictment unresolved, Foote, Ramsey and Bradlaugh were committed for trial. Even if he were unable to prosecute under the 1697 Act, Tyler still hoped for imprisonment, a heavy fine or general discrediting. Instead his own actions were widely censured, even by the *Times*. Malevolent details like the bank inquisition—a dangerous precedent that few members of the establishment wished to encourage—left a sour taste. And Tyler had been active in other ways.

He had already deprived Annie Besant of a salary as an 'authorized teacher, qualified to earn payments' from the Science and Art Department, and now he tried to disimburse the Bradlaugh girls in making another attack on the Hall of Science. As Vice-President of the Council, Mundella praised its work, and even Tyler's Tory colleagues walked out. But his campaign achieved a minor success when the secretary to the Botanic Gardens, Regent's Park, where his own daughters gambolled, refused Mrs Besant admission 'on the ground that he objects to the "opinions attributed to me" '.[101] Happily the agnostic Sir Joseph Hooker came to the rescue at Kew, where he was the director. Sharman organized and became secretary to an Association for Repeal of the Blasphemy Laws, whose vice-presidents included Arch; the Rev. R.A. Armstrong, a Nottingham Unitarian with whom Bradlaugh had debated; Conway; the Rev. E.R. Grant, a Northampton Unitarian; W. A. Hunter, professor of jurisprudence at University College; and the faithful Headlam. Lord George Hamilton put personal pressure on Headlam to give up his chairmanship of the Hall of Science classes, but he refused. Then Tyler and Father Nihill, vicar of his new parish of St Michael's, successfully urged the Bishop of London to remove him. He never gained another assistant curacy. Bradlaugh himself thought it as well to get an endorsement from his substantially devout constituents, and got it overwhelmingly.

Back in London he applied to Justice Stephen in chambers for a writ of *certiorari* transferring the blasphemy case from the Old Bailey to the Queen's Bench. After treating prosecuting counsel 'like a child'[102] he easily achieved his object, though he had to find £600 in sureties. Foote was amazed at the way he roamed the law courts, 'threading the labyrinth with consummate ease and dexterity', blandishing and blustering and cutting through red tape. Next he tried to get the indictment quashed by Field and Stephen on the grounds that the 1697 Act should have been cited, its provisions had not been observed and the persons to be proceeded against were not set out in the original document. These somewhat specious technicalities were set aside, but during the operation he secured, partly as a sop, the killing of two late counts smuggled in by the prosecution against issues of the *Freethinker* with his company's imprint on them.

This was the main object of these diversionary tactics. Meanwhile Watts's son, Charles Albert, made a scurrilous attack in the *Secular Review* on the defendants, whose main concern was now to rescue the Chief. While Ramsey was looking round for another publishing office to save Bradlaugh embarrassment, Mrs Besant proposed that they should move instead. Accordingly, impressive new premises were acquired at 63 Fleet Street, just across Bouverie Street from one of Carlile's famous offices; but they were much more expensive than Stonecutter Street. A couple of years later the whole building had to be rented by the Freethought Publishing Company to avoid its sale. To meet this new burden £5,000 worth of five per cent debenture stock was issued.

A brief lull in Bradlaugh's tempest of litigation was not soothed by leisure. In the autumn of 1882 he led a great radical denunciation of the war against Egypt and the shelling of Alexandria. He had 'too much of the fighter' in his disposition to be 'a peace-at-any-price man',[103] but he had forecast the result of Disraeli's imperialism. Ismail had become bankrupt and been replaced by his son Tewfik. Needled by Turkey and terrified of Egyptian nationalism under Arabi Pasha, Gladstone had taken time-honoured steps to 'safeguard British life and property'; and Bright had resigned from the Cabinet. Bradlaugh was still trying to get his own case raised again in the House but James reminded Gladstone that, to get his *clôture* proposals safely through, he had promised to stay with procedural matters till the end of the session. If this policy were reversed there were 'other subjects which the majority of the House would regard as of

221

more importance'.[104] A reconstituted action against Newdegate for maintenance came before Field on demurrer, but this was postponed till after the trial of fact in March 1883. For the plaintiff this was argued before Coleridge by F.O. Crump and Hunter. The judge discharged the jury, saying the facts were not in dispute and it was a question of law. Bradlaugh testified that the issue had been pursued long after he had lost his seat. Judgment was reserved.

Varley and Tyler had meantime gained fresh notoriety; one by a 'Lecture to Men' advocating circumcision to reduce sexual pleasure and prolonged lactation as a means of contraception, the other by being hooted at a shareholders' meeting of the Anglo-American Brush Electric Light Corporation and forced out of the chairmanship. As parliament was to reassemble in February 1883 great Constitutional Rights demonstrations were called in Bradlaugh's support. Opposition appeared immediately. A special meeting of the railway companies cancelled excursion tickets to London, the Duke of Bedford's agent vetoed the use of the Floral Hall, Covent Garden, and when Trafalgar Square was suggested instead the *Pall Mall Gazette* called its use illegal.[105] Notwithstanding, a highly successful rally was held there. Bradlaugh wrote to the Speaker and Labouchere secured the promise of a government Affirmation Bill. Enemies raged furiously together throughout the country. Subtlety was thrown to the winds and the *Christian Commonwealth* and a naked Anti-Bradlaugh Association flooded the land with handbills against the 'Bradlaugh Relief Bill', 'Government Atheism Affirmation Bill' and 'this dangerous enemy of the Christian religion' whose 'social views are so revolting and disgusting'.[106] Varley enjoyed his greatest sales and Sunday school kindergartens were dredged for signatures to anti-Bradlaugh petitions. For the first time the member's supporters were quite unable to compete as over half a million purported opposition signatures surged in.

The second reading debate on the Parliamentary Oaths Act (1866) Amendment Bill raged over the last week of April and into May. It was an historic occasion. Though neutral in its wording the Bill was, effectually, what the Conservatives claimed for it: a measure to allow declared atheists to sit in parliament. That infidels had sat and were sitting there they acknowledged as a fact of life, but that they should sit there as a fact of law was intolerable. Shrillest in their opposition were representatives of formerly persecuted minorities like Roman Catholics and Jews who, now that they were all right, were not going to allow any other Jacks their rights. An atheist was as disabled, explained de Worms, as 'a felon, a lunatic, or a woman'.[107] There were however sterling religious exceptions like Sergeant (later Sir John) Simon, the member for Dewsbury, who declared: 'To profess to allow a man to think for himself, and then to annex disabilities to his opinions, was to destroy religious liberty altogether.'[108] As the invective and absurdities swirled all round, a great rock of common-sense, humanity and restrained passion rose up defiantly and for a time overawed the froth. It was Gladstone, making his finest oration of that parliament and what many regarded as the grandest of his career. Sprigged with six lines from Lucretius,[109] his words rolled over the assembly with an eloquence that buried for a moment the animus of his enemies. Truly the GOM was good value at his best: 'I have no fear of Atheism in this House. Truth is the expression of the Divine mind; and however little our feeble vision may be able to discern the means by which God will provide for its preservation, we may leave the matter in His hands.'[110]

But it was all in vain. After more days of wrangling only petty spite remained, and although the whips were on, the Bill was lost 289:292. The Irish Nationalists were overwhelmingly hostile, the Tories turned up and voted with unparalleled devotion, and the government had lost an aggregate of 11 seats since the general election. Had the Bill 'been pushed through the House of Commons with comparable vigour in 1880 or 1881, it might well have passed'.[111] Symbolically it was defeated in the early hours of Ascension Day and that afternoon Bradlaugh made his fourth and last speech at the Bar.[112] He spoke of the 'considerable pain' of sitting 'within hearing of everything that has taken place in this House' without being able to intervene. Yet it was the most restrained and conciliatory of all his Bar addresses. To loud ministerial cheers he ended:

> 'The House, being strong, should be generous . . . but the constituents have a right to more than generosity . . . The law gives me my seat. In the name of the law I ask for it. I regret that my personality overshadows the principles involved in this great struggle; but I would ask those who have touched my life, not knowing it, who have found for me vices which I do not remember in the memory of my life, I would ask them whether all can afford to cast the first stone . . . then that, as best judges, they will vacate their own seats, having deprived my constituents of their right here to mine.'

Even his opponents found it moving. But Northcote had already moved that he be not allowed to take the oath and Labby's attempt to parry this was defeated 271:165.

The spring of 1883 was notable for its court decisions. First came the *Freethinker* case. In March Foote, Ramsey and Henry Kemp, their shopman, were twice tried at the Old Bailey before the Catholic Justice North and a jury. This was a fresh blasphemy prosecution citing the recent Christmas number. In festive mood Foote had really let his hair down. Among the goodies were a comic strip 'New Life of Christ', considerably more entertaining than the old one, a poem 'Jocular Jehovah' and a cartoon of 'Moses Getting a Back View'. This was based on Exodus 33, 23 ('And I will take away mine hand, and thou shalt see my back parts.') and depicted the Almighty in ragged peasant garb with one tatter looking very like a tail. Certainly to the faithful this was bad enough, but many who did not see the actual sketch assumed it was floridly obscene. The consideration which ordinarily weighs heavily in this sort of case clung to the *Freethinker*. Though no 'special publicity was given to it outside the circle of the people who approved it',[113] it was a penny publication and the poor are, of course, more corruptible than the rich. After his opening address for the prosecution Giffard left the court. North admitted evidence which should have gone to the Court of Crown Cases Reserved, constantly interrupted Foote in his defence and gave a hostile summing-up. Even so the jury failed to agree. A new trial was ordered, the defendants being remanded, contrary to all precedent in a case of this sort, in custody. At the second hearing North's hostility was, if possible, more blatant: 'You may depend upon it that, whatever the view you take, there is not a respectable paper in the country that would have sullied its pages with these passages.'[114] This time the jury did what was expected of it. When North pronounced on Foote a sentence of twelve months' imprisonment (in almost solitary confinement), a great shout of indignation rose from the gallery, with hisses and hoots and cries of 'Jeffreys' and 'Scroggs'.[115] When Foote replied 'My lord, I thank you: it is worthy of your creed', there was fresh uproar. Ramsey and Kemp got nine and three months respectively. As there was then no court of criminal appeal Bradlaugh could do nothing but pen a denunciatory open letter to the judge. It was sticking his neck out but the sentence was so unpopular no action was taken. Nevertheless, though many leading figures who, like Huxley, were critical of the *Freethinker* petitioned for clemency, the Home Secretary Sir William Harcourt refused to intervene on Foote's behalf.

At the same time *Clarke v. Bradlaugh* reached its marathon tape in the House of Lords. It was tried in the chamber before the Lord Chancellor, Law Lords and any other member of the peerage who chose to see the fun, as an appeal *Bradlaugh v. Clarke*. With many weighty precedents and learned quotations the appellant argued that the 1866 Act gave no right to a common informer to sue. Earlier statutes[116] had given the £500 penalty to 'him or them that shall sue for the same', but the new Act was notably silent on this point. He further argued, as points of law, that there was no cause of action when the writ was issued and that the courts had either no power to award costs to a common informer, unless they were specified by statute, or a discretionary power which had been wrongly exercised in his case. For the respondent, Giffard asserted that the incidental provisions of earlier statutes were still in force unless specifically abrogated and that the 1866 Act provided for the penalty 'to be recovered by Action in one of Her Majesty's Superior Courts at Westminster', thus ruling out proceedings by the Crown, which could sue only in the Court of Exchequer. Bradlaugh replied that nothing extraneous could be read into a statute and that 'the prerogatives of the Crown are not to be affected except by distinct enactment'.[117]

Giving judgment on 9 April, Lord Chancellor Selborne opined that the Crown certainly had the right to sue and that the modern tendency was to avoid common informers. He therefore found for the appellant. So too did Lords Watson and Fitzgerald. Lord Blackburn disagreed, fearing that the law might be changed 'by accidental omission of some words'. At that time any lay lord was entitled to pass judgment, but only Lord Denman (not Mr Justice Denman) had the gall to participate. In an incoherent speech he sided with Blackburn. Even so it was a victory for Bradlaugh, perhaps the greatest ever won by a lay litigant. It was also historic as the last time unqualified peers were allowed to perform.

The original blasphemy case came on the following day before Coleridge and a jury. Many leading lawyers turned up to see the maestro. First, Bradlaugh secured a separate trial. Then he made a scathing attack on Tyler and his junior counsel. The second day he intimated he wanted to call his co-defendants as witnesses. Coleridge asked him, 'Do you think it necessary?' They could either decline to give evidence or exculpate him and incriminate themselves. Already in gaol and without a parliamentary fight to wage, Foote saw it as 'clearly my duty to sacrifice myself',[118] but Bradlaugh came back after lunch and pleased Coleridge by saying he had changed his mind. Giffard then complained so bitterly that he was afraid to call his co-defendants that reluctantly he did, but put no questions to them. Bradlaugh was acquitted. The others were then tried. Foote gave a masterly defence speech, ranging over modern literature and tracing the 'blasphemies' of each religion against its rivals; Coleridge declared that free discussion was more part and parcel of the common law of England than Christianity was;[119] the jury disagreed; a *nolle prosequi* was entered; the case was struck off the list. But Foote and Ramsey went back to Holloway Gaol.

Bradlaugh's third triumph that April—one of the reasons for the intense hostility to the Affirmation Bill—was Coleridge's decision in his action against Newdegate for maintenance. This was given a fortnight after the Clarke judgement. During the hearing Giffard had asserted that the offence existed only if there were no legal right to bring the case maintained. The Lords had just decided that in fact Clarke's action was wrongly brought, but Coleridge accepted the plaintiff's submission that this point was immaterial. It was certain however that Clarke would not have proceeded without indemnity from Newdegate. So the maintainer must now pay his costs and Bradlaugh's. These amounted to several thousands. The pious member was not as wealthy as supposed, and despite many testimonials from badgered Conservatives he gratified the Land Law Reform League by having to sell the timber on his uncultivated acres. Moreover, the third testimonial was launched only on the specific understanding that he would not appeal against Coleridge's decision or sponsor the waspish clerical *Churchman* and *Guardian*. Inevitably Bradlaugh was not fully reimbursed for all the incidental expenses he had been put to, and there was a great debt from cases he had undertaken himself.

Vindictiveness against his family and associates continued. In March 1883 Hypatia and Alice were refused admission to the Somerville Club, and two months later Alice and Annie were not allowed to pursue practical botany at the Benthamite foundation, University College. Bradlaugh appealed to Lord Kimberley, President of the college's Council, but the Council endorsed the decision. Conway's son, Dana, circulated a student petition and was beaten up by orthodox students. Aveling wrote round to a number of liberal intellectuals seeking their support as requisitionists for an appeal to the Governors. As only an honorary member himself, the Unitarian theologian James Martineau declined. So, for one reason or another, did the physicist, John Tyndall, the psychiatrist, Henry Maudsley, and the publisher, William Spottiswoode. The psychologist,

Alexander Bain, was uncertain whether the governors would be more sympathetic than the council, but eventually agreed. Huxley replied that he would 'if I were a member of University College', but added that Mrs Besant 'was once a student—and a very hard-working student—of my class at South Kensington'.[120] Privately he wrote to the trade union lawyer Henry Crompton, one of Bradlaugh's supporters, that he wanted 'to be assured that in acting as they have done the Council have had no intention of interfering with religious and philosophical freedom'. He believed, however, that the Council should be 'concerned with the lives and character of those who are admitted', and he had 'a strong feeling that freedom of thought should be carefully distinguished from laxity in morals. Freethinking does not mean Free love . . . I have never been able to get hold of the "Fruits of Philosophy", but if it inculcates the principles which I am told it does with respect to the safeguards of sexual intercourse among unmarried people; and if Mrs Besant has made herself responsible for that doctrine—we are out of the region of speculation and into that of practice—and I have no objection to her exclusion.'[121] An extraordinary meeting of the college was held, opposition to the two women was led by Justice Denman and the medical graduates, and only nine, including Beesly, voted for them.

Speculation continued about 'Mrs B. and her supposed relations with Br-'.[122] But Annie was already losing hope. If Charlie were her true love, Edward Aveling was her current infatuation. While most women pass through moods and seek matching clothes, Mrs Besant passed through cyclical phases and sought matching men. Aveling was the bright new scientific proconsul of tomorrow. He was also something of a bruised reed. He had omitted to tell the secularists he was already married and there was nothing in his behaviour from which they could have deduced it. When a rumour came to light Bradlaugh tackled him with it. Ah yes, recalled Aveling, he had married Isabel Campbell Frank eight or nine years ago when 'both of us were very young' but 'we had little in common'. His employers, heads of girls' schools, had simply urged marriage prematurely upon him. Afterwards his wife became High Church, filling the house with divines and committing adultery with one of them, when at last he 'told her that we must part and indeed on that same day I left the house for ever'. He gave back the letters and promised never to mention her lapse—a 'promise I am now, I believe rightly, breaking'. On parting he told her 'that I should be alone all my time and I thought thus then'. He had not seen her since, but she had 'an income of some few hundreds a year of her own'.[123]

How much substratum of fact there may have been in this sob-story and how much of it Bradlaugh really believed is questionable. The situation was difficult. Aveling might be a notorious philanderer but he was most valuable to the secularists. Among other brilliant achievements, his Doctorate of Science—a light from which all bushels were carefully removed—was not to be underestimated in its importance or to be rejected lightly. Sceptical men of science were glad enough to use Bradlaugh to fight political and legal battles on behalf of free discussion, but few actually wanted to commit them-selves to his movement, or even to Holyoake's deliberately bland British Secular Union. Insofar as they left academic seclusion at all, a free religious chapel like Conway's or Voysey's, a positivist church such as Richard Congreve's or a Unitarian chapel like Martineau's was about as far as their teetering footsteps followed their thoughts. Aveling however had thrown caution to the winds. On the other hand, it was now more important than ever that the secularist hierarchy should face the world unsullied. It was somewhat ironic that as Bradlaugh strode through his political and legal epic, drawing arrows of outrage from those who saw in him a fearful demon-stration that, without religion, general and sexual morality alike broke down, there trotted at his side the frail and innocent-looking Dr Aveling with whose private life even the most latitudinarian moralist could have had a field-day.

The instinctive reaction of the Bradlaugh girls may have saved them from a fate worse than death; it certainly made them 'the only people he never tried to borrow money from'.[124] All around them Aveling's 'temporary loans' multiplied, legacies and other where-withal to pay being just around the corner. Sometimes, it appears, he borrowed on the strength of the Chief's name. Within the movement people were complaining. How long would the scandal of the amoral doctor stay a family affair? The original secularist 'Trinity' had been Bradlaugh-John Watts-Austin Holyoake; Charles replaced John; Annie replaced Austin; there was a person short for a while after Charles fell from heaven, then Aveling joined the triune throne. After the above calling to account early in 1882, Aveling was gradually eased out of prominence save as a science writer and teacher, where he was irreplaceable. Bradlaugh desired however 'especially to avoid the semblance even of disagreement for it would be open to the enemy to say he quarrelled with Holyoake, with Foote, with Charles Watts and now with Aveling'. As long as he could, he doubted 'if there was any intentional breach'[125] of faith on the doctor's part. Even when he was obliged to buy Aveling out of Holloway Gaol, where he had been confined as a fraudulent debtor, Bradlaugh forgave him when 'he then admitted that he had disgraced the party and solemnly promised it should not happen again'.[126] On this occasion a final breach was thus avoided, and it was Aveling who edited the *Freethinker* while Foote was in gaol. Diplomatically he dropped the offending cartoons.

He was however finding other interests. From 1882 he had been a regular reader at the British Museum, where he 'fell into the company of some of the Bohemian Socialists, male and female, who flourish there'.[127] This he found congenial. Probably there were no more eligible females among the socialists than among the secularists —you had to seek the churches for a woman-rich environment—but there clung about secularism, despite the numerous tracts on neo-Malthusianism, a strong aroma of puritan morality. If he had ever believed the Christian gibe, 'Without God anything goes', he soon found it was not true, even of the flirtatious Mrs Besant. While not lacking in intellectual sincerity and application, he soon grew tired of the Bradlaugh ethos of individual effort, community self-help and rigid morality. Having nothing to contribute but his debts, he found the doctrine of shared national wealth not unattractive, and looked forward to a revolutionary New Jerusalem with the socialization of women. Perhaps he thought that Bradlaugh was on the way to winning his battle and becoming just another Westminster politician while, in the world outside, the revolution was about to break. As he liked the centre of affairs—the main trait he shared with Annie—he soon struck up an acquaintance in the socialist firmament with Karl Marx's daughter, Eleanor. She was to prove not only clever and personable but compliant and faithful.

Mrs Besant at last moved from Oatlands to a larger establishment, a sixteen-roomed house at 19 Avenue Road, though not the one she hopefully showed the Bradlaugh girls. Aveling left the Wood for 55 Great Russell Street, convenient for his new Bloomsbury friends. But he did not wish to abandon his old associates entirely, if only because writing in the *Reformer* and functioning as the director and principal tutor of the science schools under the auspices of the National Secular Society were his main legitimate sources of income. The patience of the secularists was however near its end. Bradlaugh put up with Aveling's indebtedness as long as he could, but in June 1884, short of cash himself after his costly litigation, he was obliged to sue for £191 5s 2½d. The stone only slowly dripped blood.[128] Within the freethought movement other creditors were pressing. Aveling hoped that Annie would save him, but she avoided him. Not only was he now notorious in every way, but she had found another persecuted—and personable—young man to help.During the discussion after one of Bradlaugh's meetings she had noticed 'an Englishman who described himself as "a loafer" '.[129] It was Bernard Shaw. A fortnight later she had to apologize for 'a serious injustice' as 'Mr Shaw is very hard-working, and is also poor'.[130] Like an abandoned lover (which to some extent perhaps he was) Aveling wrote to her: 'Am I ever to see you again? If only I could be with you quietly in Scotland for an hour or a day—at rest! When do you return? Are you well? I am so tired.'[131] It was no use. 'I grieve you will not see me. But I *will* be true.'[132] Bradlaugh deemed it time to take action. Descending on Aveling by cab, he demanded the return of all her past letters to him. Then the Chief gave notice that he would move Aveling's expulsion from the National Secular Society at its August meeting, 'in consequence of repeated and increasing complaints of borrowing of moneys'.[133] Before this date the two men met privately. Aveling was allowed to tender his resignation because 'I am indebted in certain sums to certain members of that body for moneys lent. As it is not possible for me to discharge at once and completely all these obligations, I prefer to withdraw from the Society.'[134] He added his 'hope very shortly to clear them all off' and his best wishes. The resignation was accepted but not recorded in the published minutes.[135] Bradlaugh took over as director of the science classes, which were transferred to the spare accommodation at 63 Fleet Street.

Aveling's place in the secularist hierarchy was filled by Foote, though he was not yet completely trusted. And he did not get on with Annie Besant. Apart from possible jealousy, he regarded her as *dilettante* and exposed her weaknesses. She found him brash and cocksure. But he was the best of the secularist writers in overall range and literary excellence [136] and in 1883, when she established *Our Corner*, he began a monthly *Progress* of unquestioned refinement. Yet his colleagues could never quite stomach the *Freethinker*, which reverted to its 'Comic Bible Sketches' on his release.

After the latest refusal of the Commons to accept his oath and the defeat of the Affirmation Bill, Bradlaugh was in a difficult position. His legal victories in 1883 were gratifying and saved him from ruinous debt but had bypassed the original issue of whether or not he was entitled to affirm under existing statutes. Legally he had reached an *impasse* and politically he was embarrassed by the huge weight of hostile petitions. In June he assured Gladstone that this 'manufactured majority . .. did not represent the real feeling of the country'[137] and in July notified him 'I shall in compliance with the law at an early date take my seat for the borough of Northampton'.[138] Four days later Northcote moved another exclusion motion, which was passed 232:65. On the 11th Bradlaugh got Gosset to admit formally what he would do to implement it, then Lewis and Lewis began proceedings. Cluer, who had given Hypatia law lessons and advised Foote in his blasphemy case, provided counsel's opinion. The Attorney-General was instructed to represent the defendant. Bradlaugh claimed that the exclusion order was 'beyond the powers and jurisdiction'[139] of the House and asked the court to restrain the Sergeant-at-Arms. The defence demurred to the claim 'on the ground that the same does not show any matter for which an action can be maintained and does not show or ask for any relief which can be given in this action'.[140] The Treasury Solicitor refused a special tribunal and the case came before Coleridge, Stephen and Mathew in the Queen's Bench in December.

It was ominously like *Bradlaugh v. Erskine*, which Bradlaugh had lost, but Cluer suggested the earlier action could be turned to advantage. In that case Field had opined that an undertaking 'not to disturb' the House would nullify its order and in this new confrontation Bradlaugh had so assured the Speaker. As before, the plaintiff cited *Stockdale v. Hansard* empowering the courts to ascertain 'whether the authority of the House constitutes, in point of law, sufficient justification'[141] of its actions, though this precedent involved a 'stranger' in the chamber. *Clarke v. Bradlaugh* was introduced again to show that a resolution of the House could not overcome a statutory duty. It was, Bradlaugh said, as clearly established that a duly elected member must present himself to take the oath as that he must not sit and vote without taking it. The Attorney-General, however, relied on parliamentary privilege and the authority of the House over its own members. Giving judgment on 9 February 1884, their lordships somewhat reluctantly agreed. Despite Bradlaugh's 'abundant learning and ability', said Coleridge, he had not found a single direct precedent in his support, and there were many against. Stephen took the unusual step of asserting that the form of the defence demurrer admitted 'that the resolution of the House of Commons was illegal', but agreed with his colleagues that 'this court has no power to interfere'. If it could, an appeal might lie to the House of Lords and it would be invidious for one House to judge the powers and privileges of the other. The maxim held: 'Where there is no legal remedy there is no legal wrong.'[142] It was small comfort to Bradlaugh to be feted in Paris a week after the hearing as 'the valiant defender of liberty'.[143]

Two days after the judgment, by agreement with Gladstone, he repeated his performance of two years before. It was a new session and Northcote had promised to take no action before that day. He expected Bradlaugh's usual application to take the oath and was ready with the usual resolution. Suddenly however the member burst into the chamber flanked by Labby and Burt. He marched to the table. The Speaker rose and said 'Order, order', but as the crowded House splintered into disorder he sat down again to draft a rebuke. Northcote rose but could not make himself heard. By this time the infidel had whipped out his piece of paper and book, reading and signing the one and kissing the other. Depositing them on the table he returned to the Bar. Eventually Northcote gained enough calm to move, belatedly, 'that Mr Bradlaugh be not permitted to go through the form of repeating the words of the oath prescribed by the statutes'. In the debate Labouchere flayed the sacrificial words of the oath: 'To me they are just the same superstitious incantation as the trash of any Mumbo-Jumbo among African savages.'[144] Laughter mingled with cries of 'Oh, oh'. Protesting against this 'succession of coarse and gratuitous insults', O'Donnell asked if there were 'no rule to impose decency upon the honourable member'. Apparently there was not. John Morley, who had inherited Newcastle on Ashton Dilke's death in 1883, looked quietly on.

The House divided. O'Donnell shouted that Bradlaugh was about to vote. The Speaker said he had no power to stop him. Before the result was announced Healy had a conversation with Northcote, declared that the government was colluding with the junior member for Northampton, and proposed that his vote be disallowed so that the courts would have 'no data to work upon'. In vain the Attorney-General pointed out that a new resolution would itself be evidence of Bradlaugh's vote, and the motion was carried 258:161. Bradlaugh voted again. The former vote was then announced as 280:167. Northcote proposed exclusion, which was agreed to 228:120. Again Bradlaugh voted. The Attorney-General announced an action against him claiming £1,500 damages for voting three times without taking the proper oath.

BRADLAUGH AND THE BIGOTS.

233

EXIT CALIBAN

(*After "The Tempest"*).

CALIBAN . . . . MR. BR-DL-GH.   ARIEL . . . . LORD R-ND-LPH CH-RCH-LL.

[*Act IV. Sc. 1.*]

Meanwhile Bradlaugh was appointed Steward or Bailiff of the Three Chiltern Hundreds—the form of resignation—and a new writ was granted for Northampton. He commenced his campaign facetiously enough, 'speaking with the responsibilities of office upon me',[145] but then warned against Tory provocations to violence and offered £200 reward to anyone obtaining a conviction against them for bribery. Earlier in the year Churchill had called Bradlaugh's supporters 'the mob, the scum, and the dregs' and his pamphlet reply[146] sold like hot cakes. Locally the Tory candidate, a barrister Henry Charles Richards, was almost as insulting to the shoemakers as Churchill, but 'uniform good order'[147] prevailed throughout the contest. Richards took good care to be seen attending the College Street Baptist Chapel as well as St Giles's Church. Most active of Bradlaugh's clerical opponents was the Rev. Henry Bradford, who was soon to leave the Bradlaughite Princess Street Baptist Chapel to form a breakaway Union Chapel.[148] Another new opponent was the Rev. E.N. Tom, rector of St Peter's. The radical candidate cut through their prejudices: 'I am not asking you to elect me to Convocation to make your creeds, but to elect me to Parliament to make your laws.'[149] His supporters rose to new zeal and on 19 February 1884 he was returned 4,032:3,664. The following day, at Grosvenor's request, he promised Gladstone and Brand not to present himself in the House if James took early action in the courts. Nevertheless Northcote took steps to exclude him, though in March he was allowed the use of the Commons Library to prepare his legal case.

This came before Coleridge, Huddleston and Grove and a special jury at Queen's Bench in June. The Attorney-General, Solicitor-General, Giffard and Robert Wright represented the Crown. The defendant represented himself. The issue was a complicated question of fact and law, which boiled down to whether Bradlaugh was entitled to take the oath and, if so, whether his rendition satisfied the specifications. He fished out some splendid red herrings: that while it was true he had 'voted' he had not in fact 'sat'; that the Crown had failed to establish he had not taken the oath on a former occasion; and that there was no evidence before the court of his state of mind on 11 February but only inferences drawn from his earlier writings. There was even a dispute as to whether or not the case was a criminal proceeding, the Attorney-General claiming not, as it flowed from an information and not an indictment.

This affected rules of procedure and appeal. Oath-taking was regulated by Standing Order 66: 'Members may take and subscribe the

Oath required by Law, at any time during the sitting of the House, before the Orders of the Day and Notices of Motion have been entered upon, or after they have been disposed of; but no debate or business shall be interrupted for that purpose.'[150] It was agreed Bradlaugh had fulfilled the first condition, but contended by the Crown that when the Speaker rose and cried 'Order' he had introduced business which the member was interrupting. There was no business when he started, asserted the defendant, and no one had the right to come between a member and his oath. Long legal disputes pierced proceedings. How absolute were the House's powers by resolution over its members? The Attorney-General agreed it could not order an execution but was loath to draw a precise dividing line. In the matter of the oath, claimed Bradlaugh, no inquisition into personal beliefs was possible because the House had no powers of *voir dire*; i.e. no means of putting on 'oath' before formal swearing. (Perjury began only after an oath or affirmation, but what if lies were given in answer to the preliminary questions?) Was an oath invalid if unbelief was later discovered? But while no one in court was prepared to defend the anomalies and farcicalities of oaths, this did not help the defendant.

It was virtually the end of the road for Bradlaugh in possible litigation, and he was tense and quibbled a good deal. The judges were sympathetic and gave him his head. But they awarded him few points in his efforts to remove questions from the jury. In his summing-up Coleridge declared inquisitions into belief, like the select committees of 1880, 'hateful' and 'disgusting', but considered that Bradlaugh's own open letter of 20 May established his inability to swear in any meaningful definition of the word. Huddleston dissociated himself from his learned brother's 'disgusting' and 'hateful', and Grove thought 'extremely objectionable' better. But they agreed it was an issue on which 'great civil rights depend'.[151] After three hours' retirement the jury found that the Speaker had been sitting during Bradlaugh's oath-taking ceremony, but to prepare notes of rebuke and not out of deference to it; that the defendant had no belief in a Supreme Being, the Commons knew this, and an oath did not bind him; that self-administration was not 'according to the full practice of Parliament' and what he subscribed was not an oath. The Crown had won. Bradlaugh was allowed an arrest of judgment pending an appeal.

In the country at large 'scientific', as opposed to 'utopian', socialism was the talking-point of 1884. In that year the Democratic

Federation, founded three years before by a wealthy, former City man Henry Mayers Hyndman, prefixed 'Social' to its name, William Morris led a breakaway Socialist League, and the Fabian Society evolved out of Thomas Davidson's Fellowship of the New Life. At the same time socialist journals sprang from the presses. One of these was a new series of the monthly *To-Day*, edited by the barrister Ernest Belfort Bax and a former Eton master, James Leigh Joynes.[152] Another was the official Social Democratic Federation weekly, *Justice*. With his finger never off the democratic pulse, Bradlaugh was as quick as Aveling to recognize the potentialities of the new movement. But his reaction was one of misgiving and not of satisfaction. As a staunch Owenite in his youth, he was not without sympathy for many socialist aspirations. Yet he was concerned about the full-blooded—and hot-blooded—programme of the New Socialism.

In the January number of *To-Day* Eleanor 'Tussy' Marx quoted the comment of *Cri du Peuple* that bomb-throwing and the like were 'useless, and at times even harmful'. This criticism struck Bradlaugh as callously inadequate. 'If this is scientific socialism we are glad not to have any part with it.'[153] With his usual cynicism, Engels interpreted this as a purely jealous reaction:

'Bradlaugh and Mrs Besant are furious at the new Socialist "rage" in London which threatens to cut short their wittles, and so have opened an attack or two on T(ussy) and A(veling). Bradlaugh throws about the most mysterious innuendoes about Mohr's having preached assassination and arson and having been in secret league with Continental governments—but nothing tangible—I want to get him to come out a bit more, before I unmask my batteries.'[154]

Hyndman invited Bradlaugh to debate socialism with him. He was elated when able to announce that 'Mr Bradlaugh has accepted the challenge of the Socialists',[155] for he regarded the secularist as 'undoubtedly the most formidable and imposing platform figure in the country'.[156] Out streaked the ballyhoo of advance publicity. Socialists, communists, anarchists and every other group which, while mutually hostile, craved to see the revolutionary David fell the evolutionary Goliath, were drummed up; while, with their accustomed loyalty, the secularists tensed more with anticipation than trepidation as their St George took on yet another dragon. The great event filled St James's Hall on 17 April, with Beesly in the Chair. As *Justice* saw it,

'The mere occurrence of this Debate, apart from the

significant fact that St James's Hall was crowded from floor to ceiling, is an indication of the growing power of Socialism.'[157]

Hyndman began. The crux of the debate hinged, in his view, on the questions:

'Why is it that on the one hand the producers in this country are the poorest of the population? Why is it that those who do not produce are the richest? How, on the other hand, are we to give the producers a full share in that which they produce, and to teach those who live in luxury without producing, some better idea of existence?'[158]

Among the dispossessed proletariat he was careful to include 'small shopkeepers and clerks and those who live by intellectual labour'. As mankind got 'greater power over the forces of nature' and machines supplanted labour, the labourer was thrown on the streets and the new wealth which ought to benefit all was 'used by a class against a class'. Often a female labourer was thrown on the streets in every sense, while, as consumers, everyone was finding 'an increasing difficulty in buying what you may call good goods' in 'the age of adulteration'. Gluts and human need existed side by side, 'but you cannot bring the two together'. Middle-class economics had already broken down with the introduction of Factory Acts and employers' liability by the State. But the process was random. In the State Post Office workers 'compete for starvation wages' to reduce middle-class taxation. The present system stifled individuality and created slavery, as with 'the match-box-makers in the East End of London'. Action must be taken on their behalf. 'We mean if we can to stir up actual conflict', though 'it shall be the conflict of argument as far as possible'.

In reply Bradlaugh recognized the social evils described by his opponent—which he had spent a lifetime in fighting—but urged 'the individuals to remedy them'[159] and not 'some indefinite organization'. Hyndman's programme of social reform was as old as Chartism. The only new thing about 'scientific socialism' was its advocacy of revolution. In the past, however, 'no Socialistic experiment had ever yet been successful'.[160] His opponents had dodged definitions but 'Socialism' surely 'denies all individual private property, and affirms . . . that society organised as the State should own all wealth, direct all labour, and compel the equal distribution of all produce'. Socialists tried to avoid details. 'Dare you try to organise society without discussing details? It is the details which make up life.' A

238

socialist state could come about only with 'a revolution of physical force and . . . a mental revolution, and I will show you that both of them are impossible'. Through savings banks, co-operative stores, building societies, friendly societies, insurance societies and small plots of land, millions of ordinary people were 'property-owners'.[161] The greatest incentive to effort was 'the hope of private gain' in money or esteem. With state control, public meetings and publishing would be regulated by committees. He raised some silly points about the difficulty of selecting cabmen and chimney-sweeps or determining who would travel in a nationalized economy, but was on stronger ground when he dealt with the selection and provision of special facilities for creative artists, in whom 'now people speculate in a special kind of education'.

In the second round Hyndman complained of being asked to 'explain all the details of bottle-washers, cooks and cabmen in the remote future' and paid tribute to his predecessors, as Marx had done, especially Robert Owen and Bronterre O'Brien. He pointed to the 'revolution' in science and in opinion, making it possible for the first time to fill a large hall to discuss 'organized revolutionary Socialism', and the fact that Bradlaugh had 'himself been the victim of force . . . to enforce the views of the dominant class'. In reply Bradlaugh quoted from socialist pamphlets objectionable proposals for railway shareholders to be 'expropriated with or without compensation' and asserted that he did not look like a victim but was 'winning liberty for those that come after me by showing respect to the law'. In the third round Hyndman hoped the revolution would come not by force but by 'the organized education of all', while Bradlaugh asserted that factory-owners now realized that 'under comfortable conditions more is got from the labour'.

Though there was much lively heckling, the affair was on the whole courteous and well-conducted. The reaction of one independent observer was that Bradlaugh 'secured the greater portion of laurels more by the art of talking than the art of reasoning. Mr Hyndman scarcely possessed so much tact, but he was argumentative and forcible in his remarks.'[162] Two other responses to socialism were in Bradlaugh's mind at the time; responses which he was too polite to put. The New Socialism had swept in 'largely at the instance of foreigners' and, curiously, its exponents—'mostly middle-class men—declare their intense hatred of the bourgeoisie'.[163] Indeed, Bradlaugh's objections to socialism had little to do with economic theory at all. Many observers at the debate thought his confounding of personal property and capital was a simple platform trick. How could he believe anything so naive? But while Bradlaugh always liked to win debates he never used 'debating points' for their own sake. He really believed what he said. Three years later he repeated, 'I identify Socialism with Communism', [164] and of the most extreme sort. He insisted it was illogical to separate the means of production and private means. Why should it be all right for an artisan to spend £3 buying himself a silver watch and wrong for him to put the money in a bank to be used by capitalists? This sort of economic illiteracy infuriated socialists. For his part, despite his regard for Levy, he was rather contemptuous of economic literacy. Throughout his lifetime he had known rival economists anathematize one another, and he found it hard to regard abstract economics as a science at all. He appears to have read little on the subject. With the exception of legal research, he derived almost all his reading from his own library of over 10,000 volumes. Besides pamphlets there were few economics books[165] among them, though there was a good deal on fringe subjects concerned with land, taxation, national expenditure and the like. When Aveling and Samuel Moore translated Marx's *Kapital* into English in 1887, he got a copy and read at least some of it. But he regarded pure economists, especially of the socialist school, as politically naive; and many of his commonsense objections, based on the psychology of incentives and natural greed, observation of the innate conservatism of the masses, and realization of the havoc that would result from alternating revolution and counter-revolution, have been rebuked but never refuted. Even on the economic issue he did much to introduce a sense of proportion. The millennium was further away than socialist visionaries imagined. Supposing, he said, that capitalism were really living off surplus value and that socialism would be as efficient as capitalism in finding production incentives, the profit margin was really very small and there was not all that much cake to share among the workers.

By the same token, at public meetings socialists made much of other than economic abstractions. After a small boom in the early 1880s the country was already sinking into what was to become a record slump. For decades Britain had been living off an empire sustained at minimal expense, and industrialism in advance of the rest of the world. By the 1880s the empire was becoming costlier to pacify by a mixture of external force and internal reforms, and the United States had surpassed the United Kingdom in industrial potential. Germany was not far behind. In an effort to find new

240

markets, the European imperialist powers began a 'scramble for Africa', which was 'regularized' by the International Conference of Berlin, 1884-5. Economically this proved a mixed blessing and the slump worsened. When in 1887 Bradlaugh had a written debate with Bax on the same subject as the Hyndman dialogue, what his opponent stressed was 'that Socialism by *its very definition* excludes the possibility of there being any "unemployed" '.[166] Under the present system Bradlaugh could have no answer to this problem. The secularist responded that promises were easy, and leapt to the defence of the 'utopian' socialists. Their only crime was that 'they tried to reduce Socialism to actual practice in groups' while 'Modern Socialism is practical in entirely avoiding any such experiments'.[167] He was also critical when Bax asserted there was 'no possibility of the definite establishment of Socialism anywhere without a concurrent movement among the proletariat of the whole *civilised world*'.[168]

Early East End patriotism and later disenchantment with the political systems of other countries had made him something of a Little Englander. This, suggested Bax, was one of Bradlaugh's problems, wanting a scheme applicable 'to the English people *as* English'. The other was that he demanded 'a handy and portable conspectus of future society'.[169] Bradlaugh made no denial. Every country had its special problems, and over the last fifty years in her own quiet way England had made more progress than any other land. That was because her reformers had known what they wanted and told the people clearly. By contrast the socialists were maddeningly vague. Yet they did not draw back from violent revolution. This must launch 'a shocking and murderous civil war; a war which, however it ended, would leave, for more than one generation, legacies of bitter hate and of demoralizing desire for revenge'.[170] If people were asked to play a wheel that might explode in their faces, they should at least be told the stakes.

Aveling was not the only secularist sheep to wander. Many who were not able to run off to Derbyshire with Eleanor Marx and marry 'without the aid of officials, etc',[171] decided to devote themselves to fulltime political life under one or other of the socialist banners. But the loyalty of the thick-and-thin Bradlaughites was still unquestioned. At the Bradlaugh-Hyndman debate Annie Besant found the revolutionary 'very clever, very fluent, very shifty, and very shallow in his knowledge of the history of English working-class movements'.[172] In her view then, socialism was as bankrupt ideologically as it was morally. Had not the Chief weighed these questions for years and found it wanting? About this time Hypatia and Alice had a fireside chat one evening. They had 'grown more tolerant' and wondered whether 'it would have made for our father's happiness, if he had made a joint home with Mrs Besant, or if, even then, it would make him happier to do so'. In that event they felt ready to 'withdraw our opinion'.[173] He was, they knew, very attached to her. In January 1884 he made his will:

> 'As my death may leave the Freethought Publishing Company in pecuniary embarrassment I appeal to free-thinkers to rally round my loyal friend and brave co-worker Annie Besant and thus to repay to her some of the sacrifice and devotion she has made and shewn for me . . . I have nothing to leave to the true good woman who has so stood side by side with me and borne calumny and slander for my sake save my tenderest love and most earnest hope.'[174]

After consideration of all the consequences of a *liaison*, however, his daughters 'were emphatic in concluding it would not have made for his happiness, that in fact it would not only have ruined his career, but his peace of mind also'. Looking back on the events fifty years later Hypatia recalled that he had never given 'the slightest hint that he desired to make a home with Mrs Besant', and felt 'by no means sure that he did'.[175] At all events, the girls raised no objections when, in the summer of 1884, while the Avelings were in Derbyshire, Charles and Annie went for the first of many holidays together to Portincaple, at the entrance to Loch Long off the estuary of the Clyde. They stayed in the cottage of a fisherman, Finlay McNab, who spent the day rowing Bradlaugh round the loch as he fished. In the evening the McNabs were there to chaperon, but 'it was understood Mrs Besant was the housekeeper'.[176] It was some small substitute for the happy domestic life always denied her.

In the autumn it was again to Scotland that she turned to find a journalistic substitute for the polymath Aveling. Her mission was successful. John Mackinnon Robertson was born in the Isle of Arran in 1856, left school at thirteen for journalism, and by the age of twenty-two was a leader-writer on the Edinburgh *Evening News*. He was also one of a discussion circle of 'fine young men, and never a vice between them',[177] which met at John Lees's house. This was where the Bradlaugh girls discovered him. Later he contributed to *Our Corner* and *Progress*, where his panoramic vision flashed into every social nook and radical prospect. At last the persuasive Mrs

Besant paid a special visit to Scotland to attract him on to the *National Reformer* staff. Here he became a court reporter, reviewer and knowledgeable writer on scores of subjects. Since there were only Annie, her small staff and Jessie Taylor, who had assisted Hypatia in teaching German at the Hall of Science, resident at the vast house in Avenue Road, Robertson was put up there. How completely the handsome young man was intended to replace Aveling is uncertain. At any rate, it was soon apparent that the dour, uncompromising, prickly [178] egghead from Edinburgh was unlikely to adventure with a landlady and employer nine years his senior and already married. Soon, however, a somewhat less inhibited young man, the same age as Robertson, was to be a frequent visitor at Avenue Road. This was the 'loafer' Shaw. In January 1885 he had lectured on socialism at the Dialectical Society. When he noticed the formidable Mrs Besant in the audience, he expected to be demolished during discussion time. What was his astonishment when she rose to vanquish one of his opponents.

Since the Bradlaugh-Hyndman debate she had thought deeply. Apart from the drama involved over gaining Charlie his seat, passion was passing out of the radical cause. Gladstone's Administration was a bitter disappointment, able to fulfil few of its election promises. When the Tories rejected the Representation of the People Bill in June 1884, John Morley set up a cry to 'mend or end' the Lords, a cry to which Bradlaugh gave his powerful lungs. The Bill passed safely, but only with the sacrifice of other liberal legislation. And when the dust had settled, though two million new voters emerged, the measure was seen to have enfranchised only 17 per cent of the population. At the height of popular agitation a People's League against the Hereditary Principle in Legislature was formed with Bradlaugh's support, but having climbed down in time the Lords were neither mended nor ended. In 1885 a Redistribution Act on the basis of a 50,000 constituency completed the package deal. In retrospect it shines. To the masses it then seemed dull enough. Perhaps they had grown tired of waiting. And yet Mrs Besant could see no revival of republicanism or prospect of major constitutional reform. Bradlaugh and his friends were prepared to wait. She was not. Now, inspiringly, there came along an extra-parliamentary messiah with marxist trumpets at his side and 'scientific socialism' on his brow. How could the London Secular Choral Union be heard above this? She did not cease to be a secularist—the society's principles had nothing to say about economic theory, though the Chief rather

243

tended to harness his own hobby-horses to the secularist bandwagon
—but she knew that he would be hurt at this repudiation of part of
his teaching. Her 'conversion' was therefore kept quiet as long as
possible and announced by *Justice* only in July 1885.

Bradlaugh was passing through a difficult time. The financial
burden of 63 Fleet Street hung about him. Though Annie and his
daughters were supposed to manage the business side, all important
decisions had to be referred to him. Whittle had been his printer, but
when the Freethought Publishing Co. acquired additional floors he
decided to establish his own printing works. This was entrusted to
Arthur Bonner, now part of the family. He was the son of the late
Rev. William Bonner of Bradlaugh's Reform League days. The
widow, her daughter and three of her four sons stayed religious, but
Arthur lost his faith and joined the National Secular Society. When
Tyler first attacked the Hall of Science classes in 1881, he enrolled as
a gesture of solidarity. Aveling taught him theoretical mechanics;
Hypatia, mathematics. She was also vice-president of the Students'
Association and there met Arthur on social terms. They had much in
common. Apart from secularism and mathematics, they both loved
music, sang, and appreciated literature and art.[179] Their tem-
peraments were similar: rigid in morality and self-control, precise, a
little pedantic, just, family-loving. Human relations were difficult for
the Bradlaugh girls. In the world outside they felt every hand was
raised against them, and inside the secular movement they were wary
lest they be used as a route to the Chief's inner circle. Alice's high
romantic ideals, which were never realized, were something of a joke
in the family; and everyone was delighted when Hypatia and Arthur
got engaged in January 1884. In him Bradlaugh recognized and
approved another 'self-made man'.[180]

The marriage took place in June 1885 at Marylebone Register
Office. It was a strictly private family affair. The witnesses were
Arthur's eldest brother William, a pastor like his father, Bradlaugh,
Alice and Annie. Hypatia had not wanted Mrs Besant but her father's
appeal was her command. Annie had especially told him 'she very
much wished it'.[181] It was always, complained Hypatia bitterly, 'what
she wished, not what others wished'. The newly-weds went to live in
three rooms of a house in St George's Avenue, Tufnell Park. But
Hypatia wanted to be nearer her father and Alice, and when she fell
ill during her first pregnancy she gladly accepted Annie's offer of
board and lodgings at Avenue Road for 35s a week. Mrs Kenwood
did all the nursing and Mrs Besant took all the credit. A son was born

in April 1886 but died six months later. Throughout this period the house was lively with meetings of the Fabian Society. These were attended particularly by Shaw, an historian Edward Pease, a Highgate schoolmaster Graham Wallas, two civil servants Sidney Webb and Sydney Olivier, and a writer Hubert Bland. From time to time Bradlaugh met the group socially, and he was never denounced by them as violently as by other socialist bodies. This was more than good manners, as they were gradualists like himself. Shaw often dropped in alone. Annie and he played piano duets, for which she practised assiduously. Once his mother and sister came, but Hypatia 'received the impression that Mrs Shaw did not "take to" Mrs Besant'.[182]

Politically Bradlaugh was in a quandary. With parliamentary manoeuvres and litigation evaporating, it was hard to keep the pot boiling. His speeches to his constituents showed increasing concern. How long would their support last, especially without regular pep pills of notoriety? 'What they want', he said of his enemies, 'is to weary and ruin me, to weary you and make you discontented with me so that you shall return someone else.'[183] He was however still lively enough to attract petty persecution. His name was removed from an application for election to the National Liberal Club, inaugurated in 1883 to shame and defy the Whig Reform Club for blackballing Herbert and Walter Chamberlain, so that he should not suffer a like fate. At about this time Horatio Bottomley, who was a nephew of Holyoake's and a lawyer's clerk and court reporter with business plans, met Annie Besant and Bradlaugh casually. Though he was born in 1860, when she was thirteen and Bradlaugh a friend of the distant future, malicious tongues seized on a certain physical resemblance and similar aptitudes to the infidel and named Bottomley as a fruit of the couple's philosophy. In December 1884 Bradlaugh applied to his judges of June, now sitting *in banco*, for a rule ordering a new trial of *Attorney-General v. Bradlaugh* on the ground that the verdict was against the evidence. To his earlier arguments he hammered home a point from the 1867 Office and Oath Act. This allowed a range of office-holders to take an oath 'without reference to his Religious Belief'.[184] As an eye-witness of the trial, Robertson thought Coleridge sometimes showed 'nervous irritation at being persistently argued against', but at this stage the defendant knew he must 'fight with what weapons I can'.[185] Becoming an MP was not in law an 'office'; but in deciding against Bradlaugh the judges abandoned the chance words of statutes to consider the common law implications of 'oath'. At once he appealed.

A few days later Lords Justices Brett (Master of the Rolls), Cotton and Lindley decided, reasonably enough, that the verdict was not against the evidence but that there were matters of law to be determined. And so, the following January, the oath was knocked about again. Against his former pleading James now argued that the case was a criminal one and no appeal lay, but Bradlaugh successfully urged it was not. Then he set about showing that at the beginning of a new parliament the Speaker administers the oath to himself and the first forty members swear when there is not a 'full House'. The 1867 Act came up again, but their lordships decreed that 'religious belief' did not mean belief about religion, as the appellant was contending, but sectarian belief. Lindley followed the statutes to their logical conclusion and opined that many old Acts against unbelievers were 'kept alive by Parliament for the very purpose, amongst others, of keeping such people out of Parliament'.[186] On this and other grounds the appellant's case failed. Hopwood announced a new Affirmation Bill and Bradlaugh wrote to Grosvenor for support. The Chief Whip replied that this was impossible as the government was 'weaker now than we were' in 1883 and the proposal had aroused the 'bitter hostility of the Roman Catholic Irish MPs'.[187] He implored Bradlaugh not to weaken the Liberal Party at the coming election, especially after its 'sacrifices . . . to support you in your struggles'. In a second letter he explained the 'sacrifices' were of time, whereby the Liberals were 'unable to bring on much legislation, and so lost caste in the country'.[188]

Certainly they had, but the causes of their decline, national and international, were multiple. More disasters were ahead. As the Egyptian War festered up the Nile, Bradlaugh chaired a great rally at St James's Hall, including Labby, Professor James Thorold Rogers, MP, Beesly, Morris, Foote, Cremer and Mrs Besant, 'to protest against further expenditure and slaughter in the Soudan'.[189] In the country at large there was great indignation at the failure to relieve Khartoum, where General Gordon was killed. When Gladstone announced his intention of renewing the Irish Crimes Act, Churchill did a deal with Parnell whereby the Tories would renounce coercion if the Home Rulers helped them to defeat the Liberals. The opportunity came with Gladstone's proposal to increase the duty on spirits and on beer, which was regarded as 'necessarily his food'[190] by the agricultural labourer. With Harcourt and Trevelyan, Dilke threatened to resign, but Gladstone said it would be disastrous for 'anyone to retire from the Government at such a moment'.[191] Dilke yielded, but Gladstone was defeated in June 1885 and resigned.

As dissolution was impossible till the Redistribution Act took effect, Salisbury became Prime Minister without an election. There were rich prizes for the Tory commandoes. Giffard (now Baron Halsbury) became Lord Chancellor. Churchill refused to accept office unless Northcote was kicked upstairs. So one of Bradlaugh's old opponents was made Secretary of State for India as the other was created the Earl of Iddesleigh. Balfour became President of the Local Government Board, Gorst Solicitor-General, and Wolff was sent on a well-funded mission to Egypt. Just before leaving the Commons Northcote declined 'to mark my last appearance by the exclusion of another member'.[192] In fact Bradlaugh's enemies were wearier of the struggle than he feared his supporters might be. After the new ministers had been sworn in he again presented himself. Ritually, however, Sir Michael Hicks-Beach, Chancellor of the Exchequer and the new Leader of the Commons, moved an exclusion motion. In 1884 Brand had retired to become Viscount Hampden, and Sir Arthur Wellesley Peel, the youngest son of Sir Robert, became Speaker. But he had no other recourse than to accept the motion. Despite Gladstone's strong support, Hopwood's amendment was defeated 263:219 and Bradlaugh was outside again.

An election was, however, imminent. After redistribution of seats, the Hall of Science was in the constituency of East Finsbury (Clerkenwell) and R.O. Smith became Bradlaugh's election agent in his short-lived candidature to strengthen his position. If elected in both Northampton and Finsbury he would represent the former. This project naturally caused local dissension, so he confined his attention to Northampton. Apart from disestablishment and free education, Gladstone's address to the electors of Midlothian was a blend of excuses and vague promises. He ignored the main concern of the masses, 'the continued chronic depression', which Engels expected to 'prepare a crash of a violence . . . such as we have never known before'.[193] Throughout the country Bradlaughites paid less attention to party matters than to vanquishing the Tory cheer-leaders and renegade Liberals who had persecuted their hero. His enemies made a last sniping raid. A cartoon 'Moonshine' linked him, the *Fruits of Philosophy* and Dilke, who had become involved in a ruinous divorce case. A Brixham Baptist, the Rev. J.T. Almy, wrote a pamphlet *Almighty God or Bradlaugh*, urging his 'fellow Countrymen' not to 'drag down the British constitution to the low level of Atheism . . . as the Jews of old chose Barabbas and rejected Jesus';[194] and in North-ampton Richards, the only Conservative candidate, had copies distributed from door to door.

There was another wave of attacks on Bradlaugh from secular dissidents. Despite patronage by the Marquess of Queensberry, the competition of socialism finished the British Secular Union by 1884, and Charles Watts accepted a rationalist pastorate in Toronto, selling his *Secular Review* to Ross. Nursing imaginary grievances, the new editor issued a virulent anti-Bradlaugh tract, *Ananias, the Atheist's God*, the following year. Bradlaugh thought Watts had something to do with it, but his old foe assured him 'all hostilities' had ceased and he must 'utterly condemn' statements 'as false as they are foolishly wicked'.[195] In October 1885 there were two attacks on Bradlaugh in the *Beaconsfield Standard*. Its editor James Martin was a man of many parts: 'a journalist and minister of the Gospel',[196] 'Inventor of a New Religion',[197] unqualified legal adviser, author, lecturer, company promoter, arbitrator in commercial cases, commission agent, debt collector, advertising contractor and manufacturer of india-rubber stamps. He brought together his two contributors. One was Ross, then combining journalism with his country pursuit of 'milking the Bullock'.[198] Glegg Bullock was a wealthy eccentric secularist who had been persuaded to endow a secular boarding school in his grounds at Whitminster, which Ross hoped to use as his country home. The other writer, 'An Old Freethinker', turned out to be 'Anthony Collins', who Ross had 'always been under the impression . . . had been dead for many years'.[199] For ten years he had been dead to the world. A few years after relinquishing the *Investigator* he became secretary to a friendly society in Liverpool. Suddenly he absconded, printed his own death cards and resumed operations in London with his wife's brother. When he was finally tracked down the pertinent words were 'five years on each count, to run consecutively'.[200] To Bradlaugh these were all minor stings whose later swelling he was unable to foretell.

In addition to direct religious prejudice, misrepresentations of him as an Irish coercer were trumped up to influence the Catholic vote. William Platt Ball, a secularist schoolmaster who had resigned rather than teach religion, countered this campaign with *Charles Bradlaugh, M.P., and the Irish Nation*. On 25 November Bradlaugh was triumphantly returned with 4,315 votes, some 500 behind Labby but 500 ahead of Richards. Among old opponents who were casualties, or who retired to avoid defeat, were Newdegate, Wolff, O'Donnell,

Percy and Samuel Morley. Hopwood was also defeated, but Simon undertook to introduce an Affirmation Bill. 'Tory democracy' flourished in the big cities and Parnellism in Ireland. The Liberals (335) tied[201] with the Conservative (249) and Irish Nationalist (86) coalition. After the re-election of Peel as Speaker, the Liberals slipped into the minority and the Tory ministry returned to office. There was much correspondence between Bradlaugh, the Speaker, the Tory leaders and James, over the atheist's position. Bradlaugh was willing to wait if an Affirmation Bill were promised, as many candidates, including some Conservatives, had pledged themselves to its support. But the issue, when it came to the point, was in some doubt and the Speaker seemed favourable to an oath being taken. So on 13 January 1886 the infidel member presented himself. It was reported[202] that the Cabinet had decided on a three-line whip to oppose Bradlaugh's entry, either at once or when a quorum of forty was sworn in, and the excitement was intense as the Speaker ceremonially returned from the Lords with his commission, robes and full-bottomed wig. He took the oath, subscribed the roll, and announced that he had received letters from the Leader of the House and the members for Cambridge University (H.C. Raikes) and Honiton (Sir J.H. Kennaway). In his letter Hicks-Beach declared that the Court of Appeal had decided Bradlaugh was unable to take the oath and urged that the House be given an opportunity of deciding.

There was a hush as Peel gave his ruling: 'We are assembled in a new Parliament. I know nothing of the Resolutions of the past. They have lapsed, they are void, they are of no effect in reference to this case. It is the right, the legal statutable obligation, of members when returned to this House, to come to this Table, and take the Oath prescribed by Statute.'[203] He would brook no intervention. The Leader rose 'to make one observation', but the Speaker reminded him 'he has not yet, himself, taken the Oath'. Two extra tables, copies of the oath and testaments were brought in. A wild *mêlée* began as the members were put through in batches. A whisper snaked round that forty were in and Bradlaugh was not, but nothing happened. At last[204] he was handed an oath and testament at the foot of the table near the Mace. Thinking himself one of a small party sworn in by the Assistant-Clerk, he read the words and kissed the book. It was half-an-hour before he reached the Clerk to sign the roll. He told him he had already taken the oath. Perhaps, said May, he would not mind doing it again, just so there was no doubt about it. For almost six years Bradlaugh had battled for that right. His face had taken on the shade of ageing alabaster, his great shoulders sagged about his dumpling chin, his best energies had drained away. He would now gladly press a hundred hot kisses on the holy book. Repeating the oath he signed the roll. Then he shook hands with the Speaker. It was no perfunctory gesture.

'I am here only a visitor by your courtesy, a member of a great assembly, the mother of Parliaments . . . advocating the cause of those to whom I belong . . . But for whom should I work if not for the people? Born of the people, trusted by the people, I hope to die for the people. And I know no geographic or race limitations to this word "people".' — Speech to the Indian National Congress at Bombay, 29 December 1889.

There was still some doubt over Bradlaugh's position. His appeal to the House of Lords was pending, and if they should decide that he was really incapacitated from taking an oath, even in due form, he was open to further prosecution and the old charade of seat-vacating and re-election. And there were still members who wished to exclude him *pro tem*. Hicks-Beach told Raikes, however, that he did not propose such action. Bradlaugh and his friends meanwhile threw themselves into reforms. Only a week after taking his seat—below the gangway, next to T.P. O'Connor—the controversial member introduced a 'Bill to promote the better Cultivation of Land', also sponsored by Labouchere, Burt, and Arch, who had just been elected for Norfolk, North-West. Simon introduced an Affirmation Bill and the Unitarian jurist Courtney Kenny a Religious Prosecutions Abolition Bill. All these measures were aborted when the Tories fell at the end of the month, defeated on Jesse Collings's amendment to the Royal Address, censuring them for not bringing in a Labourers' Allotments Bill. Angered by a Tory Coercion Bill, the Parnellites joined the Liberals. Gladstone formed his third ministry, committed to Irish Home Rule. Hartington and other Whigs would not join. Strongly supporting Gladstone, Bradlaugh also raised the issue of market rights and tolls and called for a Labour Bureau along the lines of that established and working in Massachusetts since 1869.

The English employment situation had not improved and on 'Black Monday', 8 February 1886, two great demonstrations were held in Trafalgar Square. One was organized by Hyndman, a former army officer Henry Hyde Champion, and John Burns, a secularist engineer who had become the militant socialist 'Man with the Red Flag'.[1] The other was sponsored by the Fair Trade League. This was an association of Tories, later to be joined by Liberal manufacturers like Chamberlain, whose answer to the slump was a return to protection. When they had had technological supremacy they advocated world free trade; as overseas competition grew fiercer and markets tighter they wanted to protect those at home. Through associated organizations like the Workmen's National Association for the Abolition of Foreign Sugar Bounties, whose secretary was Samuel Peters, the league hoped to extend 'Tory democracy' with a new appeal to proletarian interests. Trouble was avoided in the square, but when Hyndman and Burns led a march up Pall Mall which was jeered at by members of the Reform and Carlton Clubs, smart windows were smashed and looting burst upon Piccadilly. Hyndman, Burns and other leaders were arrested. Despite his personal views on the socialist leadership, Bradlaugh helped Annie Besant to form a Socialist Defence Association. A secularist butcher showed him a cheque made out to Peters by a Bristol sugar-refiner, and from this and other information Bradlaugh charged Peters 'with having received large sums of money from leading Conservatives within six weeks of, and down to a few days before, the Trafalgar Square meeting'.[2] The affair fizzled out then, but exploded at the end of 1887. Speaking about the socialists in March 1886, Bradlaugh described them as 'a few poets, and a few idiots, and some of whom one could not apply as kindly words'.[3] In reply to *Justice* he explained that Annie and Headlam were not 'socialists' but 'Social Reformers'. Yet from the secularist establishment Ball gave her a resounding censure and appeal:

> 'She may find too late that it is as easy to control the sea as a mob of maddened human beings . . . Can she lead such social forces to a peaceful goal?'[4]

Bradlaugh was now seeing much less of his 'brave and loyal co-worker'.[5] As Hypatia put it: 'When the Parliamentary struggle was at an end and my father was allowed to take his seat without molestation, much of his time and thought was devoted to his Parliamentary work, often staying in the House until the small hours of the morning. His weekends and vacations were given to earning money by his lectures, so that he had little time for work in companionship with Mrs Besant, such as he had formerly carried on. There was no opening of any kind for her in Parliamentary work in those days. She was never content with a subsidiary position. She was easily attracted to Socialism through Dr Aveling and Herbert Burrows.'[6] This was a 'mild-looking but stubborn young Cambridge visionary',[7] who by 1888 was to wean her from Fabianism and Shaw to the Social Democratic Federation. By this time she was beginning to think that perhaps Shaw was a 'loafer' after all. He was certainly a *dilettante* and did not like getting too involved, especially with

252

strong-minded women. Burrows was as earnest as she, but not as self-disciplined as Bradlaugh. Annie Besant's harmless infatuations were by this time something of a merry talking-point in inner socialist and secularist circles. Annie Parris told Hypatia 'that Mrs Besant had told her (they both appeared to think it was something to be proud of!) of three men who had asked her to live with them. As a young girl with high ideals and severe judgments I felt both outraged and ashamed.' No names were mentioned, but she had a 'clear idea' who the three were.[8] 'Very sharply' she asked Mrs Parris 'what Mrs Besant could be about to allow three men to make such a proposition to her: what must have been her attitude towards them that they could venture to make such a suggestion!' Annie Parris was 'sorry she spoke'.[9]

The 'thorough' dedication of Bradlaugh moulded his success in the nation's highest debating-chamber as it had in humbler spheres. Since he was so often in his place he knew what other members had said and what had gone unsaid. If he were well-known before entering parliament, his struggle had made him an international celebrity, the John Wilkes of the nineteenth century. People sent him *gourmet* titbits on scandals and injustices throughout the empire, spicing his gluttonous consumption of white papers and blue books, reports and statistics. When he made speeches—neither too often nor too long— his colleagues trooped in from both sides of the House. He spoke only when he had something significant to say, which no one else had said, which no one else could say. When he asked questions ministers knew he could not be fobbed off with some specious answer. If he wanted a subject raised by committee or commission, debate or Bill, before long it was. In balloting for a place on the order paper he never gave up hope. He followed the simple law of averages. By applying more often he appeared more often. Though opposed to bureaucracy and 'big government' he discovered what was later credited to the Fabians: that the great 'amateur' days of politics were over, with classics men filling in odd hours of their flamboyant or scholarly lives with inspired orations on queen and country, nation and empire, even emancipation and the masses, without any real notion of the lives of ordinary people in Britain, let alone elsewhere. Much more homework had to be done; one needed figures, research and more figures. It was dull work, much of it, neglected by the ordinary member as too big for him to tackle or too little in pure intellectualism for him to notice. Yet increasingly it was what government was all about. Bradlaugh believed in a legislature

253

that did not take decisions out of the hands of the people, but was a nerve-centre for processing all the options available and a kidney for removing those waste products of tradition, inherited privilege and entrenched interests which depressed the free exercise of choice.

In March 1886 Bradlaugh obtained the first victory in a crusade which was peculiarly his. This was the appointment of a Select Committee on Perpetual Pensions. If he were not the 'discoverer of Perpetual Pensions', neither was the Financial Reform Association—as it later claimed. It was in the *Reformer* that 'the first careful detailed statement and criticism of Perpetual Pensions was published'.[10] In the same month he moved a reduction in the vote for Wolff's peripatetics, identified Tyler as a director of the Thymney Iron Company, which was prosecuted for offences against the 1831 Truck Act,[11] and was appointed to the Select Committee on the Employers' Liability Bill. Truck was a survival of feudalism whereby workers, especially in remote districts, were partly paid in kind instead of wages. It involved lump sums at irregular intervals, payment at pubs, with the inevitable temptations, and the provision of shoddy goods at top valuation in monopoly stores owned by the employer. Traditionally, said Bradlaugh, 'the labourer was not reckoned at all, except as a superior sort of animal—a kind of conscious machine. He was never treated as a human being to be reasoned with . . . In connection with all kinds of labour, the man who directed the labour was called master, the man who performed the labour was called servant; and the servant, or serf, or slave, or bond-man, was owned by his lord and master, owned as to life and to liberty—as to brain it was seldom considered.'[12] Though it was a long time since people had spoken, publicly at any rate, of workers in these terms, the law was often based on these presumptions and it was left to the late nineteenth century to cauterize the warts. Up till 1880 an injured worker was thrown on the scrap-heap like a broken vase. Then an Employers' Liability Act[13] 'started the process of assimilating the position of servants to that of the public'[14] in the right to compensation. But many jobs were not touched at all, and evasion was possible with those that were, if the injury were caused by a worker 'in common employment' with the victim. Another of Bradlaugh's lifelong interests gained parliamentary attention in April 1886 when his Land Cultivation Bill came up for its second reading, but he thought it premature to press a vote. It was in this territory of legal obfuscations and loopholes, equal rights and vested interests, that he was so intrepid and knowledgeable an explorer.

There was a great physical territory with which he was associated from the start of these parliamentary days. This was the Indian sub-continent, equal in size to Europe outside Russia, with some 250 million people, 106 distinct tongues and a congregation of religions. 'In the 1880s India was passing through the darkest period in her history. Politically disrupted, socially degraded, and economically bankrupt—she had reached her lowest ebb.'[15] The 'first and greatest'[16] of her economic difficulties was the fall in the value of silver associated with the British depression. But the 'mother country' had arranged everything to suit herself. In India, 'most of the old indigenous industries of this land are being swept off under the formidable stress of foreign competition and any new industries started have to encounter numberless obstructions in the way of their development, as much from Legislation unduly favourable to the foreign competitor as from the vastly inferior resources of skill and science available to us.'[17] While there were 'duties on Indian gold and silver plates in England' there was 'abolition of the duties on imported cotton goods in India'. As long as this proud and ancient nation had no representation at Westminster and only a toe in local legislative councils, these injustices might continue indefinitely. With his lifelong concern for the rights of all, heedless of colour or label, Bradlaugh dedicated himself to giving voice to this great mute land. The first voice he could give was his own. In 1884 Fawcett, the 'member for India', had died, and the infidel aspired to the vacant chair. There was perhaps an element of political foresight too. Already rather old for a junior member, prematurely aged by conflict, lacking commendations of birth and breeding (which were almost as prized by Liberals as by Conservatives) and still tarred with a thousand smears, his best chance of ultimate office was in some sphere of difficulty and danger, complexity and co-ordination, where he was uniquely master.

On 8 April 1886 Gladstone announced his Home Rule proposals and five days later introduced a complementary Land Bill. There was consternation among many influential Liberals, who saw it as a sell-out to Irish nationalism. A lot of Whigs had landed interests there; the big manufacturers saw it as the first bite of a wedge that would fracture the empire and prise away their markets. Hartington and Chamberlain formed the Liberal Unionists. Bright threw in his lot with them. Bradlaugh pleaded for Ireland in the Commons and agitated outside. Churchill said 'Ulster will fight and Ulster will be right' and there was little real surprise when on 7 June the Home

Rule Bill was defeated 343:313. Gladstone decided to appeal to the people. Being somewhat anxious about the national outcome Bradlaugh wrote to him seeking a *stet processus* in the hazardous appeal of *Bradlaugh v. Attorney-General*. Gladstone was sorry; his position was tenuous; the slightest controversy might be his undoing. The elections were held at the beginning of July. In Northampton the Tories got Richard Turner, a retired shoe-manufacturer, to stand as a Liberal Unionist while T.O. Hastings Lees, a barrister and former Chief Constable, made do with a Conservative ticket. But the stratagem merely took a few hundred votes from Labby. Bradlaugh was returned with 4,353, more than ever before. In the country at large however there were only 191 Liberal Home Rulers and 85 Irish Nationalists, opposed by 78 Liberal Unionists and 316 Conservatives.[18] As a last fling Bradlaugh wrote to Gladstone: 'Surely there can be no real objection now to a stay of proceedings by the Crown.'[19] But Lord Chancellor (formerly Sir Farrer) Herschell advised that there were difficulties 'in the state of things resulting from the elections'. Agreeing that the GOM could not go against this view, Bradlaugh reminded him that he was 'no new and no fair-weather adherent' and had 'a devoted tongue and not quite a powerless one'.[20]

In the new Tory administration Salisbury was again premier. As a reward for his sterling services Churchill became Chancellor of the Exchequer and Leader of the Commons. What was the infidel's astonishment when Randy Pandy's Attorney-General Sir Richard Webster granted the *stet processus* refused by the Liberals. Churchill was a complex personality. Like his famous son he was a man of moods, capable of great petulance and great generosity. Perhaps he was genuinely sorry for the St Vitus dance he had led Bradlaugh, though he justified himself at the time as a defender of his family's honour and pension, as well as on broader issues. Chief of these was a wish to swamp the Gladstone ministry in the wash of a political nuisance. He had no desire to inherit it. What the Tories had given out to the nation was a determination to uphold the prerogatives of the Almighty. This mission faded when they gained office. One day a friendly Conservative MP approached the atheist: 'Good God, Bradlaugh, what does it matter whether there is a God or not?'[21] He may not have been typical; he was far from unique. Yet however devoutly other Tories loved their Lord, they loved their property even more. Churchill and his friends were astute and well-informed. The junior member for Northampton might be a threat to their perpetual pensions and uncultivated parks, Irish estates and market rights and tolls, and his compensation might not be as liberal as his principles. But he believed in law and order and private enterprise, and he held powerful sway over the people. Wolves bloody with red revolution were already ravening over the land demanding everything for the nation, 'with or without compensation'. If Bradlaugh went, a worse might well come in his place.

In the new parliament he moved that the House not assent to the usual sessional order prohibiting the interference of peers in elections. This was one of the disabilities concomitant with the privileges of the peers, and Bradlaugh's manoeuvre was intended as the 'first step to getting rid of the House of Lords'. Churchill offered him a committee for the following year to draft another order, but he pressed the motion to a division and got 126 votes. His pursuit of his old foe did not waver. In discussing a committal for contempt of court the following month, he reminded the House that its Leader had once said that the Crown could get the right decision from the right judge. Churchill denied this: 'I am sure the honourable Member will not find any record of my having given utterance to such an opinion.'[22] And when Bradlaugh turned to *Hansard*, sure enough there was nothing there. So he apologized. In fact he was right. Randy Pandy had doctored the record. A search of newspaper cuttings later produced the missing evidence. In October Bradlaugh put together a mosaic of invective in an open letter to the Tory minister. English gentlemen, he said, 'belong to a class to which I, as well as yourself, am a stranger—I from birth, and you from habit'.[23] Churchill was undismayed. He frequently sought introductions to his fiery critic. As last he made a direct approach, joining a group and paying Bradlaugh a broad compliment. The member for Northampton merely bowed. But the ice was finally broken in the summer of 1887. Churchill was then chairman of the Army and Navy Committee. One of its members, Louis John Jennings, was approached by Bradlaugh, who said how impressed he was on reading its transcript of evidence and noting the enormously valuable work done by the chairman. 'He has done so much good that I really think I must close up my account against him.' 'Well, surely,' said Jennings, 'there is no use in keeping it open any longer. It only looks like vindictiveness.' 'Yes, I think I will close the ledger.'[24] But when he did, members of the Social Democratic Federation, about whom clung tenacious charges of accepting 'Tory gold' at the recent elections, accused him of selling out to the Conservatives; and Churchill himself wondered whether Bradlaugh or Chamberlain would be the first to sit on Salisbury's Treasury Bench. On the contrary, Bradlaugh had already been impressed by Churchill's courageous action in leaving it for the political wilderness towards the end of 1886, after failing to induce his colleagues to accept the naval and military economies he had promised. His place was taken by the Liberal Unionist George Joachim Goschen, the first step in a major realignment of British political power.

Even more than before, in the late eighties Bradlaugh's private life thinned almost to disappearance. What remained was pitted with ill health. There were more irritations and disappointments. As Victoria entered the fiftieth year of her reign and sumptuous plans were laid for a Jubilee Year in 1887, dreams of republicanism were snuffed out even in the visionary Standring. In August 1886 he announced that from the next issue the *Republican* would be called the *Radical*:

> 'Many people associate Republicanism with violent revolution, and refuse to heed the voice of its preachers; while a very large number of Radicals regard it as an academic subject of comparatively little importance ... I desire to make the paper of greater use to the members of the numerous Radical Clubs and organizations occurring in the metropolis and the provinces.'[25]

Republican feeling had 'undergone an allopathic change', many deciding 'the question of the relations of capital and labour is in truth, and has been discovered to be, far more important than the precise form assumed by the executive in a democratic State'.[26] This new political pre-occupation, which Bradlaugh associated with the two general elections, had 'somewhat hindered Freethought work during the past year'[27] as well.

Among the secularist faithful who remained, fresh rows broke out. The first came when Bradlaugh discovered that a pirated version [28] of the *Law of Population* was in circulation. He was especially distressed to find that the freethought martyr Ramsey was responsible. Immediately he broke off all business connections, instructing Alice that 'of course neither Kemp nor Ramsey will be allowed to have anything more under any circumstances'.[29] All that was ever published was that Ramsey had written a letter to the Chief: 'I beg to resign my position as a member and vice-president of the National Secular Society.'[30] The executive accepted his resignation. Worse trouble was looming on the *Secular Review* front.

'Saladin' was meeting problems in 'milking the Bullock'. For one thing, it was difficult to find enough boys to make the Whitminster school look like a going concern. For another, Bullock's adopted son, Dr Horace Walker, was getting worried about 'the machinations of that unprincipled man Ross', 'a most grasping and ill-conditioned man'.[31] To kill two birds with the one stone—i.e. fill up the student register and keep an eye on the philanthropist, who had promised large sums in endowments and bequests for the school—Ross arranged for Charles Robert Mackay to go to Whitminster as a 'pupil'. Mackay was an ambitious, but mediocre and unstable, fellow-Scot in his early twenties. He claimed to be a medical student. In fact he had worked for a wholesale chemist in Edinburgh. Soon after coming to London he met Ross through the *Secular Review*. When he turned up at the secular school and became Bullock's private secretary, Walker 'thought Mackay and Ross were partners at that time, and were to share what they got'.[32] In August 1886 Bullock had a stroke and events moved swiftly. Ross claimed Walker got a cheque for £7,000 out of the crippled man. Certainly two cheques in Ross's favour were signed, one for £5,000, another for £8,000, to be met by the sale of stock. Bullock's bank manager contacted Walker, who wired back 'Fraud expected' and wrote to one of Bullock's cousins: 'They have got all they want out of him, and now they are trying to murder him.'[33] Then he instituted lunacy proceedings. The old man was declared insane and the cheques set aside. Against Walker, Mackay brought a slander action, which was dismissed. Ross brought a slander, libel and compensation suit, which was heard by Grove and a special jury. As the judge outlined the 'painful spectacle exhibited before them, this benevolent old man being hunted during his last lucid years for his money',[34] the jury foreman interrupted to find for Ross with a farthing's damages. Grove withheld costs.

Ross's temper was not sweetened by the tensions and chagrin of this saga. Neither were his finances. For a long time he had believed that, out of jealousy, Bradlaugh was trying to sabotage his enterprises. One of these was a scheme to promote the building of secular halls. Little was actually built. And there was the celebrated school. Many members of the National Secular Society read the *Secular Review*, which had among its rodomontade, able articles and satires by 'Saladin' and 'Lara' (George Griffith-Jones, the first 'principal'[35] of Whitminster), and were influenced by its advertisements. If they were in doubt over these, as over other subjects, they turned to the Chief for guidance. He had no wish for animosity, but at last he saw it as a pastoral duty to warn his flock in answers to correspondents in the *Reformer*.[36] In his *Review* Ross raged almost incoherent. Bradlaugh declined to recant. Ross grew querulous: 'Am I too insignificant a person to apologize to, however much my feelings may be wounded?'[37] As his pages filled with scurrility, Bradlaugh and Annie Besant refused to speak at those secularist branches which displayed the *Review* for sale at their meetings. Ross was then running his popular *magnum opus, God and His Book*, and some members deemed their action 'Boycotting with a Vengeance'.[38] The Manchester branch president, who knew nothing about Ross or the years of rancour from various freethinking sources Bradlaugh had lived through, resigned in protest, though he admitted the Chief's alternative of suing 'would probably do you more harm than good, even if you won, and I can quite believe that Ross knows this and counts upon it'.[39] For the moment Bradlaugh had the last laugh when from Stonecutter Street, whence Ramsey had been removed, Forder published *Saladin the Little*, exposing 'the Farringdon school of freethought of which "Saladin" is the apostle and hierophant in chief'.[40]

During the 'boycotting' row a long contest over a secularist bequest began. With the numerical contraction of the movement such matters became even more important. As usual, Bradlaugh had to bear the brunt of the battle. Skirmishing spread from the County Palatine of Lancaster court to the Court of Appeal, but the secularists eventually abandoned a technically weak case. Towards the end of 1886 Arthur Bonner went down with typhoid, and new responsibilities fell to Bradlaugh. Weakened by overwork he succumbed to erysipelas and neuritis. Annie Besant fell ill too. Their local G P, Dr A.J. Bell agitated her for some time by diagnosing a slight valvular disorder of the heart, but eventually she forgot about it. Ill and engaged in different political activities, Charles and Annie were seen little together, and in January 1887 they had to deny a rift between them in the *Reformer*.[41] This year was to see the clear acceptance of Bradlaugh as an institution with the 'House of Commons manner'.[42] The main business of the new session was another Coercion Bill for Ireland, made more desperate by the defeat of Gladstone and Home Rule. With the resignation of Churchill, W.H. Smith became the new Leader of the House. Bradlaugh's *Reformer* was still banned on Smith's bookstalls, but there grew up between the two men a mutual esteem. From Bradlaugh came 'sincere respect'[43] for his opponent's 'sense . . . of rectitude',[44] while Smith declared there was 'not an honester man in Parliament'[45] than the infidel. Or a more hardworking one. Through his persistence the junior member for Northampton forced the publication of the confidential report of the Chief Inspector of Factories, and introduced his own Truck Amendment Bill,[46] which was passed in the summer. It extended the protection of the 1831 Act to all workmen except domestic servants and, in some things, agricultural labourers. At the same time he was granted a Select Committee on Perpetual Pensions, which he served on himself. His report, advocating their abolition by commutation, was accepted save insofar as it referred to the Prince of Wales's Duchy of Cornwall. Bradlaugh was also a member of a committee of seven appointed to look into the sessional order on peers and elections, but the majority decided against change. Equally unsuccessful was his challenge of the finance vote for Wolff's Cairo mission. Then came his Affirmation Bill, which was lost without rancour. With Howell, who had become the member for Bethnal Green North-East and lost most of his animosity towards Bradlaugh, he flew at the Corporation of London and especially at Fowler, who was Lord Mayor in 1883-5, 'alleging improper Use and Malversation of Public Funds'.[47] Hartington was the leading member of the investigating committee of five which was set up, while Bradlaugh was to 'propose and examine witnesses, but without the power of voting'. It was a perfect compromise, gaining the lay lawyer's unique talents as a bloodhound and bulldog without prejudicing the outcome, on which he had already expressed strong views. An interesting story was to emerge.

As soon as the Queen's Speech of 1882 outlined plans for reform of London local government, the Corporation, which 'remained an archaic system of guilds, livery companies and freemen, with no more than a ceremonial importance in the rest of London',[48] set up a Special Committee to fight the proposals. It was most active in 1884 when Harcourt introduced his London Government Bill, which was lost some months later during Gladstone's manoeuvres to save the Representation of the People Bill. The Special Committee was 'prepared to show that the theory of one municipality was both costly and ineffective'.[49] In its campaign it floated an Anti-One-Municipality League to oppose the Municipal Reform League, and promoted petitions to create a municipality for South London, charters for every ancient London borough and other diversions. All this was somewhat dubious in a corporation supposedly controlled by, rather than set up to manipulate, the spontaneous will of the people; but as the City of London was not subject to the 1882 Municipal Corporations Act,[50] it was a nice legal point and the Select Committee found malversation had not been established. The Corporation had, however, gone far beyond organizing petitions. It hired a journalistic wide boy who became secretary of a bogus Metropolitan Ratepayers' Protection Association. This paid strong-arm 'stewards' and attenders at its own meetings, many of which were notified only to the press at the last moment, though later described as public; sent paid hecklers on forged tickets to meetings of the Municipal Reform League; and even called meetings in the name of the Reform League, where an organized opposition outnumbered the supposed promoters. Thus the charges of Bradlaugh and Howell were proved up to the hilt, and Hartington's committee found the Corporation responsible for hiring agents who spend money 'for improper and indefensible purposes . . . calculated to mislead Parliament'.[51]

Though not appointed to the Royal Commission on Market Rights and Tolls, which he was influential[52] in setting up, Bradlaugh was in frequent communication with C.E. Ritchie, President of the Local Government Board. In a matter of 'such vital importance as affecting the food supply of the poor',[53] he fought to get working-class representatives, such as Henry Broadhurst, on to the commission and to secure the appointment of assistant-commissioners to range the country gathering evidence. Much of this he was able to supply from his own correspondence. Not only the vast ducal estates with their mediaeval privileges, but modern companies were in on the racket of grabbing excessive rents from market stall-holders, who were evicted and replaced if they complained. Railway companies often owned market halls at their London terminals and refused to carry goods that were not sold there. All these charges were of course passed on to the consumer, as Bradlaugh demonstrated. Abroad he was no less vigilant. He was now reaching a *modus vivendi* with another old foe, Gorst, who had become Under-Secretary of State for India. When unable to answer the backbencher's searching questions, Gorst wrote privately and explained why. In 1887 a great talking point for those in the know was alleged corruption involving a ruby concession in Upper Burma. Bradlaugh was sent a folio of confidential correspondence[54] establishing the innocence of the officials concerned, despite their temptations. He was a radical and a newspaper editor with an eye to scoops, but the Tories knew that secret material could not be in more scrupulous hands.

In the continued distress his old friends the Northumberland miners were heavily burdened and came out on a hopeless seventeen-week strike. Bradlaugh put three searching questions in the House on mining conditions and, though 'terribly embarrassed by my debts',[55] contributed over £11 to the miners' strike fund. At their melancholy gala at Blyth that summer—the London radical held the record of invitations to address galas of both the Northumberland and the Durham miners[56]—he chided the men for their lambasting of a hard-working Commons, and pointed out that while they were on strike the Welsh mine-owners rejoiced. England was no longer 'the work-shop of the world', he explained, some eighty years before the country as a whole was prepared to acknowledge the fact, and socialists could not make 'manufactures profitable by simply saying it shall be so'. The burden of taxation should be put on land and capital, with large estates reduced, but tactfully. Perceptively he saw that 'all parties were changing in this country, the Whig and Tory were dying away'[57] and the middle ground was being cultivated. With the rise of the labour movement in the twentieth century political polarization was for a time restored under new labels, but by the middle of the century the trends Bradlaugh recognized were resumed.

Varley meanwhile gained fresh publicity by a horrified appraisal of West End prostitution in *The Great London Flesh Market*. When Bradlaugh called attention to this pamphlet in the House, Varley wrote a leaflet *Mr Charles Bradlaugh, M.P., and Mr Henry Varley*: 'You, sir, voluntarily entered, some years since, into business partner-ship and association with the wife of a clergyman contrary to his will and in violation of all family and social propriety.' He was not alone in this feeling. In happy oblivion, however, Mrs Besant chose this moment to censure the 'indiscretion' of a walk together by Robertson and Mrs Mary Reed, an old friend of the Bradlaughs. 'I wonder', wrote Alice to Hypatia, '*what* word she would use to qualify some of her own performances. Talk about *bourgeois*, Mrs Besant is really so in its narrowest sense when it comes to dealing with other people's conduct.'[58] The following month part of her association with Bradlaugh was terminated. With the impoverishment of a section of his supporters, the competition of socialist literature and the disappearance of past dramas, the *National Reformer*'s cir-culation was in decline and 'the expenses of Fleet St are as great as the income'.[59] Looking for internal explanations, the editors decided that, reminiscent of its Barker days, the paper's editorial divisions were working against it. To the regret of them both Annie resigned because of 'the divided editorial policy of this paper on the question of Socialism'.[60] She remained a co-proprietor, and was still second to the Chief in the secularist hierarchy. As he presided at the second congress of the International Federation of Freethinkers held in London—in September 1887—she was at his side. And, in the forthcoming 1888 *Almanack*, always a subtle index of secularist status, her contribution appeared immediately after his. Her position was, however, becoming increasingly anomalous, though she had not followed her socialist friends in rejecting neo-Malthusianism which they held to be 'the first article of the capitalist creed today' designed by the bosses 'to keep down the numbers of the labouring class to their requirements'.[61] Giving advance signals of future discord, Robertson's name appeared in this *Almanack*, for the first time, after hers and before Foote's.

On 13 November 1887 the Metropolitan Radical Federation, to which the National Secular Society was affiliated, called a protest meeting in Trafalgar Square against unemployment. Supporting marches were promised by the socialist bodies. An anxious Home Secretary banned it, relented and banned again. The protest went on regardless, and the police lashed it into history as 'Bloody Sunday'. With William Thomas Stead, the radical Congregationalist editor of John Morley's *Pall Mall Gazette*, Annie formed the Law and Liberty League. Bradlaugh, who had been out of town on a lecturing engagement and so branded by the socialists as a coward, gave evidence at Bow Street on behalf of the demonstration's leaders, notably Burns and Cunninghame Graham, a pompous Scottish writer and member for West Lanark. Boldly vindicated in his City of London allegations, Bradlaugh seized the opportunity of returning to his attack on Salisbury. The noble marquess had himself sent a cheque for £25 to Thomas Martin Kelly, secretary of the Riverside Labourers' Association and a friend of Captain Peters. Of course the association was supposed to be a charitable organization for distressed dockers, but everyone knew, said Bradlaugh, what that meant. It was simply a front to pay hired Tory trouble-makers. In December Salisbury denied, and Bradlaugh repeated, these charges in the *Times*.[62] Salisbury's secretary wrote to Kelly accusing Bradlaugh of 'wilful perjury'. At Bow Street Peters applied for a summons against the radical member for perjury. When this was refused, he brought a libel action in the Lord Mayor's Court. With his customary skill Bradlaugh got this transferred to the High Court. In *Truth* a lie was called a 'Salisbury'. Meanwhile plots were maturing against Bradlaugh elsewhere, and 1888 was to be an *annus mirabilis* of libel actions.

For some months 'Saladin' had garnished the *Secular Review* with hints of a public unfrocking of what the *Sozial Demokrat* called the 'Atheistic Pope'.[63] In January 1888 Foote met 'a Radical pressman', probably the ubiquitous Morrison Davidson, who had seen proofs of a book about Bradlaugh. The 'ostensible author' was Mackay. 'Behind this fellow' were Ross and Brewin Grant, and 'behind these', the informant thought, 'though he is not sure, are one or two Tories, who are finding cash, and one or two Socialists who are also promising support'.[64] No evidence of the direct implication of Grant (though he supplied 'evidence'), the Tories (apart from the paper-makers, printers and steam-rollers, who may or may not have regarded the book as an ordinary commercial transaction) or the Socialists ever came to light, though all of them tried to benefit from the 'revelations'. Its true aetiology was less spectacular and more squalid. It appears that Ross persuaded Mackay, now back in London after the balloon had gone up at Whitminster, that fortune and fame, after which the drifting young man vainly hankered, would come from a 'frank' biography of the great radical, who was then being tipped as Gladstone's next Under-Secretary of State for India. Lytton Strachey was not, as he has often been hailed, the pioneer of the modern debunking biography. 'Tay Pay' O'Connor did Disraeli; Louis Jennings, Gladstone; 'Junius', the Duke of Bedford. If the Bradlaugh venture succeeded it was hoped Davidson would produce a Life of *Albert Edward, Prince of Wales* and 'Julian' a *Life of Jehovah*.

Ross's only interest in Mackay was to find a 'stool pigeon' to take the blame when Bradlaugh brought the inevitable libel action. In July 1887, therefore, 'Saladin' brought together the 'medical student', Selkirk Charles, one of his many legal advisers and probably the only qualified one, and 'Dodo' of the socialist *Reynolds's Newspaper*.[65] 'Dodo' was to get advance proofs if he would 'hammer away at the — Bradlaugh'[66] in his paper. Ross then brought Mackay and Johnson together. Mackay was to pay 'Anthony Collins' £50 for legal documents and other 'information' about Bradlaugh's early life; though Johnson later claimed he ghosted all the book save the 'Introductory', 'interpolations as marked on pages 355-9 and occasional epithets such as "dirtites" '.[67] Knowing that no reputable London printer would touch the finished masterpiece with a barge-pole, Ross found paper-makers in Dumfriesshire, his home county, and printers, Colston & Co., in Edinburgh, which he thought far enough away to escape detection. He corrected the proofs and added several eulogies of himself. When the job was done he found a publishing and dispatch office at the celebrated 84 Fleet Street,[68] handy to 'Ye Olde Cheshire Cheese' gossips. This was taken over by 'D.J. Gunn & Co.', the book's 'publishers', and converted into an 'Agnostic Depot'. Ross promised the first half-quarter's rent. It was claimed the company consisted of Charles Mackay and a supposititious brother David James (Gunn), but Mackay's solicitors later stated: 'There is no such person as D.J. Gunn. Mr Mackay carries on business as D.J. Gunn & Co.'[69] Probably Ross originated the phrase 'gunning for Bradlaugh'. He also asserted that when the Chief was on the warpath Mackay lived on the premises with a revolver to protect himself and his stock, saying: '*This* is the Mr *Gunn* I had resolved should speak to him.'[70] The stage was set; the gossip grew; two evening newspapers offered ten guineas for advance copies of the book.

And so, on 3 February 1888, the *Life of Charles Bradlaugh, M.P.* was published. 'Lara' urged the erection of 'a white stone in the Secular Calendar by every Secularist to whom the sacred cause of intellectual progress and mental freedom is more dear than the meretricious reputation and flatulent vain-glory of the uncouth "Standard-bearer" who, some thirty years ago, seized the banner of Freethought by brute force, and then—so that all better men should shrink from the disgrace of touching it—wiped his blasphemous lips on the flag, and branded his ill-omened name on the staff'.[71] Behind this outburst there was, inevitably, a personal grudge. In response to many enquiries Bradlaugh had told his *Reformer* readers he knew nothing about the Whitminster school but was prepared to 'report' on it. The offer had been indignantly declined by the proprietors. In February 1888 Bradlaugh put a note in his paper: 'The North West London Branch is now announcing a lecturer who, a few months ago, professed to be a Christian.'[72] That month the speakers were Dr Allinson, Foote, Bradlaugh, and 'Lara', whose invitation was promptly withdrawn. Whereupon Griffith-Jones retaliated with two pamphlets, *Mokanna Unveiled* and *The Bounciad*[73], a Popesque epic beginning:

> Still must we hear? Shall still great BUNKUM bawl
> His windy rubbish in the Old Street Hall,
> And none denounce—lest, haply legal pains
> At their expense shall swell his ill-won gains?

When the Peters libel action was decided he produced a third polemic, *Peters v. Ananias M.P.*[74] 'Gunn' was again the fearless publisher.

This spate of libels did Bradlaugh remarkably little harm, though the *Life* was to involve him and Hypatia in litigation and inconvenience for the rest of their lives. The pamphlets achieved little circulation or publicity outside the freethought movement. The 'biography' achieved more publicity than circulation, but not of a very favourable kind for its authors. It was so obviously a 'job' of private spleen, full of smears and insinuations but very few hard facts, clumsily packaged by many soiled hands. Whatever the exertions of 'Dodo', *Reynolds's* went out of its way to say of Bradlaugh, 'We entertain the highest opinion of his ability, his honesty, his consistency, and his character in general . . . All those we have met, and they are many, who were engaged with Mr Bradlaugh in matters of a private character, spoke in the highest terms of his probity and straightforwardness.'[75] He was indeed already something of an elder statesman. When he spoke in the House, peers, even on occasion the Prince of Wales, slipped into the gallery. In an age notorious for its mistresses and prostitution and incompletely purged of eighteenth-century bribery and jobbery, the grossest insinuations against Bradlaugh dwindled before the facts about many public figures. Ross had declared that if 'the subject of the work could, after its appearance, socially, live, he would certainly be immortal'.[76] Bradlaugh was immortal.

His friends rallied round. John Lees discovered the Edinburgh printers and began proceedings there. Bradlaugh applied for an injunction against the book's sale, and issued a writ for libel against Mackay, Ross and 'Gunn'. He proposed to add C.A. Watts after Gunn was traced. This eventuality did not arise. Almost immediately the conspirators fell out. Johnson wanted to handle the legal side. He urged the defendants to 'justify' and offered to testify himself. Ross thought otherwise. He told his *Review* readers he had nothing to do with the book and would not review it. Instead, he republished comment made elsewhere. This humbug was the last straw for 'Lara', who had quarrelled with 'Saladin' in the past and now injuncted and sued him for the return of various manuscripts. Mackay brought an action against Ross for slander, then a £570 claim for writing the *Life* and contributing towards the publishing expenses. Anxiously Ross sent various cronies round to persuade Mackay to settle out of court, and agreed to pay the 'author' £225 for incriminating manuscripts. Claiming they were not all given up he prosecuted these intermediaries and Mackay for return of the money and criminal conspiracy. When the case was dismissed all the defendants sued Ross for malicious prosecution. 'Saladin' would not pay the fees of one of his many solicitors, who sued him for them, or the rent of 84 Fleet Street, or the bills of his printers and decorators. Meanwhile Bradlaugh brought successful actions against the *Dumfries Standard* and *Warrington Observer* for quoting from the *Life*. By February 1889 Mackay, made bankrupt by his landlord, expressed regret for the libel before Master Gordon and Bradlaugh allowed him to leave the action. Ross's new solicitors advised their client that Mackay had shown Bradlaugh's solicitors the incriminating manuscripts and was ready to give evidence for the Chief. The game was up. Before Master Butler, 'Saladin' agreed to destroy all copies of the *Life* that came his way and to pay £50 to the Masonic Boys' School, plus plaintiff's costs (over £190). Then he coolly explained to Bradlaugh, 'The book was part of a plot to "smash" both you and me and put Mr Jones in our place.'[77]

The Peters case turned out less satisfactorily for Bradlaugh. In a personal statement to the House he called for a Select Committee to investigate the affair. The government rejected this on the grounds that a law suit was pending. Salisbury declined to endorse his secretary's letter to Kelly alleging perjury, so Bradlaugh was unable to attack the prime minister 'either before a select committee or in a court of law'.[78] In April 1888 *Peters v. Bradlaugh* was to be heard at Queen's Bench before Huddleston and a special jury. The editor of the Tory *St Stephen's Review* tried to influence the decision by a libellous attack on the defendant, and was fined £20 with costs before Justices Manisty and Hawkins. When the Peters case came on, it was at once clear that Bradlaugh had been precipitate in his allegations. Kelly had in the past taken money to whip up agitation against municipal reform and it was more than likely his venality persisted. But the defendant had no real evidence against Peters and his references to Salisbury were more than a little reckless. He argued however that there was nothing libellous in accusing someone of organizing a propaganda association and collecting subscriptions from sympathetic individuals, whether this was true or not. Huddleston, who asked the jury to consider what value they could give to the evidence of one of Bradlaugh's witnesses, who had objected to the oath, thought there had been a 'libellous' statement against Salisbury: that he was a liar. Though the plaintiff in the action was Peters, the award to him of £300 damages plus costs was clearly influenced by this consideration. Bradlaugh was now so hard-pressed financially he thought he would have to sell his library, even more precious to an *autodidacte* than to a don, but a friend gave him a timely £100.

The debts incurred by *Attorney-General v. Bradlaugh* had not yet been cleared. With the growth of socialism, the rise of the 'New Unionism' during the matchgirls' strike in July 1888 and militant follow-up by Annie Besant and Burrows, and a certain religious revival, secularism was facing stiffer competition. Nor could the *Reformer* now advertise itself as the horse's mouth of one side in a constitutional epic. As a national figure Bradlaugh was much in demand as a lecturer and review journalist, and his last bestseller, *Humanity's Gain from Unbelief*, was commissioned that November by the *North American Review*.[79] But sales were dropping all round and his time was largely consumed with unpaid parliamentary duties and attending to problems in some 1,200 letters a year. In August he mentioned he was too poor to take a holiday. Stead took this up in the *Pall Mall Gazette*, whence it leapt to other journals. An appeal raised £2,490 by his birthday, when he asked for it to close. Mrs Besant, who had forgiven him for getting the National Secular Society to rescind its affiliation to the Law and Liberty League when he read about its anarchist Ironside Circles, was elected in November to the London School Board. It seemed that life was fresh again. Then tragedy disrupted it.

Alice, still helping her father at Circus Road, fell ill with typhoid. Meningitis developed. To escape the traffic she was moved to Avenue Road. Her sister devotedly nursed her. One evening Hypatia was having supper. A nurse and Annie were with the patient. There was a meningitis scream and she rushed upstairs. Alice 'sat up and, in a peculiar high monotonous voice, said that "there is someone in the room who wishes me ill, someone who is watching, watching all the time".'[80] She was of course delirious, but Mrs Besant was watching with a 'still intentness'. Unknown to the Bradlaughs or the world at large she was already dabbling in spiritualism and theosophy, and apparently hoped to see Alice's 'astral body' departing. Whatever she saw, life departed on 2 December 1888. The family, who had been so close, were devastated. Gayest and best-looking of them all, clever, courageous, a fine teacher, she died strangely unfulfilled, leaving only a penny tract *Mind considered as a Bodily Function* behind. Even in death she was defeated. It was her wish to be cremated but the furnace was out of order. Privately and silently she was buried at Brookwood Necropolis.

Annie told Charles it was Hypatia's wish for him to take over the Avenue Road lease. To his relief his daughter assured him it was not.

The expense was too great. But she felt they should be together, so the Bonners moved to Circus Road. Hypatia closed the Hall of Science classes, which Mrs Besant had already left. With Burrows, Annie moved closer to theosophy. She was coming to realize the force of Bradlaugh and Ball's censure of her socialist friends and mob passions. Only religious idealism was the way out, she felt. But not Christianity, with its intolerance and persecution. The following spring she was sitting in the *Reformer* office when a voice asked: 'Are you willing to give up everything for the sake of truth?' 'Yes, Lord.' 'In a short time you will know it.'[81] Two weeks later Stead gave her *The Secret Doctrine* to review anonymously. She asked to meet the author. It was Helena Petrovna Blavatsky, a woman of 'rude and massive' power, with 'the manners of a man, and a very un-conventional man',[82] who had teamed up with Olcott in 1875 to form the Theosophical Society. In May 1889 Mrs Besant formally joined the theosophists. Charlie knew she was 'dabbling in Theosophy, and had sometimes tried to discuss it with her, but her only reply was just a smile'.[83] He learned of her actual conversion through the press. It was his last great disappointment. Whatever HPB might say, he believed 'an Atheist certainly cannot be a Theosophist'.[84]

Throughout this period his parliamentary life flourished. During the debate on the Address in 1888 Balfour admitted that the chief difficulty in the Highlands was overpopulation. Bradlaugh reminded the House how long he had been saying that, and showed how foolish was Balfour's solution of emigration. Britain no longer mono-polized the world's empty spaces, and indigent immigrants were not often welcomed by sovereign states. Bradlaugh himself believed in a humane approach to this subject, and demonstrated it soon after when he was appointed to a Commons Committee on the im-migration of destitute aliens. Most of the immigrants to Britain at that time were refugees from European pogroms. Bradlaugh deplored the hysteria being whipped up by the anti-immigration lobby, which was 'fostering a kind of anti-Jewish cry'.[85] When the Trafalgar Square demonstrations were debated, Bradlaugh forced the Home Secretary to promise an investigation into charges against the police, and also showed that most of the square was not ancient Crown land—the King's Mews—but had been bought with public money. He had another victory when Smith put forward a small amendment to the Perpetual Pensions report and the House then passed it. In politics, however, little is finally won. On 20 July there was a Treasury

Minute naming termination of pensions 'on the same terms as have been accepted in the numerous cases already commuted'. This was twenty-seven years' purchase, which the committee, with the approval of the Attorney-General and then of the House, had declared far too high. It took Bradlaugh almost a year to challenge the minute. A Conservative said to him, 'I agree with you in principle, but it is a small matter.' 'Nothing', he replied, 'is too small to be honest upon, and if you require honesty from the people, you must be honest towards them in all matters, whether they affect £10,000 or £10.'[86]

In May 1888 his motion on the compulsory cultivation of waste lands came up again. In a conciliatory speech Bradlaugh pointed out that the government had accepted the principle of confiscation in Cyprus. The ownership of land carried a moral but not yet a legal duty of cultivation or mining; tenants needed security of tenure before effecting improvements; and the best way to meet the socialist 'storm' was by remedial measures. 'My desire is to avert in England what in Ireland has already become, and in Scotland is gradually becoming, a fearful war between one class of society and another.'[87] But the motion was talked out. The following year he tried again, this time taking advantage of the formation of the county councils, by the 1888 Local Government Act, to put the responsibility for supervising land utilization on the local authorities; but his motion was not discussed. Another disappointment of 1888 was when Smith and the Opposition Front Bench combined to defeat his motion for a new Rule obliging the Speaker to call forward any new member duly presented to take the oath.

One of Bradlaugh's successes, which did little to endear him to the new unionists, was his influence in defeating Sir John Lubbock's Shop Hours (Early Closing) Bill, which sought to limit hours to twelve on five days and fourteen on Saturday. Perhaps overlooking how little bargaining power many of these indentured drudges really had, he argued that the Bill was 'immoral', striking 'a blow at the self-reliance of the individual' and 'opening the door to legislation which might be of the most terrible character'.[88] As usual his enemies oversimplified his objections, representing him as an old-time *laissez faire* man. His basic position was:

'I submit that the Legislature ought not to directly limit the freedom of the adult except in matters of crime, or in matters which, being less or other than crime, are clearly injurious to the life, health, or property of other members of

271

the community.'[89]

To this he added a lawyer's concern to scrape away sentiment and examine the words actually on the paper. If legislation was always to safeguard people's health, then smoking should be banned. There was no appreciation, he said, of the possibility of shift work or the desires of one-man retailers. Public-houses and tobacconists were arbitrarily excluded; while the 1677 Sunday Observance Act, concerned to uphold 'the duties of piety and true religion'[90] and not the rights of man, was renewed with increased penalties.

Fiercer winds in radical circles eddied round the Employers' Liability Bill.[91] Backed by Harcourt, Broadhurst denounced it as 'this sham, misleading, mischievous Bill, than which a worse one had never been presented to the House'.[92] It was a modest enough measure, extending the general provisions of the 1880 Act without radical changes. The unions objected to employers' contracting-out and seemed to believe the alternative of compulsory insurance would encourage negligence. Particularly did they condemn the 'common employment' loophole. While agreeing he was not satisfied, Bradlaugh supported the Bill. It was, he said, an improvement on Broadhurst's own Trade Unions Bill of 1886 and he suspected the opposition was mere party manoeuvring, which he disliked whoever was responsible. But his accusation that this response 'tried to set the employed against the employer'[93] was certain to be quoted out of context.

What became a popular cyclone, however, twisting through the last years of his life, was an agitation for the eight-hour day. This reached a peak in 1890. In May, Burns challenged him to a debate to be 'heard' by 200,000 and voted upon. When Bradlaugh declined such impossible conditions Hyndman, now in dispute with Burns, who was working with Champion and Tom Mann outside the Social Democratic Federation, issued a friendlier invitation, which Bradlaugh accepted. The debate was fixed for 23 July at St James's Hall, with Sydney Buxton, MP, in the chair. Bradlaugh had written an influential article the previous year setting out his position: he was 'thoroughly and earnestly in favour of shortening hours of labour to the lowest point consistent with the profitable conduct of each industry' but 'most decidedly opposed'[94] to legislation. A noisy opposition which nagged at his now failing health turned up. Hyndman conceded 'that in certain respects what he has done in the House of Commons has been beneficial with regard to the workers'. That was because 'the moment Mr Bradlaugh very much wished to

272

carry something which he considered for the benefit of the working classes, he dropped all his talk about Trade Unions, and at once appealed to the Legislature to enforce that which he knew Trade Unionists could not by themselves do'.[95] This was the true position with the eight-hour day. As distinct from the debate on socialism with its large abstractions, Bradlaugh was now on the ground of practical politics and it was his opponents who often swam in naive economics.[96] He argued that with sudden intervention 'the bulk of the textile industries in this country would be ruined at once'; 'no hard and fast rule can be made which could apply or ought to apply to all industries'; thrift is 'the life and soul of our country'; and to regulate cottage industries you must 'allow the police spies to come into your home and say how long you shall work'.[97] In a subsequent article he remained unrepentant: 'Much still may be gradually achieved alike for skilled and unskilled, if men will rely more on themselves and look less for salvation to paper statutes.'[98]

In July 1888 he had given evidence before the Royal Commission on Market Rights and Tolls. His main submission was that they should be purchased by county councils or county boroughs, which had adequate purchasing power, and administered by the local district or small borough. Tolls 'ought never to be in relief of the rates'[99] but only to cover expenses. If no market accommodation at all had been provided by the present owner there should be no compensation; if inadequate, payment up to seven times the net annual receipts; if adequate, purchase at full freehold value. In the same month he again attacked *laissez-faire* when appointed to a seventeen-member Select Committee 'to inquire into and report upon the operation of section 30 of "The Friendly Societies Act, 1875", as amended by subsequent Acts',[100] and of the collecting societies and industrial assurance companies that handled insurance. Originating as pools of friendly co-operative endeavour, they had been invaded by sharks who found the fishing better than in ordinary limited liability companies. With imperfect supervision they had, in extreme cases, harboured octopi of multiple insurance, baby farming and mass poisoning. They were supposed to handle sick pay benefits as well as life assurance, but found the latter more profitable. Not paying out immediately, they could cream off much of the takings as 'expenses'. The assurance companies were worse as the policy-holder had no vote. Decrepit companies were kept alive and sold to speculators, 'thus getting outside the provision of the Life Assurance Companies Act requiring a deposit of £20,000'.[101] Some agents liked old business to lapse as new business brought them higher fees. Others paid some premiums out of their own pockets, fell into difficulties, and had to sell their books for a song to a paid official, who collected a transfer fee and then farmed the business out to collectors on commission. These officials also got an 'enormous amount paid in salaries' and 'when once in office they seem immovable'.[102] It was the sort of investigation for which Bradlaugh was ideally suited and for which, with its surface dullness, there were few rival candidates.

But his greatest parliamentary achievement of 1888, and the only one generally remembered, was the Oaths Act. Among its sponsors, which included Conservative and religious members, were Burt, Simon, Courtney Kenny, Collings, and the Non-conformists, Alfred Illingworth and Henry Richard. In Bradlaugh's second reading speech on 14 March he cited many omissions and difficulties of the existing law. Otherwise suitable jurors were unable to take the oath or affirm; if they did so without entitlement, verdicts might be set aside; JPs' commissions might be similarly challenged; there were painful wrangles in coroners' courts over the oath; the 1869 and 1870 Acts did not technically include religious witnesses who considered an oath had a 'binding effect' on their consciences (and thus could not affirm) but had no belief in 'a future state of rewards and punishments' (and thus could not swear); the Acts did not extend to Scotland; affirmation of allegiance was available only to Quakers, Moravians and Separatists, though other Christians opposed the oath too. He scarcely mentioned his own past occupancy of 'a position which often becomes intolerable'.[103] The vote in favour of 250:100 'surpassed his most sanguine expectations',[104] though his undertaking to allow an inquisition into the reasons for affirmation, so that Christians could not simply dodge the oath, caused later unexpected bother from certain Liberals, including Hunter, John Morley and his own constituency organization. James Allinson Picton, MP, a heretical, former Congregationalist minister, said the new qualification for affirmation—'either that he has no religious belief, or that the taking of an oath is contrary to his religious belief'[105]—would not help him as he had a religious belief but his objection to the oath was on intellectual, not religious grounds. Freethinking witnesses have since met prejudice by avowing they have 'no religious belief'. Bradlaugh would like to have abolished the oath altogether, but the time was not ripe.[106] On third reading the Bill passed 147:60. In the absence of Herschell, Earl Spencer, briefed by Bradlaugh and helped by Coleridge, piloted it through the Lords. Halsbury abstained and the

Archbishop of Canterbury, Edward Benson, supported it. Bradlaugh demanded a vote of confidence from his constituents. It was carried unanimously.

On 21 August 1888 another great meeting was held at Northampton Town Hall. In the chair was Covington, the new mayor. Two eminent Indians, Dadabhai Naoroji and W.C. Bonnerjee, addressed the people in the heart of England's 'tight little isle'. They told them of the plight of distant millions whom they would never see, exploited and disenfranchised, undernourished and often starving. Charles Bradlaugh knew of their plight. He had studied it for years. He was anxious to be their voice in the mother of parliaments. But, they admitted, it was complex and difficult work. It would take up much of his time and reduce what was available for his Northampton constituents. In one of those rare acts of political generosity, the people said they would gladly make the sacrifice and Bradlaugh was 'nobly consecrated ... "Member for India" '.[107]

Next session the new member was responsible for 'saving lakhs of human lives'[108] when he raised the question of famine in Ganjam. Both the British Government and the Madras Presidency, on the basis of their briefing, denied its existence, but Gorst, 'knowing Mr Bradlaugh would not persevere unless he had good information, wired to the Governor of Madras to make special and immediate inquiries'.[109] The governor found that Bradlaugh was correct and took immediate relief measures. Then the British watchdog asked how such things could go unnoticed, and what about the Famine Insurance Fund. At first it was denied that such a fund existed, but Bradlaugh had no difficulty in showing that since 1878 a special annual tax of £1,500,000 had been levied 'for the purpose of providing ... an insurance against famine, and for no other purpose whatever'.[110] Instead the money had, over the years, been spent on 'war and annexation and the erection of costly buildings at Simla, and for similar purposes, while the people of India have been starving'.[111] He passed on to denounce the whole British attitude to India. It was the end of August, with the House in committee and most of its members off for the recess, the only occasion year by year when time could be found to discuss the destinies of between 200 and 300 million people. He gestured scathingly round the chamber. Only the Under-Secretary for India to represent the government, none of the leaders of his own party present. If more suitable opportunities were not provided he would raise Indian questions by an amendment to the Address. He had other complaints. Salt duty had been raised 25%; mining concessions were granted in secrecy; the provincial councils of India had too few native representatives and powers; there should be a Committee of the House or a Joint Standing Committee of both Houses to study Indian questions.

In his speech Bradlaugh quoted the Marquess of Dufferin and Ava, a former Viceroy and now the ambassador to Rome. During the Jubilee celebrations at Calcutta Dufferin had said of educated Indians: 'Nor do I regard with any other feelings than those of approval and good-will their natural ambition to be more extensively associated with their English rulers in the administration of their own domestic affairs.'[112] In November 1888 he gave his farewell address. A garbled version of his mild criticism of the Indian National Congress appeared in the *Times*. Bradlaugh attacked this at Newcastle and another garbled version reached Dufferin at Rome. His secretary assured the member for India that the ambassador had been misrepresented, sent a transcript of his speech, and added in confidence 'that he himself has been doing his very best to forward such a reform of the Provincial Councils in India as Mr Bradlaugh appears to advocate'.[113] This was the Congress proposal that at least half the members should be elected and the remainder consist equally of officials and government nominees. Both Bradlaugh and Congress wanted the same arrangement for the Governor-General's Council too, but Dufferin thought it best to wait and see how the provincial reforms turned out.

Following a friendly reply from Bradlaugh the ambassador said he 'should esteem it a great pleasure if I might be allowed to make your acquaintance',[114] which he did the next time he was in London. A most cordial confidential correspondence proceeded. Dufferin was delighted that Indian matters were 'in the hands of a prudent, wise, and responsible person like yourself, instead of having been laid hold of by some adventurous *frais tireur*, whose only object might possibly have been to let off a few fireworks for his own glorification'.[115] With absolute impartiality Bradlaugh pursued his brief, trying to approach every question as the Indians themselves would. Though an atheist and republican, he protested at misappropriation of the foundation funds, jewels and other property belonging to the *chattra* and temples of Benares, and at the deposition of Maharaja Pratap Singh of Jammu and Kashmir with 'neither judicial, nor Parliamentary, nor Governmental inquiry'.[116] Among Indian moderates he thus became 'one of the immortals of history',[117] though Indian revolutionaries did not appreciate this old-world regard for

276

their *ancien régime*.

After the triumph of his Oaths Act in 1888, he essayed two new Bills the following year. That for abolishing political pensions soon came to grief. His Religious Prosecutions Abolition Bill inspired an interesting second reading debate in April. It was the Kenny Bill modified to exclude the 'Indian clause'. In an attempt to conciliate religious opposition, this clause had been imported from the Penal Code of a country peculiarly sensitive to religious riots and obsessively anxious for everyone to avoid 'wounding with deliberate intention the religious feelings of his neighbours by words, gestures, or exhibitions'.[118] While sympathetic to the spirit of this provision, English freethinkers considered a literal enforcement could stifle free discussion altogether. When he looked again at Blackstone and Stephen, Bradlaugh was forced to question Coleridge's liberal interpretation of the Blasphemy Laws in *R. v. Foote and others*. These laws the infidel considered both dangerous and unnecessary, since truly offensive behaviour was always actionable as likely to cause a breach of the peace. What he sought was abatement of 'that kind of unfortunate spirit which treats opinion as if it were a crime'.[119] This attitude drew out its own vicious circle, so that when he tried to moderate the anticlerical zeal of his French friends they replied: 'The Church shows us no mercy.' Bradlaugh's Bill was, however, defeated 141:46. He was equally unsuccessful in his efforts to secure a Royal Commission on Indian grievances, or to persuade the Public Service Commission significantly to increase native Indian personnel. At the same time and in the same spirit of reconciliation, Annie Besant tried to persuade English socialists and radicals to unite. She also failed.

At the beginning of June 1889, encouraged by a Darlington friend, Bradlaugh accepted an invitation to sit on the Royal Commission on Vaccination, the establishment of which he had first urged over twenty years before. With that remarkable flair for adaptation to change which characterized her later years, Victoria found it possible to designate the atheist republican as 'Our Trusty and Well beloved' adviser. Vaccination was still a field over which medical and libertarian controversy raged, as with fluoridation of drinking water today. Many laymen continued to regard it—as, alas, was sometimes the case—as 'poisoning the blood with diseased pus'[120] by admitting 'a loathsome virus derived from the blood of a diseased brute'.[121] Some parents preferred prison to allowing their 'poor innocent and helpless children to be poisoned, tortured, and killed without the power of thinking, judging, and refusing for themselves'.[122] These libertarian

277

arguments were especially strong among secularists and other radicals. Apart from anthropology, in which Bradlaugh did a lot of reading in 1882, when the subject reached England as a new revelation of human unity in diversity, Bradlaugh had made no special study of science. But he had excellent advisers and was always anxious to avoid well-meaning crankiness. As a colleague on the commission, Dr W.J. Collins, said of him, he was not only admirable with witnesses but had a fine 'grasp of even pathological intricacies'.[123] This new responsibility he faced with his accustomed integrity, and he declined to open up to lobbyists or even to his own family. 'I do not think when sitting in a quasi-judicial position', he said, 'I ought to express opinions until the conclusion of the evidence.'[124] His own death, however, supervened and whatever conclusions he may have formulated died with him.[125]

Meanwhile his kaleidoscopic interests whirled faster. He was invited to speak at a peace demonstration in Milan. Watching Europe flexing for war, 'a most fearful demoralizer of human kind', he urged her peoples 'to unite to compel permanent disarmament'.[126] Asquith transmitted to him a report on South African prisons, assuring the atheist that its author, the Rev. J.F. Philip, 'is known to me to be a person of respectability'.[127] This comment was a curious inversion of former attitudes. The next tribute to Bradlaugh came when the South Shields branch of the newly formed National Amalgamated Sailors' and Firemen's Union of Great Britain presented him with a framed address 'as a mark of respect for his services in bringing forward the grievances of Seamen in the House of Commons'.[128] In London the great event of the late summer of 1889 was the dock strike organized by Burns, Mann, and especially Ben Tillett, a young Congregationalist who was secretary of the small Tea Operatives and General Workers' Union. The non-unionist who got all the credit for assistance—and he did work hard in the negotiation of a settlement—was Manning; but Tillett later acknowledged it was Mrs Besant and 'the great Charles Bradlaugh' who 'helped me in drawing up the rules of the Dockers' Union'[129] which was then formed. To finance all this voluntary work, and his constituency duties, Bradlaugh also had to cope with ceaseless editing, lecturing and review journalism. Olcott called on him at this time and thought how old he was looking. Unlike Holyoake, who always recouped his strength inside welcoming country houses and who had married again and moved into a comfortable home at Brighton, Bradlaugh would not relax, or concentrate on remunerative activities, or move to more congenial quarters. The inevitable happened. He fell seriously ill. Ramskill and Collins poured out their medical skill, and the devoted Hypatia her care. Annie told public meetings she was exhausted looking after him, though Hypatia recalled that 'she did not nurse him for a single hour'[130] but worried him by saying she was going on a lecture tour of the States and might not live to return. At last he pulled through, but Foote was 'shocked by his appearance. He looked twenty years older, grey, and infirm.'[131] His doctors insisted he go away and he was too weak to resist.

They suggested a long sea voyage to India. Indeed, he had always wanted to visit his 'constituency' and address Congress, but there was the expense. A parliamentary colleague, William McEwan, delicately sent a cheque for £200 and Bradlaugh set sail. In his absence Annie edited the *Reformer*. On 23 December 1889 he reached Bombay. As soon as he was installed like a visiting potentate, a river of distinguished individuals and deputations from all the provinces began to flow past him, depositing their addresses and scrolls, silks and caskets of silver, sandalwood and ivory. As he wrote to Hypatia, 'The poor Hindoo folk seem inclined almost to worship me.'[132] The financial difficulties of Bradlaugh and his family could have been permanently resolved. Wealthy businessmen and envoys of the princes called with money and jewels; but he took the precaution of having an English friend in the room with him, and the compromising tributes were taken away again. As he said to Foote on his return: 'No, I cannot do that. I'll live like the old Bradlaugh, or I'll go under.'[133] Fiercely independent, he had already declined Labby's offer of a company directorship or the financing of his reading for the bar. In the caskets and the scroll-holders came the formal messages of adulation. Captious minority voices were later to question 'whether Mr Bradlaugh really did anything for India which deserved the extravagant praise which was allotted to him both on his demise and during the later years of his life';[134] but most observers agreed that, within the traditions of Indian hyperbole, the appreciations were richly justified. They stressed the people's loyalty to Britain and to their native princes, satisfaction with English justice and technological help, but concern at the expense, centralization and undemocratic structure of the administration. Bradlaugh was placed in the tradition of Burke, Macaulay, Fawcett and Bright, and, by at least seven of the deputations, in the loving care of the Almighty.

Five days after his arrival in Bombay the election meeting of the fifth Congress[135] took place under the presidency of the retired

Indian civil servant, Sir William Wedderburn, an Englishman who had travelled out with Bradlaugh. Four thousand delegates were present from every part and most of the races and religions of India. But dissident groups flashed grim portents of trouble. 'At an outside meeting of Mahommedans, it was resolved "that the Mahommedans, as a community, are opposed to the Indian National Congress".'[136] While Muslims inside the Congress repudiated this attitude, the *Times* was able to assert that it was a British duty 'to keep the peace between these traditional combatants'.[137] Dissident Rajpoots, Parsees and Mahrattas also opposed Congress. The following day, far from well and almost suffocated by goodwill, Bradlaugh, the first MP to visit Congress, gave its closing cheer-drenched speech. Though some delegates thought his Indian Bill did not go far enough and Sir Madhava Row believed his proposed House Committee on Indian affairs would lack both knowledge and authority, his policies had been overwhelmingly endorsed. Calling for unity across the subcontinent and across the sea to Britain, he expressed delight that 'in its infancy so many have joined' Congress and pledged himself to 'speak that which seems to me to be right and true'.[138] Too weak to travel round India as he would have liked, he returned home in early January.

His illness had shown he must shed some of his work burden and financial responsibilities. He at once resolved to give up publishing and the Fleet Street lease and make Bonner the owner of the printing works he ran. He told his daughter he would also resign from the secularist presidency. She begged him to pause; she knew how much it had meant to him down the years. But chiefly she thought of the way a sudden departure during grave illness would be misinterpreted. He urged that the work was too much and he would not be a president in name only, but agreed to wait till his return from India. Perhaps there was disappointment as well as overwork. In the secular movement he had known and worked with thousands of sterling people from all walks of life, who seemed to incarnate his thesis that secular was superior to Christian morality. But he had also met very different characters, and so often they were its most vocal and self-righteous prophets. There was a limit to the vilification an honorary worker could take. And there was the disappointment of contraction in the movement. He had never minded joining two or three gathered together in the name of truth; indeed he liked the challenge of rocketing earth-bound payloads into space. But he was also success-oriented and did not like causes to crumple in his hands. So much of the secular programme was unfulfilled, and yet people were already drifting off into socialism or unionism, even theosophy. He had been so proud to refer year by year to the growing membership of the National Secular Society. By the time the 1890 *Almanack* went to press his annual message made no reference to the society at all.

In the broad freethought movement more serious fissiparous influences were at work. When Conway resigned from South Place in 1885 there was difficulty in finding a successor. Two years later he suggested Stanton Coit, a philosopher and disciple of Felix Adler, the founder of Ethical Culture in New York. Coit made no effort to study English conditions and imported grandiose plans to take over, 'rationalize' and 'ethicize' the Church of England. Though ostensibly he had abandoned theology altogether, his 'ethical society' was more liturgical than the old 'religious society'. And, as a by-product rather than a calculation, he attracted a new type of member. Conway's flock were mainly well-to-do professional people. But while the Conwayites were middle-class as a matter of sociology, the Coitites, generally poorer and less intellectual, were bourgeois as a matter of conviction. In a genteel way the 'class struggle' entered a movement from which it had hitherto been absent. Accompanying this was a rise of Holyoake's type of mental fuzziness. To some extent this reflected the late nineteenth-century discovery that the world was more complex than mechanistic science had thought. But it included less sophisticated and creditable considerations. At the very time that Bradlaugh had won through and made atheism more or less respectable, agnosticism was taken up by more and more people as 'a mere society form of Atheism'. [139] The Agnostic Depot crowd was no challenge. Just as ambitious, but free of scandal and a better organizer, was C.A. Watts, who in 1885 established the *Agnostic Annual* and a shortlived *Agnostic*. Three years later Holyoake and he conceived a modest Propaganda Press Committee, [140] which was to become a new, and viable, off-Fleet Street House.

On his return from India Bradlaugh went ahead with his plans for resigning the secularist presidency. 'He would have wished to nominate J.M. Robertson, but he did not think organizing and directing a Society was at all in his line.' [141] In the 1889 *Almanack* Robertson had already slipped back in the hierarchy. Mrs Besant was still second. Despite her theosophy she expected Bradlaugh to nominate her. It was, of course, quite out of the question. So he chose Foote 'because there was no one else'. Despite competition and contraction in the movement, there was still no shortage—and is not today—of able secular writers, lecturers and debaters prepared to devote their time. But Foote was the only one to combine the right practical and intellectual gifts, to be nationally known, and to edit a prospering weekly. On 16 February 1890 a special meeting was called at the Hall of Science. Members flooded in from London and the provinces. Tears swam down many faces. Bradlaugh rose to speak. Only a sob came out and he sat down. Again he tried, and broke down. But there was no emotion he could not crush in his hand like an egg, and the third time he succeeded. He spoke with a quiet compulsive earnestness that thrilled them all. Whatever his enemies might say, he wanted them to know that the sun of freethought still shone upon him and only his physical powers were in the shade. He nominated his successor, the meeting approved, and he handed over his gavel— Richard Carlile's gavel, that had passed down the apostolic succession—to Foote. Then he tried to vacate the chair. Foote would not let him, so he presided till the end of the meeting. Two weeks later Mrs Besant resigned. Bradlaugh continued as 'the Chief' to every member.

It was another crammed year politically. His Indian Councils Bill had a rival in that of Viscount Cross, the Secretary of State for India. With a former Viceroy, the Marquess of Ripon, a Catholic who had been one of Gladstone's most successful as well as controversial appointments, Bradlaugh discussed an amendment: 'That the House expresses its regret that in proposing by this Bill to increase the number of the additional Members of the Indian Councils for making laws and regulations, no recognition is given to the Elective Principle.'[142] Then he turned to revenue questions. When he had imported his Indian gifts, Congress paid the £19 duty. Later he managed to persuade the government to remove duties on works of art, but not the duty on and hallmarking of gold and silver, an issue he raised for the Financial Reform Association. Increasingly, however, as Bright's disease[143] crept on him, he grew obsessively anxious for the House to expunge its resolution of 22 June 1880, denying him both the oath and an affirmation, as being (after the precedent of a century before with Wilkes) 'subversive of the rights of the whole body of electors of this Kingdom'.[144] The Tories demurred. Yet other advances in tolerance were made. Smith's company now offered to handle the *Reformer*, though this was declined as alternative arrangements had been made. Gladstone sent Harcourt to sound Bradlaugh out on joining a future government. 'I will not,' he said, 'accept office and become a Minister of the Crown so long as the Resolution concerning my expulsion from the House remains on the

Charles Bradlaugh in later years

Records. Let Mr Gladstone promise that its removal shall be one of the first things he will accomplish on entering office, and I shall be proud to accept a seat in his administration.'[145] The promise was given. Hitherto Bradlaugh's political career had been a one-man, one-constituency crusade. This year, for the first time, he attended the National Liberal Federation rally at Sheffield, where he was called on to speak. He was now a member of the National Liberal Club, which had quietly accepted him the year before. At the next election the Northampton Tories intended to oppose only Labby. But he felt death already bustling around him.

It was a great satisfaction when, in April, Hypatia bore a son, who was called Charles. Mary Reed took over as his secretary. Digby and Mabel returned to Annie, who denounced Parnell's adultery with Kitty O'Shea, which killed him politically. Bradlaugh was anxious to save his business partner from financial disasters. He drove himself on, lecturing like a record, writing like a computer. The interest was somehow paid on the debentures, but how could he ever free the capital? In August he swallowed his pride and wrote round to the holders proposing a scheme of buying them out at some sacrifice to themselves. The answer was almost unanimous. They would like to help, but they had their own responsibilities. Towards the end of the year the Fleet Street shop was closed and the partnership between Bradlaugh and Mrs Besant dissolved. Their shares in secular halls went to the National Secular Society, the publishing business to Forder and the printing to Bonner. Bradlaugh totted up his estimated assets and liabilities, making the one (including 'legacies due to be paid') £8,623 and the other £6,673. Hypatia, who had just fitted up a sitting room on the first floor, suggested selling some books to finance a holiday. 'Ah! my daughter, when I have to part with my books . . . '[146] He gave his last lectures: 'My Heresy—its Justification' to the Chatham Secular Society, to show his living unbelief, and a testimonial to Forder on 'The Evidence for the Gospels', which was where he came in.

The winter of 1891 was particularly cold. On 10 January he went out on a foggy afternoon. Cold seeped into him and would not leave. At home his vast correspondence continued. The order papers of the new parliamentary session were already filling up with notices in his name: 26th—a question on the closing of a Board infant school at Rawnsley, Staffordshire; 27th—a question on 'certain specific charges of grave character' at Portsmouth Dockyard, and the expunging motion; 28th—questions on the value of the French system of registering and recognizing prisoners and on the trial and exile of Sultan Abdullah of Perak, and the second reading of his Indian Councils Act (1861) Amendment Bill; undated—motions on the appointment of thirteen Select Committees to examine the estimates prior to the Committee of Supply, removing the 'common employment' loophole in employers' liability, abolishing compulsory hallmarking, giving local authorities powers over unused land. On the 11th Gladstone sanctioned the issue of a three-line whip to support the expunging motion.

Two days later Bradlaugh had 'a terrible attack in the night'[147] of cardiac asthma. Reluctantly he had to take to his bed in the new sitting-room and cancel his engagements. Still he could not rest. So he set about mastering the latest accounts of the Salvation Army, which had of recent years tried to provoke disturbances at secularist rallies and was suspected of tycoonery behind a mask of poverty. But a crushing weariness was on him, and he wished to be spared visitors. He particularly asked for Annie, who often 'worried him with her own personal matters',[148] not to be allowed in. This put Hypatia in an embarrassing position as her excuses became increasingly threadbare. At last Mrs Besant wrote:

> 'Certainly I will do nothing to disturb your father, though, if he goes, it will be hard enough not to have seen him during the last days. You say he has "not even seen Mrs Reed". But I do not think that seeing his secretary and the admission for a moment of the nearest and dearest friend he has had through all his life are quite on a par. However let it be so. You might tell the servant, when I send, to let me know how he really is: not the answer given to the press or strangers.'[149]

As Hypatia read through Annie's letter at her father's bedside, he noted her embarrassment and insisted on hearing the reason. 'Oh! let her come in', he sighed. Hypatia wrote and Annie delightedly promised to call on her way back from the School Board, if that was no bother. It was no bother. Hypatia left the two alone.

What was to be said? Ideologically they had drifted a long way apart. And personally? If they had lived in a less censorious age, if they had been plain Charlie and Annie of back-street seclusion, if they had not themselves been wedded to vows and responsibilities that coupled past to future, shutting out the present, if . . . Would Mrs Annie Bradlaugh have put on the red scarf of revolution or trodden the paths of mysticism? Now it was too late. But from the moment they met it had been too late. 'She did not remain many minutes. I believe my father hardly spoke to her, if at all. She did not ask to see him again until after his death.'[150]

It became clear that Bradlaugh would be unable to present his expunging motion on the 27th. The Speaker sent his sympathy and prayers were offered up in many churches. Hunter was deputed to introduce the motion. The Commons Librarian believed it was 'a bad precedent and practice for one Parliament to review and erase from the Journal of the House any resolution of a previous Parliament . . whatever injustice may have been done . . . It is right that the Journals of the House should bear what was *actually done* at the time.'[151] This was the view the government took. When the debate came on, Hunter spoke with his usual lucidity. Edward Clarke opposed the motion. The 'infamous scoundrel' Wilkes, he said with a measure of justification, was no fit precedent. In that case the action was taken after thirteen years—longer than in the present instance— and only through his 'importunity'. To Clarke it seemed 'childish to strike out from the records of the House an incident which must remain celebrated in the history of this House'. Gladstone urged the justice of the motion, but suggested omitting its 'subversive' climax. Iddesleigh's son, the new Sir Stafford Northcote, rose to declare an 'hereditary interest'. As the members strained eagerly forward, he urged the government not to quibble over technicalities and 'to recognize fully the good service which the junior Member for North-ampton has rendered in the House'. Smith relented. Praising Bradlaugh as 'undoubtedly a valuable addition to this House', he offered to accept the motion with Gladstone's amendment. On be-half of Bradlaugh, Labby said he would be quite content. Hunter agreed. While expressing 'deep regret' at the member's illness, the Catholic Edwin de Lisle rebuked an 'assembly which legalizes atheism and whitewashes treason'; but Sir Walter Barttelot called for unanimous support of 'a generous act to a man who has endeavoured to do his duty'.[152] The motion was put and carried *nem. con.* amid cheers.

Hunter telegraphed the news to Circus Road, but Bradlaugh was too ill to be disturbed. Gladstone's son Herbert at once wrote 'to congratulate you most warmly on the historic triumph which you have won'.[153] The following morning 'Old Morality' Smith, who in times of crisis always showed real fatherly interest in the whole House, went round to the simple lodgings to deliver the an-nouncement personally. Ritchie also called; and the Prince of Wales, who appreciated a 'doughty assailant',[154] had anxious enquiries made. From the Colonial Office de Worms sent a message hoping soon to have him back in the House 'as it is always a pleasure to cross swords with so fair and courteous an opponent as yourself'.[155] Bradlaugh now had constant attention. There were two nurses and frequent visits from Doctors Bell, Ramskill and Bristowe, another colleague on the Vaccination Commission. Hypatia worked incessantly, co-ordinating their activities, recording that throughout his illness her father spoke on religious subjects only with herself—'he merely uttered a few words as to the futility of the Design Argument'[156]—and controlling the vultures who clustered and croaked on the threshold for hot news when he was cold.

On the evening of the 29th his condition suddenly deteriorated. At about 6.30 a.m. the following morning the long vigil was over. Bell certified chronic renal disease and uremia. Messages of sympathy flashed in. Obituary comment flashed out. Most of it was sane, informed, sympathetic, eulogistic. Some was enlivened with reminiscence and anecdote. A few French rags[157] said he had many children by Annie Besant. Charles Watts and Ross paid glowing tributes in their journals. Holyoake joined Foote and Forder at a memorial service in the Hall of Science.

In his will of 1884 Bradlaugh had specified: 'I direct . . . that my body be buried as cheaply as possible and that no speeches be permitted at my funeral.'[158] Though this was not repeated in his last will, Hypatia felt it was still his wish. She also knew he would want to lie beside his wife, sister-in-law, grandson and daughter at Brookwood. The funeral was announced for 2.30 p.m. on 3 February. It was expected that it would be no ordinary event and a special train was advertised from the necropolis platform at Waterloo. Meetings were held throughout the country. Without embarrassment the Victorians faced up to death, enacted their grief and prepared for life again. This time they would do it with a certain difference. Bradlaugh wanted no artificial trappings. As Chief Priest of Secularism he had pricked the ceremonies and set-piece orations and let the flatulence escape. In his ministry to the needy, Coit complained, 'he never stopped to speak words of sympathy for the destitute—he was always rushing to remedies'.[159] Bradlaugh knew there would never be a shortage of eloquent sympathizers whose practical help was always cut short by the call of a waiting dinner. In death protestations were yet more futile. Mourning clothes and mummers were mute. It was the heart that spoke.

The day of the funeral came. Some had perhaps thought that a special train for a backbencher's ceremony was excessive, especially for a man who was far from clubbable, who had few close friends. They were mistaken. As the mourners turned up in twos and threes from all over the country and all walks of life it became clear that not one, but three special trains would be needed. Charlie's wishes were well advertised and they came as if for a special Sunday excursion or a miner's gala. There was a great contingent from Northampton, gay with rosettes of green, mauve and white. The legislature was represented by Queensberry and Liberal MPs including Picton, Hunter, Burt, Labouchere, Cremer and a lively newcomer David Lloyd George. John Morley wondered whether or not to come, but arrived just before the train left at 1.30 p.m. Gertrude, Countess Schack, Mrs Emmeline Pankhurst and Mrs Herbert Burrows represented the Women's Franchise League. Among a large contingent of Indians was a studious-looking law student Mohandas Gandhi. Soldiers were usually absent from public funerals save those state occasions to which they were drafted, but the Queen's uniform was prominent that day. Bret Ince, secretary of the Vaccination Commission, was there with Henry Rooke, secretary of the Market Rights and Tolls Commission, who had been planning to enter into business with Bradlaugh. One Conservative member had regretted being unable to be present because he did not know 'what my clergyman would say',[160] but clergymen like the faithful Headlam came themselves. Other battles stirred to life with the approach of Casson, Truelove, Burrows, Maxse, the secularist leadership and Holyoake.

But mostly the mourners melted into a crowd of anonymous grief. There were miners from the north of England, his traditional friends, and even from Hamilton in Scotland, grateful for the collapse of truck. There were sailors and firemen, journalists on and off duty, outdoor customs men, postal telegraph clerks, jobbing printers, upholsterers, machine workers, stalwarts from trades councils and working men's clubs. The Christian Social Reform League, Good Templars, Financial Reform Association, Cobden Club, of which he was a member, International Arbitration League, Royal Masonic Institution for Boys, so richly endowed by successful litigation it had made him a patron, the Brighton Anarchists and Toynbee Hall were all represented. Liberal and Radical Associations and secular societies from up and down the country sent their delegates and unofficial members. Shortly after 1.0 p.m. the chief mourners arrived: the Bonners, his sisters Elizabeth Norman and Emma Bradlaugh, Annie Besant. Though her life was eviscerated by the loss, Hypatia stepped along with the bravery she knew he expected of her. Only Mrs Besant in the whole vast crowd came in black and heavily veiled. Hypatia recalled suggestively it was 'the only time I ever saw her wearing a veil and it made her conspicuous'.[161] But this was the only time Charles Bradlaugh had ever died.

The trains reached Brookwood and the procession to the grave began. There were six pall-bearers: four Northampton veterans of the 1868 campaign,[162] William Digby and Robertson. Digby represented the British Committee of the Indian National Congress; Robertson, British freethought. Not surprisingly, Foote turned up expecting to occupy the sixth place; but Hypatia had chosen Robertson 'as one who loved her Father, was ever loyal and devoted to him, and was most closely connected with him in many ways—and who stood high in his personal affection and esteem'.[163] Oblivious of these arrangements, wondering how much his own past defection had added to the burdens which dragged the Chief into premature death, and feeling miserably isolated at the head of an eroded and rebellious freethought empire, the creation of which he saw as Bradlaugh's greatest achievement, Foote in his confusion put himself at the head of the procession. Hypatia scarcely noticed. But, asking 'how he dared come between the daughter and her dead father',[164] Annie thrust him aside, pushing harder than was strictly necessary. Then she grabbed Hypatia's arm and they set off for the graveside. There the *papier-mâché* earth-to-earth coffin with its simple brass plate was laid down. White flowers heaped upon it. The finest were from Her Majesty's Customs and the Nottingham secularists, with an inscription 'Brave, honest, incorruptible, thorough'. W.R. Bradlaugh sent a wreath labelled 'Robert's last token of a brother's love' and quoting Job 33, 15-16. No words were spoken as the coffin was lowered. The family stood a few moments at the graveside, then moved away.

Fifty marshals, mostly from the secular society, guided the other mourners in single file round the grave. Hardly a person was there out of a sense of duty, or to see a good show. They came with simple gratitude and love. A few were loyal co-workers. Most of them had little personal knowledge of him but knew what he had done. On the whole they were from the working or lower middle classes. By no means affluent, they could yet look back on a life of progress. Their children were better fed and clothed and went to better schools than themselves; building and friendly societies were giving many of them the security of homes and life assurance; most of the men among them had the vote and a strong trade union. Less tangibly, they had a new sense of dignity and a place in society, and were freer to think for themselves, say what they thought, do what they wanted to on Sunday, and even get buried as they liked. The national cake had risen with the yeast of the industrial and scientific revolutions and the spices of empire—great forces attributable to no individual. Yet the wider sharing out of the cake was largely due to the man in the grave at their feet. The more perceptive of them could see struggles and difficulties ahead. In the popular firmament there were shooting stars that promised greater victories, but would they ever come to earth with the pot of gold? As the mourners shuffled round, lost in speculation, one of them suddenly cried out, 'Oh, Charlie, this is no place for you yet.'[165] The Northamptonites cast their rosettes into the open grave. There would be other elections, but none like those they had known. After an hour and a quarter the last step had gone, and gravediggers and devoted volunteers closed the account.

POSTSCRIPT

Many of those who came together at Brookwood fell apart afterwards. Even efforts to raise memorials to their common hero built up little but disappointment and bitterness and, as the contestants wrangled, the work of the man they hoped to honour faltered and stumbled. It was soon apparent that Bradlaugh's estimate of his liabilities was accurate enough, but that of his assets was wildly optimistic. First casualty was the sum set aside for expected legacies, but other items were almost equally nugatory. The *Reformer* copyright was still valued at £1,000; but it was largely a personal journal and Robertson, who took over the editorship, had to abandon it in 1893. Even Bradlaugh's own copyrights—exhaustive tracts on causes already won, abandoned, or increasingly needing to be 'jazzed up' for the naughty nineties—slumped heavily in demand when the author was no longer there to invest them with his own charisma. His library was of unique value to a social historian, but, contrary to his own opinion, had little in it for which bibliophiles of the day were prepared to pay good money. The printing business largely depended on the skill of Arthur Bonner and had little goodwill in its own right. When Hypatia left the National Secular Society before the year was out, it had even less. There was the lease of 63 Fleet Street, but at a forced sale it would realize only part of its value of £1,000. The Bonners managed to borrow enough to pay urgent debts, such as £34 in taxes, to avoid distraint, but wondered what to do about the debenture-holders, who were creditors to the tune of £5,926.

At the beginning of March Annie, though angry that Hypatia had been made sole executrix, joined her in an appeal to them to forgo part of their claim, pointing out that a forced sale would realize only part of the liabilities and deprive Mrs Besant of her copyrights, Mrs Bonner of her father's, and her husband of the means of supporting his wife, child and Abraham Hooper, whose life savings had all gone to Charlie. As in answer to the earlier appeal, most of them pleaded inability to help or offered only marginal concessions. In April, however, while Annie happened to be in America, Hypatia's solicitor Thomas Harper called them together and persuaded the majority to accept 10 shillings in the pound. Even this was substantial on almost £6,000, but appeals had already been launched: by Burt and Mrs Cobden Unwin, a daughter of Richard Cobden, with a message written by the novelist 'Edna Lyall' (Ada Ellen Bayly), for the House of Commons; by Reynolds for the National Secular Society; by Annie for £1,000 to purchase the library and vest it in trustees. This last appeal was largely in retaliation against Foote's £10,000 appeal on behalf of a Bradlaugh Memorial Hall Co. Ltd, whose board was entirely in secularist hands.

When Annie came back from America she received plaintive letters from dissident shareholders and accused Hypatia and the solicitors of waiting till she was out of the country to come to terms. By promising to pay them in full because they had trusted Charlie and herself implicitly, she jeopardized the whole arrangement and assumed a responsibility that Bradlaugh had dissolved the partnership to relieve her of. Hypatia was impatient at this quixotry, especially when Mrs Besant herself demanded the full £100 which she had lent from the funds of the Matchmakers' Union and questioned whether Mrs Bonner had really spent on the estate, out of her own pocket, what she said she had. It was inevitable the two women would slip apart when all that had united them was gone, but the separation was unexpectedly acrimonious. They met three times later. At the conclusion of one of Mrs Besant's addresses at South Place, Hypatia introduced her son Charles. Annie came out of her abstraction, said 'He has his grandfather's eyes', then slipped back into theosophy. The next meeting was at a *Tribune* rally for children at the Queen's Hall, where Annie seemed not to recognize Hypatia and merely asked 'Can I get out this way?' The last contact was in 1927 at the Malthusian Jubilee Dinner, where Mrs Besant was the guest-of-honour. Contraceptive beliefs that had withstood her socialist phase had yielded at last to theosophy, and she further insisted on the absence of wine and smoking. But she gave a tactful address, full of her old eloquence. She recognized Hypatia, but had to be told the name. Then her face lit up. 'I have seen him', she said. 'I am not a Spiritualist, but I have seen him.'

Mrs Besant's scheme for the library fell flat. Instead it was sold by catalogue to individual buyers and realized £550 net. Friends bought the Indian gifts for £50 but returned them to the family. The

Reynolds appeal raised £1,125. Great things were expected of the 'Edna Lyall' appeal, especially from the Labouchere fortune. He gave £10 and the thing limped on to £710. Two years later there was another attempt, backed by the novelist, Mrs Unwin, and Digby. Eventually about £1,000 was raised, of which £900 purchased a freehold house for the Bonners in Streathbourne Road, Tooting Bec. F. Verheyden executed a bronze bust for Brookwood and a marble bust for the Pitfield Street Library, Hoxton. It was hoped to erect a marble statue of the celebrated member in Northampton, but the appeal fell short. George Tinworth thereupon worked wonders with Doulton terracotta. At a huge rally in 1894 the figure was set up in Abington Square on a plinth round which was carved James Wilson's famous song, and, despite objections and alternative suggestions from time to time, has remained there ever since.

Soon after the memorial hall appeal was opened, R.O. Smith announced he wished to dispose of the lease of the Hall of Science. If the secular party, which so much depended on it, wished to retain their claim they would have to purchase it themselves. This would cost £2,000, half of it to be found almost immediately, plus £2,500 for rebuilding. Because of legal difficulties the society had never been able to build up capital of its own, so Foote proposed turning a renovated Hall of Science into the 'Bradlaugh Memorial Hall'. This did not please Hypatia, Robertson and their circle. They nursed resentment at slights heaped on the modest building down the years, and disapproved of Smith's dancing classes and smoking-and-drinking concerts, 'music-hallism' and 'club' atmosphere, as unworthy of the dignity of secularism and the memory of Bradlaugh. Supported by Reynolds, Forder, Standring and Truelove, Foote walked out of the Memorial Hall Company board and set up his own National Secular Hall Society Ltd to acquire the Old Street Hall, saying that the money already collected by the society would be used for this purpose unless otherwise specified. His opponents accused him of irregularity and dictatorship. It was almost certainly what Bradlaugh himself would have done in the circumstances, but whereas the Bradlaughites could take 'dictatorship' from the Chief, they could not from Foote. Some six years, much acrimony and many resignations later, the Memorial Hall Co. Ltd wound itself up, handing back its subscriptions, less 10% expenses; while the National Secular Hall Society Ltd fell into the hands of the Offical Receiver. The Hall of Science was taken over for commercial purposes and nothing was ever built in Bradlaugh's honour. In 1960 however the National

"THOROUGH"

CHARLES BRADLAUGH.
BORN: SEPT. 26, 1833.
DIED: JANY. 30, 1891.

M.P. FOR NORTHAMPTON 1880-1891.

FOUR TIMES ELECTED TO ONE
PARLIAMENT. IN VINDICATION OF
THE RIGHTS OF CONSTITUENCIES.
INDIA, TOO, CHOSE HIM HER
REPRESENTATIVE.
A SINCERE FRIEND OF THE PEOPLE.
HIS LIFE WAS DEVOTED TO
PROGRESS, LIBERTY, AND JUSTICE.

Bradlaugh's Statue in Northampton

Secular Society acquired premises at 103 Borough High Street, Southwark, and named them Bradlaugh House. There was to be another attempt at a Bradlaugh memorial, this time a tablet in the House of Commons. Colonel Josiah Wedgwood, MP, chose the centenary year, 1933, to make his request. Nothing was done. It was argued Bradlaugh was only a backbencher.

The year 1891 also saw the deaths of Hooper, who went to pieces when 'the boy' had gone, Granville, W.H. Smith, Parnell and Madame Blavatsky. Annie Besant took her place in the theosophy hierarchy. Two years later she settled in India to become its 'white priestess', founder of the Home Rule League and first woman president of Congress. Almost to the end she worked constantly from 5 a.m. daily, keeping five secretaries fully engaged. By 1933 her great generators were running down into the amplitude of a dream, but they were galvanized when she was invited to the Bradlaugh Centenary. She was not dead yet; of course she would come. Six days before the event, however, her currents ceased to flow. In July 1891 Charles Watts returned from Canada and rejoined the National Secular Society. Despite dissensions and further resignations, Foote remained its president till his death in 1915. Hypatia's biography of her father led to libel threats from her Uncle Bob and to Holyoake's bitter *Warpath of Opinion*, which denounced the Chief's 'restive ambition', 'needless machinations', 'immoral casuistry' and 'superb sense of his own importance'. He sent a copy to Ingersoll, who approved it. The Propaganda Press Committee flowered into the Rationalist Press Association Ltd in 1899. As its chairman till his death in 1906, Holyoake was at last associated with a viable rival to the National Secular Society. Hypatia was not especially fond of C.A. Watts, but she liked Foote even less. Finding a freethinking organization useful to her, she gladly became a director of the association in 1916 and remained one till she died in 1935. Arthur died four years later. In 1929 their son Charles became a director, but failed in an attempted *coup* after a sub-publishing row and left in 1954. From 1946 till his death in 1966 he was president of the World Union (International Federation) of Freethinkers. His younger son Basil, for a time one of the union's vice-presidents, presented the Bradlaugh Collection to the National Secular Society, for so long his great-grandfather's first love.

The political was as troubled as the freethought arena after Bradlaugh's death. Who was to inherit his seat at Northampton? In the country at large many hoped it might be a way to get Dilke back into politics. Aveling hoped to stand with Social Democratic Federation backing, but no one turned up with the £100 deposit. He was now writing unsuccessful plays and scrounging with the help of Engels. When news came of his wife's death he married an actress in 1897. Shocked, Eleanor suicided the following year, when he too died. The Northampton Bradlaughites wanted Robertson as a candidate, but Manfield persuaded the Liberal and Radical Association to endorse him on the understanding that he would retire at the general election in 1892. Once elected, he repudiated the promise. A Bradlaugh Radical Association then split off. Just before the 1892 election Labby pledged that he would retire at the following election if Manfield would not. Robertson agreed not to split the vote, Labby and Manfield were re-elected and the Bradlaugh Radicals came back into the fold. But the manoeuvrings continued. A Bradlaughite eventually got in in 1900: Dr J.G. Shipman, a son of Bradlaugh's old supporter. Robertson finally made parliament for Tyneside in the 1906 Liberal landslide. In 1911 he became Parliamentary Secretary to the Board of Trade. Four years later he was eased out by the coalition and compensated by becoming a Privy Councillor and chairman of the Liberal Publication Department. He lost his seat in 1918 and died in 1933.

Robertson's seat collapsed when effective Liberalism collapsed. In Northampton, and the country at large, it lingered on for four more years as a Co-Lib coalition; but the end was in sight. Some commentators have attributed the *débâcle* chiefly to the short-term calculations of the Lloyd George-Simonite compromisers, who ditched the Asquith-Samuelite true vehicle of the faith. But the real causes lie deeper. Briefly, nineteenth-century Liberalism was a strange coalescence of forces. Some of them, like teetotalism and Nonconformism, despite a brief upsurge in 1906, never gained a firm hold on the twentieth century. More importantly, the great class centrifuge, whose action Bradlaugh and a handful of contemporaries just managed to confine, quite defeated their successors. At the 1892 election working-class candidates began to stand independently and not as radical Liberals. In time most of the wealthy Liberals reactively changed into Conservatives so that upper-middle-class interests might have a unified defence. Led by idealism many intellectuals turned socialist and came to support the Labour Party in the quixotic belief that the two things were related. Only the rump of the old whig-radical-representative-of-labour caucus stayed Liberal. The Bradlaugh family has, largely out of loyalty, though in later life

Charles Bradlaugh Bonner gained renewed interest and gladly took the chair at the Wandsworth Central Liberal Association. Yet the family's history shows well the trends that, without loyalty, led many to stop voting Liberal altogether. Increasingly Hypatia, and especially the women who married the Bonners in succeeding generations, saw virtue in security and social status. These were to be gained by association with the right institutions, academic and otherwise. Charles and his two sons, Edmond and Basil, went to preparatory and public schools before university. Edmond is well-established as a botanist in Switzerland, out of touch with British politics and apolitical in his attitudes. Educated as a statistician at the London School of Economics, Basil votes Liberal but thinks anarcho-syndicalist. On a new social wave his younger children are in state schools.

What would Charles Bradlaugh himself be were he alive today? It is hard to say. Could a hot potato with the savour of Margaret Knight, John Calder and Tariq Ali find a place in the deep-frozen supermarkets of Smith Square, or even off the Strand? Denied radio and television facilities, how would he fare as a market square orator? With all his ability, running on, say, an 'independent radical' ticket, would he even save his deposit? Perhaps it is these considerations that have led some twentieth-century observers to dismiss him as an interesting curio from another epoch, with nothing to say to our pre-packaged generation. On the other hand, there are those who insist he would have come to terms with modern life and been a noted Queen's Counsel or a television-personality or a Secretary of State for Employment and Productivity in a Labour government. Whatever the value of these speculations, those who look back into the real life of Bradlaugh will find interesting comments on the plaintive problems of today in practical and in general matters.

His individualist creed may have given no answer to the sweat-shops and the childless widows, the junkies and alcoholics, cripples and other casualties of life. But there are very few items in his specific programme which are not relevant still, as either achievements or aspirations. His Chartist demands have mostly been met. For the rest—secular education, affirmation instead of the oath, penal reform, housing, reform of the House of Lords, abolition of cultural censorship, sex instruction, devolution and federation within the United Kingdom, a multi-racial commonwealth of nations, world disarmament, international arbitration, equal rights for the sexes, the channel tunnel, economies in bureaucracy, family planning, fear of the socio-political influence of the Roman Catholic Church, conciliation in industry—they all have a strangely modern ring. Against those issues about which less is now heard—republicanism, the primacy of land law reform, proportional representation, disestablishment of the Church of England—how many can claim an intellectual *coup de grâce*? Never resolved, they have never dissolved. Would those progressives who vilified him in his last ailing years for questioning the universal prudence of state intervention in industrial bargaining be so confident had they lived to see a British Labour government try to force through a punitive Prices and Incomes Bill? What would they say—if they were allowed to talk at all—as citizens of the workers' paradises in the modern socialist world? In his day academic agnostics sneered at his attacks on popular superstitions, which were said to be already outmoded. Are they quite dead today, even in the universities? Does his attitude to Disraeli's triumphant purchase of Suez Canal shares look quite so pettifogging since the 'incident' of 1956?.

Yet he has a significance for our generation above and beyond particular issues, and for people who have made no study of traditional politics or perhaps reject them outright. The man who first put large, perfectly disciplined forces of ordinary men and women into the streets when there was no other way for their feelings to be known, the man who urged co-operation and community help, freedom of speech and freedom of assembly, speaks down the years to those young people who are tired of ancient conventions and frightened authoritarianism, and are struggling, sometimes with incoherence and confusion, slowly towards participation and responsible permissiveness.

APPENDIX 1

Acknowledgements

My interest in Bradlaugh began when, in 1963, I became his successor in the radical humanist movement. From that time my absorption in the whole range of political and social reforms he championed has mounted steadily. It therefore concerned me to find how little by or about him is now in print. A number of monographs appeared during his lifetime or after his death, and are listed in the bibliography. Most late Victorian and Edwardian political memoirs say something about him. A useful volume of essays and quotations appeared in his centenary year, 1933. The standard biography by his daughter Hypatia and a leading disciple, John M. Robertson, came out four years after his death in 1891. Two such distinguished writers and personalities could not fail to produce an interesting and thoughtful book and I am greatly indebted to it, but it is, as Professor Walter Arnstein has aptly described it, a 'work of hagiography'. Important questions are left unanswered, considerable space is devoted to trivia, and certain material was suppressed in the interests of the living. It has at any rate long been out of print. Many recent volumes have touched on, or even featured, certain aspects of Bradlaugh's life and work. Among the most painstaking of these are Arnstein's *The Bradlaugh Case* (1965) and Arthur H. Nethercot's *The First Five Lives of Annie Besant* (1960). They rely however on secondary sources (as far as Bradlaugh the man is concerned) and inevitably present a lopsided picture of him.

Apparently on the authority of the late Charles Bradlaugh Bonner, Arnstein has asserted that there is no Bradlaugh Collection. Fortunately this is not so. I am immeasurably indebted to Bradlaugh's great-grandson, Mr Basil Bradlaugh Bonner, and to his wife Beryl and their household, for finding this collection in sundry forgotten attic trunks and generously and hospitably making it available to me without restriction during long months of research. Mr Bonner has in no way attempted to influence and is in no way responsible for my conclusions, but I am also indebted to him for the remarkable candour with which he has spoken about the generations of his family and for his most generous gift and loan of unique Bradlaugh material.

It is impossible to name all of those who have assisted me in the furnishing of other materials. Among respondents to my published appeals I would particularly like to thank Mr Gustavo Duran, who from Greece sent me photocopies of some interesting Thomas Huxley letters in his possession. In the Bradlaugh Collection is a sheaf of letters from Prince 'Jérome' (Joseph) Napoleon and Charles Tissot. I am indebted to M. Jean-Pierre Schweitzer for invaluable assistance in the deciphering and translation of the more illegible of them. In trying to capture, so far as one can today, the atmosphere of the various places with which Bradlaugh is associated, I have been there and spoken to numerous anonymous inhabitants. As interlocutors with special knowledge or access to special documents I must name the following for particular usefulness:

Suffolk: Mr and Mrs Hector Moore, Mrs Vera Abbott and Mr Allan Pearce (all distant cousins of Bradlaugh, and most kind); Rev. S.F. Minchin (vicar of Brandeston with Kettleburgh); Rev. R.A. Marchant (vicar of All Saints, Laxfield); Rev. Alex L. Rigg (rector of Kelsale with Carlton); Olive, Lady Hambling.

Hoxton: Mr Stanley Tongue and Mrs Brenda Hough (archivist and assistant at Shoreditch Central Library); Mr John Bellamy; Rev. J.O. Hutchinson (vicar of St John's); Miss May Scott (warden of Hoxton Hall Friends' Neighbourhood Centre).

Bethnal Green: Mr James Fordham (research assistant at Bethnal Green Museum); Rev. Cyril A. Rowe (priest-in-charge of St Matthew's); Rev. Albert Jones and Mr Noel P. Mander (former priest-in-charge and churchwarden of St Peter's with St Thomas's); Mr Arthur L. Hellicar (local history librarian of Central Library, Tower Hamlets); Mr William Brown (schoolkeeper of Robert Montefiore School Annexe).

Tottenham: Mr Ian Murray and Miss Jean Pegram (archivist and assistant of Haringey Libraries, Museum and Arts Department); Rev. Raymond Avent (vicar of St Paul's).

City of London: Guildhall Library; Public Record Office.

Stepney: Master Kenneth Gavens (29 Turner St); Mr David Sherren (treasurer of London Hospital); Mr Edward Marsh (churchwarden of St Augustine's with St Philip's).

United States: Mr Sherman D. Wakefield (grandson-in-law of Robert

Ingersoll).

Finsbury: Mr Graham Melville (Finsbury branch librarian of Islington Public Libraries).

St John's Wood: Miss Vada Readman (assistant archivist of the City of Westminster Libraries).

Northampton: Messrs D. Howard Halliday and John Stafford (chief and local librarian of the Central Public Library); Mr Victor A. Hatley (librarian of the College of Technology); Mr C.E. Vivian Rowe (Town Clerk); Mr George Franklin (secretary of the Northampton Board of Conciliation and Arbitration for the Boot and Shoe Trade and of the Northampton Town Footwear Manufacturers' Association); Ald. Arthur Lyne (president of the local branch and on the national executive of the National Union of Boot and Shoe Operatives); Mr George Attewell (general secretary and agent of the Northampton Labour Party); Mr Thomas Hood (Conservative agent); Messrs Kenneth Kennedy and Graham Knight (secretary and organizer of the Northampton Liberals); Ald. Percy Adams (grandson of Bradlaugh's election agent Thomas Adams); Mrs Annie Ball (remarkable 97-year-old lady who personally remembers Bradlaugh); Cllr David Walmsley (member of the majority group on the Borough Council); Cllr Caroline Trusler and Ald. Ruth Perkins (leader and member of the minority group on the Borough Council); Lovell William Dickens (chief features writer and former editor of the *Mercury and Herald*); Ald. Fred Watts; Canon Edward Elcock (Rural Dean of Northampton and vicar of St Michael and All Angels); the Earl Spencer; Mr Norman Collings (publicity manager of Anglia Building Society); Mr Richard Rutledge (verger of St Giles's); Mr T. C. Lees (formerly senior history master of Northampton Grammar School); Mr N.C. Wright (Town Hall Keeper); Mr W. Neville Terry and Miss June Swann (curator and shoe specialist of the Borough Museums Department); Mr Albert Wright (guide at Messrs Church & Co. Ltd); Mr Harold Cousins (general secretary of Men's Own). Alds. Adams, Lyne and Watts are former mayors.

Houses of Parliament: Brigadier Sir Francis Reid (Speaker's Secretary); Mr Maurice Bond (Clerk of the Records, House of Lords); Mr D.C.L. Holland (Librarian of the House of Commons).

For general or subject reference I have also found the following libraries helpful and extend special thanks to individuals named: the British Museum Reading Room, Newspaper Library, State Paper Room and Department of Manuscripts; the Members' Library and Greater London Records Office, County Hall (Messrs J. Darlington and Michael Pearce, head and assistant archivists); Marx Memorial Library (Messrs Andrew Rothstein, John Williamson and Frank Walker); National Secular Society (Mr William McIlroy, always helpful); Rationalist Press Association Ltd (Mr Hector Hawton); South Place Ethical Society (Miss Edwina Palmer); the University of London Library; the London School of Economics Library; National Liberal Club (Mr George Awdry, for access to portraits of Bradlaugh and George Jacob Holyoake and the Bradlaugh pamphlet collection—the core of his library—now in the club's Gladstone Memorial Library); Theosophical Society (Mrs Nan Walker, librarian with personal recollections of Annie Besant); Royal Botanic Gardens, Kew (Mr Nigel Sinnott); Westminster Central Reference Library; Bishopsgate Institute (Mr D.R. Webb, reference librarian); General Register Office; National Portrait Gallery (Miss Caroline Brown); Central Reference Library, Newcastle upon Tyne; Messrs Penningtons and Lewis & Lewis (Mr Cyril Maby); Dr Edward Royle of Selwyn College, Cambridge, a Holyoake specialist; the Rev. Dewi Morgan, rector of St Bride's, Fleet Street.

Ireland

In 1840 'Liberator' Daniel O'Connell, the Roman Catholic MP whose refusal to take the Protestant Oath of Supremacy in 1828 was an important factor in the agitation leading to the Roman Catholic Relief Act of 1829, founded an Association for the Repeal of the Union (of England and Ireland). O'Connell was particularly interested in increasing the power of the Catholic Church, but religion was only one of the boils that in 1884 Disraeli diagnosed on the Irish body politic: a weak executive, absentee landlords and an alien church. The great famine of the next five years brought things to a head. Children died and adults emigrated[1] in vast numbers. By 1851 the population had dropped from eight to five and a half million. Among those who stayed, violent crime, both nationalist and indiscriminate, broke out; and the Westminster Parliament was induced to pass a Coercion Bill in 1847. The following year, under the impetus of Continental revolution, especially in France, Young Ireland, inspired by Mazzini's Young Italy and Young Europe, came into its own. It had originally been founded in 1842 by the Catholics Sir Charles Gavan Duffy and John Dillon and the Protestant Thomas Davis as a reaction against the divisive Catholic-Celtic orientation of O'Connell's movement. Feeling that 'no practical good was done to the rack-rented peasantry by denunciations of Cromwell's tyranny', Young Ireland aimed at 'a purely political and secular movement for emancipating the peasantry from landlordism, and Ireland from English government'.[2] It was an attempt to nail the splintering factions together.

Originally preferring evolution to revolution, under the leadership of Smith O'Brien and John Mitchel the movement changed direction. Parliament suspended Habeas Corpus and an abortive insurrection broke out. It was soon suppressed, but the discontent remained and distress grew worse. The 1848 rising 'had one disastrous result. It dried up English sympathy for victims of the Famine.'[3] The Irish had

305

another problem. There was no agreement as to how Ireland's difficulties should be solved. No reformer supported the establishment of the Protestant Church of Ireland, but should the country become Catholic or secular? Should it cut adrift from Britain, or should it continue to send members to Westminster? The one thing about which everyone was agreed was the land question. In 1850 the Tenant Right League was formed to advocate the three Fs: fair rent, fixed tenure and free sale. It aimed at a return to the constitutional[4] methods of O'Connell. But he himself had now died and Isaac Butt was yet to come to prominence. The peasants soon saw that help from Westminster would be a long time coming, and so 'the 1850s were marked by a series of small local riots with unhappy tenants burning crops and property'.[5] This was what had brought the guardsmen to Ireland.

Republicanism

From the earliest times a leader who emerged from the tribe, strongest or wisest to save it from its enemies, might with luck swell from chieftain to king. The obedience he was gladly given as dangers raged became an obedience he exacted as of right when peace returned, and claimed for his firstborn. But a vision of the public good still flickered in the tribe; the passion for participation simmered. The Latin *res publica* or public matter has been equated with the Greek *ta koinonia* or common property. It implies government for the benefit of the governed and not the governors, supported by public money. But who are the public? Historically republicanism has been dated from Sparta and the Greek city-states, or from Rome after the expulsion of the Etruscan Tarquins. It has been contrasted with 'democracy', or rule by village council, as the conduct of national affairs. Clearly a whole city, or something larger, cannot sit in legislation. There must be representatives. But whom and how do they represent?

Plato believed the interests of all were served by an oligarchy of mostly hereditary philosophers combining 'justice with prudence',[1] and all the ancient civilizations had large slave populations without civil rights. The historian Polybius admitted there could be monarchical elements in society without a king and rather liked 'mixed' government. Could there be republican elements with a king? To the political theorist there were three 'pure' forms of government: (1) monarchy (2) aristocracy (3) democracy. Aristotle[2] believed they could be corrupted into, respectively, (1) tyranny (2) oligarchy (3) mob rule. Cicero, a student of the Academy founded by Plato, spread patrician republican ideas throughout the Roman world. He was killed by Mark Antony, and his avenger Augustus established the Roman Empire. In a derelict and divided form, overgrown by barbarous kingdoms on the pre-classical pattern and by a clamant post-classical Papacy, it crumbled away for centuries. In the tenth and eleventh centuries new towns coalesced round tiny merchants and master craftsmen, who, as they grew in wealth in Germany and north and central Italy, gained more or less independence from emperor, pope or princeling. Sometimes these *haut bourgeois* republics drifted, as in Florence, into autocracies claiming noble titles. In Venice, however, from the twelfth to the eighteenth century, an elected Doge graced a constitution that was 'a work of art much abused, much envied and much admired'.[3]

These early capitalist republics developed without much theory. Their organizers were businessmen. Niccolo Machiavelli of Florence was the first modern political theorist. In his *Discourses* he developed a schedule of checks and balances from Plato's *Politicus*, and in his *Il Principe*, based on Cesare Borgia, he dissected the anatomy of pragmatic power, preferring it to arise from a manipulated republic rather than a dynastic monarchy. A ruler should be energetic and at least seem to be virtuous. The Tudors cleverly agreed he should seem to be democratic. 'We at no time stand so high in our estate royal', said Henry VIII, 'as in the time of Parliament, when we as head and you as members, are conjoined and knit together into one body politic.'[4] George Buchanan, tutor to the youthful James I, revived the old idea of social contract that had fluttered round the Sophists and the Old Testament, viz. that there was some past compact between the people and the government. From his biblical researches James came to believe that he held power by the 'Divine Right of Kings', which was an overriding contract. Republicans like Algernon Sidney were satisfied with a governed-government contract, so long as the government was prepared to obey the terms. But most republicans said that this presupposed the government to be some power always independent of the people. The most popular form of social contract theory therefore made the people the original sovereign power. Yet how could they contract with themselves?

First stated in Richard Hooker's *Ecclesiastical Polity*, this theory was better developed in Thomas Hobbes's *Leviathan*. At first sight it might suggest instability whereas Hooker and Hobbes were devoted to the Tudor and Stuart establishments. Hobbes made the government not only stable but also absolute through a universal relinquishment of power by the people so as to set up a Sovereign authority outside. Its sway would be permanent unless overthrown by revolution. In a democratized form this view influenced John Milton's *Tenure of Kings and Magistrates* and John Locke's *Treatises on Civil Government*, which emphasized the key role of an independent judiciary in resolving disputes between the executive and the people. It became the cornerstone of newly erected nations without an established power. On the *Mayflower* the Pilgrim Fathers determined to 'solemnly and mutually, in the presence of God and of one another, covenant and combine ourselves together into a civil body politic'.[5] Most famous of all the writers influenced by Hobbes was Jean Jacques Rousseau, who had been secretary to the French Ambassador to Venice. In his *Social Contract* Rousseau sought to provide two contracting parties: the people as a group of individuals and the 'collective moral person' formed by their 'General Will'. This alienated power from their individual wills but did not abandon the essential freedoms guaranteed by the natural law. These were Paine's *Rights of Man*. They fired the Marquis de Lafayette and the American and French Revolutions, and have inspired the Universal Declaration of Human Rights and the world's millions to this day. But political theorists have often thought the notions of social contract and natural law equally unreal. The Baron de Montesquieu preferred to concentrate on checks and balances; the English Utilitarians, under Jeremy Bentham, on the empiric pursuit of happiness. What really made Paine so valuable were his practical vision and blunt common sense, which have continued to influence the popular democratic movement. To him it owes unanswerable polemics like:

> 'The idea of hereditary legislators is as inconsistent as that of hereditary judges, or hereditary juries; and as absurd as an hereditary mathematician, or an hereditary wise man; and as ridiculous as an hereditary poet-laureate.'[6]

In the seventeenth century Britain had led the rush of republican revolutions with that 'episode in English history', the Commonwealth. Though Sir John Eliot wanted *The Monarchie of Man*, the other parliamentary leaders were perfectly contented with the monarchy of Charles I if only he would behave. 'Hampden, like his party, had no aversion to monarchy.'[7] 'The commonwealth men declared openly for a republic, but Cromwell declined to pledge himself; not, as he explained to Ludlow, because he did not think it desirable, but because he did not think it feasible.'[8] By 19 May 1649, however, it was decreed that 'England . . . shall from henceforth be governed as a Commonwealth and Free-State—by the supreme authority of this nation, the representatives of the people in Parliament, and by such as they shall appoint and constitute officers and ministers under them for the good of the people, and that without any King or House of Lords'.[9] Change was desired by the country gentry and merchants, Presbyterians and Independents. The Fifth-Monarchy Men expected Jesus to come down to secure the empty throne, while John Lilburne, leader of the Levellers, suspected Cromwell would rise up and seize it. Very soon Lilburne and his lieutenants were seized. 'No sooner had the House of Lords been demolished than a second Chamber was found necessary in the establishment of the all-powerful Council of State.'[10] From being its president in 1649, Cromwell became Lord Protector in 1653. A colleague Sir Henry Vane strongly disapproved, and was imprisoned. By 1655 the Diggers and Fifth-Monarchy Men were suppressed.

As Cromwell's despotism grew so did plots against his life from the extreme right and the extreme left. In 1657 'Silas Titus' (William Allen) published Britain's most influential tyrannicide pamphlet *Killing No Murder*. The following year, somewhat to his surprise, Cromwell died of natural causes. Vane went to the Long Parliament to oppose the hereditary accession of Richard Cromwell. The new ruler was incompetent and the people grew restive. Milton fought hard to protect the republic against a return to 'burdensome, expensive, useless and dangerous'[11] kingship. If men valued monarchy for its seeming stability they could have instead an 'immortal' Grand or General Council, where as one member died another was elected. In a few months Richard Cromwell resigned. Prince Charles became Charles II. His statutes were dated from the death of his father as if the Commonwealth had never been. Wise men cursed or avoided the name of Cromwell.

Yet, despite his 'Puritan mercilessness of judgment', the Protector had had, as Bradlaugh recognized, great qualities:

> 'Cromwell was no Republican; but he was a grand Englishman, who pushed to the front by virtue of his sturdy thoroughness, and who did mighty service for the nation whose authority he took, whose power he wielded.'[12]

Soon after the Merry Monarch's accession, Vane was executed for alleged treason. Twenty years later Henry Marten died in prison. Algernon Sidney followed Lord William Russell to the scaffold for the dubious 'Rye House Plot' and entered republican literature as the last English martyr for the cause. Indeed, it almost seemed like the end of the cause. Not that a golden age of monarchy ensued. Charles II had all the vices of his family, somewhat redeemed by his sense of humour. James II was impossible. By a Bloodless Revolution in November 1688 he was pushed out. The subsequent Convention

Parliament declared 'That King James II, having endeavoured to subvert the constitution of the kingdom by breaking the original contract between King and people, and by the advice of Jesuits and other wicked persons having violated the fundamental laws, and having withdrawn himself out of this kingdom, has abdicated the government, and the Throne is thereby become vacant.'[13] It had taken good care to get itself summoned by letters from William of Orange, declared him and Mary King and Queen, got itself formally constituted and then endorsed its former actions. William and Mary, followed by Anne, pursued wars of which republicans disapproved, but their full wrath broke upon the four Georges:

> 'George the First was always reckoned
> Vile, but viler George the Second;
> And what mortal ever heard
> Any good of George the Third?
> When from earth the Fourth descended,
> (God be praised!) the Georges ended.'[14]

Yet the explosion was purely intellectual and even as literature most of it appeared after the rule of the Georges was over. Republican echoes rang round utopianist volumes of the late seventeenth and eighteenth centuries: *The Common-Wealth of Oceana* (1656) by James Harrington, who was influenced by Venice, Henry Nevill's *Plato Redivivus; or, a Dialogue Concerning Government* (1681), John Toland's pamphlets, Walter Moyle's *Essay on the Lacedaemonian Government* (1698) and *Essay upon the Constitution of the Roman Government* (1726), Dean Swift's *Gulliver's Travels* (1726) and Thomas Hollis's republications. Even where they were culturally influential they made no real political impact. A great timidity had settled upon the British people. Before the Commonwealth the middle and the lower classes, even some of the aristocracy, came together because they knew what they hated. Severally they knew what they wanted, but these things were incompatible. The Whig aristocrats, like King John's barons, wished to curb the power of the king and little more; the wealthy merchants opposed the aristocrats; the Levellers, the wealthy merchants; the Diggers, the Levellers. Paralleling the social divisions were the sects, with theological divisions more bitter still. William Walwyn wanted a secular republic, but most of the commonwealth men were perfectly happy with an established church so long as it reflected their own point of view. The Westminster Assembly of Divines merely supplanted Parliament and the Convocations, and replaced orthodox Anglicanism with orthodox Presbyterianism. Further to the theological left were the Independents, Quakers, Anabaptists and Fifth-Monarchy Men.[15] In exasperation Cromwell at last shouted at the factions, 'A plague on all your houses' and ruled despotically. With monumental gifts this policy might work. But what when the dictator died?

And so, as the Commonwealth receded into ancestral memory, though the several interests in the country loved one another no better, they drew back at the thought of any new, violent overthrow of the *status quo*, plunging the land again into turmoil. There was some hope of republican agitation in 1768 when the cry 'Wilkes and liberty' rose outside the gaol which caged John Wilkes, the radical member for Middlesex, for publishing obscenity and treason.[16] Three times he was expelled from parliament, three times re-elected. But in 1774 he was allowed to take his seat and advocate shorter parliaments and more equal representation. Later he became a very reactionary City Chamberlain and Lord Mayor of London. At the height of the excitement in 1769, 'Parson' Horne (John Horne Tooke) formed a Society of Supporters of the Bill of Rights, which two years later became the Constitutional Society demanding 'full and equal representation of the people in Parliament'. It gained no great popular following. From that time, despite the country's endemic grievances and injustices, British revolutionary movements largely reflected the situation in France. When the 1789 revolution broke, the Whigs split. They had been generally sympathetic to the American revolution. It involved a country whose potentialities were unrealized and which was a safe distance away. But France was too near home. Continued advocacy of reform emphasized the need for it; and a stimulated appetite might not easily be satisfied. Apart from a rump of New Whigs under Charles James Fox, the middle classes threw in their lot with the upper. This deprived the masses of those who, in the Commonwealth and at most times in most places, provided leadership, direction, advice and money. In 1794 Horne Tooke, Thomas Hardy and John Thelwall formed the working-class London Corresponding Society. It was supported by Place, who had worked his way up but not forgotten the route. The next hundred years showed strange ebbs and flows of agitation, middle- and working-class, maximal when they worked together, minimal when they fell apart. On the latter occasions it was always the working class which suffered more.

The republican movement[17] lived off this agitation. Its leaders were dedicated and richly vocal. They have left behind a powerful literature, which is almost entirely forgotten. Apart from the Commonwealth the movement is forgotten. The British are pragmatic. In reviewing their history they recall the things which seem to matter. English republicanism is not included because—save for a few heady years in the seventeenth century—it never seemed to matter much at the time. It saw politics as a grand design and Anglo-Saxons are interested in spots of damp rot. It was cosmopolitan and Anglo-Saxons are insular. It was idealistic and Anglo-Saxons are practical. Very often republican journals were kept alive more for the gratification of their editors than for the zeal of their readership. And yet there were many occasions when the concatenation of events almost turned the combination that would have opened out the face of politics and shone on the republic.

When the French Revolution passed into the Napoleonic Wars, all classes in Britain loyally coalesced. With shortage of overseas supplies and general inflation, local corn commanded high prices. After the war imports tended to force prices down. The aristocratic government of the Earl of Liverpool, with its hated Viscounts Castlereagh and Sidmouth, gladly obliged landowners by controlling the import of foreign and colonial corn.[18] Great distress was caused, especially among the urban masses in the industrialized north. By 1817 Cobbett's well-established *Weekly Political Register* was joined by other protest prose. Wooler began his *Black Dwarf* as a popular Sunday. Charged with libelling Ministers, he was twice tried but acquitted on a technicality. Sidmouth issued a circular which caused 'a general damp among the pamphlet-vendors',[19] and Habeas Corpus was suspended. Early in 1817 a young prison officer, William Sherwin, had come to London with a political pamphlet. He presented it hopefully to William Hone, the publisher of *Parodies on the Book of Common Prayer*, and to other radical imprints, but 'they were all afraid of it as too strong'.[20] So he set up shop as his own printer and publisher and on 1 March issued the weekly *Republican*.

At its masthead were the slogans 'For a nation to love liberty, it is sufficient that she knows it; and to be free, it is sufficient that she wills it' and 'The laws are, in fact, the conditions of THE SOCIAL CONTRACT; the People submit themselves to the Laws, in order to enjoy the right of making or changing them'. The editorial asserted that

'a REPUBLICAN GOVERNMENT does not imply any particular form, is not confined to any peculiar nomenclature, but includes all and every description of Public Administration, wherein the weal of the great mass of the population is consulted and openly enforced, under whatever appellation it may be discriminated: and may be defined to be a GOVERN-MENT OPENLY ACTING IN BEHALF OF, AND FOR THE BENEFIT AND ADVANTAGE OF THE PEOPLE ... The Nation, therefore, in its collective capacity, is the natural sovereign; the prince, or magistrate, is the depository of this sovereignty, which he exercises in behalf of the people.'[21]

After offering to become Wooler's publisher and being turned down, Carlile was accepted by Sherwin as his publisher and general risk-taker. After five numbers Sherwin changed his journal's title to *Sherwin's Weekly Political Register.* 'Republican' was 'objectionable to a few friends'.[22] Cobbett was one of those opposing republicanism, but the plagiaristic new title angered him even more. Soon his protests were distant, for to escape either the authorities or his creditors he again[23] fled to the United States.

On 16 August 1819 Henry Hunt organized a huge reform meeting in St Peter's Fields, Manchester. Some of his supporters, including Carlile, expected trouble from the police and thought the people should come armed in self-defence, but Hunt countermanded this. Accompanied by Yeomen Cavalry the police met Carlile's expectations. Sabres were used, eleven people were killed and hundreds injured. Carlile had come to deliver 200 pamphlets to Hunt, got caught up in the thick of battle but incredibly escaped between the horses' legs. Arriving back in London hot-foot with this scoop, he decided to turn editor himself. His view of Sherwin was that he 'found more in his title than in his pages',[24] so he resurrected the *Republican*. Before the first number went to press he was in gaol, and it was there that most of the paper was produced over seven years. He began from a Sherwinite position:

> 'The word Republican ... really means nothing more when applied to government, than a government which consults the public interest—the interest of the whole people ... it does not argue the necessity of abolishing monarchy to establish a Republican government ... let us have a fair and equal system of representation without excluding the suffrage of any one of sound mind and unimpeached conduct.'[25]

But, he continued:

> 'I hold as opinion, that an expensive hereditary system of monarchy as existing at present in this country would not be countenanced by the representatives of the whole people.'

Established religious creeds had their place so long as they were not established politically; then they became 'disgusting, degrading, and injurious'.

At this time Carlile, greatly under the influence of Paine, was a deist. Later, 'That I have, since my imprisonment, avowed what is vulgarly called *Atheism*, I confess'.[26] He would be a 'blind creature' to be 'opposed' to God; his position was 'that no such a personified God does, or ever has existed'.[27] He took up the French revolutionary slogan of 'liberty, equality, fraternity', carefully defining its most difficult part as 'abolishment of all exclusive privileges, and an equality of rights', not 'an equality of riches'.[28] In later years his comments ranged further. He supported astrology, and took great delight in revealing the rituals, passwords and signs of the various orders of freemasonry. In 1821 a Constitutional Association—very different from the earlier Society—was formed to put him out of business, but so devoted were successive shopmen it went out of business itself.[29] His journal was very much a one man's view of the world, sometimes cranky, full of rows with Hunt and Cobbett[30] as well as with the establishment; but he felt entitled when he abandoned the *Republican* in 1826 to say 'the work is complete'.[31]

What Carlile had done was to break down the walls of repression and let free discussion out. Moreover, he established the pattern for mainstream republicanism in Britain for a century. All the essential ideas of the movement led by Bradlaugh came from this source. Carlile had shocked and entertained a wide readership. He did not, could not, and did not perhaps desire to, lead a movement. Either in or out of gaol he was no organizer. Inside he was a martyr. Only slowly did the authorities learn their lesson. As they over-reacted physically at Peterloo, so they over-reacted legalistically afterwards. Hunt and several others were indicted for conspiracy. The wealthy radical Sir Francis Burdett was prosecuted for libel for telling the electors of Westminster about the massacre. These trials publicized it further. At last governments grew wiser. Silence was best. It was left to the reformers and republicans to keep Peterloo alive.

Their next chance for mass demonstrations came with the next French revolution. In 1830 Charles X was forced to abdicate and Louis Philippe, the 'Citizen King', took his place, subscribing a declaration of rights and asserting that republican institutions would take root in his monarchical soil. In Britain Hetherington's Metropolitan Political Union blew up into the National Union of the Working Classes and Others, but it was soon swamped by the bourgeois Political Unions pioneered by Thomas Attwood in

315

Birmingham. On this wave, cresting to the Great Reform Bill, fresh republican bubbles broke. On 26 March 1831 Hetherington published his first weekly *Republican; or, Voice of the People*.[32] It was a halfpenny paper, unstamped like his *Poor Man's Guardian*, to salute 'Year of the People I'. Week by week there was a piece on the 'Rotunda. The House of the Unrepresented—Theatre of Free Discussion', where all the speakers were named as 'Citizen'. In August the journal was joined by a weekly penny *Radical*, 'devoted to the advocation of *Universal Suffrage*, or the right of every man (not incapacitated by crime or extreme ignorance) to vote in electing the law-makers'.[33]

This *Republican* evolved into the *Republican: The Sovereignty of the People* in the 'Year of Christ, 1832'. Hetherington, a well-known atheist, was still its publisher. The editor was J. H. B. Lorymer. It remained anticlerical. A special target was the established Church of Ireland, whose 'Protestant rogues rob the doubly-humbugged Catholics of the pay'.[34] But 'Republicans belong to no particular party or sect in politics or religion. The object of the sincere Republicans is the PUBLIC GOOD . . . If they adhere to any party, it is to that which advocates JUSTICE and HUMANITY in all parts of the civilized globe, whatever may be its political or religious denomination.'[35] The co-operative movement was deemed the best system and the profit motive a 'tormenting malady'.[36] After merging with its twin paper, the combined *Republican and Radical Reformer* devoted itself to trying to persuade the political unions not to disband with their job of enfranchisement half done, even though their role was the reverse of revolutionary. For they could rightly claim credit 'for the preservation of the country from anarchy and civil war'.[37] Hetheringtonian republicanism was in the bland Carlile-Bradlaugh tradition.

In the spring of 1836 Place and Dr J. R. Black established an Association of Working Men to Procure a Cheap and Honest Press. When the newspaper stamp was presently reduced to 1d, the association was absorbed, with the help of Lovett and Hetherington, into the London Working Men's Association. 'Its leaders were tough, middle of the road radicals, gradualists, who laid great stress upon education'[38] and were soon in conflict with the militant East London Democratic Association. Under the leadership of Bronterre O'Brien and his disciple on the *Poor Man's Guardian,* George Julian Harney, 'a Jacobin in an English setting',[39] the militants became the core of Chartism's 'physical force'[40] and its hostility to the middle classes.

They were especially opposed to the Anti-Corn Law League, whose creators were millowners like Bright and Cobden, and declared that low wages hurt more than dear bread. In 1841 the Quaker Joseph Sturge formed a Complete Suffrage Union for reconciliation between the classes, but when the Chartist leaders wanted it to adopt the Charter by name, he walked out. In the same year a shortlived *Atheist and Republican* was formed by an Owenite lecturer Frederick Hollick. After 1843 Chartism declined as the country prospered and factory legislation was introduced. In 1845 Harney launched the Society of Fraternal Democrats. A year later he urged 'the oppressed classes of every land to unite for the triumph of the common cause'.[41] In 1847 the League of the Just became the Communist League and Marx came to London for its congress. He met Harney and a new wave of English republicanism stirred.

Just at this time a mainstream *Republican*, advocating 'the Sovereignty of the People', sprang to life. Its publisher was Watson, its editor a gas inspector Cornelius George Harding, its slogan that of the Commonwealth lawyer John Selden, 'Above all things, Liberty'. Unusually it 'chose this state of quietude, rather than a more exciting period',[42] to emerge. It skated over its 'opinions concerning the form of Legislature which is best adapted to the sustentation of the spirit of Liberty', but advocated the exposure of 'statecraft and priestcraft'; though occasionally a correspondent said republicanism was not infidelity. It advocated a graduated property tax and abolition of the Bank of England's monopoly. If the paper began in quietude it soon entered the fire storms of 1848. They started in Switzerland the year before and reached Sicily in January. But it was the third French revolution of February which set Europe alight and burnt through Vienna, Milan, Berlin, Schleswig-Holstein, Lombardy, Prague, Hungary, Rome, Tuscany, Genoa, Dresden and Baden in the next fifteen months. Another year, and the *anciens régimes* were back. During this period in Britain Chartism radiated a new heat, but cooled down as quickly. Harding's *Republican* died as quietly as it was born. The 1848 Aliens Act, with increased powers of deportation, encouraged Continental *émigrés*, who during the quiet times had kept revolution smouldering in London, to go to earth. But they were not forgotten. When British republicanism was kindled again it was beneath the red flag of Harney and Ernest Jones, not the green flag of the National Charter Association.

The Red Republican was unfurled by a committee, whose secretary was the radical poet Gerald Massey, on 22 June 1850. Its editor Harney wrote as 'L'Ami du Peuple'. His slogan was 'Equality, Liberty, Fraternity'. At the masthead were the *bonnet rouge* and 'the red flag, dyed in the lifestream of the martyrs of June'. Ledru Rollin's programme in *Le Proscrit: Revue de la République Universelle* was commended. This included adult suffrage, education, a single tax, credit, the right to work and form voluntary associations. Rather more iconoclastically a correspondent advocated the 'Abolition of Money'.[43] Running through its volumes were the proposals of the National Reform League founded the year before by Bronterre O'Brien. These became gradually more radical until the 'expropriation of railways, canals, bridges, docks, gas-works, etc.[44] was advocated. The main attack on monarchy was economic. Emerging bodies like the National Parliamentary and Financial Reform Association, which tried to combine modified Chartist demands with bourgeois interest in free trade, were despised for their 'big names and subscriptions'.[45] And when a 'Democratic and Social Conference' proposed a merger of progressive organizations, the league opposed it. Because of its name the paper was boycotted by booksellers, and on 7 December 1850 it euphemistically became *The Friend of the People.* Harney was ill and Holyoake edited the first number. Discussing the old title, he had 'no doubt it was a name which, in this country, would always keep those who bore it a small party'. But Harney was soon back in his stride, damning with faint praise the trades unions and co-operative movement. They would merely 'advance the discussion of social principles, and thereby prepare the way for those Social Revolutionists who seek, through Universal Suffrage, THE ABOLITION OF CLASSES AND THE SOVEREIGNTY OF LABOUR'.[46] For a time he tried to arrange a merger with Ernest Jones's *Notes to the People.* When this bid failed the paper folded.

A regular contributor to the *Red Republican* was Linton, who was able to take advantage of the change of name to publish his *English Republic: God and the People* in December 1850. It had its own tricolour of blue, white and green: for the world to come, Freedom's home and worldwide republicanism. At first he published the mystical utterances of the Central European Democratic Committee which had been formed by Ledru Rollin, Mazzini, Arnold Ruge and Albert Darasz the previous summer. After the most visionary opening of any republican journal came Linton's proposal for a republican organization, the most practical suggestion to emerge hitherto. This was for a number of chiefly educational associations formed 'only with the trustworthy'[47] which would circumvent restrictive laws by meeting and corresponding privately. This fiendish scheme was denounced by *John Bull* as 'a kind of Methodism of Republicanism'. The following month Linton listed an imaginative array of 'Republican Measures'[48] for the reform of education, government, land laws, taxation, empire and the armed forces. There was some of the Welfare State and humanitarian programme of Paine; and a significant variation of one of Harney's recommendations: 'appropriation' of crown, church and waste lands, streams, mines, roads, railways and canals, 'giving equitable compensation to the present holders'. With the exception of his 'revolutionary measures'—the abolition of monarchy, the House of Lords, the peerage and laws of primogeniture and entail—these proposals, somewhat re-arranged, were adopted by the 1851 Chartist Convention in London. Linton's call for organization was answered almost immediately by the Bethnal Green Republican Propagandist Society, which was formed by local Chartists. Associations in Cambridge and Liverpool were detected on the way. Cambridge arrived, with Cheltenham, in April. Northumberland and Durham looked promising. Scotland and Ireland joined in. But it does not appear that there was ever much activity outside Bethnal Green, and by 1852 the section 'Republican Chronicle' in the *English Republic* was quietly dropped. The editor's defensive New Year message for 1855 was 'We are utopians, theorists, dreamers, enthusiasts, fanatics, madmen; in a word, we are Republicans'. Inside four months the dreams faded. He had to 'leave off because the response I meet with is not sufficient to justify the farther continuance of my endeavour . . . The time of words has passed, the time for action is come.'[49] This he was unable to give. It was no disgrace. Better organizers than he were to fail.

Harney and Cowen were in the process of failing with their newly-formed Republican Brotherhood at Newcastle. It had been

'organized for mutual instruction in Republican principles, and the general diffusion of information in connection with those principles—not to conspire against the present system, not to attempt any act overt or secret against the existing Monarchy. The members of the Republican Brotherhood will seek, by instructional means, to indoctrinate their fellow countrymen with Republican principles, leaving to the national will of the future to determine the means of reforming or changing the institutions of the country.'[50]

The national will was to be slow in forming. But the brotherhood went out splendidly. In 'A Welcome to Emperor Bonaparte!', ' "by the grace of God" and gunpowder, Emperor of the French', it looked forward to the 'resurrection' of France:

> 'At the trumpet-blast of thy awaking all nations will arise, and hurling thrones and tyrannies to the dust, will join in one thundering acclaim of brotherhood, freedom, and victory:— Vive la République!'[51]

In early societies morality, politics and religion were intimately associated. It was feared that ethics, law and order would break down without external guarantees. The crux of the social nexus in Christendom was the oath, the solemn 'appeal to a Supreme Being as thinking him the rewarder of truth, and avenger of falsehood';[1] whether it be the truth of legal evidence or the truth of protestations of loyalty. The first promissory oath in England was the oath of fealty to the king in the sheriff's torn before holding suit in any court leet. During the Anglo-Saxon era all males over twelve had to swear allegiance to the king and submission to the laws before fellow-citizens in a hundred court. Only the pope as Christ's vicar could absolve a citizen from these solemn vows, and throughout the Middle Ages this was the trump card of Vatican diplomacy. After the Reformation the Tudors continued the system without reference to the pope. With the people now confronted by a rivalry of politico-ecclesiastical allegiance, the precise form of the oath assumed greater importance.

Henry VIII instituted his Oath of Supremacy in 1534. Following Bloody Mary, Elizabeth introduced a new Oath of Allegiance at the beginning of her reign.[2] On the discovery of recusant (Roman Catholic) plots she declared a special oath for MPs in 1563.[3] Following the Gunpowder Plot of 1605 an Oath of Allegiance and Abjuration was exacted by James I[4] on the admission of MPs, 'upon the true Faith of a Christian'. Similar Acts[5] were passed four years later. Catholics had thus to renounce the political power of the pope to depose princes, and Jews were excluded altogether. In 1614 Attorney-General Francis Bacon's possible disqualification from the Commons as a practising barrister was investigated. It was decided to leave 'their Oath, their own consciences to look into, not we to examine it'.[6] In 1678, after the Titus Oates allegations, an Oath of Abjuration[7] of Roman Catholic doctrines was introduced, thus excluding Catholics from both Houses.

The 1689 Toleration Act[8] simplified the old oaths and allowed

Quakers to make a solemn declaration together with a profession of faith in the Trinity and the Scriptures. In 1696 they were allowed in civil court cases to make a simple declaration 'in the presence of Almighty God'.[9] Three years later the Quaker John Archdale was refused an affirmation in the Commons and refused to take an oath. The Quakers were the best-known of many sects which, in the period of biblical fundamentalism that came with the Puritan revival, insisted on following Matthew 5, 34 and 37: 'Swear not at all . . . But let your communication be, Yea yea; Nay nay: for whatsoever is more than these cometh of evil.' During Old Pretender trouble in 1701 a fourth oath[10] was introduced, renouncing the Stuart claim. Thirteen years later a fine of £500 was imposed on members of parliament for voting without taking the prescribed oaths. In 1721 the affirmation—wherever it might apply—was established in its modern form: 'I, A.B., do solemnly, sincerely, and truly declare and affirm.'[11] Throughout the nineteenth century freedom slowly broadened down from statute to statute, and in 1858[12] 'the true Faith of a Christian' vanished from the oath.

NOTES

Abbreviations:
BC: Bradlaugh Collection, National Secular Society
BMMS: British Museum's Department of Manuscripts
F: *Freethinker*
H: *Hansard*
I: *(London) Investigator*
IH: *International Herald*
MSAB: Hypatia Bradlaugh Bonner's manuscript memoir of Annie Besant
NL: Northampton Central Public Library
NR: *National Reformer*
NSS: National Secular Society
PRO: Public Record Office
R: *Reasoner*
Rep: Republican
SC: *Secular Chronicle*
SR: *Secular Review*

CHAPTER ONE

1. Variously spelt Bradlaugh, Bradlaughe, Bradlaw, Bradley, Bradlow, Bradlowe, Bradlough; pure Anglo-Saxon meaning 'broad mound'. East Anglian information derived from sources acknowledged in Appendix 1, articles in the *East Anglian Daily Times* for 1923 and Joan Corder's *Dictionary of Suffolk Arms* (1965). The Bradlaugh coat of arms included three *fleur-de-lis Argent.*
2. Composed by Francis Genius and Francis Goodwill.
3. Smithy and cottage behind still in family's possession.
4. Later the site of a board school, now the Pitfield Youth Centre and London College of Furniture, Borough of Hackney. Bacchus Walk and nearby Bradlaugh Street are now swallowed up in a housing estate, London N.1.
5. Writings on Bradlaugh represent his birthplace not in its modest gentility of 1833 but in its decrepit state described at his death in, e.g., A. Osborne Jay's *Story of Shoreditch* (1896), Sir Walter Besant's *Children of Gibeon* (1888), Arthur Morrison's *Tales of Mean Streets* (1894) and *Child of the Jago* (1896), and Charles Booth's *Life and Labour of the People in London* (1902-3).
6. 'Charles Bradlaugh' by Anne Besant (*Review of Reviews,* March 1891).
7. At St Leonard's, the old parish church of Shoreditch, not the nearby St John the Baptist. St Leonard's *Baptism Register*, 8 December 1833; Shoreditch Central Library; BC.
8. Now Columbia Road, London E.2.
9. *The Autobiography of C. Bradlaugh* (1873), p. 5.

10. Now Mansford Street, London E.2.
11. From 8,872,980 to 13,894,574 and from 818,129 to 1,358,541 (*Population*, 1831).
12. The rent was seven shillings a week. Now the site of Tower Hamlets Borough's Wyndham Deedes House.
13. In the 1740s over 60% of the population were weavers or dyers; by the 1840s this percentage had halved (research based on a sample of 400 entries in St Matthew's *Baptism Register*). For this and later periods see George F. Vale's *Old Bethnal Green* (1934) and George Lansbury's *My Life* (1928) and *Looking Backwards and Forwards* (1935).
14. *Review of Reviews*, March 1891.
15. Now Buckfast Street, London E.2., in the Greater London Council's Hereford Estate.
16. Built by the British and Foreign School Society, originally the Royal Lancastrian Institution (1808) after its founder Joseph Lancaster. The Abbey St Schools (infants, boys and girls) were founded in 1837; later became Sunday schools and are now the Robert Montefiore School Annexe (Inner London Education Authority).
17. All the Bradlaugh biographies and obituaries, save that of the *Echo* (30 January 1891), perpetuated this. J.M. Robertson asserted (*Charles Bradlaugh*, 1920, p.2.) there were no other available schools in Bradlaugh's day; but apart from 'dame' and other private schools and British foundations there was a sprinkling of Society for Promoting Christian Knowledge charity schools (1699) and Shaftesbury's 'ragged' schools (1844). The National Society 'for promoting the education of the poor in the principles of the Established Church' was created by Dr Andrew Bell in 1811 and remains the custodian of Anglican voluntary maintained schools.
18. Now Ravenscroft Street, London E.2.
19. His Paymaster Sergeant in the army, who otherwise gave a favourable account of his ability, claimed his arithmetic was dubious (*Englishman's Overland Mail*, 8 September 1891). His daughter disputed this. In adult life he showed an accountant's ability to analyse figures.
20. See Appendix 3.
21. *The Growth of the British Party System*, I, 1640-1923 (1965) by Ivor Bulmer-Thomas, p. 58.
22. *Political Unionist*, 30 June 1832.
23. *Annual Register* for 1833, p. 205.
24. E.P. Thompson's *Making of the English Working Class* (1963), p.807.
25. Founder of the Brahmâ Samâj, a modernist Hindu movement.
26. Founder of the Religious Tract Society and strenuous opponent of Thomas Paine.
27. See Andrew Rothstein's *House on Clerkenwell Green* (1966), scrapbooks at the Central Library, Tower Hamlets, William Combe and William Henry Pyre's *Microcosm of London* (1904), Henry Mayhew *et al.*'s *London Characters* (1874), A. R. Hope Moncrieff's *London* (1910) and J.J. Sexby's *Victoria Park* (1936). The park was created as a 'Hyde Park of the East End' under an Act of 1840 which sanctioned the spending of £72,000 realized by

the sale of York House, St James's Park. Some 290 acres were laid out by Sir James Pennethorne in 1842-5.

28. Called after Bloody Mary's persecuting Bishop of London, Edmund Bonner, though what had been an episcopal palace was sold by his hapless predecessor Nicholas Ridley. 'Bishop Bonner's Palace' was finally demolished in 1845 and the site was used for religious and political outdoor meetings till occupied by the City of London Hospital for Diseases of the Chest (1855) in an attempt to cope with tuberculosis.

29. Always described as the *Political Gridiron*. In fact *Cobbett's Gridiron* (1822) is a hostile pamphlet and Cobbett's projected daily of this name was never issued. Probably Cobbett's *Political Proteus* (1804), which was in Bradlaugh's possession at his death. May have been a bound volume of Cobbett's weekly *Political Register*, which often had a gridiron at its masthead after 13 November 1819 when he issued his challenge to Castlereagh, Sidmouth and Canning on their return to the gold standard at pre-Napoleonic War parity.

30. *The Biography of Charles Bradlaugh* (1880) by Adolphe S. Headingley, p.3.

31. City Road Basin, London E.C.1.

32. An autographed copy of the *Life and Struggles of William Lovett* (1876) later became his most cherished book; author's collection.

33. Now, respectively, St Matthew w. St Philip, St Matthias, St Paul and St Andrew, and St Peter w. St Thomas.

34. *Christian Commonwealth* (5 February 1891), *Manchester Guardian* (26 September 1933) and all the Bradlaugh biographies.

35. *Autobiography*, p. 7.

36. As related by Annie Besant (*Weekly Dispatch*, 1 February 1891), who never lost anything in the telling; but plausible in that Bradlaugh's iron discipline in public, often indeed betrayed by tears, masked tempestuous private struggles.

37. *Diegesis* (1829), p. 4. In Bradlaugh's copy of the book (author's possession) a portion of this paragraph is underlined. The phrase 'better or worse for belief' is doubly underlined: so too are 'if it be true' in another passage relating to Christianity and 'the evidence of moral demonstration shall offer to our conviction'. It is uncertain whether these markings appeared before or after the book's dispatch to Packer.

38. Headingley's *Biography*, p. 5.

39. Letter to the Rev. Brewin Grant, 19 April 1860 (Charles S. Mackay's libellous *Life of Charles Bradlaugh, M.P.,* 1888, p. 43).

40. Pamphlet *First Letter from 'Iconoclast' to Rev. Brewin Grant*, June 1860.

41. Summary of Chapter 18 in *Diegesis*, p. vii.

42. Announcement, October 1824 (*Carlile's Rep*, 29 April 1825).

43. *British Weekly*, 19 January 1891.

44. *Autobiography*, p. 8.

45. Numbers 183, 55, 84, 135 and 62, at the last of which he drew great crowds by displaying in the first-floor window great effigies of a 'temporal broker' and a bishop arm-in-arm with the devil as 'spiritual brokers'. See his *Rep* (1819-26), G.J. Holyoake's *Life and Character of Richard Carlile* (1849), William Kent's *London for Heretics* (1932) and J.M. Wheeler's *Biographical*

Dictionary of Freethinkers of All Ages and Nations (1889).

46. For publishing No. 3 of the *Prompter* (27 November 1830).

47. Letter from Eliza Sharples Carlile to Thomas Cooper, 23 April 1850; BC.

48. His legal wife Jane died a few months after him.

49. Letter from Eliza Sharples Carlile to Thomas Cooper, 28 July 1849; BC.

50. He had previously been a Methodist and ended as a Baptist minister.

51. See note 49.

52. Headingley's *Biography*, p.13. A similar but less fulsome version is in Hypatia Bradlaugh Bonner's *Charles Bradlaugh: A Record of His Life and Work* (1895), I, p. 19.

53. *Autobiography*, p. 9.

54. Now the site of miscellaneous clothing manufacturers and wholesalers.

55. According to his first press notice, a report in the *British Banner* (31 July 1850), a religious journal hostile to Chartism.

56. *Benny on Bradlaugh and Hyndman* (1884) by J. Benny, p. 1.

57. The original MS (BC), which was never published, has a note 4 years later: 'I would not defend the existence of Jesus as a man at all though I have not sufficient evidence to deny it.'

58. Or Essene. A novel hypothesis then, quite common today through the writings of John Allegro and others.

59. Probably 'Dr' John Brindley, originally master of the National School at March, who lectured against Owen and later against Bradlaugh.

60. Headingley's *Biography*, p. 12. Bradlaugh's daughter observed (*Record*, I, p.44) that he later lectured on Burns and Byron and also loved Whittier, Marlowe, Spenser and Sidney.

61. *A Few Words on the Christians' Creed* (1850) p.15.

62. See note 55.

63. The title may have been inspired by the article 'Past, Present, and Future' in No. 10 of the *Black Dwarf* (2 April 1817), for which Thomas Wooler was unsuccessfully prosecuted for libel.

64. First published 1801 and, apart from Paine's *Age of Reason* and *Rights of Man*, the most prosecuted work of that period. See Carlile's *Rep*, 9 May 1823.

65. Everyone testified to his amiability. With a pointed reference to George Jacob Holyoake, their sister Henrietta wrote to Bradlaugh's daughter (31 January 1895; BC): 'I had so often heard of you from my friend and brother *Austin* Holyoake.'

66. Holyoake was editor and Watson publisher of the *R*, launched 3 June 1846 and described in C.G. Harding's *Rep* (Introduction to I, 1848) as 'fearless, bold, independent, and always on the side of humanity'. Its name probably inspired by Wooler's *R* (July 1813 to July 1814), this principle of reincarnation being popular among radical nineteenth-century editors. Similarly the *Oracle of Reason* echoed Charles Blount's collection *The Oracles of Reason,* of 1693.

67. BC. First reproduced in G.J. Holyoake's *Life and Career of Charles Bradlaugh, M.P.* (1891), p. 3.

68. *ibid*, p. 4.

69. 'J.J.' in the *Hereford Times*, 4 April 1891.
70. *R*, 30 October 1850.
71. The essay has some 22,000 words. It is not certain which parts he copied out, but the above extracts, taken at random, have particular significance.
72. Now Goldsmith's Row, London E.2.
73. Letter from M.A. Keeves Record to Hypatia Bradlaugh Bonner, 21 March 1891; BC.

CHAPTER TWO

1. Founded as Devonshire's Horse in 1688, merged with the 4th Royal Irish Dragoon Guards in 1922. The 'Virgin Mary' was Empress Maria Theresa, for whom it had fought in the eighteenth century.
2. *British Weekly*, 19 January 1891. Bradlaugh and his daughter often had occasion to amend W.R. Bradlaugh's accounts of Charles's heartlessness and his family's concern, but this report is probably correct.
3. *ibid.*
4. See Appendix 2. In 1690 the regiment had fought for King Billy at the Battle of the Boyne.
5. *Echo*, 2 March 1875.
6. Further sidelights in NSS's *Almanack* for 1876, pp. 51-3.
7. He remained a temperance advocate throughout his life. Was a complete abstainer till 1861, when his physician told him he was drinking too much tea (*Record*, II, p.30).
8. *Englishman's Overland Mail*, 8 September 1891.
9. Headingley, p.21.
10. *Record*, I, p. 39.
11. See note 8.
12. Robertson's *Charles Bradlaugh*, p. 14.
13. Bradlaugh retained the mythical professor's disinterest in food. 'His meals had to be punctual to the moment, or, if asked for at an unaccustomed hour, they had to be promptly served; if that was done, he was content with whatever was given him' (*Record*, II, p. 32). His daughter also recorded that at his death his chest measurement was 46½ inches, though he was then overweight.
14. Headingley, p. 22.
15. Accusations in *Land and Water* (17 February 1891) and *Daily Chronicle* (29 September 1891). Bradlaugh's Paymaster Sergeant said the opposite: 'He was in no sense a badly affected or insubordinate soldier, but on the contrary most steady and law-abiding' (*Englishman's Overland Mail*, 8 September 1891).
16. *Autobiography*, p. 9.
17. In later years shadow-fighting with his heavy sabre (BC) was the only

exercise he took.

18. Letter to Bradlaugh from Scotland, then a lieutenant-colonel, 26 March 1883 (BC), a courteous, almost moving plea to the now celebrated atheist to 'stay your powerful voice and pen from disseminating your views, and causing others to believe what will eternally ruin them'.

19. *Review of Reviews*, March 1891.

20. Suppressed in 1855.

21. 'Memoir' by John M. Robertson appended to Bradlaugh's posthumously published *Labour and Law* (1891), p. xxvi. Overlooking this incident his daughter came to attribute his tendency to erysipelas to injuries later sustained in worthier combats. Bradlaugh's half-jocular assessment of this disability was probably not exaggerated. We now know there is a close connection between erysipelas, rheumatic fever, of which he was also subject to recurring attacks, and Bright's Disease (toxaemic kidney), from which he died. They are caused by the toxins of *Streptococcus pyogenes*, a Group A haemolytic streptococcus, whose effects are stimulated by debility due to overwork and anxiety.

22. See Appendix 2.

23. *Autobiography*, p. 10.

24. *New York Tribune*, 7 October 1873.

25. 'Memoir' by Bertram Dobell to James Thomson's *Voice from the Nile* (1884), p. 10. Thomson was nicknamed 'Co' (precocious). He was brought up in Scottish puritanism. His mother, an Irvingite, was emotionally un-balanced. His father's paralysis in 1840 impoverished the family.

26. *The Life of James Thomson ('B.V.')* (1889) by H.S. Salt, p. 10.

27. A letter to Elizabeth (14 March 1853; BC) mentions a seven-month absence.

28. Somewhat improbably his grand-daughter attributed this to 'the agony of mind which he must have endured from the time when his son was first denounced to him as an "Atheist" ' (*Record*, I, p. 28).

29. *British Weekly*, 19 January 1891.

30. 'Dedication' to 1861 edition of *The Bible, What it is!*

31. *A Proem* 'Carouse in the Past' (1853) to Robert Browning's *Saul* (BC). See *Poetical Works of James Thomson* (1895), II, p.438. Bertram Dobell at-tributed Thomson's later alcoholism and pessimism to the loss of his young love, but a close associate of the poet in his declining years, G.W. Foote, rightly observed: 'She was, I hold, merely the peg on which he hung his raiment of sorrow; without her another object might have served the same purpose. He carried with him, his proper curse, constitutional melancholia' (*Progress*, 1 April 1884, and Thomson's *Satires and Profanities*, 1884, p. viii). She also provided an excuse for having no wife or girl-friends.

32. See note 29.

33. Letter 14 March 1853; BC.

34. Letter 22 June 1853; BC. The whole purchase system, involving purchasing commissions, was abolished by Gladstone in 1871. Bradlaugh's calumniators later made the inevitable assertion that his sudden departure was connected with his foreseeing the 1854-6 Crimean War.

35. Letter from Lieutenant E.T. Rowbiggin, 23 September 1853; BC.

36. *Morning Post*, 31 January 1891.

37. Letter 28 December 1853 to her solicitors (author's collection). Unaware of this letter Bradlaugh's daughter blamed Lepard for trying to hold up the purchase (*Record*, I, pp. 37-8). Packer declared his mother had come forward 'with money she had saved' (*Anti-Infidel*, July 1899).

38. Letter to mother, 6 October 1853; BC.

CHAPTER THREE

1. *Stepping Stone*, April 1862.

2. Indeed the journal *Red Republican* had changed its name to *Friend of the People* on 7 December 1850, just before Bradlaugh left England.

3. In December 1850 he established the *English Republic*, which lingered till 15 April 1855, but it was a paper without a movement.

4. *English Republic*, 22 October 1851.

5. *London Phalanx*. See *Benny on Bradlaugh and Hyndman*.

6. Thesis (quoted by kind permission) *George Jacob Holyoake and the Secularist Movement in Britain, 1841-1861* (1968) by Edward Royle, pp. 42-3. The wave of prosecutions which put four of the five editors of the *Oracle of Reason* in gaol receded in 1844. In its wake came public apathy. Even the excitement of 1848 failed to establish Holyoake as a great popular leader. His *R* had limited though loyal support, but his collaborations in 'popular' journalism with Maltus Questell Ryall (*Movement*, 16 December 1843 to 2 April 1845) and Linton (*Cause of the People*, 20 May to 22 July 1848) were unsuccessful.

7. Holyoake's *Principles of Secularism Illustrated* (3rd edition revised), p.10.

8. Proprietor of the *Spirit of the Age* and other radical papers, and solicitor to Owen, Holyoake and Rowland Hill. Holyoake himself attributed secularist guidance to G.H.Lewes, but this is questionable.

9. This number was first given in 1858 (*PO Directory*), when William Bendall was listed as proprietor and a coachmaker and an academy as neighbours. Now the site of Lummus Co. Ltd.

10. This was foreshadowed a generation before, in 1820, when three comrades in adversity—Carlile in Dorchester Gaol, Wooler in Warwick Gaol and Henry Hunt in Ilchester Gaol—almost forgot their common foe as they hurled anathemas at one another like fifteenth-century antipopes.

11. *R*, 15 October 1851.

12. Letter 7 February 1852 (No. 464 Holyoake Collection, Co-operative Union Library, Manchester). Southwell apparently knew nothing of the will. Holyoake later asserted that on Southwell's emigration 'Mr Fletcher, in his disappointment, bequeathed it to the present writer... who held Mr Fletcher's will two years' (*History of Co-operation in England: its literature and its advocates*, 1875, I, p. 239). McCabe, who had access to the Holyoake papers, accepted some time before the end of 1853, two years

before Southwell's departure, as the date of Holyoake's accession to the will (*Life-Stories of Famous Men: George Jacob Holyoake*, 1922, p.32).

13. *The Impossibility of Atheism Demonstrated, with Hints to Nominal Atheists* (1852).
14. *R*, 4 August 1852.
15. *R*, 11 August 1852.
16. Cooper had Salford origins, was educated at the socialist school established by Lloyd Jones and became a teacher himself at 14.
17. *R*, 14 January 1852.
18. Letter to Holyoake, 13 September 1852 (No. 524 Holyoake, Co-operative Union Library, Manchester).
19. *Leader*, 13 November 1852.
20. *R*, 6 October 1852.
21. *English Republic*, 26 March 1853.
22. *R*, 15 December 1852.
23. Said by Southwell in *R*, 7 December 1853.
24. Letter from his mother to her solicitors, 28 December 1853 (author's collection).
25. *Times*, 31 January 1891.
25. See *Law List* for 1854 and 1855. For some reason he had none by 1864.
27. *Record*, I, p. 42.
28. Lecture at John St Institution, 16 October 1853. Its significance recalled in *NR*, 20 August 1865. Maccall had been working on his theory 'for more than a dozen years' (*Outlines*, p. 3) and published *The Elements of Individualism* in 1847.
29. *R*, 16 November 1853.
30. *R*, 7 December 1853.
31. *ibid.*
32. *R*.1 January 1854.
33. *SR*, 3 June 1877.
34. Letter from Bradlaugh to Susannah, 17 November 1854; BC.
35. *Review of Reviews*, March 1891.
36. *R*, 26 October 1853. These criticisms are not borne out by Cooper's published writings.
37. *R*, 31 March 1858.
38. *I*, 1 April 1854.
39. Now St Augustine w. St Philip. Original church consecrated 1823. A good indication of population growth and the Victorian craze for christianizing the East End is the fact that 9 churches were built in Stepney in the whole period before Bradlaugh was born and 25 in his lifetime. See *Stepney Churches. An historical Account* (1967) by Gordon Banes.
40. Now Braintree St and Malcolm Rd, London E.1-2.
41. Sarcastically known as the 'Saints' Bill' because it was intended to come into force on 1 November, All Saints' Day.
42. Evidence in Report of the Royal Commission 'to inquire into the alleged disturbances of the public peace in Hyde Park, Sunday, July 1st, 1855; and the conduct of the metropolitan police in connection with the same' (*Par-

liamentary Blue Book, XXIII, 1856, p. 147). Extracts given in Headingley, p. 40, and *Record*, I, p. 59. Later quotations in text are from the same source.

43. *Autobiography*, p. 12. The 1936 Public Order Act has given the police almost unlimited powers over public demonstrations and an action such as Bradlaugh's, however justified, would not be treated so indulgently today.

44. Both the French and Russian Revolutions, and Indian and African independence movements, have had this foundation.

45. *H*, 2 July 1855, Third Series, CXXXIX, 369. In the 1960s the Lord's Day Observance Society asserted the Sunday Entertainments Bill would let big business exploit entertainers.

46. Still in existence, though inactive for many years.

47. Respectively 1860 and 1862.

48. With Voltaire he was convinced that those who believe absurdities will commit atrocities.

49. *NR*, 29 December 1860.

50. Despite this Kantian terminology Bradlaugh was most influenced by Spinoza and his monism was very similar to that later popularized by the German physician Ludwig Büchner and biologist Ernst Haeckel.

51. This was particularly hidden from his own family. Compare the writings of Robertson and Hypatia Bonner with the not unfriendly memoirs of his political contemporaries.

52. Letter from W. J. Birch to G. J. Holyoake, 25 September 1856 (No. 865 Holyoake, Co-operative Union Library). 'You always say myself and the cause, the cause and myself.'

53. In fact he took it in 1850 and tried to take it in 1852. His explanation was that he did so on his own terms.

54. Holyoake declared many associates Wesleyans after falling out with them; e.g. Wilks, who hotly denied it. He claimed—quite erroneously—that Southwell edited a Wesleyan journal in New Zealand in his later years.

55. Letter from Bradlaugh to Thomas Cooper, 24 October 1855; BC.

56. *R and London Tribune*, 15 June 1856. The *London Tribune* disappeared three weeks later.

57. History *of the Fleet Street House*, p. 8.

58. As many of Holyoake's regular contributors used pseudonyms, Johnson professed indignation when Holyoake sneered at 'Anthony Collins' 'as he calls himself' (*R*, 17 March 1858). But Johnson had assumed the name of a real person, a highly respected deist friend of John Locke's.

59. *R*, 17 March 1858.

60. This was in April 1857. Johnson dropped 'London' from the title, which Cooper had doubtless used to distinguish his from Southwell's *I* (April to October, 1843).

61. *I*, March 1858.

62. Bradlaugh intended to extend Cooper's work and produce a secularist encyclopaedia of biblical comment and criticism. This could occupy, as the *I* reviewer observed, 'years of study and a prodigality of loss'. *The Bible, What it is!*, originally in weekly parts of 8 pages at 1d each, extended from Genesis to Isaiah. As his own studies and the knowledge explosion grew, he

decided not to continue but to revise. An amplified version appeared in 1865 covering only the Pentateuch. By 1882 a still longer *Genesis: Its authorship and authenticity* covered just the first 11 chapters.

63. *I*, February 1858.
64. *ibid.*
65. Holyoake had said that 'one gentleman unconnected with Secularism advanced a loan of £388' (*History of the Fleet Street House*, p.8), and he often spoke of his liberal Christian friends.
66. *I*, July 1857.
67. *ibid.*
68. Libellous *Life* of Bradlaugh, p. 231.
69. Even in personal letters in the BC, Dr George Drysdale always signed himself 'G. R.' and gave Truelove's address. The authors of the libellous *Life*, with their beagle's nose for 'revelations', failed to discover his identity, though they got as close as his younger brother Charles.
70. Their liaison began in the same year as the book, 1854.
71. Of 17 May 1857. Holyoake later explained he reviewed the book 'without looking carefully into his pages' (*Warpath of Opinion*, 1896, p. 30). Austin Holyoake recommended the book in his *Large or Small Families* (1870).
72. *I*, August 1857. Insofar as he was the prime author of the libellous *Life* he later claimed 'he had seen only the Malthusian part in the "proof-sheets" sent to him by Mr Truelove' (p. 231).
73. Letter to William Hilton, Bolton, 29 September 1859; BC.
74. Later Hedger's Grove, London E.9, now swallowed up in a housing estate.
75. *I*, March 1858.
76. He gave a simple factual statement (p. 36) about the change of publisher, but Holyoake later spoke of his 'grievous-mongering tongue' (*R*, 21 April 1858).
77. Till 1873 this dealt with financial matters. They are now the province of county courts or the High Court.
78. Of 24 February 1858.
79 *I*, 15 April 1858.
80. *I*, 1 May 1858.
81. *I*, 1 January 1859.
82. Of January 1858.
83. *R*, 6 and 13 January 1858.
84. *I*, February 1858.
85. *R*, 24 February 1858.
86. *R*, 17 March 1858.
87. *R*, 31 March 1858.
88. *I*, 15 April 1858. Holyoake said he had spent £2,745 on the House and received £1,221.
89. *I*, 1 April 1858.
90. Robertson's comment in his 'Account of' Bradlaugh's 'Parliamentary Struggle, Politics and Teachings' (*Record*, II, p. 427).
91. *I*, 1 April 1858.
92. The *R* once praised *George Jacob Holyoake and Modern Atheism*, a pamph-

let by an 'independent publisher', who was in fact John Watts using his home address.

93. *R*, 14 April 1858.

94. Holyoake's official view of tyrannicide was 'I have no sympathy with this doctrine. I deem it far nobler and more useful to society, to submit to be the victim than to victimize others' (*Life and Character of Richard Carlile*, p. 37). But he wrote much more ambiguous material as the anonymous 'Editor of Literature of Tyrannicide'; e.g. in his Preface to *Killing No Murder* (1864 ed.), p. iv: 'It is Tyranny alone that creates Tyrannicides.'

95. Holyoake later claimed (*Warpath*, pp. 64-6) that he refused to publish because of the original title and Adams's insistence on anonymity, and that Mazzini was not mentioned.

96. The publisher was Stanislaus Tchorzewski, the tract *Letter to Parliament and the Press*. The Bill was popularly called the 'French Colonels' Bill'.

97. Letter from Hugo to Bradlaugh, 31 March (?) 1858; BC. This sneer at Louis Napoleon ('the Little') was invented by Hugo.

98. Before the Criminal Justice Act 1967 unanimous jury verdicts were required.

99. W. E. Adams in *Record*, I, p. 71. See also his *Memoirs of a Social Atom* (1903), II, p. 368.

100. Addendum by 'Saladin' to *Sexual Economy—as Taught by Charles Bradlaugh, M.P.* (?1885) by Peter Agate MD.

101. *I*, 1 May 1858.

CHAPTER FOUR

1. During his parliamentary career people asserted he had been uncouth in language and appearance before he turned respectable at Westminster. In the 1880s there was arising a class of socialist agitators (not including their founder H. M. Hyndman) who believed the masses respected them as 'one of us' if they looked as scruffy as possible.

2. A lifetime of outdoor speaking somewhat hardened this and he sometimes spoke too loudly in the House of Commons. In 1881 he wrote to the *New York Herald*, 'I never sang in my life'. Culture did not interest him particularly, except as relaxation or 'self-improvement'.

3. His enemies pretended this remained Cockney, e.g. Sir Alfred E. Pease's caricature: 'Hi 'OPE the 'Ouse will 'ear me' (*Elections and Recollections*, 1932, p. 66). Probably the truth was that Bradlaugh did not worry about the affected articulation which up till recently distinguished 'where' and 'wear'.

4. Mrs W. Pitt Byrne in *Social Hours with Celebrities* (1898), I, pp. 320-1.

5. cf. 'Hitler' (*Observer*, 22 September 1968) and the Leni Riefenstahl film *Triumpf des Willens* (1934).

6. T.P. O'Connor in *John O'London's Weekly*, 21 October 1933. At least two

of his opponents in debate, Dr Brindley and Brewin Grant, are recorded as imploring him not to look at them as he denounced their matter and their manners.

7. It was necessary for an infidel lecturer, especially a self-educated one, in those days and till recent times to carry his reference books about, including the bible. Many of his quotations he knew by heart and most could have been copied out with little trouble, but without a text to flourish he would have been accused of lying.

8. At his suggestion the NSS adopted as its motto a quotation from the German playwright Gotthold Lessing, 'We seek for truth'.

9. Bradlaugh did not believe in free lectures or collections and thought people valued only what they were prepared to pay for in advance. His admission charges were usually 2d. and 4d., though the best seats might command 1s. or more. The Rev. Dr Charles Maurice Davies observed: 'I could not help asking myself the question, How is it Mr Bradlaugh can get these people to pay fourpence and listen to an abstruse subject, while we cannot "compel them to come in"?' (*Heterodox London: or Phases of Freethought in the Metropolis*, 1874, II, p. 122). Davies shrewdly spoke of Holyoake and Bradlaugh as 'the typical Pharisee and Sadducee of the Secular ranks' (I, p. 375). The American Unitarian Charles W. Wendte made similar observations on Bradlaugh's meetings (*The Wider Fellowship*, 1927, I, pp. 285-6).

10. *Autobiography*, p. 14 (expanded in Headingley, pp. 42-4).

11. *ibid.*

12. Headingley, p. 49.

13. *ibid*, pp. 51-2.

14. Letters in the BC show she remained devoted to the family till her death. In retrospect it is clear that, though kind, they had the Victorian disregard for the independence and proper remuneration of domestics.

15. *I*, 1 July 1858.

16. Draft of letter in BC.

17. *Law List* for the 1850s. By 1858 Harvey is not shown.

18. *I*, 1 November 1858.

19. *I*, 1 December 1858. This was an enduring aspiration of reformers. In 1835 Owen formed an Association of All Classes of All Nations.

20. 'B.' for Bysshe in Percy Bysshe Shelley; 'V.' for Vanolis, an anagram of 'Novalis', the pseudonym of the German poet Friedrich von Hardenburg. Thomson admired one for his politics, the other for his pessimism, and both for their beauty.

21. In 1966 it amalgamated with the Leicestershire Building Society (1870) to form the Anglia Building Society.

22. *Rules*, adopted at general meeting, 12 December 1848. Until incorporation under the Building Societies' Act in 1923 it had power to buy and sell land. One of its prime purposes was to offer 'the forty shilling freehold and a vote for the county'. Gurney became secretary in 1853 and remained so till 1890. He was president from 1891 till his death 3 years later.

23. *Times*, 7 March 1859.

24. Letter to a friend, 16 March 1859 (*Record*, I, p. 83).

25. The real cause of papal anathemas against freemasonry was the nature of Continental orders as revolutionary, anticlerical secret societies. Up till 1877 the Grand Orient of France invoked, like Anglo-Saxon masonry, the Grand Architect of the Universe, but was never a mere social club for the wealthy. In *What Freemasonry is, what it has been, and what it ought to be* (1885) Bradlaugh said 'true Freemasonry should be of no religion' (p. 11) but admitted 'there are two Masonic currents drifting in very opposite directions' (p. 9).

26. *I*, 1 April 1859.

27. Libellous *Life*, p. 94.

28. *ibid*, pp. 94-5. The author of this section was probably Johnson, who knew both Bradlaugh and the law at this time and whose tactic was to build a vast tissue of innuendo on a frail skeleton of fact.

29. *Yorkshire Post*, 31 January 1891.

30. Until the 1868 Compulsory Church Rate Abolition Act, Anglican churches could levy rates on all householders in their parish regardless of belief. Truelove's premises at 240 Strand were in the parish of St Clement Danes.

31. Report of trial at Middlesex Sessions (*I*, 1 July 1859).

32. *I*, 1 August 1859.

33. The last chapter (13) of *The Compleat Angler, or the Contemplative Man's Recreation* (1653-5) is devoted to Tottenham.

34. Tottenham *Rate Book* for May 1861. Rates were 1s. in £1 half-yearly. The rooms were of moderate size, the top two being dormer attics. The house is now demolished but similar villas survive nearby. For background to Tottenham see William Roe's *Ancient Tottenham* (1949) and Fred Fisk's *History of Tottenham in the County of Middlesex* (1933) and *History of the Ancient Parish of Tottenham in the County of Middlesex* (1923).

35. *Halifax Courier*, 26 November 1904.

36. *Glasgow Herald*, 26 September 1933.

37. *Autobiography*, p. 16.

38. *Bradford Review* (*Record*, I, p. 158).

39. *Record*, I, pp. 49-50.

40. BC. Punctuation supplied. In letters and personal notes Bradlaugh disregarded most punctuation. His daughter recorded her surprise that someone so businesslike often omitted the dates of letters.

41. Letter from Holyoake to Cowen, 4 February 1859 (no. C 464, Cowen Papers, Newcastle upon Tyne Central Reference Library). The testimonials raised £642 and £500 towards the debts of the House-Institute.

42. With 'Malthusianism' this was a euphemism at the time for birth control.

43. *R*, 12 February 1860. Bronterre O'Brien had started a *NR* in 1837 (7 January to 18 March) and again in 1844.

44. *NR*, 6 June 1863. See Barker's *History and Confessions of a Man, as put forth by Himself* (1846) and *Life of Joseph Barker: Written by Himself* (1880).

45. Circular April 1860 from Elysium Villa; BC. Bradlaugh said therein his lectures were 'more successful than those of any other secular lecturer (excepting perhaps Mr Barker)'. Barker later claimed the Sheffield com-

mittee pressed him to join Bradlaugh and no members 'supposed that they were doing *me* a favour; but considered that I was doing *them* one' (*NR*, 27 July 1861).

46. An ancient British prince famous for his resistance to the Romans.
47. Probably the notorious 'G.R.' or Dr George Drysdale, author of the *Elements*.
48. *NR*, 9 June 1860.
49. Three 'taxes on knowledge' were imposed by the notorious Six Acts of 1819. These were gradually repealed in the middle of the century: duty on advertisements (1853), newspaper stamp (1855) and paper duty (1861). The *R* was the last unstamped publication to be summonsed under the old law.
50. *NR*, 2 June 1860.
51. *NR*, 21 July 1860.
52. Barker cannily described himself as a sceptic, saying 'I do not even ask my own wife and children what their religious opinions are. I never bother anybody about their religious opinions' (*NR*, 29 December 1860).
53. *NR*, 20 October 1860.
54. *Record*, I, p. 279.
55. *NR*, 27 July 1861.
56. *NR*, 16 March 1861.
57. Common Law Procedure Act (17 & 18 Vict. cap. 125), s. 20.
58. Shorthand report in *NR*, 27 April 1861. Bradlaugh was referring to the 1697 Blasphemy Act (9 Will. III cap. 35), which made it a criminal offence for anyone brought up as a Christian who then 'denies the Christian religion to be true, or the Holy Scriptures of the Old and New Testament to be of Divine authority' (s.1). This Act was repealed by the Criminal Law Act 1967.
59. *NR*, 9 March 1861.
60. *NR*, 23 March 1861.
61. Quoted in G.H. Taylor's *Chronology of British Secularism* (1957), p.6. A fairly rare example of florid Bradlaughana.
62. Letter from Trenaman to Hypatia Bonner, 16 March 1891; BC.
63. *Western Morning News*, 31 July 1861.
64. *Tablet*, 3 August 1861. An important object of the *Tablet* was to slate the 'jury of British Protestants' in an Anglican cathedral city.
65. *NR*, 9 November 1861.
66. *Jesus, Shelley, and Malthus* (1883 ed.), p. 10. In the 1877 edition he first mentioned 'some points of ethics on which I dissent'. In the 1861 edition he did not qualify the statement: 'His work I especially recommend'.
67. *Record*, II, p. 171.
68. *NR*, 18 May 1861.
69. *NR*, 1 June 1861.
70. *NR*, 15 June 1861.
71. *Life of Joseph Barker*, p. 336.
72. *NR*, 20 July 1861.
73. *ibid*.
74. *NR*, 27 July 1861.

75. *NR*, 3 August 1861.

76. *NR*, 10 August 1861.

77. *NR*, 24 August 1861.

78. *NR*, 7 September 1861.

79. *Autobiography*, p. 17.

80. *Pathfinder*, 16 November 1861.

81. *NR*, 31 August 1861. John Watts called *Barkers' (Barker's) Review* 'eight pages of vituperative effusion' (*NR*, 19 March 1864). In it Barker denounced anyone who could recommend the *Elements* 'as a greater criminal, as a deadlier foe to virtue and humanity, than the vilest murderer that ever plotted or sinned against mankind' (28 September 1861).

82. *NR*, 23 November 1861, and *Counsellor*, December 1861.

83. The Joint Stock Companies Act of 1844 began the boom. Acts of 1855, 1856 and 1862 made vain attempts to regulate it. The industrial revolution was demanding more and more minerals of all sorts and gold finds in California and Australia excited the world. Harvey was said to own the Tal-y-Sarn Slate Quarries in North Wales. Bradlaugh's connection with him probably terminated late in 1859. Headingley stated that 'from 1858 to 1861 Bradlaugh worked in the provinces, visiting town after town, establishing Secular Societies' (p. 61). At first these were merely weekend visits.

84. cf. Dickens's *Martin Chuzzlewit* (1844). Largely because of his exposures the Debtors Act of 1869 somewhat ameliorated the position.

85. Headingley, p. 61. The details of Bradlaugh's legal and business career are vague. Mostly writing in propagandist journals (even his *Autobiography* first appeared in the *NR*) he probably felt it of slight interest. His daughter added little because he seldom brought his worries home and tended to destroy all private correspondence. Naturally this enabled enemies to say later the family had something to hide. I have been able to shed some light through research in company files at the PRO. The incident involving Harvey's son is from the libellous *Life*, which implies a Heep-Wickfield (*David Copperfield*, 1850) relationship. As a tainted source it is generally to be avoided but here has a ring of truth. It suggests the Harvey family did not impute malpractice to Bradlaugh.

86. BT 31/593, 2470; PRO.

87. By 18 November 1862 1,087 shares were subscribed for.

88. *Record*, I, p. 156.

89. Entry on Mazzini in *Encyclopaedia Britannica* (1969), XV, p. 21. The writer seemed unaware of Bradlaugh's role.

90. *'Thorough': The Late Charles Bradlaugh, M.P., and Northampton* (1894), p. 7. Gedge was vicar from 1859 to 1877.

91. Bates was a strong radical who later led an independent Radical Association and stood against Thomas Adams in a county election. See Northampton *Mercury*, 17 February 1922, and election poster in NL.

92. *NR*, 12 October 1861.

93. Memorandum of agreement between Leverson and Bradlaugh, 11 January 1862; BC.

94. BC.

95. Austin Holyoake's boy said he delivered the copies but George Jacob claimed not to have received them. When he later challenged Bradlaugh's version of the agreement he was thus unable to provide any evidence.

96. *Mr Holyoake's Disconnection with the 'National Reformer' and the Correspondence Which Accounts for It* (1862); tract in BC and Bishopsgate Institute. In his first *NR* Holyoake said he was 'not implicated in any responsibility of editorial duties' (4 January 1862), but claimed later there was a private arrangement overriding this.

97. *Minutes of Meetings* of the arbitrators (1863), para. 500; BC. *Moral Physiology* (1831) was a birth control book by Robert Dale Owen.

98. *Minutes*, para. 632.

99. After denying this, Holyoake said he agreed to be editor to the company, not of the paper, as he proposed to change its name and form.

100. During the arbitration Bradlaugh complained Holyoake often gave short measure on original material and simply reproduced his lecture notes and letters to other papers.

101. Letter from Bradlaugh to Holyoake, 29 March 1862.

102. This had no effective existence and was unrelated to Bradlaugh's NSS of 1866.

103. *Minutes*, para. 548.

104. Raised £5,614 1s. 9d. Ashurst became solicitor to the GPO.

105. *Minutes*, para. 57.

106. Even if Bradlaugh were responsible for payment, Holyoake claimed a sum for these wages which he had to admit was never paid.

107. Letter from Crawford to Linton, 6 March 1863; BC. *The New Moral World* was a journal established 1 November 1834 by Robert Owen.

108. Letter from Linton to Hypatia Bonner, 20 March 1892; BC. Apart from *Mr Holyoake's Disconnection*, his version of the dispute is given in James Dodworth's *Account of the Proceedings at the Shareholders' Meeting of the National Reformer Co., Held at Sheffield, March 23, 1862*, William Turley's *Mr Holyoake and his Detractors*, and James Robertson's *Secularists and their Slanders* and *Mr Holyoake and his Assailants* (all 1862).

109. Now the site of the new Leathersellers' Hall, London E.C.3.

110. *Newcastle Weekly Chronicle*, 7 February 1891.

111. *NR*, 16 August 1862.

112. On 7 September 1862.

113. This was how Cardinal Wiseman described them after they had been routed by a counter-attack.

114. *Morning Advertiser,* 29 September 1862

115. *NR*, 4 October 1862.

116. *Record*, I, p. 131. This is doubtless true. But Bradlaugh's health frequently broke down and he carried on. It seems likely that other considerations were in his mind at this time when he largely withdrew from active propagandism.

117. *NR*, 28 February 1862.

118. cf. the film *The Bofors Gun* (1968).

1. The 1860 *Law List* names the Great Ship Co. Ltd, Ecuador Land Co. Ltd and Telegraph Cable Co. Ltd.
2. Now the site of the Commercial Union Insurance Co., London E.C.3. After the move Jacob Elkin became manager of the Italian Coal and Iron Co. Ltd. Leverson went to 66 Bishopsgate in 1864, before the crash.
3. He vanished overseas. By 1873 his address in the books of the Italian Coal and Iron Co. is given as New York; that of his wife as Hanover. In 1868 Bradlaugh is listed for the first time as a shareholder (with ten shares) at 23 Great St Helens, with his profession given as 'articled clerk'.
4. He was described technically as a merchant.
5. Among the companies were the St Nazaire Co. Ltd (1864), Caerhun Slate Co. Ltd (1865) and Naples Colour Co. Ltd (1866).
6. Bradlaugh urged all freethinking parents to withdraw their children from indoctrination at school and provide books giving both sides freely at home as they grew older. Today the NSS advises parents to put the happiness of the child at school first and consider possible embarrassment or victimization withdrawal may cause.
7. His admission was made easier by membership of the Loge des Philadelphes. Garibaldi was simultaneously Grand Master of the Grand Lodge of Italy and president of the Società Atea (atheist society) of Venice. Sir Charles Dilke was a member of the Ranelagh Lodge No. 834 at Hammersmith (Dilke Papers, Add. 43910; BMMS).
8. *Parish of Tottenham: Minutes of Vestry*, 13 September 1864.
9. *ibid*, 20 February 1865. At this time the provision of essential services was one of vital concern to the proliferating metropolis. In the decade or two before steps had been taken to reform, reduce, rationalize and circumscribe the powers of the ancient vestries. The 1848 Public Health Act had set up a General Board of Health under Edwin Chadwick, with local boards responsible for disease prevention, pure water supply and other matters. A Metropolitan Board of Works (which yielded to the London County Council in 1889), with local boards, was set up by the Metropolis Management Act in 1855, mainly to build sewers and better roads. By 1865 there were still demarcation disputes.
10. *Life and Letters* of Holyoake, I, p. 330 and following.
11. On 28 September 1864. Marx was the guiding light from the first (see *SC*, 4 August 1878, and *Progress*, May 1883) and drew up its Inaugural Address and General Statements. Other revolutionary intellectuals came into IWMA from the Continent. Britain, on the other hand, interpreted the association to mean what its name implied, and put forward working trades unionists like George Odger and W. R. Cremer. As a City financier Bradlaugh hardly qualified, though the inaugural meeting was presided over by the bourgeois positivist historian E. S. Beesly. In a MS note to an article in the *Westminster Gazette* (4 November 1918) Hypatia Bonner wrote: 'Charles Bradlaugh and Karl Marx were antagonistic. I do not think CB was ever a

member of the International: although it is possible he was present at a meeting' (BC).

12. Howell had been the first secretary of the London Trades Council, 1860-2. He became a Christian and the first secretary of the TUC Parliamentary Committee in 1871. In 1878 he wrote a *History* of the International hostile to Marx as an atheist.

13. He resigned in 1871 after it endorsed Marx's *Address on the Civil War in France.*

14. Cremer became the organizer of the Workmen's Peace Association (later International Arbitration League), MP for Haggerston and a knight.

15. Lucraft resigned from the International for the same reason as Odger.

16. Edmund Burke's *Reflections on the Revolution in France* (1790), p. 117.

17. Suggestions were an £8 or £6 tenant suffrage, respectively without and with the poor law rate. Lord John's Bill was related to the poor rate. Unfortunately many otherwise eligible tenants gladly contracted with an interested landlord that he should pay the rate, and thus they lost their vote.

18. John Bright's Bill would have enfranchised only 200,000 more.

19. See Newman's *Permissive Bill more urgent than Parliamentary Enfranchisement* (1865).

20. See Mill's *Thoughts on Parliamentary Reform* (1859).

21. *The Liberal Situation: Necessity for A Qualified Franchise* (1865), pp. 9-10.

22. *The Real Representation of the People* (1863), pp. 4-5.

23. See Hare's *Treatise on the Election of Representatives, Parliamentary and Municipal* (1859). Proportional allocation was to involve the whole country, not separate regions. The preference scheme proposed that when a candidate secured a specified number of votes, enough to ensure his election, the next preferences should be allotted to other candidates.

24. *Real Representation*, p. 3.

25. i.e. United States (*NR*, 8 October 1865).

26. BT 31/1182, 2594C; PRO. For mining in Caerhun, Caernarvonshire. Registered 14 November 1865 with nominal capital of 2,500 £10 shares and 5,000 £1 shares, of which 880 £10 shares and 3,007 £1 shares were taken up.

27. His daughter stated that he was building stables at the bottom of the garden in this period (*Record*, I, p. 108), and it was presumably then that he acquired the fine mahogany, rosewood and walnut furniture, damask furnishings and Brussels carpets listed in the auctioneers' *Catalogue* of 1870; BC.

28. In later years Hypatia was a well-known children's story writer and acknowledged the stimulation he gave her (*Our Corner*, 1 August 1886).

29. BT 31/1220, 2810C; PRO. Presumably the company worked in association with the Italian Coal and Iron Co. 'The paint that this company sold was a good paint' (*Star*, 12 February 1891).

30. Potterton, another struggling intellectual helped by Bradlaugh, became a schoolmaster 2 years later.

31. Robertson's 'Memoir' with *Labour and Law*, p. xxxviii.

32. *Annual Register* for 1866, p. 185.
33. *ibid*, p. 183.
34. *Utopia Unlimited* (1893). See *The Savoy Operas* (1926), p. 601.
35. He added 126 to his shareholding of 99 in Caerhun.
36. He died the following October. Bradlaugh gave benefit lectures for the widow.
37. At 10s. 6d. per week, he complained bitterly later. But Bradlaugh was hard-pressed, his own luxuries were curtailed and the stables never finished, As the paper expanded Austin Holyoake was made a second sub-editor.
38. The following reconstruction is based on Fisk's *History* (2nd series 1923), pp. 197-8, and documents at Bruce Castle.
39. Vicar from 1862 to 1870. Tottenham Vestry met at All Hallows under the chairmanship of Hale. The minutes do not show any particular animosity between him and Bradlaugh, but Hypatia Bonner believed the odd press report showed there was and, confusing the two parishes, named McSorley as the vestry chairman and gave this as a motivation for the libel.
40. Vicar from 1861 to 1892. He made collections of evangelical hymns and wrote regularly for the ultra-Protestant *Rock*. The only time he appears to have attended the vestry was when a faculty was to be applied for to alter the east end of All Hallows.
41. No. 365, 21 April 1866.
42. *Tottenham and Edmonton Weekly Herald, Southgate Messenger, etc.,* 29 December 1866. The complainant was a local tradesman, who claimed his trade suffered from other assertions in the article.
43. *Standard*, 22 May 1866.
44. *How are we to abolish the Lords?* (1884), p. 6.
45. *NR*, 29 April 1866.
46. *Times*, 3 July 1866.
47. *NR*, 15 July 1866.
48. *NR*, 5 August 1866.
49. *NR*, 12 August 1866.
50. *NR*, 9 September 1866.
51. G.W. Foote's *Reminiscences of Charles Bradlaugh* (1891), p.5.
52. The only one to survive is that at Leicester, endowed with valuable property mainly through the wealthy Gimson engineering family.
53. In *The Late Charles Bradlaugh* it is stated that he spoke there although 'the local wire-pullers were not quite pleased at his advent, and . . . endeavoured to make him feel that he was *de trop*' (p.6).
54. In *About Myself* (1930) he described his educational debt to the secular Sunday school of his youth.
55. *NR*, 13 January 1867.
56. Letter from Voysey to Bradlaugh, 16 January 1867; BC.
57. *NR*, 16 June 1867.
58. Letter from Bradlaugh to Howell, 15 February 1867; BC.
59. Letter from Beales to Bradlaugh, 17 May 1867 (*Record*, I, p. 236).
60. Letter from Bradlaugh to Beales, 10 June 1872; BC. The International opposed a show of strength, believing the people were 'not yet ripe' and

should not fight brethren in the police and army (IWMA General Council *Minute Book*, 30 April 1867). Or perhaps it would not support what it did not lead.

61. *Daily Telegraph*, 7 May 1867.
62. Letter from Howell to Bradlaugh, 10 May 1867; BC.
63. See note 59.
64. Derby called it 'dishing the Whigs'.
65. Headingley, p. 104. Bradlaugh always regarded the Fenian movement as a native product, not an American importation (*NR*, 19 January 1868).
66. Lecture at Steinway Hall, New York, 6 October 1873 (*Champion of Liberty: Charles Bradlaugh* (1933), p. 245).
67. Lecture in Ireland in 1878 (Headingley, p. 108).
68. Fenian Manifesto.
69. *NR*, 22 December 1867.
70. Letter from Gladstone to Bradlaugh, 17 July 1868; BC.
71. In 1868 he became Gladstone's Lord Chancellor as Baron Hatherley. Three years later he heard Voysey's unsuccessful appeal to the Privy Council.
72. Cheques of £200 payable monthly; BC. See entry on dos Santos in *Grande Enciclopédia Portuguesa & Brasileira* (1940), XI, p. 198.
73. Constant Van den Brouck; BC.
74. Shorthand notes in *NR*, 22 December 1867.
75. Preamble to Evidence Further Amendment Act 1869, 32 & 33 Vict. cap. 68. There had been an Evidence Amendment Act the year before on a different subject.
76. Section 4.
77. 33 & 34 Vict. cap. 49, s.1.
78. More accurately 60 Geo. III & 1 Geo. IV cap. 9. This was one of the Six Acts passed in 1819 when Cobbett's and Sherwin's *Weekly Political Registers* and Carlile's *Rep* were agitating Lord Liverpool's Cabinet.
79. 11 Geo IV & 1 Will. IV cap. 73. The third Security Law was 6 & 7 Will. IV cap. 76; it did not alter the law in this particular but reduced the newspaper stamp from 6d. to 1d.
80. *NR*, 7 February 1869.
81. *History of the Taxes on Knowledge* (1899), II, p. 195.
82. *NR*, 9 May 1869.
83. Gilbert and Sullivan's *Iolanthe* (1882). See *The Savoy Operas*, p. 234.
84. The Liberal Registration Association (1861) and National Union of Conservative and Constitutional Associations (1867) existed chiefly to get votes registered. See H. J. Hanham's *Elections and Party Management: Politics in the time of Disraeli and Gladstone* (1959), John Vincent's *Formation of the Liberal Party 1857-68* (1966), Sir Henry Slesser's *History of the Liberal Party* (1944), Robert McKenzie's *British Political Parties. The distribution of power within the Conservative and Labour parties* (1955) and Ivor Bulmer-Thomas's *Growth of the British Party System*, I, 1640-1923 (1965).
85. Representation of the People Act 1867, 30 & 31 Vict. cap. 102, Schedule C.

86. *Socialists, Liberals and Labour: The Struggle for London 1885-1914* (1967) by Paul Thompson, p. 13.

87. See A. P. White's *Story of Northampton* (1914), Reginald W. Brown's *Guide to Northampton (Together with Historical Notes) and Its Surroundings* (1927), Barry Wake and Edwin Weeks's *Ned Weeks of Northampton: The Story of His Life* (1902), Alan Fox's *History of the National Union of Boot and Shoe Operatives, 1874-1957* (1958) and Alfred Scott's *Northampton through the Ages with Reference to the County* (1931).

88. A. P. White's *Story*, p. 115.

89. Blake's sole-sewing machine was introduced in 1858. In America in 1872 Goodyear developed the first machine for imitating 'hand-sewn' work, which reached Britain some years later. 'From that time rapid progress has been made' (British United Shoe Machinery Co. Ltd's *Special Brochure*, p. 11).

90. William Blake's 'Jerusalem'.

91. This figure is based on author's 10% sample survey (974 individuals) of some 10,000 householders listed in an 1870 Northampton directory (NL). The streets are nothing like as socially segregated as in most industrial towns of the period. Manufacturers and their skilled operatives lived side by side; labourers are found next door to professional men. In this century socially segregated private or council estates have been built outside the original borough boundary. The ancient industry is still important and 'practically one-fifth of the national production of footwear comes from the area' (*Official Handbook*, 1965, p. 73), though since this date engineering has become the dominant industry.

92. *A Century of Shoemaking, 1844-1944* (1944) by E. W. Burnham, I, p. 5.

93. *Graphic*, 7 February 1891.

94. *Bradford Observer*, 28 March 1882. *The Sheffield Daily Telegraph*, on the other hand, claimed that 'Atheism and Radicalism are rampant' (29 May 1880) but also revealed much Nonconformist support for Bradlaugh. In *Ned Weeks* Barry Wake observed it was 'idle to submit that secularism, freethought, or rationalism, alias infidelity, in one form or another, had not obtained for this ancient and really respectable midland town an unenviable notoriety' but 'to his agreeable surprise, Bradlaugh found among the Christian public at Northampton many supporters of his political views' (p. 40).

95. *Truth*, 8 April 1880.

96. *ibid*, 1 April 1880.

97. *Daily Chronicle*, 31 January 1891.

98. *NR*, 5 July 1868.

99. *Compulsory Cultivation of Land: What it Means, and Why it Ought to be Enforced* (1887), p. 5.

100. cf. letter from 'F. Rosher' (Engels) to N. F. Danielson, 13 November 1885 (Add. 38075, f. 38; BMMS).

101. *ibid*.

102. Engels admitted the primacy of the Scottish lairds, who, after 1745, came to 'own' land when the tribute money paid to them was called 'rent'.

103. *State-Tenants versus Freeholders* (1887), p. 1.
104. Of 23 January 1864. Radical land law reform in Britain was in the tradition of 'Digger' Gerrard Winstanley's *Declaration of the Wel-affected in the County of Buckinghamshire* (1649), Thomas Spence's *On the Mode of Administering the Landed Estate of the Nation as a Joint Stock Property in Parochial Partnerships by Dividing the Rent* (1775), William Ogilvie's *Essay on the Right of Property in Land* (1781), Thomas Paine's *Agrarian Justice, opposed to Agrarian Law, and to Agrarian Monopoly* (1797) and Patrick Dove's *Elements of Political Science* (1854).
105. *NR*, 8 February 1862.
106. A variation of these—green, white and purple—was adopted by the suffragist movement.
107. Letter to James Wells, 29 June 1868 (election poster, 'Dr Lees and Mr Bradlaugh'; NL).
108. Letter from Bradlaugh to Howell, 4 July 1868; Bishopsgate Institute.
109. In 1768 Northampton had itself seen a 'Spendthrift election' where £500 a vote was paid and each side spent £160,000.
110. *The Late Charles Bradlaugh*, p. 9.
111. In 1865 the highest vote (for Henley) was 1,274. In 1868 (for Gilpin) it was over 2,600 (precise figure varies in different sources).
112. Boston *Unitarian*, March 1891.
113. Northampton *Mercury*, 4 July 1868.
114. *The Churches and the Labour Movement* (1967) by Stephen Mayor, p. 15.
115. *Sketch of the Political and Social Programme of the National Party* (1868).
116. *Daily Telegraph*, 3 August 1868.
117. *ibid*, 6 August 1868.
118. Letter from Bright to Thomas James, 17 September 1868 (election poster; BC).
119. Letter to Northampton Whig, 25 September 1868 (*Record*, I, p. 272).
120. The last time it surfaced was in a feature in the *Observer Magazine*, 16 July 1967. With his puckish wit Shaw later said that he could never understand why atheists did not give such a demonstration and that he once announced it himself at a private gathering but everyone left the room.
121. First applied to Abner Kneeland, founder of the freethinking Boston *Investigator*.
122. So obscure is this that it is not listed in the *British Union Catalogue of Periodicals* and no copies seem to have survived anywhere.
123. *NR*, 20 December 1868.
124. The only occasion this was actually mentioned at home was with McSorley (*Record*, I, p. 106).
125. *NR*, 20 December 1868.
126. J. S. Mill's *Autobiography* (1873), p. 311.
127. Election placard (*NR*, 16 August 1868).
128. Text with music (G major march); NL and BC. Minus 2 choruses it is reproduced on plinth at base of Bradlaugh's statue in Abington Square, Northampton.
129. Hill's obituary (NL). It said that Bradlaugh made his final decision to stand

after a conversation with him about his prospects.

130. In a circular 'Men and Women of Northampton' (NL) he stated it was the wish of his General Committee but proudly emphasized 'I do not come to beg your vote'.
131. Address 'To the Electors of Northampton' (NL). Another poster claimed Lees was paid to intervene by a wealthy local radical, Starmer.
132. 'Words to the Wise' (anon); NL.
133. The most quoted figure is 1,086. The *Northampton Guardian* cited Bradlaugh as a 'republican' not a 'radical' candidate.
134. Now a forecourt, London E.C.2.
135. *The Autobiography and Conversion of W. R. Bradlaugh* (1881), p. 9.
136. *NR*, 20 December 1868.
137. *Secularist's Manual of Songs and Ceremonies* (1871).
138. Letter from Mill to Bradlaugh, 7 May 1869; BC.
139. *Sir Charles Dilke: A Victorian Tragedy* (1958) by Roy Jenkins, p. 57. See also *The Life of the Right Honourable Sir Charles W. Dilke, Bart., M.P.* (1917) by Stephen Gwynn and Gertrude Tuckwell. For Fawcett see Leslie Stephen's *Life of Henry Fawcett* (1885).
140. *Primitive Methodist Quarterly Review*, July 1891.
141. Now the site of miscellaneous workrooms and the distribution office of the *Jewish Chronicle* and other publications, London E.C.1. For background to Finsbury see the *Official Guide* (1963), G. E. Milton and Sir Walter Besant's *Clerkenwell and St Luke's* (1906), John Timbs's *Curiosities of London* (1885) and Henry Wheatley's *London Past and Present* (1891).
142. By George Standring, a vice-president of the NSS, in his *Rep*, June 1880.
143. By T. P. O'Connor, recalling his youthful debate on Catholicism, in *TP's Weekly*, 21 August 1903.
144. By Bradlaugh's successor, G. W. Foote, in *F*, 6 November 1892.
145. Letter, 2 January 1870 (*Letters of George Meredith*, 1912, I, p. 202).
146. *Secularism, Scepticism, and Atheism* (1870), p. 66.
147. Letter from Allsop to Bradlaugh, 19 September 1869; BC.
148. *NR*, 17 April 1870.
149. *NR*, 22 May 1870.
150. The only house with Bradlaugh associations to survive, London E.1. It now has an LCC plaque 'Charles Bradlaugh 1833-1891. Advocate of Free Thought lived here 1870-1877.'
151. Robertson's 'Memoir' with *Labour and Law*, p. xxxvi.
152. *Annual Register* for 1870, p. 3.
153. A disease process similar to his father's and probably with hereditary predisposition.

CHAPTER SIX

1. *Rep*, 1 November 1870.

2. *Rep*, 1 April 1870.
3. See Appendix 3.
4. *Autobiography*, p. 31.
5. *NR*, 14 September 1870.
6. Uncertainty in Western Europe whether to support Turkey or Russia in their confrontation over the Balkan dependencies.
7. Letter, 18 September 1870; BC.
8. Her real name was Emma Elizabeth Crouch. The Prince of Orange was another lover. See Cyril Pearl's *Girl with the Swansdown Seat* (1955).
9. Letter, 4 September 1870 (Prince Napoleon's *La Vérité à Mes Calomniateurs* (1871). See printed and MS documents in BC.
10. Unnamed cutting; BC.
11. Letter of 21 October 1870 from a delegation of the Government of National Defence at Tours, signed by Léon Gambetta, Adolphe Crémieux, Al Glais Bizoin and Admiral Fourichon; later Emmanuel Arago, originally 'shut up in Paris'; BC.
12. Letter, 29 October 1870 (Vol. 754, 1870, p. 232; Archives des Affaires Etrangères, Correspondance Politique, Angleterre; Paris).
13. Letter, 29 November 1870; do.
14. Letter, 4 February 1871; BC.
15. *Life* of Fawcett, p. 286.
16. *Rep*, February 1881.
17. *SC*, 17 March 1878.
18. Foote's *Reminiscences*, p. 6.
19. Built in Cleveland St, London W.1., to replace the John St Institution.
20. *Reminiscences*, p. 7.
21. These quotations are abstracted from *London Republican Club—The Inaugural Address of the President, Mr Charles Bradlaugh* (1871).
22. In April 1871 from Bright's disease, the familial disease process.
23. *Record*, I, p. 322.
24. Foote on 'The Fall of the Commune' (*NR*, 11 June 1871). Foote also said a lot of little communes would be economically unsound.
25. *NR*, 9 July 1871.
26. *Rep*, 15 May 1871.
27. *NR*, 24 December 1871.
28. *Eastern Post*, 16 December 1871.
29. *ibid*.
30. *ibid*, (2nd ed.) and 23 December 1871.
31. *ibid*, 23 December 1871.
32. *ibid*, 6 January 1872.
33. *ibid*.
34. Probably J. G. Eccarius, the minutes secretary of the General Council.
35. *ibid*, 13 January 1872.
36. *ibid*, 20 January 1872.
37. *ibid*.
38. *ibid*, 3 February 1872.
39. Letter from Marx and Engels (*IH*, 11 January 1873).

40. *NR*, 10 December 1871.
41. *Rep*, 1 May 1871.
42. *Rep*, 12 August 1871.
43. *Evening Standard*, 2 June 1871.
44. *Life and Times of Queen Victoria*, III, p. 411. His constituency was Birmingham.
45. Advocating a working day of 9 hours. Earlier the International had advocated 8 (*The History of the T:U.C. 1868-1968. A Pictorial Survey of a Social Revolution*, 1968, pp. 8-9), but this had made little impact.
46. On 26 September 1871 (*NR*, 1 October 1871).
47. *NR*, 22 October 1871.
48. *Record*, I, p. 310.
49. *NR*, 1 October 1871.
50. *The Cost of the Crown* (1871), p. 23. Also pp. 7, 9, 16, 17, 20.
51. p. 121.
52. Gwynn and Tuckwell's *Life* of Dilke, I, p. 305.
53. *Annual Register* for 1871, p. 122.
54. *Impeachment of the House of Brunswick*, p. 94.
55. *ibid*, p. 93.
56. Published as *George Prince of Wales, with Recent Contrasts and Coincidences*.
57. *Annual Register* for 1871, p. 122.
58. *Life and Times of Queen Victoria*, III, p. 414.
59. *Life of the Rt. Rev. Samuel Wilberforce, D.D.* (1882) by Reginald G. Wilberforce, III, p. 394.
60. Letter from Odger to Bradlaugh, 29 January 1872; BC.
61. Its printer was then John Vail, originally William Dever. I have been unable to trace the editor.
62. *Rep*, 1 March 1871.
63. *Rep*, 1 February 1871.
64. *Rep*, 1 June 1871.
65. *Rep*, 1 July 1871.
66. *IH*, 11 May 1872.
67. *IH*, 2 March 1872.
68. *IH*, 8 June 1872.
69. *National Secular Almanack* for 1873, p. 15.
70. Letter, 20 May 1872; BC.
71. *SC*, 1 August 1872.
72. *National Secular Almanack* for 1873, p. 16.
73. *De Morgan's Monthly*, September 1876.
74. Letter, 22 August 1872; BC.
75. *IH*, 25 January 1873.
76. Letter, 21 October 1872; BC.
77. Letter from W. R. to C. Bradlaugh, January 1873; BC.
78. Similar, 23 July 1873; BC.
79. Letter from Thomson to Hypatia Bradlaugh, 28 February 1873; BC.
80. *Autobiography*, p. 34.

81. *NR*, 22 December 1872.
82. *Gentleman's Magazine*, November 1872.
83. *ibid*, January 1873. Bradlaugh did not complain of any 'violent attack' (Hypatia Bonner in *Record*, I, p. 306) by Hopkins.
84. *ibid*, February 1873.
85. *IH*, 25 January 1873.
86. *IH*, 14 December 1872.
87. *ibid*.
88. *IH*, 21 December 1872.
89. *NR*, 8 December 1872. 'De' Morgan himself used 'De' instead of 'de'.
90. *NR*, 15 December 1872.
91. *NR*, 22 December 1872.
92. *NR*, 5 January 1873.
93. *IH*, 25 January 1873.
94. *IH*, 30 August 1873.
95. *IH*, 8 February 1873.
96. *IH*, 15 February 1873.
97. *IH*, 11 January 1873.
98. *Birmingham Morning News*, 12 April 1873.
99. *NR*, 4 May 1873.
100. *NR*, 20 April 1873.
101. *IH*, 10 May 1873.
102. *NR*, 15 June 1873. Probably Maxse.
103. *IH*, 21 June 1873.
104. *IH*, 23 August 1873. The publisher was Frederick Farrah.
105. *IH*, 30 August 1873.
106. First number just after the Sheffield Conference (*IH*, 7 December 1872).
107. *IH*, 12 April 1873.
108. *IH*, 26 April 1873.
109. *IH*, 4 January 1873.
110. *NR*, 27 April 1873.
111. *NR*, 4 May 1873.
112. *SC*, 1 June 1873.
113. *IH*, 24 May 1873; a report of the conference by J. Sketchley of Birmingham. See also *NR*, 18 May 1873.
114. *NR*, 15 June 1873.
115. See note 113.
116. *IH*, 31 May 1873; also 24 May and 21 June 1873.
117. *Examiner*, 17 May 1873.
118. Mackay's libellous *Life* of Bradlaugh asserted that he was also deputed to represent Hillel in a commission relating to litigation in England, and that through going to Spain first he arrived in Portugal too late.
119. Headingley, p. 144.
120. *Madras Times*, 3 April 1891. Hypatia Bonner dismissed all of Castelar's account as spiteful lies.
121. 'Entre deux et trois heures' and 'deux heures' (2 o'clock), which could be 2 a.m.; letters 23 and 25 May 1873; BC.

122. *New York Herald*, 18 September 1873.

123. See note 120.

124. See note 122.

125. Auckland *Truth Seeker*, 20 August 1933.

126. *NR*, 29 June 1873.

127. *Autobiography*, pp. 34-5.

128. Letter to John Mack, 7 August 1873; BC.

129. *To the Electors of the Borough of Northampton* (1873); NL.

130. See note 122.

131. Also General Kilpatrick, Andrew Jackson Davis, Theodore Tilton, Victoria Woodhull, O'Donovan Rossa, Rev. Octavius Brooke Frothingham, Hester A. Benedict, David Goodman Croly and Jane Cunningham Croly.

132. *Germantown Chronicle* (Philadelphia), 8 October 1873.

133. New York *World* and *New York Evening Mail*, 4 October 1873. *The New York Herald* (18 September 1873) had announced his theme as 'The Impeachment of the House of Brunswick in Conjunction with French and Spanish Republicanism'.

134. Preston S. Brooks from South Carolina.

135. *Weekly Dispatch*, 16 November 1879, where Sumner and Phillips were confused. Samuel Adams was the first American to protest against monarchical tyranny in 1776.

136. During a visit to Boston a little earlier the writer J.E. Jenkins attributed these words to Dilke.

137. *Boston Transcript*; undated cutting in BC.

138. In 1888 Harney returned to England and became columnist on the *Newcastle Weekly Chronicle*.

139. *Traveller*, 1 January 1874.

140. Compare with 'Goodbye-e-e!' (*Observer*, 4 January 1970) by Malcolm Muggeridge, who had similar experiences lecturing there.

141. Article 'Emigrants and Immigrants' by Hypatia Bonner in *Morning Leader*, 30 May 1907.

142. Francis E. Abbot's freethought *Index*, 6 January 1872. Miner was the president of Tuft's.

143. *Life* of Dilke, I, p. 152.

144. A man of conspicuous piety inherited by his son, who endowed St Matthew's Northampton (1891-4) in his honour. It was called 'Phipps's Fire Escape'.

145. Letter to Bradlaugh from Vicomtesse de Brimont, 2 July 1873; BC.

146. Letter, 5 April 1874; BC.

147. pp. 15-16.

148. The *National Secular Almanacks* of 1872, 1873 and 1874 respectively showed that, out of 29, 28 and 19 clubs listed, only 6, 4 and 4 of them had an *obvious* connection with the NSS through their secretary or meeting place; 7, 11 and 8 were in towns without a secular society.

149. The League was omitted from the 1875 *National Secular Almanack*, compiled in the autumn of 1874. The Brotherhood was not mentioned in the surviving numbers of the *Rep Chronicle* (11 April to 20 June 1874).

150. *Rep Herald*, 23 May 1874.
151. *ibid*, 20 June 1874.
152. *ibid*, 25 April 1874.
153. *ibid*.
154. *ibid*, 30 May 1874.
155. *ibid*, 11 April 1874.
156. *SC*, July 1874.
157. p. 78.
158. NSS's *Almanack* for 1876, p. 30.

CHAPTER SEVEN

1. Given in *Times* obituary, 21 September 1933.
2. *Annie Besant—An Autobiography* (1893), p. 94. See also Gertrude Marvin Williams's *Passionate Pilgrim* (1932), Geoffrey West's *Mrs Annie Besant* (1927), Sri Prakasa's *Annie Besant: As Woman and as Leader* (1941), Theodore Besterman's *Mrs Annie Besant* (1934), 'Besant Centenary Issue' of *Theosophist* (October 1947) and Arthur H. Nethercot's *First Five Lives of Annie Besant* (1960).
3. Annie Besant's *Autobiography*, p. 116.
4. He became Sir Henry Trueman Wood of the Royal Society of Arts.
5. Digby Besant's 'Memories of My Mother—Annie Besant' (*Sunday Reporter*, 24 September 1933).
6. *Autobiography: Memories and Experiences of Moncure Daniel Conway* (1904), II, p. 261.
7. Annie Besant's *Autobiography*, p. 133.
8. *ibid*, p. 134.
9. *NR*, 2 August 1874.
10. Annie Besant's *Autobiography*, p. 178.
11. *MSAB* (MS *Mrs Besant—Personal Reminiscences, by Hypatia Bradlaugh Bonner, jotted down at intervals without exact chronological order*), p. 11; Bradlaugh family papers.
12. Undated letter; BC. 'Ajax' was taken from 'Ajax Crying for Light' in the Crystal Palace, then at Upper Norwood.
13. Election poem 'The Defeat of Bradlaugh'; NL. 'The George', beside All Saints' Church, was Bradlaugh's campaign HQ and also that of the Tory Merewether. It is now the site of Lloyds Bank.
14. Election poster; NL.
15. *Northampton and County Independent*, 23 September 1933.
16. Poster 'Circus'; NL.
17. e.g. G.A. Mantz (letter, 22 November 1874; BC), whose father later vilified Bradlaugh in the House of Commons.
18. Letter, 19 December 1874; BC.
19. Letter from Hypatia Cooke to Hypatia Bonner, 25 January 1875; BC.

Hypatia Carlile had married Edward Cooke and Theophila, Colin Campbell, both friends of the teenage Bradlaugh.

20. Letter to Bertram Dobell, 18 January 1875 (Salt's *Life* of Thomson, p. 125).
21. Letter from Headlam to the Rev. George Sarson, 4 April 1875 (F.G. Bettany's *Stewart Headlam: A Biography*, 1926, p. 49).
22. *Rep Chronicle*, May 1875.
23. Letter from Maxse to Bradlaugh, 24 May 1875.
24. Letter from Thomson to Dobell, 9 July 1875 (Salt's *Life*, p. 126).
25. Do, 24 August 1875 (Salt's *Life*, p. 127).
26. NSS's *Almanack* for 1876, p. 21.
27. e.g. concerning the drafting of policy statements and other important writings. See NSS *Minute Book* of this period; Bradlaugh House.
28. Letter from Watts to Bradlaugh, 7 October 1875; BC.
29. *Agnostic Journal*, 14 March 1891.
30. *NR*, 21 November 1875. It is likely the 'hymn' was satirical and inspired by Foote and Holyoake.
31. The personalities who entertained him were mostly freethinkers like Horace Seaver, editor of the Boston *Investigator*.
32. In 1879 this was collated as *Hints to Emigrants to the United States of America*.
33. Conway's *Autobiography*, II, p. 362.
34. *Correspondence respecting the purchase by HM Government of the Suez Canal Shares belonging to the Egyptian Government*, C 1391 (1876), p. 9.
35. *Bradford Observer*, 11 September 1882.
36. *Secularist*, 5 February 1876.
37. *To the subscribers of the 'Secularist' Guarantee Fund*; BC.
38. *Life* of Holyoake, II, p. 79.
39. *Secularist*, 26 February 1876.
40. *ibid*, 13 May 1876.
41. *Record*, I, p. 350.
42. Unnamed cutting; BC.
43. *Secularist*, 17 June 1776.
44. *MSAB*, p. 2.
45. *ibid*, p. 4; plus first draft of document, p. 4a.
46. See Pearl's *Girl with the Swansdown Seat*, Alan Montgomery Eyre's *St John's Wood: Its History, Its Houses, Its Haunts and Its Celebrities* (1913), Ethel G. Merston's MS *Cloth of Bits and Pieces: The Story of a Scattered Life through Five Reigns* (undated), scrapbooks of cuttings and photographs in the Marylebone Road branch of Westminster Libraries.
47. *Pall Mall Gazette* (Pearl's *Girl*, p. 100).
48. Philip Hope-Wallace in 'Ageing in the Wood' (*Guardian*, 5 April 1962).
49. This moderated, by all accounts, in her later years as 'white goddess' to the Indian theosophists.
50. *MSAB*, p. 20.
51. Undated answer to begging letter from George Green; BC. See also *Record*, II, p. 97 and prologue to many NR appeals.

52. Libellous *Life*, p. 343 and opposite p. 346. This action is not referred to in the *Record*, but it is unlikely that the libellers would dare to forge a legal document or that if they had no criminal prosecution would have followed.
53. *MSAB*, p. 4.
54. *MSAB*, pp 2 and 15.
55. *MSAB*, p. 2.
56. *MSAB*, pp 2-3.
57. *MSAB*, p. 20.
58. Letter to Hypatia, 17 March 1876; BC. See also letter to both daughters, 11 July 1876; BC.
59. *Fruits of Philosophy* (Freethought Publishing Co. ed., 1877), p. 54.
60. *NR*, 11 February 1877.
61. Summons to H. Cook, 9 Walter St, Bristol; BC.
62. Letter from Watts to Cook, 11 December 1876; BC. Cook sent this to Bradlaugh some time later after Watts had claimed he had not read the book and blamed Bradlaugh for the decision to defend it.
63. In 1877 G.W. Hunt's anti-Russian 'Jingo' song became popular in London music-halls:
    > We don't want to fight,
    > But by Jingo if we do,
    > We've got the ships, we've got the men,
    > And we've got the money too.

    Holyoake coined the name 'Jingoes' for these noisy patriots (*Daily News*, 13 March 1878).
64. Letter from Watts to Cook, 19 December 1876; BC.
65. Leaflet *Evidence for the Defence in the case at Bristol* (1877); BC.
66. Later Sir George Lewis. The firm, now Penningtons and Lewis & Lewis, retains the same interests.
67. *Mrs Watts's Reply to Mr Bradlaugh's Misrepresentations* (February 1877), p. 3.
68. *NR*, 11 February 1877.
69. Once the site of a plague pit and now the site of Gordon and Gotch, London E.C.4.
70. *Mr Bradlaugh's Trial and the Freethought Party* (anon. 1877), p. 1.
71. *SC*, 28 January 1877.
72. *SR*, 21 January 1877.
73. Letter from Watts to Annie Besant, 31 January 1877 (*Mrs Watts's Reply*, p. 10).
74. *MSAB*, p. 15.
75. Appendix to *The Queen v. Charles Bradlaugh and Annie Besant* (1877), p. 322.
76. *The Late Charles Bradlaugh*, p. 19.
77. Conway's *Autobiography*, II, p. 262.
78. This rose to £75 after 1880, when he acquired the large first-floor room as his library. The owner of the building was Thomas Welch; George Rogers, the occupier, paid all the rates (£24 1s 5d).
79. Now the site of the St John's Wood branch of the Westminster Libraries,

London N.W.8.

80. Letter from Bradlaugh to Kate Watts, 9 March 1877; BC. It is a copy sent to Hypatia Bonner by George Stewart and filed by her as authentic.
81. Letter from Annie Besant to Booth, 6 April 1877; BC. See note 80.
82. *MSAB*, p. 21.
83. Article 'The Hall of Science—The Propagandists' by E.D.J. (probably Evelyn Jerrold) in 'Red London' series (unnamed cutting, probably *Weekly Dispatch*, 1879); BC.
84. *MSAB*, p. 24.
85. Laid down in *R.v. Hicklin* (1868) in action against a pamphlet *The Confessional Unmasked; Shewing the Depravity of the Roman Priesthood, the Iniquity of the Confessional, and the Questions Put to Females in Confession.*
86. *British Secular Union Almanack* for 1879. The reason later given for the BSU's formation was 'strengthening the ranks of that ever-increasing party . . . convinced that the questions of God's existence and the future life of man are insoluble problems' (*SR*, 10 January 1880). To assist 'in advertising the chapel for public meetings'(*Minute Book*, 27 September 1872), South Place committee added 'Institute' to its title. Conway spoke there most Sunday mornings and in the evening at a chapel in St Paul's Rd, Camden Town.
87. *Record*, II, p. 24.
88. The guild, founded in 1877, retained this name till it closed down in 1909 under competition from the Church Socialist League.
89. The High Courts moved to the present Temple Bar site in 1882.
90. *Queen v. Charles Bradlaugh and Annie Besant*, p. 56.
91. *ibid*, p. 267.
92. Undated letter from Hypatia Cooke to Hypatia Bonner just after Mrs Bradlaugh's death; BC.
93. *MSAB*, p. 22.
94. *Passionate Pilgrim*, p. 97.
95. *MSAB*, p. 16.
96. Judgment (*NR*, 2 June 1878).
97. Conway's *Autobiography*, II, p. 264.
98. Descriptions of Bradlaugh and Annie Besant first applied by Maccall. More obliquely Holyoake announced that a Princetown (Mass.) 'Free Love paper' *The Word* had 'taken Mr. Bradlaugh and Mrs Besant under their wing'(*SR and Secularist*, 28 July 1877).
99. *Ought Charles Bradlaugh to be an M.P.?* (1877), p. 1.
100. Letter from Herbert to Bradlaugh, 20 March 1878; BC.
101. i.e. the 1881 *Almanack*, which went to press in autumn 1880, p. 47. The *SR* of 21 February 1880 was unable to report anything more tangible.
102. The issue for 23 February 1878 baldly announced that 'no "Jottings" have arrived from Mr Foote' and the following week only Watts was billed as editor.
103. Letter from Foote to Bradlaugh, 19 February 1881; BC.
104. Annie Besant's *Autobiography*, p. 218. Hypatia complained of the omission

in *MSAB*, p. 16.

105. *The Hall of Science Libel Case* (1895), edited by G.W. Foote, pp. 12-13.

106. January 1879. Standring pioneered in photographic reproduction as Brad-laugh did in new type faces.

107. *MSAB*, p. 9. Aveling was the model for Dubedat in Shaw's *Doctor's Dilemma* (1906). See also Hesketh Pearson's Introduction to Feliks Topolski's *Portrait of G.B.S.* (1946), Nethercot's *First Five Lives* and *Rep*, December 1881.

108. *MSAB*, p. 25.

109. *NR*, 27 July 1879. The title means 'I think, therefore I shall work'.

110. NSS's *Almanack* for 1882, p. 20.

111. viz. £1,056 7s 0d to be paid back at 5 guineas monthly.

112. F. Sheehy-Skeffington's *Michael Davitt* (1908), subtitle. His type of Irish nationalism was called 'necessarily anticlerical' (p. 220).

113. *SR*, 14 February 1880.

114. *ibid.*

115. *Rep*, March 1880.

116. Letter from Bradlaugh to Gladstone, 7 August 1879 (Gladstone Papers, Add. 44111, f. 77; BMMS).

117. So called because they met in a room used by the Church of the New Jerusalem (Swedenborgians). Bradlaugh warned Dilke his friends could 'prevent the return of 5 or 6 moderates and render doubtful the return of 10 or 12 more' (Dilke Papers, Add. 43910, f. 326; BMMS).

118. Algar Labouchere Thorold's *Life of Henry Labouchere* (1913), p. 129.

119. Letter from Labouchere to Hypatia Bonner, 30 January 1891; BC.

120. *To the Electors of the Borough of Northampton*; NL.

121. After being attacked for his action when Bradlaugh's return was announced he hastened to 'deeply regret the step I took' (*Record*; see *NR*, 25 April 1880).

122. Local clergymen estimated there were 3,000 Churchmen, 3,000 Dissenters and 2,000 atheists (*Sheffield Daily Telegraph*, 29 May 1880).

123. Winston Spencer Churchill's *Lord Randolph Churchill* (1906), I, p. 124.

CHAPTER EIGHT

1. There is a great discrepancy in the figures cited: 351 Liberals, 237 Tories, 65 Home Rulers (*Life and Times of Queen Victoria*, IV, p. 591); 347, 240, 65 (R. H. Gretton's *Modern History of the English People, 1880-1922*, 1930, p. 38 and Bulmer-Thomas's *Party System*, 1, p. 126); 349, 243, 60 (*Annual Register* for 1880, p. 30). Despite the first set of figures, the total of MPs then was 652.

2. Letter to her private secretary, Sir Henry Ponsonby, 4 April 1880.

3. Circular by W.C. Bennett, *The London and Provincial Radical Club* (1883); National Liberal Club.

4. Letter from Dilke to Gladstone, 4 January 1883 (Dilke Papers, Add. 44149, f. 126; BMMS).
5. Speech by Gladstone (*Daily Telegraph*, 3 May 1883).
6. There are striking parallels between the early years of Gladstone's Administration of 1880 and the Wilson Administrations of 1964 and 1966.
7. For full details of the political manoeuvring see Walter Arnstein's *Bradlaugh Case: A Study in Late Victorian Opinions and Politics* (1965) and Robertson's 'Parliamentary Struggle' (*Record*, II, pp. 203-367 and *Charles Bradlaugh*, pp. 66-98). Arnstein did not have access to the court briefs, full transcripts of cases and legal notes made by Bradlaugh; while Robertson, who apparently did, lacked Bradlaugh's legal sense, made minor errors in processing the material and attributed to some of the judges a bias there is no evidence of. Hypatia similarly attributed to her father a saintly forgiveness which could better be described as a generously impartial awareness that, on strictly legal grounds, his case was not as strong as his supporters would have liked.
8. Letter from A. Dilke to Bradlaugh, 7 April 1880; BC.
9. Letter from Bradlaugh to Brand, 29 April 1880 (Gladstone Papers, Add. 44194, f. 194; BMMS).
10. Letter from Brand to Gladstone, 30 April 1880 (*ibid*, f. 190; BMMS).
11. *Journals of the House of Commons*, 3 May 1880.
12. *Life, Letters, and Diaries of Sir Stafford Northcote, First Earl of Iddesleigh* (1890) by Andrew Lang, II, p. 154.
13. To allow Nonconformist services at burials in parish churchyards; passed later in the year.
14. Also written Edgcome and Edgcumbe. The man had other aliases. The *British Empire* had been the *Monetary Gazette*. In the BC are letters re debts and frauds in his early life.
15. *Daily Chronicle*, 31 January 1891. The paper said Wolff's 'personal hatred of Mr Gladstone at this period was almost monomaniacal'.
16. 29 Vict. cap. 19.
17. See Appendix 4.
18. 31 & 32 Vict. cap. 72, s. 2.
19. Said to Labouchere by Bradlaugh (New York *Recorder*, 19 February 1891, from *Truth*).
20. Many newspapers of 21 May 1880 and Bradlaugh's *True Story of My Parliamentary Struggle* (1882), pp. 75-8.
21. s. 4.
22. John Morley's *Life of William Ewart Gladstone* (1903), III, p. 14. Wolff later denied he had used quite those words, but all his auditors heard what Gladstone did.
23. Letter from Victoria to Gladstone, 22 May 1880 (*The Queen and Mr Gladstone*, 1933, by Philip Guedalla, II, p. 96).
24. H, CCLII, 339.
25. *ibid*, 347.
26. Bradlaugh's description at a speech in Northampton (*Northamptonshire Guardian*, 29 July 1882).

355

27. *Report from the Select Committee on Parliamentary Oath (Mr Bradlaugh)*, 16 June 1880, 226, Session 2, p. iv.
28. *Life*, of Northcote, II, p.168. Gladstone agreed it was a uniquely 'ecstatic transport' (Morley's *Life*, III, p. 16).
29. This is a brass bar, usually down, between the Cross Benches opposite the Speaker at the southern end of the House, 'where the tribune would be if one were elected' (*Daily News*, 31 January 1891). Since Charles I's attempted arrest of the Five Members in 1642, this has been the place beyond which 'strangers' cannot pass.
30. *Speeches by Charles Bradlaugh* (1890), pp. 1-8.
31. Letter from Gladstone to Victoria, 23 June 1880 (*Letters of Queen Victoria*, 2nd series, III, 1928, p. 115).
32. *Stewart Headlam*, p. 60.
33. Letter from Victoria to Gladstone, 23 June 1880 (Guedalla, II, p. 105).
34. Letter from Plimsoll to Bradlaugh, 25 June 1880; BC.
35. *Daily News*, 28 June 1880.
36. *H*, CCLIII, 972.
37. Report of *Clarke v. Bradlaugh* (*NR*, Special Extra Number, Vol. 38, No. 7).
38. The solicitor and his clerk were unrelated. Almost as frequently the name of both is written in official records as 'Stewart'.
39. Also written 'Barber'.
40. This figure is based on the divisions listed in the NSS's *Almanacks* for 1881, pp. 52-4 (91), and 1882, pp. 53-5 (127); i.e. 218 minus 1, at £500 each. Arnstein made the total liability £355,000. £347,500 is quoted in other places.
41. *H*, CCLIII, 1472.
42. Called 'Hyram Travers' Great Song' after the singer who owned the rights; BC.
43. 'An Englishman's Protest' (*Nineteenth Century*, August 1880). He was referring somewhat inaccurately to the 1697 Blasphemy Act.
44. *Charles Bradlaugh, M.P., and the Irish Nation: what Charles Bradlaugh has said, and how he has voted, in regard to Ireland* (1885) by 'Humanitas' (W.P.Ball), p.10.
45. *The Ethics of Punishment*, (1886) by Annie Besant and Charles Bradlaugh, p. 16.
46. *H* for 28 March 1881, CCLX, 35.
47. *Reply*, 26 November 1880; BC.
48. *NR*, Extra Special Number, Vol. 37, No. 12.
49. 34 & 35 Vict. ch. 83.
50. Memorandum, March 1881 (Gladstone Papers, Add. 44219, f. 41; BMMS).
51. See note 48. He added: 'It is a little hard that with my heavy parliamentary and other work I should have all the expense and annoyance of this harassing litigation.'
52. Bramwell in the main decision (*Judgement*, 31 March 1881).
53. Widely supposed to be the origin of 'G.O.M.' for Gladstone. But Bradlaugh had already used the phrase in the *NR* (27 March 1881) and there are reports he used it first in a speech in Edinburgh early in 1881: 'But he

would not say a word against the Grand Old Man' (*NR*, 18 December 1892). It is suggested that he adapted it from the phrase 'Grand Old Knight' used of New Zealand's governor and premier Sir George Grey. 'G.O.M.' has also been dated from Harcourt's speech to his Derby constituents in 1880 (*NR*, 25 December 1892).

54. *Speeches*, pp. 8-13, and *H*, CCLX, 1207-12.
55. *H*, CCLX, 1559.
56. Letter from Bradlaugh to Gladstone, 6 May 1881 (Gladstone Papers, Add. 44111, f. 86; BMMS).
57. *Order* signed T. Erskine May, 10 May 1881; BC.
58. *Life and Times of Queen Victoria*, IV, p.563. Former phrase was Harcourt's.
59. Foote's *Reminiscences*, pp. 21-2. Percy later claimed Bradlaugh's friends had forged tickets for the event.
60. *Order*, 17 May 1881; BC.
61. *Judgement*, 21 June 1881.
62. Letter from Bradlaugh to Speaker, 4 July 1881 (*Journal of the House of Commons*, 5 July 1881).
63. This account is derived from the transcript of evidence, Aveling's colourful comments in the *NR* (Special Extra Number, Vol. 38, No. 7) and Foote's *Reminiscences*, pp. 25-6.
64. Letter from the famous constitutional lawyer W. Ivor Jennings to Hypatia Bonner, 16 September 1933; BC. This arose from his article in *Champion of Liberty* (pp. 309-26), where he asserted on good grounds that Bradlaugh gave too much attention to 'legal subtleties and petty objection' and not enough to appeals for justice. In support of Jennings it may be said that Bradlaugh over-played legal technicalities—which were as likely to be against as for him and should have been subservient to common sense and equity—and in cross-examination had an irritating trick of picking on witnesses who said 'It would be' instead of 'It was' (Bradlaugh: 'Why do you say it would be? I put it to you that you are making all this up.') But it must be admitted that Bradlaugh sometimes got out of tricky situations by the skilful use of technicalities; and while he might have irritated judges by quibbling over witnesses' idioms, this often unnerved lying opponents.
65. This offence—providing money for someone else to go to court—was abolished by the 1967 Criminal Law Act.
66. *Daily News*, 28 June 1880.
67. He estimated at one stage there were only 2 hostile votes out of 75,000 (*Record*, II, p. 284). This impression is borne out by many contemporary accounts (cuttings; BC).
68. Annie Besant's *Autobiography*, p. 265.
69. *Standard*, 4 August 1881. Most of the foregoing description is derived from this source.
70. *The Memoirs of Sir David Erskine of Cardross, KCVO (1926)*, edited by Mrs Steuart Erskine, p. 188.
71. *T. P. O'Connor in The Million (Northampton Reporter*, August 1892).
72. He said that night at the Hall of Science: 'Violence would only be justi-

fiable if I meant revolution. I do not mean revolution; I hope I never may'
(*Standard* 4 August 1881).

73. Press comment on this was the first the British public heard of this new invention.
74. Bradlaugh's MS note on Appeal brief; BC.
75. Written in the heyday of republicanism, 1873.
76. Taken from Leo Taxil's *Bible Amusante.*
77. *F*, 15 January 1882.
78. *F*, 12 March 1882.
79. *F*, 16 July 1882.
80. *Speeches*, pp. 13-23, and *H*, CCLXVI, 70-5.
81. *The Channel Tunnel: Ought the Democracy to Oppose or Support it?* (1887), p. 5.
82. This account is mainly based on the *Daily Telegraph* of 22 February 1882. The information about Waugh comes from an unnamed cutting; BC.
83. Richard Harte's *On the Laws and Customs relating to Marriage* (1870), a book in favour of easier divorce or common law marriages (if not 'free love'), was reviewed in *NR*, 28 August 1870.
84. *NR*, 5 March 1882.
85. *Northamptonshire Guardian*, 27 February 1882.
86. *NR*, 12 March 1882.
87. Letter from Bradlaugh to Northcote, 5 March 1882 (Iddesleigh Papers, Add. 50041, f. 96; BMMS).
88. Speeches in the Lords, 7 and 23 March 1882 (*H*, CCLXVII, 319 and 1647).
89. David Collis has a copy of this volume with notes purportedly by the author and not in Holyoake's writing. But 'Ion' was a Holyoake pseudonym and the style and sentiments are his.
90. *Blasts*, p. 18.
91. *ibid*, pp. 10 and 12.
92. They handled the Bradlaugh family's private affairs.
93. *Law Times*, November 1882.
94. *Statement of Claim* in *Bradlaugh v. Erskine*, (1882B, No. 2487), 23 May 1882.
95. *Statement of Defence*, 24 June 1882.
96. Transcript, 18 December 1882; BC.
97. Transcript, 29 March 1882.
98. London and South Western Bank. See letter of apology from head office to Bradlaugh, 23 April 1883; BC.
99. Respectively 1 Edw. VI cap. 1, s.1; 2 & 3 Edw. VI cap. 1, s.3; 1 Eliz. (I) cap. 2, s.3; 60 Geo. III & 1 Geo. IV cap. 8, s.1. By the criminal Law Act (1967 c. 58) the 1697 Act was repealed, not the operative sections of the other Acts. In the Middle Ages there was a Statute of Heretics allowing for the burning of blasphemers, but this was repealed in 1677.
100. *The Reports of Sir Peyton Ventris Kt* (1696), p. 293. Sir William Blackstone's *Commentaries*, IV (1769), says: 'This is a Christian country, and the laws of England are founded on the Christian religion' (p. 59).
101. Letter from Annie Besant to Sir Joseph Hooker, 23 October 1882; Archives

of the Royal Botanic Gardens, Kew.

102. Foote's *Reminiscences*, p. 28.
103. *Northamptonshire Guardian*, 14 October 1882.
104. Memo from James to Gladstone, 14 November 1882 (Gladstone Papers, Add. 44219, f. 76; BMMS).
105. 57 Geo. III cap. 19, s.23 prohibited meetings within a mile of the Houses of Parliament to petition 'for alteration of matters in Church or State'. The Bradlaugh meeting fell outside it.
106. *A Protest against the Admission of Mr Bradlaugh into Parliament* and other documents in BC.
107. *H*, CCLXXVIII, 962.
108. *ibid*, 1488.
109. Lucretius II, 646-51.
110. *H*, CCLXXVIII, 1196.
111. *Bradlaugh Case*, p. 242.
112. *Speeches*, pp. 23-30, and *H*, CCLXXVIII, 1844-51.
113. Foote's *Defence of Free Speech, being a Three Hours' Address to the Jury in the Court of Queen's Bench before Lord Coleridge on April 24, 1883* (1932 ed.), p. 52.
114. *F*, 8 April 1883.
115. *Record*, II, p. 326. The references are to 'Bloody Jeffreys' of the Monmouth Rebellion Assize in 1685 and Charles II's corrupt Lord Chief Justice, Sir William Scroggs, impeached in 1680. North and Huddleston had earlier refused a writ of *certiorari*.
116. e.g. 1 Geo. I Stat. 2 cap. 13 and 22 Vict. cap. 32.
117. Bradlaugh's *Brief*, citing *ex parte* Bishop of Exeter *in re Gorham*, 10 CB 102, 19 LJCP 200.
118. Foote's *Reminiscences*, p. 33.
119. This was put more strongly by Lord Sumner in *Bowman v. Secular Society Ltd* (1917): 'The phrase "Christianity is part of the law of England" is really not law; it is rhetoric.'
120. Letter from Huxley to Aveling, 30 May 1883; BC. On the strength of his letter to Sir M. Foster, 18 July 1883 (*Life and Letters of Thomas Henry Huxley*, 1900, II, p. 56) Huxley is supposed to have given his support.
121. Letter from Huxley to Crompton, 16 July 1883; possession of Gustavo Duran.
122. Letter from W. Gibson to Crompton, 16 December 1898, suggesting this is what Huxley really had in mind in the foregoing; do.
123. Letter from Aveling to Bradlaugh, 26 January 1882; BC.
124. *MSAB*, p. 10.
125. Letter from Bradlaugh to Hypatia, undated; BC.
126. Notes by Bradlaugh on Aveling's resignation from the NSS; BC.
127. Comment by Annie Besant, dating the event to 1882, after she had definitely broken with him (*NR*, 4 May 1884).
128. Another £100 was owing on William Robinson's account. By 27 January 1887 only £75 had been paid and Bradlaugh was anxious about Aveling's father's estate, from which 'you led me to believe a considerable sum was

coming' (letter in BC).

129. *NR*, 11 May 1884.

130. *NR*, 25 May 1884.

131. Undated, unsigned letter in BC; filed by Hypatia Bonner in section relating to Aveling.

132. Similar.

133. Circular to NSS Council, 10 August 1884; BC.

134. Letter, 26 August 1884 (circular by NSS secretary Robert Forder, 2 September 1884; BC).

135. *NR*, 7 September 1884.

136. Including the prose of 'B.V.'. At his best Ross wrote the best invective, but he was a most uneven and unreliable writer. George Meredith was a great admirer of Foote.

137. Letter from Bradlaugh to Gladstone, 11 June 1883 (Gladstone Papers, Add. 44111, f. 134; BMMS).

138. Do., 5 July 1883 (f. 137).

139. *Statement of Claim*, 26 July 1883 (1883B, No. 3931); BC.

140. *Demurrer*, 30 July 1883 (do.).

141. 9 A & E 231.

142. *Weekly Reporter*, 19 April 1884.

143. *Moniteur de Meurthe et Moselle*, 29 January 1891.

144. *H*, CCLXXXIV, 455.

145. *Northamptonshire Guardian*, 19 February 1884.

146. *John Churchill, Duke of Marlborough, the Mob, the Scum, and the Dregs* (1884).

147. *Newcastle Daily Chronicle*, 20 February 1884.

148. Memorial stone laid by Admiral Sir W. King Hall. Now a factory and workshop.

149. See note 145.

150. No. 66, 30 April 1866 (*Standing Orders*, 1884).

151. *Transcript of Evidence*, pp. 238, 246 *et al*; BC.

152. In 1883 Joynes founded the *Christian Socialist* with H. H. Champion.

153. *NR*, 13 January 1884.

154. Letter from Engels to Laura Lafargue, 5 February 1884 (*Friedrich Engels, Paul and Laura Lafargue—Correspondence*, I, 1868-86, 1959, p. 168).

155. *Justice*, 16 February 1884.

156. Hyndman's *Record of an Adventurous Life* (1911), p. 336.

157. *Justice*, 19 April 1884.

158. *Will Socialism Benefit the English People?* (1884), p. 5 *et seq.*

159. *ibid*, p. 12 *et seq.*

160. See Bradlaugh's series on 'Socialism' (*Our Corner*, March to May 1884).

161. Joynes showed from Bradlaugh's own figures that each member of a friendly society earned 2s a year (*Our Corner*, June 1884).

162. *Benny on Bradlaugh and Hyndman*, p. 2.

163. Bradlaugh's *Some Objections to Socialism* (*Atheistic Platform VII*, 1884), p. 100.

164. C. Bradlaugh and A. Besant's *Socialism: For and Against* (1887), p. 3 (*Our*

Corner, 1 March 1887).

165. e.g. Fawcett's *Manual of Political Economy* (1876) and his wife's *Political Economy for Beginners* (1872).
166. Bax and Bradlaugh's *Will Socialism Benefit the English People?* (1887), p. 32.
167. *ibid*, p. 12.
168. *ibid*, p. 19.
169. *ibid*, p. 32.
170. Bradlaugh's *Socialism: its Fallacies and Dangers* (1887), p. 11. Reprinted from the *North American Review*, January 1887, his first essay into international review journalism, for which he was much in demand until his death.
171. Letter from Engels to Eduard Bernstein, 6 August 1884 (*Die Briefe von Friedrich Engels an Eduard Bernstein* 1925, p. 151).
172. *NR*, 27 April 1884.
173. *MSAB*, p. 23.
174. *Last Will and Testament*, 30 January 1884; BC.
175. See note 173.
176. *Glasgow News*, 22 September 1933.
177. Said by Charles Drysdale (*Literary Guide*, July 1926).
178. In a letter to Hypatia Bonner on 10 January 1933, just after Robertson's death, E. Maddison, secretary of the International Arbitration League, said he 'did not mellow with age'; BC. Atheist and mythicist in Christology, Robertson supported free trade when most had abandoned it and, as a syncretist, conflicted not only with orthodox Shakespearean scholars but also with the supporters of every rival claimant.
179. Arthur Bonner became a well-known amateur antiquarian and FSA.
180. His grandson Basil Bradlaugh Bonner testifies that this image never quite left him.
181. *MSAB*, p. 26.
182. *ibid*, p. 12.
183. *Northamptonshire Guardian*, 12 July 1884.
184. 25 & 26 Vict. cap. 37, s1.
185. *Record*, II, p. 354.
186. *NR*, 7 February 1885.
187. Private letter from Grosvenor to Bradlaugh, 4 February 1885; BC.
188. Do., 9 February 1885; BC.
189. *Daily News*, 3 April 1885.
190. Letter from Dilke to Gladstone, 24 April 1885 (Gladstone Papers, Add. 44149, f. 343; BMMS).
191. Secret letter from Gladstone to Dilke, 21 April 1885 (*ibid*, f. 337).
192. Northcote's *Life*, II, p. 214.
193. Letter from Engels to Danielson, 13 November 1885 (Add. 38075, f. 38; BMMS).
194. p. 21.
195. Letter from Watts to Bradlaugh, 31 July 1885; BC.
196. *Weekly Dispatch*, 5 July 1891. He had written *Antipas F. D.'s Fruits of*

Philosophy.

197. Charles R. Mackay's *Balak Secundus* (1888), p. 4.
198. *ibid*, p. 16.
199. 'At Random' proof which C. A. Watts, printer of the *Agnostic Journal* (formerly *SR*), 'very reluctantly' declined to set up in February 1889 after taking legal advice. See letter from Watts to Ross and proof in BC.
200. This information is based on a letter from George Reid to Charles R. Mackay (*Balak Secundus*, p. 7). In his MS notes in one of the copies of the libellous *Life* in the British Museum Reading Room, Johnson asserted that he 'obtained verdict and "damages" ' against Mackay for this pamphlet. I can find no record of this case. Johnson did not say whether it was the letter of Reid's or other material to which he objected.
201. The figures usually given. *The Life and Times of Queen Victoria* (IV, p. 726) gave 333 Liberals, 251 Tories and 86 Parnellites.
202. *NR*, 17 January 1886. Today a 3-line whip is the strongest.
203. *H*, CCCII, 23.
204. The following report is taken from the *Times Parliamentary Debates* for the week ending 30 January 1886.

CHAPTER NINE

1. Published title of Burns's defence speech at his trial.
2. *NR*, 26 February 1886. See also *Times*, 1 March 1886.
3. *H*, 2 March 1886, CCCII, 1772.
4. *Mrs Besant's Socialism* (1886), p. 36.
5. *NR*, 14 March 1886. This contains the reply to *Justice*, 6 March 1886.
6. *MSAB*, p. 32.
7. *First Five Lives*, p. 237.
8. Presumably Aveling, Shaw and Burrows.
9. *MSAB*, p. 24.
10. *NR*, 24 August 1890.
11. 1 & 2 Will. IV cap. 37. The *Rep Herald* had claimed that 'most wives prefer part payment in kind' (9 May 1874) and objected to Macdonald's attempt to abolish truck (25 April 1874).
12. Speech at Northampton Town Hall on 'Capital and Labour', 7 January 1886 (*Speeches*, p. 47).
13. 43 & 44 Vict. cap. 42.
14. *An Economic History of Modern Britain*, II, *Free Trade and Steel, 1850-1886*, (1932) by J. H. Clapham, p. 418.
15. Vidya Sagar Anand's *Savarkar* (1967), p. 19.
16. Bound speech of the Marquess of Dufferin and Ava, retiring Viceroy, at Calcutta, 30 November 1888, p. 2.
17. *Address* to Bradlaugh by the Poona Mercantile Association during his visit

to Bombay in December 1889; BC.

18. Figures quoted in the *Annual Register* for 1886. Bulmer-Thomas gave 194, 85, 75, 316 and the *Life and Times of Queen Victoria* 192, 86, 76, 316 respectively.

19. Letter from Bradlaugh to Gladstone, 6 July 1886 (Gladstone Papers, Add. 44111, f. 146; BMMS).

20. Do., 16 July 1886 (*ibid*, f. 147).

21. *Record*, II, p. 426.

22. *H*, 19 October 1886, CCCIX, 652.

23. *Letter to the Rt. Hon. Randolph Churchill, M.P., Chancellor of the Exchequer.* It was considered Bradlaugh had 'scored off long-standing account' (*Punch*, 14 May 1887) when he finally confronted 'Grandolph' with the cooked *H*.

24. *Lord Randolph Churchill*, II, p. 321.

25. *Rep*, August 1886. The *Radical* suddenly disappeared in September 1889.

26. H. A. L. Fisher's *Republican Tradition in Europe* (1911), p. 275.

27. NSS's *Almanack* for 1887, p. 15.

28. Sample in BC superficially convincing but with detectible minor differences.

29. Undated letter; BC.

30. *NR*, 5 September 1886.

31. Letters from Walker to Bullock cited in libel action by Ross (*Times*, 11 June 1887).

32. *Times*, 13 June 1887.

33. *ibid*, 11 June 1887.

34. *ibid*, 13 June 1887.

35. See George Minson's *Whitminster Secular School Inauguration* (1884), p. 14. He often signed himself G. Chetwynd Jones.

36. *NR*, 22 February and 1 March 1885.

37. *SR*, 21 August 1886.

38. *SR*, 4 September 1886. Here the critic was Joseph Taylor, a former Unitarian.

39. Letter from George Payne to Bradlaugh, 18 October 1886; BC.

40. *Saladin the Little* (1887) by T. Evan Jacob, p. 14. Mainly based on the lunacy hearing and Ross's suspect scholarship. My account draws on revelations added by the *Ross v. Walker* libel action, pamphlets issued during the libellous *Life* controversy, and a probate case after Bullock's death (*Weekly Dispatch*, 5 July 1891).

41. *NR*, 16 January 1887. A reply to press comment that they had 'parted company' (e.g. in *Manchester Evening News*, 12 January 1887).

42. 'Toby, MP' (Sir Henry Luce) in *Punch*, 3 September 1887.

43. *Record*, II, p. 425.

44. *Leeds Mercury*, 16 October 1891.

45. See note 43.

46. Truck Amendment Act (50 & 51 Vict. cap. 46).

47. *Report of the Select Committee on London Corporation* (*Charges of Malversation*), 20 May 1887, No. 161.

48. Thompson's *Socialists, Liberals and Labour*, p. 77. In 1889 London County Council was formed. Metropolitan local government was finally rationalized in 1900 when 28 borough councils replaced the old vestries. The City still has many anomalies.

49. *Second Report of the Special Committee*, 18 April 1884, No. 1371, p.iii.

50. 45 & 46 Vict. cap. 50. This set out the sort of expenditure justified for London boroughs. Malversation is the illegal use of public funds.

51. Select Committee *Report*, p. xiv.

52. Moved at a speech in the Commons on 22 April 1887 (*Speeches*, pp. 64-73, and *H*, CCCXIII, 1642-51), 250,000 copies of which were distributed by the Cobden Club.

53. Letter from Bradlaugh to Ritchie, undated; BC.

54. In BC.

55. Letter from Bradlaugh to Hypatia, 9 July 1887; BC.

56. Michael Foot, MP, tells me 9 times. Speakers are selected by ballot.

57. *Newcastle Daily Leader*, 1 August 1887.

58. Letter from Alice (at Darnstadt) to Hypatia, 7 September 1887; BC.

59. See note 55.

60. *NR*, 23 October 1887.

61. Joseph Lane's *Anti-Statist Communist Manifesto* (1887), p. 23.

62. *Times*, 2 and 3 December 1887. See also R. T. Gunton's 'wilful perjury' letter (*Times*, 7 December 1887).

63. *NR*, 11 May 1884.

64. Letter from Foote to Bradlaugh, 23 January 1888; BC. The following account is the most plausible construction from many conflicting versions, not only from each protagonist, but from the same protagonist at different times.

65. On 8 January 1888 it declared that socialists were the only 'scientific' politicians, 'active, conscientious, and intelligent'. I am uncertain who 'Dodo' was.

66. *Balak Secundus*, p. 5.

67. MS notes in copy of the libellous *Life* bought by the British Museum in 1932.

68. When Ross acquired the *SR*, he ran it from 41 Farringdon St and 84 Fleet St passed to the London Educational Trading Co. 'Ye Olde Cheshire Cheese' was, and is, the favourite rendezvous of Fleet St reporters, especially from the populars, and hangers-on.

69. Letter from Fred Bradley to Harper and Battcock, 27 April 1888; BC.

70. See note 199, chapter 8.

71. G. C. Griffith-Jones's *Mokanna Unveiled: An Essay on Charles R. Mackay's 'Life of Charles Bradlaugh, M.P.', with an addendum on Secularism and Politics* (1888), p. 3.

72. *NR*, 12 February 1888.

73. An amalgam of Pope's *Dunciad* (1728-43) and Maccall's 'Breezy Bouncer'.

74. After a 'lie to the Holy Ghost', Ananias 'fell down, and gave up the ghost' (Acts 5, 3 and 5).

75. *Reynolds's Newspaper*, 12 February 1888.

76. *Balak Secundus*, p. 5.
77. Letter from Ross to Bradlaugh, 27 February 1889; BC.
78. *NR*, 26 February 1888.
79. The piece appeared in March 1889 and was then published as a booklet.
80. *MSAB*, p. 30.
81. *Theosophist*, October 1931. Her earlier versions of this event are less colourful.
82. Estelle W. Stead's *My Father: Personal and Spiritual Reminiscences* (1913), p. 155.
83. *MSAB*, p. 25.
84. *NR*, 30 June 1889.
85. *Keighley News*, 3 November 1888.
86. Speech in the Commons, 16 May 1889 (*H*, CCCXXXVI, 273, and *Speeches*, p. 134).
87. Do., 1 May 1888 (*H*, CCCXXV, 1085-6, and *Speeches*, p. 89).
88. Do., 2 May 1888 (*H*, CCCXXV, 1132 and 1128).
89. Bradlaugh's *Labour and Law* (1891), p. 29. In *Roads to Ruin: The Shocking History of Social Reform* (1950), E. S. Turner argued that Bradlaugh was 'forgetting the example of the Factory Acts' (p. 78). But these Acts were basically concerned with children and inspectors, where he welcomed special measures, and insofar as they were not he was not forgetful but opposed.
90. 29 Car. II cap. 7, s. 1.
91. 51 & 52 Vict. cap. 58.
92. Speech in the Commons, 7 December 1888 (*H*, CCCXXXI, 1432).
93. *ibid*, 1440.
94. 'The Eight Hours' Movement' (*New Review*, 1 July 1889).
95. *Eight Hours' Movement: Verbatim Report* (1890), p. 10.
96. In *What a Compulsory Eight Hour Working Day Means to the Workers* (1885), Tom Mann naively argued that if on a 9-hour day there were 900,000 unemployed out of 7 million workers, 750,000 could find jobs if it were reduced to 8.
97. *Report*, pp. 17, 23, 31 and 34. A heckler made a pertinent point: 'Thrift on 18 bob a week? Bosh!' (p. 31).
98. 'Eight Hours a Day by Law' (*Universal Review*, 15 August 1890).
99. *Speeches*, p. 91.
100. *House of Commons Paper*, 5 July 1888.
101. *Memorandum* to Committee from William Sutton, actuary to the Registry of Friendly Societies, p. 4; BC.
102. *Life Assurance Agents' Journal*, 28 July 1888.
103. *H*, CCCXXIII, 1191, and *Speeches*, p. 81.
104. *Record*, II, p. 388.
105. 51 & 52 Vict. ch. 46, s. 1.
106. It seems to be ripe now. Backed by the Magistrates' Association there is strong opposition to the oath on the further grounds that it is often cheapened by perfunctory administration and complicated by the many forms and scriptures sacred to immigrant religions.

107. *Address* to Bradlaugh from the inhabitants of Nagpur in Central Province, December 1889; BC.
108. *Address* to Bradlaugh from the Benares Association, December 1889; BC. 1 lakh equals 100,000.
109. *Manchester Evening Chronicle*, 8 May 1901.
110. *Parliamentary Paper*, No. 37 (1878), p. 5. See also No. 118 (1878), p. 5.
111. Speech in the Commons, 27 August 1889 (*H*, CCCXL, 630, and *Speeches*, p. 143).
112. Bound *Speech* of Lord Dufferin, 30 November 1888, p. 17.
113. Letter from Dufferin to Bradlaugh, 7 February 1889; BC.
114. Do., 22 February 1889; BC.
115. Do., 2 April 1889; BC.
116. Speech in the Commons, 3 July 1890 (*H*, CCCXLVI, 700, and *Speeches*, p. 158).
117. *Charles Bradlaugh: A Sketch of His Life, and His Services to India* (undated), probably by publisher G. A. Natesan, p. 61.
118. Note J to the original draft of the Indian Penal Code.
119. Speech in the Commons, 12 April 1889 (*H*, CCCXXXV, 455, and *Speeches*, p. 124).
120. A. Trevelyan on 'Vaccination a Delusion' (NSS's *Almanack* for 1875, p. 58).
121. Letter from John Gibbs to Sir B. Hall, President of the Board of Health, 30 June 1855; BC.
122. Chandos Leigh Hunt's *Vaccination Brought Home to the People* (1876), p. 34.
123. *Pall Mall Gazette* (*Vaccination Inquirer*, 2 March 1891).
124. Letter from Bradlaugh to A. Wheeler, 4 June 1889; BC.
125. Alfred Milnes of the 'anti' lobby asserted Bradlaugh was against compulsion.
126. Letter from Bradlaugh to organizers (*Stockport Express*, 12 October 1933).
127. Letter from Asquith to Bradlaugh, 14 August 1889; BC.
128. *Address*, 18 August 1889; BC.
129. *Empire News*, 24 September 1933.
130. *MSAB*, p. 34.
131. *Reminiscences*, p. 37.
132. Letter, 26 December 1889; BC.
133. *Reminiscences*, p. 39.
134. Allahabad *Morning Post*, 13 March 1891.
135. The other Congresses were at Bombay (1885), Calcutta (1886), Madras (1887) and Allahabad (1888).
136. *Broad Arrow*, 28 December 1889.
137. *Times*, 30 December 1889.
138. *Speeches*, pp. 155 and 157.
139. *NR*, 15 July 1883.
140. The actual members were Watts, Frederick James Gould, Richard Bithell and Frederick Millar. Holyoake was too ill to join.
141. *MSAB*, p. 26.

142. Letter from Bradlaugh to Wedderburn, 20 March 1890 (Add. 43618, f. 15; BMMS).

143. The terminal phase of his old disease process.

144. Resolution of 3 May 1782 (*Commons Journal*, XXXVIII, p. 977). The original resolution against Wilkes declared him 'incapable of being elected a Member'.

145. Confidentially told to William Digby, secretary of the Indian Political Agency in London (*Native States*, 5 October 1903).

146. *Daily News*, 17 August 1891.

147. Letter from Bradlaugh to Mrs Sewell, 14 January 1891; BC.

148. *MSAB*, p. 34.

149. Letter from Annie to Hypatia, 20 January 1891; BC.

150. See note 148.

151. Letter from James Caldwell to George Faulkner, 23 January 1891; BC.

152. *H*, CCCXLIX, 1161, 1162, 1170, 1171, 1174 and 1175. 'Infamous scoundrel' is not in *H*, but reported at the time.

153. Letter, 27 January 1891; BC.

154. *East Anglia Daily Times*, 30 January 1891.

155. Letter from de Worms to Bradlaugh, 29 January 1891; BC.

156. Circular letter by Hypatia Bonner, November 1893; BC.

157. e.g. *l'Estafette* and *L'Echo de Paris*, 1 February 1891.

158. *Last Will and Testament*, 30 January 1884; BC.

159. *F*, 22 March 1891.

160. *Halifax Courier*, 7 February 1891. The following account is derived from letters in the BC, contemporary press reports, of which the *Standard* (4 February 1891) is most informative, and pamphlets like *The Late Charles Bradlaugh*.

161. *MSAB*, p. 35.

162. Richard Roe, James Benford, John Yorke, James Smith.

163. Letter from Annie Besant to Foote, 4 February 1891; BC.

164. See note 161. In *An Apology for his Resignation of the Office of Vice-President of the National Secular Society* (1896) J.P. Gilmour described the same incident but located it at the graveside. He emphasized the rebuff to Foote in being excluded from the main party. With unwonted blindness or delicacy the press does not seem to have referred to it at the time.

165. *Halifax Courier*, 7 February 1891.

APPENDIX 2

1. This set the pattern of later Irish Catholic politics in the United States and Australia. Among the migrants to America was Patrick Kennedy, founder of the Kennedy dynasty. See Edward M. Levine's *The Irish and Irish Politicians* (1966).

2. *Life and Times of Queen Victoria*, I, p. 339.

3. *Ireland's Story* (1967) by Désirée Edwards-Rees, p. 141.
4. In the *English Republic* of 22 February 1851 W. J. Linton blamed the Tenant Leaguers for being too moderate in recognizing the landlords' right to the land. Fintan Lalor was saying this in Ireland. In the issue of 22 May 1851 'Spartacus pointedly asked the Irish: 'Have you none but Englishmen among the priests and police who persuade you to remain slaves? Are there none but Englishmen in the Imperial army which overawes both you and us?'
5. *Ireland's Story*, p. 143.

APPENDIX 3

1. *Republic*, first English translation by H. Spens (1763), Book X, p. 430.
2. *Politics*, III vii and IV ii.
3. *The Medieval World, Europe 1100-1350* (1961) by Friedrich Heer, p. 57.
4. J. W. Allen's *English Political Thought 1603-1660*, I, 1603-44 (1938), p. 4.
5. 'Introduction' by G. D. H. Cole to the 1955 ed. of *The Social Contract—Discourses* by Jean Jacques Rousseau, p. xii.
6. *Rights of Man* (1791), Part I, p. 71.
7. *Dictionary of National Biography* (1890), XXIV p. 258. This was the moderate Puritan (Presbyterian) party. The army Independents were republican, while the Anabaptists and other extremist sects were communistic. See H. N. Brailsford's *Levellers and the English Revolution*, edited by Christopher Hill (1961), 'Joseph's' *Fifth Monarchy of the Bible—What is it?* (1885), Zara S. Fink's *Classical Republicans: An Essay in the Recovery of a Pattern of Thought in Seventeenth Century England* (1945) and Christopher Hill's *Century of Revolution, 1603-1714* (1961).
8. *DNB* (1888), XIII p. 166.
9. *Acts and Ordinances of the Interregnum, 1642-60* (1911), II, p. 122.
10. *Daily Telegraph*, 28 January 1891.
11. *The Readie and Easie Way to Establish a Free Commonwealth, and the Excellence thereof, compar'd with The inconveniences and dangers of readmitting kingship in this nation* (1659), p. 1.
12. *Cromwell and Washington: A Contrast* (1875), p. 21.
13. On 28 January 1689. See *The Political History of England* VIII, 1660-1702 (1923) by Richard Lodge, p. 303.
14. W. S. Landor in the *Atlas*, 28 April 1855. Prompted by W. M. Thackeray's lectures on the *Four Georges: Sketches of Manners, Morals, Court and Town Life* (1855).
15. The hostility of these divisions was well shown when parties of the different sects settled America in the seventeenth and eighteenth centuries and imposed their own creed on each colony.
16. The obscenity was good old-fashioned pornography, Thomas Potter's *Essay on Woman* (1763) (Add. 30887; BMMS). The treason charge involved No. 45 (23 April 1763) of the *North Briton*, attacking the King's speech of 1763.

17. Apart from the Commonwealth period, most books on which do not have an entry 'republicanism' in their indexes, no volume appears to have been written on the English republican movement. This appendix and chapter 6, based on original research in ample periodical literature, are first steps in the production of a serious study.
18. All imports were banned when the price of local corn fell below 80s a quarter.
19. *Rep*, 1 March 1822.
20. *Rep*, 3 March 1820. Hone tried to withdraw the *Parodies* but Carlile republished them and forced Hone and himself into a prosecution. Hone was acquitted and Carlile then released.
21. Carlile said of Sherwin that he 'afterwards learned that he did not write the first number himself' (*Rep*, 1 March 1822).
22. *Rep*, 3 March 1820.
23. Cobbett's first flight was in 1794.
24. *Rep*, 1 March 1822.
25. Introduction to Vol. I, p. ix. Three years later he said that 'England was a perfect Republic under the reign of Alfred, but has never been so since' (*Rep*, 4 January 1822).
26. *Rep*, 28 March 1823. In 1819 he had started another weekly, the *Deist*.
27. *Rep*, 14 May 1824.
28. *Rep*, 4 February 1820.
29. The older and more powerful Society for the Suppression of Vice and the Encouragement of Religion and Virtue (1802) carried on the pious work.
30. Hunt accused him of running away at Peterloo. Cobbett opposed his Malthusian *Every Woman's Book* (1825-6), free trade and republicanism, and resented the exposures of his own vacillations.
31. *Rep*, 29 December 1826.
32. Many of its issues are unobtainable. Journalistically the French were behind the English. *Le Républicain* began in April 1833.
33. Hetherington's *Rep*, 20 August 1831. The *Radical* soon became the *Radical Reformer*. A merger late in 1832 brought the *Rep and Radical Reformer*.
34. *Rep*, April 1832. The Catholic priests vend the superstition while the Protestant clergy collect the tithes.
35. *Rep*, 1 May 1832.
36. *Rep*, No. 3, May 1832.
37. *Political Unionist*, No I, 30 June 1832.
38. Introduction to *The Red Republican and The Friend of the People* (1966 ed.) by John Saville, p. iii.
39. *ibid*.
40. Feargus O'Connor and Ernest Jones jumped on this bandwagon. In later life Carlile said in his *Christian Warrior* that as a young man he might have taken up physical force but saw it was impracticable.
41. *Northern Star*, 14 February 1846.
42. Preface to Vol. I, p.i. Linton described its editor as 'gentle as a child, pure as a girl, irreproachable as a saint' (*English Republic*, 22 September 1851).
43. *Red Rep*, 27 July 1850.

44. *ibid*, 31 August 1850.
45. *ibid*, 19 October 1850.
46. *Friend of the People*, 25 January 1851.
47. *English Republic*, 27 January 1851.
48. *ibid*, 22 February 1851.
49. *ibid*, 15 April 1855.
50. Tract No. I, January 1855 (B31; Cowen Collection, Newcastle upon Tyne Central Reference Library).
51. Broadsheet, 19 April 1855 (A335; do.).

Appendix 4

1. Judgment of Lord Chancellor Hardwicke in *Omichund (Omychund) v. Barker* (*Atkyns's Reports* 1765-8, I, p. 48). The best sources on the oath question are the transcripts of evidence in the major Bradlaugh cases, *Clarke v. Bradlaugh* and *Attorney-General v. Bradlaugh*. See also E. and A. G. Porritt's *Unreformed House of Commons* (1903), Frederick Pollock's *Essays in Jurisprudence and Ethics* (1882), Erskine May's *Constitutional History of England* (Francis Holland's ed., 1912), Michael MacDonagh's *Parliament: Its Romance, Its Comedy, Its Pathos* (1902) and the Select Committee *Reports* for 20 May 1880 (159 Session 2) and 16 June 1880 (226 Session 2).
2. 1 Eliz. (I) cap. 1, s. 19.
3. 5 Eliz. (I) cap. 1, s. 16.
4. 3 Jac. I cap. 4, ss. 13, 15, 21, 41 and 42.
5. 7 Jac. I cap. 2, s. 2 and 7 Jac. I cap. 6, s. 8.
6. *House of Commons Journal*, I, p. 460.
7. 30 Car. II, Stat. II, cap. 1, s. 3.
8. 1 Will. & Mary, Sess. I, cap. 18, s. 13.
9. 7 & 8 Will. III cap. 34, s. 1.
10. 13 Will. III cap. 6, s. 1. This was passed immediately after James II's death. A similar measure (1 Anne, Stat. I, cap. 22, s.1) was passed after William III's.
11. 8 Geo. I cap. 6, s.1.
12. Jewish Relief Act, 21 & 22 Vict. cap. 48, s.4.

The following is a complete list, in chronological order, of all the separately published works by Bradlaugh and non-libellous works specially devoted to him, that I have been able to trace. I have omitted material with useful references but primarily devoted to other subjects: biographies (e.g. Arthur and Charles Bradlaugh Bonner's *Hypatia Bradlaugh Bonner. The Story of Her Life*, 1942, and Arthur H.Nethercot's *The First Five Lives of Annie Besant*, 1960); social histories (e.g. Collet Dobson Collet's *History of the Taxes on Knowledge* , 1899, Norman E. Himes's *Medical History of Contraception*, 1936, and Peter Fryer's *The Birth Controllers*, 1965); freethought histories (e.g. my own *100 Years of Freethought*, 1967); political and journalistic memoirs, and unpublished juvenilia by Bradlaugh himself. Whatever is important in all these categories is referred to in the text and notes. Many of his 'works' are penny pamphlets reprinted from periodical sources like *The National Reformer*, *The North American Review*, *The New Review*, *Our Corner* and *The Northern Guardian*. Some of them ran through several editions but I have confined myself to what I believe to be the first. Collections such as *Polemical Essays: Political and Theological* (1864 and 1865), *Humanity's Gain from Unbelief, and Other Selections from the Works of Charles Bradlaugh* (1929) and the volumes collected after his death by his daughter and son-in-law, that purported to be his complete works, are excluded.

Works edited by Bradlaugh

The Investigator; a Journal of Secularism: from 15 March 1858 to 1 August 1859.
Half-hours with Freethinkers (1858): with John Watts and W.H.Johnson.
The National Reformer: with Joseph Barker from 14 April 1860 to 31 August 1861; alone from 7 September 1861 to 28 February 1863 and from 29 April 1866 to 25 January 1891.
Robert Cooper's *The Holy Scriptures Analysed* (1868): plus an 'introductory sketch'.
Charles Knowlton's *The Fruits of Philosophy* (1877): with Annie Besant.
Baron von Holbach's *The System of Nature* (1884): plus a 'memoir'.
National Secular Society's *Almanacks*: with Austin Holyoake from 1870 to 1874; with Charles Watts from 1875 to 1877; with Annie Besant from 1878 to 1890.

Works Written by Bradlaugh

1850
A Few Words on the Christians' Creed

1854-6
The Bible not Reliable
What does the Bible Teach?
What does the Bible Teach about God?

What is Christianity?
Does the Bible contain a Perfect Code of Morality?
Poor Saints and Rich Sinners
Who Helps the Poor?
The Apostles' Creed

1857
The Bible, What it is!

1858

The God of the Bible, Revengeful, Inconstant, Unmerciful and Unjust: 4-night debate with Rev. Brewin Grant

1859

What is Faith?
What shall a Man do to be Saved?
Has Man a Soul?

1860

Who was Jesus Christ?
The Atonement
Letter to John Brindley, LLD
First Letter from 'Iconoclast' to Rev. Brewin Grant
Is there a God?
New Life of David
New Life of Abraham
What Did Jesus Teach?
God, Man, and the Bible: 3-night discussion with Rev. Dr Joseph Baylee
Discussion on the Gospels: 4-night debate with Robert Court
Important Discussion: 4-night debate with John Brindley
Are the Doctrines and Precepts of Christianity, as taught in the New Testament, calculated to Benefit Humanity?: 3-night debate with Reverend J.H. Rutherford

1861

New Life of Jacob
New Life of Moses
A Few Words About the Devil
Jesus, Shelley, and Malthus; or Pious Poverty and Heterodox Happiness
Were Adam and Eve our First Parents?
The Existence of God
Prohibition of Free Speech. A Letter to the Rt Hon. LCJ Erle, and to the Hon. Mr Justice Williams, Mr Justice Byles, and Mr Justice Keating
Genesis
Is the Bible a Divine Revelation?: 4-night discussion with Rev. Woodville Woodman

The Existence of God: do
Has or is Man a Soul?: written debate with Rev. Thomas Lawson
What does the Bible Teach about God?: discussion with Rev. Alexander Mackie
Christianity and Secularism Contrasted: debate with Rev. W.M. Hutchings

1863

Real Representation of the People
Poverty and its Effect on the Political Condition of the People

1864

A Plea for Atheism

1866

Exodus

1867

When were our Gospels Written?
Reform or Revolution. An Address to the Lords and Commons of England in Parliament Assembled
Leviticus
Numbers
The Authorship and Credibility of the Four Gospels: written debate with B.H. Cowper
Atheism or Theism?: written debate with William Gillespie

1868

Heresy: Its Utility and Morality; a Plea and a Justification
The Irish Question
To the present and future electors of the borough of Northampton

1869

A Letter from a Freemason to General HRH Albert Edward, Prince of Wales

1870

George, Prince of Wales, with Recent Contrasts and Coincidences
The Twelve Apostles
The Land Question
Deuteronomy
The Existence of God: 2-night debate with Alexander Robertson
Secularism, Scepticism, and Atheism:

2-night debate with G.J. Holyoake
Exodus xxi, 7-11: written debate
with B.H. Cowper
Christianity v. Secularism: discussion
with David King
1871
*The Land, the People and the
Coming Struggle*
*Christianity in Relation to Free-
thought, Scepticism, and Faith:
Three Discourses by the Bishop of
Peterborough, with special Replies
by Charles Bradlaugh*
*London Republican Club—Inaugural
Address of the President, Mr Charles
Bradlaugh*
*The Impeachment of the House of
Brunswick*
1872
What Does Christian Theism Teach?:
2-night discussion with Rev. A.J.
Harrison
Atheism or Theism?: debate with
W.H. Gillespie
1873
*Modern Spiritualism. Human Im-
mortality Proved by Facts*: 2-night
debate with John Burns
The Autobiography of C. Bradlaugh
The Inspiration of the Bible: 6 letters
to the Bishop of Lincoln
1874
National Secular Society *Tracts*:
  Address to Christians
  Who was Jesus?
  A New Life of Jonah
1875
*Letter to Edward Vaughan Kenealy,
MP for the Borough of Stoke*
*Cromwell and Washington: A Con-
trast*
American Politics
*Letter to the Prince of Wales on His
Indian Visit*
*Five Dead Men Whom I Knew when
Living*
*Great South Place Debate (Is
Atheism or is Christianity the true*

*Secular Gospel, as tending to the
improvement and happiness of mankind in this life by human efforts and
material means?)*: 6-night discussion
with Rev. Brewin Grant
1876
Can Miracles Be Proved Possible?:
2-night debate with W.R. Browne
*Disestablishment and Disendowment
of the English Church*: 2-night
debate with W. Simpson
Is the Bible Divine?: debate with
Robert Roberts
The Freethinker's Text-Book: Part 1
1878
*The Laws Relating to Blasphemy and
Heresy: An Address to Freethinkers*
*Taxation: How it originated, how it
is spent, and who bears it*
Has Man a Soul?
Is it Reasonable to Worship God?:
2-night debate with Rev. R.A. Arm-
strong
1879
*Hints to Emigrants to the United
States of America*
Toryism from 1770 to 1879
Has, or is, Man a Soul?: 2-night
debate with Rev. W.M. Westerby
1880
Perpetual Pensions
*Is Atheism the True Doctrine of the
Universe?*: written debate with Rev.
Thomas Lawson
1881
Appeal to the People
*Secularism: Unphilosophical, Immoral,
and Anti-Social*: 3-night debate with
Rev. Dr James McCann
1882
Anthropology
*The True Story of My Parliamentary
Struggle*
*An Address to the Majority of Mon-
day* (6 March)
*The Civil List and Cost of the Royal
Family*
A Cardinal's Broken Oath. A Letter

to His Eminence Henry Edward, Cardinal-Archbishop of Westminster.
To the Electors
Genesis: Its authorship and authenticity

1883

The Rights of Constituents
May the House of Commons Commit Treason? An Appeal to the People
India and the Ilbert Bill
Lecture by Mr Bradlaugh, MP, on India

1884

An Address to the People
Northampton and the House of Commons
John Churchill, Duke of Marlborough. 'The Mob', 'the Scum', and 'the Dregs'
England's Balance Sheet
Some Objections to Socialism
How are we to Abolish the Lords?
To the Electors
Will Socialism Benefit the English People?: debate with H.M. Hyndman

1885

To the Electors who may Vote on January 1st, 1886
The Radical Programme
What Freemasonry is, what it has been, and what it ought to be

1886

Capital and Labour
Appeal to the Electors. Mr Gladstone or Lord Salisbury: Which?
A Letter to the Rt Hon. Lord Randolph S. Churchill, MP, Chancellor of the Exchequer
England's Balance Sheet for 1886, with exact details as to the Perpetual Pension to the Prince of Wales
Supernatural and Rational Morality
The Ethics of Punishment: with Annie Besant

1887

Lying for the Glory of God: A Letter to the Rev. Canon Fergie, BD, ex-posing his Gross Slander of a Dead Man
Market Rights and Tolls Restrictive of Trade
Compulsory Cultivation of Land: What it Means, and Why it Ought to be Enforced
Socialism: Its Fallacies and Dangers.
Notes on Christian Evidences. Being Criticisms on 'The Oxford House Papers'
The Channel Tunnel: Ought the Democracy to Oppose or Support it?
Will Socialism Benefit the English People?: written debate with E. Belfort Bax
Socialism: For and Against: written debate with Annie Besant

1888

Workmen and Their Wages. The Truck Law and How to Enforce It
Mr Gladstone in Reply to Colonel Ingersoll on Christianity
The Civil List
Employers' Liability Bill. Letter to Thomas Burt, MP
Royal Grants
Eternal Torment: written debate with Rev. John Lightfoot in 1876
India

1889

The Right to Affirm. Instructions to Witnesses, Jurors, and others
Northampton's Voice on Royal Grants
The Rules, Customs and Procedure of the House of Commons
Parliament and the Poor: What the Legislature Can Do: What it Ought to Do
Humanity's Gain from Unbelief
Indian Money Matters: The story of a famine insurance fund and what was done with it
The Eight Hours' Movement
Has Humanity Gained from Unbelief?: 2-night debate with Rev. Marsden Gibson

1890	H.M. Hyndman

The Oaths Act

1891

Speeches by Charles Bradlaugh

Doubts in Dialogue

Eight Hours' Movement: debate with

Labour and Law.

(*Note*: In the foregoing I have taken the title which appears on the title page and is often different from those on the cover and other pages. Bradlaugh had many more oral debates than those recorded, but the ones shown are the only ones of which I can trace printed transcriptions.)

Works about Bradlaugh (also in chronological order)

The Queen v. Charles Bradlaugh and Annie Besant, London, 1877.

HEADINGLEY, ADOLPHE S. *The Biography of Charles Bradlaugh*, London, 1880.

ANON. *Mr Bradlaugh, the Member for Northampton. An Answer to Mr Henry Varley's 'Appeal to the Men of England'*, London, 1882.

MAWER, W. *The Latest Constitutional Struggle*, London, 1883.

A HINDOO. *Mr Bradlaugh and the House of Commons*, London, 1884.

'HUMANITAS'. *Charles Bradlaugh, MP, and the Irish Nation*, London, 1885.

PARRY, EDWARD. *Charles Bradlaugh and the Parliamentary Struggle*, London, 1885.

STANDRING, GEORGE. *Biography of C. Bradlaugh, MP*, London, 1888.

CARTWRIGHT, J.H. *Some Lessons from the Life of Mr Bradlaugh*, Bristol, 1891.

GASQUOINE, T. *In Memoriam: Charles Bradlaugh*, Northampton, 1891.

HOLYOAKE, G.J. *Life and Career of Charles Bradlaugh, MP*, Buffalo, NY, 1891.

FOOTE, G.W. *Reminiscences of Charles Bradlaugh*, London, 1891.

ROBERTSON, J.M. 'Memoir' with *Labour and Law*, London, 1891.

ANON. *'Thorough'. The Late Charles Bradlaugh, MP, and Northampton*, Northampton, 1894.

BONNER, HYPATIA BRADLAUGH and ROBERTSON, J.M. *Charles Bradlaugh: A Record of His Life and Work, with an Account of His Parliamentary Struggle, Politics and Teachings*, 2 vols, London, 1895.

BONNER, ARTHUR and HYPATIA BRADLAUGH. *Did Charles Bradlaugh Die an Atheist?* London, 1898.

HEADLAM, STEWART D. *Charles Bradlaugh. An Appreciation*, London, 1907.

ANON. *Charles Bradlaugh. A Sketch of His Life and His Services to India*, Madras, c. 1910.

ROBERTSON, J.M. *Charles Bradlaugh*, London, 1920.

Champion of Liberty: Charles Bradlaugh, Centenary Volume, London, 1933.

Bradlaugh and Today, Speeches at Centenary Celebration, London, 1933.

ARNSTEIN, WALTER L. *The Bradlaugh Case. A Study in Late Victorian Opinion and Politics*, London, 1965.

INDEX

Abdullah of Perak (d. 1916), Malayan sultan, 286
Abolition, 75, 84, 150, 162
Adam, W.P. (1823-81), Liberal statesman, 189
Adams, J.P. (fl. 1850s), secularist organizer, 42, 53, 96, 176, 181
Adams, Samuel (1722-1803), US patriot, 150
Adams, Thomas (d. 1890), civic leader, 69, 105, 198, 206
Adams, W.E. ('Caractacus') (b. 1832), journalist, 55, 62, 68, 75, 83, 85-6, 93, 150
Address on the Civil War in France, Karl Marx, 124, 126
Adler, Felix (1851-1933), ethicist leader, 281
Affirmation, 16, 71, 75, 100-1, 192-223, 226, 230, 246, 249, 251, 261, 274, 282, 298
Age of Reason, The, Thomas Paine, 21
Agnostic Annual, The, 281
Agnostic Dépôt, 266, 281
Agnostic, The, 281
Agnosticism, 10, 19, 281, 299
Agricultural labourers, 125, 136, 153, 160, 188, 246, 261
Ainslie, C.P. (fl. 1850s), army officer, 30, 33, 36
Albert, Prince (1819-61), Victoria's Consort, 123, 131
Ali, Tariq (b. 1943), Trotskyist agitator, 298
Aliens, 270
All the Year Round, 92
Alliance, 125, 127
Allotments, 239, 251
Allsop, Thomas (1795-1880), republican businessman, 55, 57, 114
Almanack, National Secular, 153, 185, 264, 281
Alma-Tadema, Sir L. (1836-1912), painter, 170
Almighty God or Bradlaugh, J.T. Almy, 247
Ananias, the Atheist's God, W.S. Ross, 248
Anarchists, 84, 89, 125, 127, 237, 269, 289, 298
Andrews, S.P. (1812-86), US reformer, 149
Anglicans, 15-6, 46, 64, 66, 68-9, 103, 107-8, 111, 122-3, 150, 152, 157, 162-3, 181, 189, 204, 227, 235, 281

Another 'Fourpenny Wilderness', Charles Southwell, 40
'Anthony Collins', see Johnson, W.H.
Arch, Joseph (1826-1919), farm workers' leader, 136, 188, 206, 220, 251
Argyll, 8th Duke of (1823-1900), Liberal statesman, 215
Army, British, 28-37, 202, 257-8, 289
Arnold, Matthew (1822-88), poet, 212
Arthur, Prince (1850-1942), Victoria's son, 128
Ashurst Junior, W.H. (fl. 1860s), solicitor, 81-2
Ashurst, W.H. (1792-1855), solicitor and publisher, 39
Asquith, Herbert (1st Earl of Oxford and Asquith) (1852-1928), Liberal Prime Minister, 163, 278, 297
Atheism, 10, 18-9, 21, 38-9, 41, 47, 58, 73, 75-6, 80, 82, 85, 99, 100, 103, 108, 114, 132, 141-2, 151, 156, 158-9, 190, 192-223, 247, 270, 281, 287
Attorney-General v. Bradlaugh, 232, 235-6, 245-6, 256, 269
Australia, 48
Autobiography of C. Bradlaugh, The, 12, 58
Aveling, E.B. (1851-98), writer, 186-8, 206-7, 210-1, 227-30, 237, 240-4, 252, 297
Ayrton, A.S. (1816-86), Liberal statesman, 50, 101-2, 136, 189
Baggallay, Sir Richard (1816-88), High Court judge, 204, 212
Bain, Alexander (1818-1903), psychologist, 227
Baines, Sir Edward (1800-90), Liberal MP, 89
Bakunin, Michael (1814-76), Russian anarchist, 84, 125
Balfour, 1st Earl of (1848-1930), Tory Prime Minister, 193, 205, 247, 270
Ball, W.P. (1844-1917), secularist writer, 248, 252, 270
Ballot, secret, 103, 155
Baptist, The, 192
Baptists, 46, 60, 65, 69, 108, 161, 235, 247
Barker, Joseph (1806-75), journalist, 67-70, 75-7, 80, 263
Barker's (or *Barkers'*) *Review*, 77
Barttelot, Sir Walter (1820-93), Tory MP, 287
Bates, John (fl. 1870s), secularist bookseller, 79, 108, 160
Bax, E.B. (1854-1926), socialist journalist, 237, 241

376

Baylee, Joseph (1808-83), Anglican theologian, 66

Bayly, A.E. ('Edna Lyall') (1857-1903), novelist, 293-4

Beaconsfield, 1st Earl of, see Disraeli, Benjamin

Beaconsfield Standard, The, 248

Beales, Edmond (1803-81), barrister, 89, 93-4, 96-7, 107, 113

Becket, Thomas à (? 1118-70), Archbishop of Canterbury, 104

Beesly, E.S. (1831-1915), historian, 121, 138, 227, 237, 246

Bell, A.J. (fl. 1880s), medical practitioner, 260, 288

Benn, A. Wedgwood (renouncing 2nd Viscount Stansgate) (b. 1925), Labour statesman, 9

Benson, Edward (1829-96), Archbishop of Canterbury, 275

Bentinck, A.C. (1819-77), army officer, 33

Bernard, Simon (1817-62), French republican, 55-6, 73

Besant, Annie (1847-1933), theosophist leader, 156-90, 197, 203, 206, 209-10, 212-3, 216, 219-20, 226-30, 237, 242-6, 252, 260, 263-4, 269-70, 277-9, 281-2, 285-93, 296

Besant, Digby (1869-1960), actuary, 157-8, 285

Besant, Frank (1840-1917), Anglican vicar, 157-8, 163, 181, 183

Besant, Sir Walter (1836-1901), novelist, 157

Besant-Scott, Mabel (b. 1870), theosophist, 157-8, 163, 183, 186, 285

Bible, What it is!, The, Charles Bradlaugh, 50, 52, 54-5

Biggar, Joseph (1828-90), Irish MP, 181

Bimetallic League, 11

Birmingham Morning News, The, 141, 144

Birth control, 10-11, 14, 51, 67-70, 74-7, 80, 83, 110, 172-84, 209, 222, 227, 229, 264, 270, 293, 298

Bismarck, Prince Otto von (1815-98), German Chancellor, 119, 126

Blackburn, 1st Baron (1813-96), High Court judge, 109, 225

Blackie, John (1809-95), classicist, 114

Blackmore, R.D. (1825-1900), novelist, 178

Blackstone, Sir William (1723-80), jurist, 277

Blanc, Louis (1811-82), French socialist, 58, 63, 87

Bland, Hubert (1856-1914), socialist writer, 245

Blasphemy, 101, 185, 189, 195, 213, 219-21, 224-6, 231, 251, 277

Blasphemy Act (1697), 201, 212, 219-21

Blasts from Bradlaugh's Own Trumpet, G.J. Holyoake, 216

Blavatsky, H.P. (1831-91), theosophist leader, 270, 296

Boa, Andrew (fl. 1870s), trade union leader, 155

Bomba (Ferdinand II) (1810-59), Two Sicilies king, 78

Bonner, Arthur (1861-1939), printer, 244, 260, 270, 280, 285, 289, 292, 294

Bonner, Basil Bradlaugh (b. 1920), Bradlaugh's great-grandson, 296

Bonner, Charles Bradlaugh (1890-1966), Bradlaugh's grandson, 69, 285, 293, 298

Bonner, Edmond Bradlaugh (b. 1915), Bradlaugh's great-grandson, 298

Bonner, Hypatia Bradlaugh (1858-1935), Bradlaugh's daughter, 56, 66, 69, 115, 135, 159-61, 168-72, 177-8, 180-3, 186-7, 209-10, 212, 220, 226, 228, 231, 242, 244-5, 252-3, 263, 269-70, 279-80, 285-6, 288-90, 292-5, 298

Bonner, William (d. 1869), radical pastor, 89, 244

Bonnerjee, W.C. (b. 1844), Indian lawyer, 275

Bonner's Fields, 16-8, 22, 27

Bottomley, Horatio (1860-1933), fraudulent financier, 245

Boudicca (Boadicea) (d. 62), early British queen, 12

Bovill, Sir William (1814-73), High Court judge, 100

Bowen, 1st Baron (1835-94), High Court judge, 206

Bradlaugh, Alice (1856-88), Bradlaugh's daughter, 49, 115-7, 135, 159-61, 168-72, 180-3, 186-7, 209-10, 220, 226, 228, 242, 244, 263, 269, 288

Bradlaugh, Charles (1859-70), Bradlaugh's son, 65, 115, 117

Bradlaugh, Elizabeth, *née* Trimby (d. 1871), Bradlaugh's mother, 13, 35-6, 43-4, 161, 168

Bradlaugh, James (1780-1811), Bradlaugh's grandfather, 13

Bradlaugh, Mary (d. 1852), Bradlaugh's grandmother, 28, 35

Bradlaugh Norman, Elizabeth (1835-1907), Bradlaugh's sister, 13, 15, 27, 36, 43, 289

Bradlaugh Senior, Charles (1811-52), Bradlaugh's father, 13-4, 18-20, 26,

28-9, 35

Bradlaugh, S.L., *née* Hooper (1831-77), Bradlaugh's wife, 43-4, 66, 112, 115-6, 134, 171-2, 182, 288

Bradlaugh, W.R. (1845-1917), Bradlaugh's brother, 20, 28-9, 35, 87, 90, 112, 116, 135, 161, 168, 202, 290, 296

Bramwell, 1st Baron (1808-92), High Court judge, 102, 182, 204

Brand, Henry (1st Viscount Hampden) (1814-92), Commons Speaker, 192, 195, 197-8, 210, 222, 231-2, 235-6, 247

Brett, W.B. (1st Viscount Esher) (1815-99), Master of the Rolls, 100, 182, 212, 215, 219, 246

Bright, Jacob (1821-99), Liberal MP, 160

Bright, John (1811-89), Liberal statesman, 88-9, 97, 109, 129, 144-5, 158, 191, 196, 205, 211, 221, 255, 279

Brimont Brassac, Vicomtesse de (fl. 1870s), French republican, 120, 135, 153

Brindley, John (d. 1873), evangelist, 23, 66, 150

British Banner, The, 24

British Empire, The, 193, 203

British Monarchy, The, 109

Broadhead, William (1815-79), trade union militant, 109

Broadhurst, Henry (1840-1911), trade union leader, 262, 272

Browne, Robert (? 1550-1633), Nonconformist pioneer, 104

Bryson, J. (fl. 1870s), miners' leader, 183-4

Büchner, Ludwig (1824-99), German physician, 149, 212

Buckle, H.T. (1821-62), social historian, 76

Bullock, Glegg (1800-90), secularist philanthropist, 248, 258-9

Bureau of Statistics of Labour, 164, 251

Burials Act (1880), 192

Burke, Edmund (1729-97), independent statesman, 89, 279

Burns, John (1858-1943), Liberal-Labour statesman, 251-2, 264, 272, 278

Burrows, Herbert (1845-1922), socialist, 252-3, 269-70, 289

Burt, Thomas (1837-1922), miners' leader, 113, 152, 188, 232, 251, 274, 289, 293

Buxton, Charles (1823-71), Liberal MP, 89

Buxton, Sydney (1st Earl) (1853-1934), Liberal statesman, 272

Byles, Sir J.B. (1801-84), High Court judge, 74

Calder, John (b. 1927), controversial publisher, 298

Callan, Philip (b. 1837), Irish MP, 215

Campbell, 1st Baron (1779-1861), Lord Chief Justice, 56

Canada, 98, 248, 296

Canute II (?994-1035), Anglo-Danish king, 9

Capitalism, 91, 106-7, 116, 118-9, 133, 143, 238-40, 258, 263

Capper, Charles (fl. 1860s), Tory MP, 109

'Caractacus', see Adams, W.E.

Cardinal's Broken Oath, A, C. Bradlaugh, 202

Carlile Campbell, Theophila (b. 1837), Richard's daughter, 22, 38, 151

Carlile Cooke, Hypatia (1836-78), Richard's daughter, 22, 38, 151, 162

Carlile, Eliza Sharples (? 1805-?1852), Richard's common law wife, 21-2, 38

Carlile, Jane (1783-1843), Richard's wife, 21-2

Carlile, Julian (1834-?1862), Richard's son, 22, 38

Carlile, Richard (1790-1843), republican journalist, 21-4, 42, 86, 133, 155, 174-5, 221, 282

Carlyle, Thomas (1795-1881), man of letters, 89, 114

Casson, W.A. (fl. 1880s), reformer, 206, 289

Castelar, Emilio (1832-99), Spanish dictator, 146-7, 153

Catholics, Roman, 16, 32, 55, 63, 83-4, 98-9, 103, 108, 113, 142, 151-2, 159, 198, 203-4, 222, 246, 248, 282, 287, 299

Cattell, C.C. (fl. 1870s), secularist republican, 62, 122, 138, 140-1, 145, 163, 181

Chamberlain, Joseph (1836-1914), Liberal Unionist statesman, 103, 113, 131, 160, 191, 251, 255, 258

Champion, H.H. (1859-1928), socialist, 251, 272

Channel tunnel, 214, 298

Charles I (1600-49), Stuart king of England, 104, 118

Charles Bradlaugh, M.P., and the Irish Nation, W.P. Ball, 248

Chartism, 16-7, 38-9, 46, 62, 67, 70, 82, 114, 141, 155, 216, 238, 298

Christian Commonwealth, The, 222

Christian Evidence Society (evangelical), 114, 181

Christian Evidence Society (Robert Taylor's), 20

Christian Globe, The, 204

Christian Herald, The, 168
Christianity, see separate denominations
Church of England, see Anglicans
Church of Ireland, 16, 32, 84, 99, 189
Church rate, 64, 68, 79
Churchill, Lord Randolph (1849-94), Tory statesman, 193, 195-6, 205, 214, 235, 246-7, 255-8, 260
Churchman, The, 226
Citizens' Advice Bureau, 202
City of Dreadful Night, The, James Thomson, 152, 168
Civil War, American, 75, 84, 88, 98
Clarke, Sir Edward (1841-1931), barrister, 287
Clarke v. Bradlaugh, 201-4, 206-7, 212, 215, 218-9, 224-5, 231
Cleasby, Sir Anthony (1804-79), High Court baron, 102
Clerkenwell Green, 16, 99, 103, 115
Clifford, W.K. (1845-79), mathematician, 121
Clôture (closure), 214, 221
Cluer, A.R. (1852-1942), judge, 163, 231
Cluseret, G.P. (1823-1900), republican general, 98
Cobbett, William (1763-1835), radical journalist, 16, App. 3
Cobden Club, 289
Cobden, Richard (1804-65), free trader, 293
Cockburn, Sir Alexander (1802-80), Lord Chief Justice, 101, 180-2
Coercion, Irish, 16, 28, 98, 188, 202, 248, 251, 260
Coit, Stanton (1857-1944), ethicist leader, 281, 288
Colenso, J.W. (1814-83), modernist bishop, 46
Coleridge, 1st Baron (1820-94), Lord Chief Justice, 206, 212, 222, 225-6, 231, 235-6, 245, 274, 277
Collet, C.D. (1813-98), reformer, 101
Collier, Robert (1817-86), High Court judge, 73-4
Collings, Jesse (1831-1920), Liberal MP, 251, 274
Collins, W.J. (fl. 1880s), medical practitioner, 278-9
Collins, Wilkie (1824-89), novelist, 149
Common Law Procedure Acts (1852-60), 41
Commons, House of, 10, 16, 89, 93, 96-7, 149, 192-224, 230-6, 247, 249-58, 260-3, 268, 270-7, 280-8, 293
Commune, Paris, 105, 118, 123-6, 133
Communism, 119, 133, 143, 154, 237, 240

Congregationalists, 22, 38, 63, 104, 108, 111, 186, 215, 264, 274, 278
Congreve, Richard (1818-99), positivist, 228
Conservatives, see Tories
Constituency rights, 9, 191-250
Constitutional Rights, League for the Defence of, 205-6
Conway, Ellen D. (d. 1897), Moncure's wife, 158, 167, 178, 183, 206
Conway, Moncure D. (1832-1907), radical pastor, 114, 158-9, 164, 171, 178, 183, 187, 220, 226, 228, 281
Cook, Henry (fl. 1870s), bookseller, 172-5
Cookson, John (?1832-?1913), birth control advocate, 74-5
Cooper, R.A. (fl. 1870s), secularist republican, 144-6
Cooper, Robert (1819-68), secularist journalist, 40, 42-3, 48-50, 53-4, 59-60, 86, 94
Cooper, Thomas (1805-92), Chartist polemicist, 21, 23, 60, 104
Co-operative movement, 39, 67, 119, 141, 154, 239, 273, 299
Corbett, Edward (fl. 1880s), Tory, 205, 215
Corporation of London, 261-2, 264
Cotton, Sir Henry (1821-92), High Court judge, 182, 215, 219, 246
Counsellor, The, 77
Covington, Frederick (fl. 1880s), civic leader, 160, 275
Cowen Junior, Joseph (1831-1900), republican industrialist, 55, 130, 169, 211
Crawford, John (fl. 1860s), barrister, 77, 81-2
Cremer, Sir W.R. (1838-1908), Liberal MP, 89-90, 93, 246, 289
Cri du Peuple, Le, 237
Crompton, Henry (1836-1904), solicitor, 227
Cromwell and Washington, C. Bradlaugh, 118
Cromwell, Oliver (1599-1658), Lord Protector, 12, 60, 104, 118
Cross, 1st Viscount (1823-1914), Tory statesman, 282
Crump, F.O. (1840-1900), barrister, 222
Daily Chronicle, The, 204
Daily News, The, 39, 189
Daily Telegraph, The, 109
Dale, R.W. (1829-95), radical pastor, 215
Danton, G.J. (1759-94), French revolutionary, 9
Darwin, Charles (1809-82), evolutionist, 76, 181

379

Davenport, Allen (b. 1775), radical shoe-maker, 105
Davidson, Morrison (fl. 1880s), radical journalist, 265
Davidson, Thomas (1840-1900), reformer, 237
Davitt, Michael (1846-1906), Irish patriot, 187-8
De Rin, Bradlaugh v., 99-101
Debt, National, 122
Denman, George (1819-96), High Court judge, 101, 206, 212, 215, 227
Denning, Inspector (fl. 1880s), police officer, 209-11
Derby, 14th Earl of (1799-1869), Tory Prime Minister, 38, 56, 93, 97
Derby, 15th Earl of (1826-93), Tory statesman, 185
Descartes, René (1596-1650), philosopher, 49
Dialectical Society, London, 113, 129-30, 183, 243
Dickens, Charles (1812-70), novelist, 44, 92
Diegesis, The, Robert Taylor, 19, 20
Digby, William (1849-1904), Anglo-Indian publicist, 290, 294
Dilke, Ashton (1850-83), journalist, 188, 192, 211, 232
Dilke, Sir Charles (1843-1911), Liberal statesman, 113, 122, 129-32, 138, 140, 150, 152, 155, 188, 191, 246-7, 296
Disarmament, 278, 298
Disestablishment, 75, 99, 105, 145, 189, 247, 299
Disraeli, Benjamin (1st Earl of Beacons-field) (1804-81), Tory Prime Minister, 96-7, 128, 152, 167, 184-5, 188, 191, 197, 205, 221, 265, 299
Dixon George (1820-98), educationist, 128
Dock strike, 278
Doddridge, Philip (1702-51), Noncon-formist pastor, 104
Domestic servants, 61, 170, 261
Dowsing, William (?1596-?1679), Puritan iconoclast, 12
Drysdale, Charles (1829-1907), birth con-trol advocate, 181, 183, 206
Drysdale, George ('G.R.'), (1825-1904), birth control advocate, 68, 75, 175, 178
Dufferin and Ava, 1st Marquess of (1826-1902), diplomat, 276
Dumfries Standard, The, 268
Early Closing Bill, 271-2
Eastern Post, The, 125-6
Eastern question, 120, 173, 185

Education League, National, 113, 128
Education, national, 105, 113-4, 130, 145, 239
Education, secular, 88, 94, 114, 124, 135, 248, 259
Edwards, Superintendent (fl. 1860s), police officer, 70, 72-3
Eight hours movement, 272-3
Elements of Social Science, The, George Drysdale, 50, 74-5, 77, 80, 173, 203
Eleusis Club, 127, 145
Eliot, George (1819-80), novelist, 51, 169
Elliott, Ebenezer (1781-1849), radical poet, 23
Ellis, Sir John (1829-1912), Lord Mayor of London, 219
Emerson, R.W. (1803-82), US poet-essayist, 26, 62, 151
Empire, British, see Imperialism
Employers' liability, 238, 254, 272, 286
Engels, Friedrich (1820-95), socialist writer, 106, 127, 237, 247, 297
English Church Union, 102
English Churchman, The, 79
English Republic, The, 55
Erle, Sir William (1793-1880), Lord Chief Justice, 74
Erskine, Sir H.D. (1838-1921), Commons Sergeant-at-Arms, 210, 217-8, 231
Esquiros Alphonse (1814-76), French poet, 88
Essays and Reviews, 46
Ethical Culture, 281
Evening News, The, (Edinburgh), 242
Evening News, The, (London), 216
Evidence Amendment Act (1870), 101, 192, 194, 203, 274
Evidence Further Amendment Act (1869), 100-1, 192, 194-5, 203, 274
Examination of the four Gospels, C. Brad-laugh, 23-4
Examiner, The, 146
Exclusion motion, 197, 205-6, 213, 218, 231-2, 235, 247, 282
Expulsion, 210-1, 214, 217
Expunging motion, 282, 285-7
Fabian Society, 237, 245, 252-3
Factory Act (1833), 16, 238
Fair Trade (Protection), 251-2
Fall of Prince Florestan of Monaco, The, Charles Dilke, 155
Family planning, see Birth Control
Favre, Jules (1809-80), French statesman, 121, 124
Fawcett, Henry (1833-84), radical econo-mist, 113, 121-2, 155, 169, 181, 255, 279
Fawcett, Millicent (1847-1929), feminist,

181

Fellowship of the New Life, 237

Fenians, 98-9, 136, 187

Ferry, Jules (1832-93), French Premier, 124

Few Words on the Christians' Creed, A, C. Bradlaugh, 24

Field, 1st Baron (1813-1907), High Court judge, 169, 217-8, 221-2, 231

Financial Reform Association, Parliamentary and, 254, 282, 289

FitzGerald, J.D. (1816-89), Law Lord, 225

Fleet Street House, 42, 48-50, 53-4, 57, 81, 142

Fletcher, Samuel (d. 1856), secularist philanthropist, 40, 48-9

Foote, G.W. (1850-1915), secularist journalist, 122, 124, 137-9, 141, 144, 146, 152, 160, 163, 167-9, 176, 181, 186, 206-8, 213, 219-21, 224-6, 228, 230-1, 246, 264-6, 277, 279, 281-2, 288, 290, 293-4, 296

Forder, Robert (b. 1844), secularist publisher, 83, 188, 260, 285, 288, 294

Forster, W.E. (1818-86), Liberal statesman, 114, 202

Fortescue, 3rd Earl (1818-1905), Whig peer, 128

Fortnightly Review, The, 114

Fourth Party, 193

Fowler, Sir R.N. (1828-91), Lord Mayor of London, 195-6, 210, 261

Fowler, William (b. 1828), Liberal, 160-1

Fox, W.J. (1786-1864), radical pastor, 55

France, 14, 56, 63, 100, 119-21, 123, 143, 147-8, 153, 214, 232

Franchise, see Reform, parliamentary

Franco-Prussian War, 118, 120, 123

Free trade, 251-2

Freemasonry, 63, 88, 164, 169, 268, 289

Freethinker, The, 206, 219, 221, 224, 229-30

Freethinkers, International Federation of, 212, 264, 296

Freethinker's Text-Book, The, 168, 173, 178

Freethought, 11, 18-21, 25, 40-2, 46, 48, 51, 59-60, 62, 67, 70, 83, 85, 88, 94-5, 105, 109, 167, 170-2, 174, 176, 184, 195, 213, 227, 230, 258, 266, 277, 281-2, 290, 296

Freethought Publishing Company, 176-7, 187, 219, 221, 242, 244, 285

Frere, Sir Bartle (1815-84), diplomat, 206

Friendly societies, 239, 248, 273-4, 290

Fruits of Philosophy, The, C. Knowlton, 172-84, 193, 201, 203, 205, 214, 227, 247

Gambetta, Léon (1838-82), French Premier, 153

Game laws, 107, 136, 153

Gandhi, Mohandas (1869-1948), Indian patriot, 289

Garibaldi, Giuseppe (1807-82), Italian revolutionary, 56, 63, 69, 75, 77-8, 81, 83-4, 88

Garrison, W.L. (1805-79), US abolitionist, 40, 88, 150

Gedge, Sydney (1802-83), Anglican vicar, 79, 111

Gentleman's Magazine, The, 136

George IV (1762-1830), Hanoverian king of England, 131

Gibson, Milner (1806-84), Liberal statesman, 101, 111

Giffard, Sir Hardinge (1st Earl Halsbury) (1823-1921), Lord Chancellor, 181, 193, 197, 203, 206-8, 224-6, 235, 275

Gilbert, Sir W.S. (1836-1911), librettist, 91

Gilpin, Charles (d. 1874), Liberal MP, 107-9, 111, 152, 160

Girard, Pierre (fl. 1870s), US journalist, 148

Girardin, Émile de (1806-81), French journalist, 126

Gladstone, Herbert (1st Viscount) (1854-1930), Liberal statesman, 287

Gladstone, W.E. (1809-98), Liberal Prime Minister, 88, 96-7, 99, 101-2, 109, 121, 129-30, 144, 152, 173, 188-9, 191-3, 195-8, 204-6, 211, 214, 221, 223, 231-2, 235, 243, 246-7, 251, 255-6, 260-1, 265, 282, 286-8

God and His Book, W.S. Ross, 260

Gordon, C.G. (1833-85), army general, 246

Gorst, Sir John (1835-1911), Tory statesman, 193, 198, 203-4, 247, 262, 275

Goschen, 1st Viscount (1831-1907), Liberal Unionist statesman, 258

Gospel according to St John, The, Annie Besant, 157

Gospel of Atheism, The, Annie Besant, 183

Gosset, Sir Ralph (d. 1885), Commons Sergeant-at-Arms, 197, 205, 231

Graham, Cunninghame (1852-1936), socialist writer, 264

Grant, Brewin (1821-92), Anglican vicar, 22, 60-1, 65, 163, 170, 265

Grantham, Sir William (1835-1911), High Court judge, 195

Granville, 2nd Earl (1815-91), Whig states-

381

man, 120, 191, 296

Grey, Sir George (1799-1882), Whig statesman, 44

Grey, 3rd Earl (1802-94), Whig statesman, 89

Griffith-Jones, George ('Lara') (fl. 1880s), secularist journalist, 259, 266-8

Grosvenor, Lord Richard (1837-1912), Whig statesman, 198, 235, 246

Grosvenor, Lord Robert (1801-93), Whig MP, 44, 46

Grove, Sir W.R. (1811-96), High Court judge, 203, 207-8, 212, 218, 235-6, 258

Guardian, The, 226

Guernsey Mail, The, 71

Guild of St Matthew's, 181, 211

Gurney, Joseph (d. 1894), civic leader, 62, 105, 108, 111, 152, 188, 206, 216-7

Habeas Corpus, 98

Haeckel, Ernst (1834-1919), German biologist, 212

Hale, Sir Matthew (1609-76), Lord Chief Justice, 220

Hales, John (fl. 1870s), socialist, 125-6, 129

Half-hours with Freethinkers, 49

Hall of Science (City Road), 39, 90

Hall of Science (Old Street), 113-4, 127, 132, 134, 158-9, 162-3, 176, 182, 187, 202, 211, 216, 220, 243-4, 247, 266, 282, 288, 294

Hallmarking, 282, 286

Hampden, John (1594-1643), Puritan statesman, 60

Hansard, 191, 257

Harcourt, Sir William (1827-1904), Liberal statesman, 224, 246, 261, 272, 282

Hardy, Thomas (1752-1832), radical bootmaker, 105

Hare, Thomas (1806-91), political theorist, 90

Harney, G.J. (1817-97), republican journalist, 150, App. 3

Harper, Thomas (fl. 1880s), solicitor, 216, 293

Harrison, Frederic (1831-1923), positivist writer, 121, 138

Harte, F.B. (1836-1902), US writer, 149

Hartington, Marquess of (8th Duke of Devonshire) (1833-1908), Whig statesman, 191, 251, 255, 261-2

Harvey, Thomas (fl. 1850s), solicitor, 61, 63, 77, 87

Haughton, James (1795-1873), Irish reformer, 32

Hawkins, Henry (1st Baron Brampton) (1817-1907), High Court judge, 212,

215, 268

Hay, John (1838-1905), US statesman, 149

Headlam, Stewart (1847-1924), Christian socialist, 162, 181, 184, 187-8, 197, 206, 220, 252, 289

Healy, Tim (1855-1931), Irish leader, 219, 232

Henderson, Sir Edmund (1821-96), police commissioner, 209

Henley, 3rd Baron (1825-98), Whig MP, 107-8, 111, 152, 160

Henry VI (1421-71), Lancastrian King of England, 220

Herald and Helpmate, The, 162

Herald, The, 160

Herbert, Hon. Auberon (1838-1906), reformer, 138, 185, 189

Herschell, 1st Baron (1837-99), Lord Chancellor, 235, 256, 274

Herzen, Alexander (1812-70), Russian republican, 84, 87

Hetherington, Henry (1792-1849), radical publisher, 25, 39, 52

Hicks-Beach, Sir Michael (1837-1916), Tory statesman, 247, 249, 251

Hill, Robert (1832-1908), radical shoemaker, 110-1

History of the Fleet Street House, The, G.J. Holyoake, 49

Holker, Sir John (1828-82), High Court judge, 215

Holyoake, Austin (1826-74), secularist printer, 25, 48, 77, 80-1, 100-1, 108, 112, 129-30, 134, 152, 163, 173, 228

Holyoake, G.J. (1817-1906), radical journalist, 18, 21, 25, 38, 40, 42-3, 48-57, 59, 64, 67-8, 75, 77-8, 80-1, 84-6, 89, 102, 119, 134, 149-50, 152, 155, 162-3, 167-8, 173, 176, 180-2, 184, 194, 213, 216, 228, 245, 278, 281, 288-9, 296

Home colonization, 114-5

Home, D.D. (1833-86), spiritualist medium, 113

Home Rule, Irish, 191, 202, 209, 246, 249, 251, 255-6, 260

Hooker, Sir Joseph (1817-1911), botanist, 220

Hooper, Abraham (d. 1891), Bradlaugh's father-in-law, 23, 43-5, 115, 171, 292, 296

Hopkins, J.B. (fl. 1870s), journalist, 136-7

Hopwood, C.H. (1829-1904), Liberal MP, 193, 246-7, 249

Howell, George (1833-1910), trade union leader, 89, 96-7, 107, 113, 121,

261-2

Huddleston, Sir J.W. (1815-90), High Court judge, 218, 235-6, 268

Hughes, Thomas (1822-96), novelist, 97, 189

Hugo, Victor (1802-85), French novelist, 56, 58

Humanism, 39, 85

Humanity's Gain from Unbelief, C. Bradlaugh, 269

Hume, David (1711-76), Scottish philosopher, 10

Hunt, J. Leigh (1784-1859), poet, 40

Hunt, Thornton (1810-73), radical journalist, 40

Hunter, W.A. (1844-98), lawyer, 220, 274, 287, 289

Huxley, Thomas (1825-95), biologist, 170, 224, 227

Hyde Park, 44-5, 62, 83, 93, 96, 124, 128, 132, 136, 148, 185

Hyndman, H.M. (1842-1921), socialist leader, 237-9, 241, 243, 251-2, 272-3

Hypatia (d. 415), Neoplatonist scholar, 22, 56

Hypothesis, C. Bradlaugh, 23

Illingworth, Alfred (1827-1907), Liberal MP, 274

Impeachment of the House of Brunswick, The, C. Bradlaugh, 128, 131, 136, 195

Imperialism, 15, 36, 118, 206, 221, 240-1, 253, 255, 275, 279, 291

Ince, Bret (fl. 1880s), civil servant, 289

Independents (early Congregationalists), 104, 161

India, 16 28, 67, 113, 206, 255, 262, 275-7, 279-80, 282, 286, 296

Indian National Congress, 251, 276, 279-80, 282, 290, 296

Individual, Family and National Poverty, J.H. Palmer, 181

Individualism, 42, 107, 143, 238, 298

Industrial arbitration, 105, 299

Ingersoll, Robert (1833-99), US reformer, 134, 296

International Herald, The, 133, 139-40, 142, 144, 162

International Working Men's Association (First International), 88-90, 118, 124-7, 129, 133, 135, 141, 144, 155

Investigator, The (London), 43, 49-50, 53-4, 61-4, 66, 68, 74, 248

Ireland, 16, 29-35, 98-9, 107, 122, 187-8, 201, 205, 255, App. 2

Irish Nationalists (Parnellites or Home Rulers), 191, 198, 201-2, 214, 223, 246, 249, 251, 255-6,

Irish Reform League, 99, 110

Irish Revolutionary (Republican) Brotherhood, see Fenians

Is the Bible Indictable? A. Besant, 183

Is there a God?, C. Bradlaugh, 159

Italian Coal and Iron Co. Ltd, 78, 87, 112

Italy, 55, 63, 75, 78-9, 83, 120, 214

James, Edwin (1812-82), barrister, 56

James, Henry (1843-1916), novelist, 151

James, Sir Henry (1st Baron) (1828-1911), Liberal statesman, 202, 204-5, 217-8, 221, 231-2, 235-6, 246, 249

Jennings, L.J. (1836-93), Tory MP, 257, 265

Jessel, Sir George (1824-83), Master of the Rolls, 183

Jesuits, 124

Jesus, Shelley, and Malthus, C. Bradlaugh, 74, 80

Jevons, Stanley (1835-82), orthodox economist, 106

Jews, 16, 62, 64-5, 103, 109, 222-3, 248, 270

Jingoes, 173, 185

John Street Institution, 25, 42, 61-2

Johnson, W.H. ('Anthony Collins') (fl. 1850s and 1880s), secularist journalist, 49-51, 54, 61, 248, 265-7

Jones, Ernest (1819-69), Chartist barrister, 46, 62, 90, 99, 108, 188

Joynes, J.L. (d. 1886), socialist journalist, 237

Junta, 67

Justice, 237, 244, 252

Kapital, Das, K. Marx, 213, 240

Keating, Sir H.S. (1804-88), High Court judge, 74, 100

Keevil, Edward (fl. 1860s), Irish reformer, 110

Kelly, Colonel (fl. 1860s), Irish patriot, 98-9, 102

Kelly, Sir Fitzroy (1796-1880), Lord Chief Baron, 101

Kelly, T.M. (fl. 1880s), Tory, 264, 268

Kennaway, Sir J.H. (1837-1919), Tory MP, 249

Kenny, Courtney (1847-1930), jurist, 251, 274

Khedive of Egypt (Ismail) (1830-95), 167, 221

Khedive of Egypt (Tewfik) (1852-92), 221

Kimberley, 1st Earl (1826-1902), Liberal statesman, 226

Knight, Margaret (b. 1903), secularist propagandist, 298

Knowlton, Charles (1800-50), birth control advocate, 172

Kossuth, Louis (1802-94), Hungarian

revolutionary, 23, 38

Kropotkin, Prince (1842-1921), Russian anarchist, 114

Kydd, Samuel (b. 1821), barrister, 198, 203, 207, 218-9

Labouchere, Henry (1831-1912), Liberal MP, 189-90, 196-8, 205-6, 208, 211, 214-5, 222-3, 232, 246, 248, 251, 256, 263, 279, 285, 287, 289, 294, 297

Labour Party, 297-9

Labour Representation League, 112

Labour Union, International, 185

Laissez-faire, 90, 271, 273

Land and Labour League, 114-5, 118, 121, 145

Land law reform, 11, 105-8, 136, 153, 187-8, 205, 251, 254, 271, 299

Land Law Reform League, 188, 226

Land nationalization, 107, 114-5, 188

Land, the People and the Coming Struggle, The, C. Bradlaugh, 127

Landseer, Sir Edwin (1802-73), painter, 170

Lansbury, George (1859-1940), Labour statesman, 114

Law and Liberty League, 264, 269

Law, Harriet (1832-97), secularist journalist, 94, 109, 122, 160, 162, 169, 172, 181, 185

Law of Population, The, A. Besant, 183-4, 258

Law Times, The, 217

Lawson, Sir Wilfrid (1829-1906), reformer, 138, 211

Ledru-Rollin, A.A. (1807-74), French revolutionary, 58, 63

Lees, Frederick (fl. 1860s), radical, 111

Lees, John (fl. 1880s), secularist manufacturer, 171, 242, 267

Lees, T.O.H. (1846-1924), barrister, 256

Lenin, V.I. (1870-1924), Soviet leader, 136

Lepard, J. (fl. 1850s), solicitor, 35-6

Leverson, M.R. (fl. 1860s), solicitor, 56, 73, 78-80, 82-3, 87, 109, 174

Levy, J.H. (1838-1913), political economist, 186, 240

Lewes, G.H. (1817-78), man of letters, 51, 169

Lewis, Sir George (1833-1911), solicitor, 163, 174, 176, 208, 231

Libel actions, 55-6, 79, 92, 109-10, 168-70, 193, 203, 259, 264-8

Liberal, The, 186

Liberals, 94-5, 102-3, 105, 107-9, 111, 149, 152, 160-1, 189, 191-223, 243, 246-9, 251, 255-6, 274, 289, 297-8

Lincoln, Abraham (1809-65), US President, 117, 149

Lincoln, Bishop of (C. Wordsworth) (1807-85), 181

Lindley, 1st Baron (1828-1921), High Court judge, 203, 208, 212, 246

Linton, W.J. (1812-97), republican engraver-writer, 38, 41, 55, 81-3, 138, 143

Lisle, Edwin de (1852-1920), Tory MP, 287

Lloyd-George, 1st Earl (1863-1945), Liberal Prime Minister, 289, 297

Local government, 261-2, 271, 273, 286

London Labour and the London Poor, Henry Mayhew, 14

London School Board, 269, 286

Lords, House of, 10, 16, 68, 92-3, 105, 119, 122-3, 130, 145, 149, 153, 204, 215, 218-9, 225-6, 232, 243, 247, 249, 251, 257, 261, 274-5, 298

Loring, George (1817-91), US statesman, 150, 152

Lotos Club, 149

Louise, Princess (1848-1939), Victoria's daughter, 122

Lovett, William (1800-77), Chartist leader, 17, 39

Lubbock, Sir John (1st Baron Avebury) (1834-1913), banker, 271

Lubez, P.A.V. Le (fl. 1870s), secularist, 125-6, 188, 212

Lucraft, Benjamin (fl. 1860s), trade union leader, 62, 124

Lucretius, Titus (?96-55BC), Roman poet, 223

Lush, Sir Robert (1807-81), High Court judge, 181, 204

Macaulay, 1st Baron (1800-59), historian, 279

Maccall, William (1812-88), polemicist, 42, 107, 118, 154-5

Macdonald, Alexander (1821-81), miners' leader, 152, 188

MacDonald, J. Ramsay (1866-1937), Labour Prime Minister, 114

Mackay, C.R. (b. 1865), agnostic writer, 259, 265-8

Maintenance, 207-8, 218, 222, 226

Malthus, Thomas (1766-1834), political economist, 76, 83

Malthusian League, 74-5, 183

Malthusianism, see Birth control

Manchester Guardian, The, 188

Manchester Martyrs, 99

Manfield, Sir Philip (1819-99), Liberal MP, 189, 297

Manisty, Sir Henry (1808-90), High Court

judge, 217, 268

Mann, Tom (1856-1941), socialist, 272, 278

Manning, H.E. (1808-92), RC cardinal, 136, 201-2, 204, 212, 278

Marjoribanks, Edward (2nd Baron Tweed-mouth) (1849-1909), Liberal states-man, 215

Market rights and tolls, 251, 257, 262, 273, 289

Marlborough, 7th Duke of (1822-83), Tory peer, 193, 205

Martineau, Harriet (1802-76), writer, 55

Martineau, James (1805-1900), Unitarian scholar, 226, 228

Marx Aveling, Eleanor (1856-98), socialist journalist, 229, 237, 241-2

Marx, Karl (1818-83), socialist economist, 106, 124, 126, 129, 213, 228, 239-40

Matchgirls, 238, 269, 293

Materialism, 53, 155

Mathew, Sir J.C. (1830-1908), High Court judge, 203-4, 217, 231

Matthias, T.D. (1822-1904), pastor, 65

Maudsley, Henry (1835-1918), psychi-atrist, 226

Maughan, John (d. 1875), secularist organ-izer, 50, 53-4, 62, 76

Maxse, Frederick (1833-1900), republican admiral, 121, 133, 160, 289

May, Sir T.E. (1st Baron Farnborough) (1815-86), Clerk of Commons, 192, 196, 214, 249

Mayhew, Henry (1812-87), social writer, 14

Mayne, Sir Richard (1796-1868), police commissioner, 44, 93

Mazzini, Giuseppe (1805-72), Italian pat-riot, 24, 55, 63, 78-9

McCulloch, J.R. (1789-1864), political economist, 76

McEwan, William (1827-1913), brewer, 279

McSorley, Hugh (fl. 1860s), Anglican vicar, 92

Mellor, Sir John (1809-87), High Court judge, 181

Memorial Hall, 293-4

Mercury, The, 108, 161, 184

Meredith, George (1828-1909), man of letters, 114

Merewether, C.G. (fl. 1870s), barrister, 160-1, 190

Metaphysical Society, 113

Methodist New Connexion, 67, 71

Methodist Old Connexion, 67

Methodists, Primitive, 108, 113, 136, 189

Mill, J.S. (1806-73), utilitarian philo-sopher, 42, 50, 55, 76, 89, 94, 97, 101, 110-1, 113, 129, 175

Milton, John (1608-74), poet, 60

Miner, A.A. (1814-95), US Universalist, 152, 164

Miners, 59, 113, 152, 161, 184, 206, 209, 262-3, 289

Mitty, Walter, cinematic daydreamer, 57

Monarchy, 9, 105, 109, 118-56, 163

Montfort, Simon de (1st Earl of Leicester) (?1208-65), parliamentary institutor, 104

Moore, Samuel (fl. 1880s), socialist, 240

Moral Physiology, R.D. Owen, 181

More, Hannah (1745-1833), Christian apologist, 16

Morgan, John De (fl. 1870s), agitator, 134, 137-43, 154-5

Morley, John (1st Viscount) (1838-1923), Liberal statesman, 114, 212, 232, 243, 264, 274, 289

Morley, Samuel (1809-86), Liberal MP, 63, 136, 142, 189-90, 215, 249

Mormons, 64

Morning Advertiser, The, 182

Morris, William (1834-96), poet-artist, 237, 246

Mundella, A.J. (1825-97), Liberal states-man, 169, 220

Murphy, William (d. 1871), Orangeman, 99

Music hall, 70, 294

Mutual Help Association, 154-5, 162

Naoroji, Dadabhai (1825-1917), Indian MP, 275

Naples Colour Co. Ltd, 90, 99, 112, 115-6

Napoleon Bonaparte, Louis (1808-73), French emperor, 55-6, 75, 119-20, 153

Napoleon, Prince Joseph (Jérome or 'Plon Plon') (1822-91), Bonapartist repub-lican, 114, 120-1, 142, 152-3

National Liberal Club, 245, 285

National Liberal Federation, 285

National Reformer, The, 38, 67-9, 74-7, 79-81, 83, 85, 91, 93, 96, 101-2, 107, 120, 122, 125, 127, 129, 133-5, 138-9, 142, 152, 158-60, 162-4, 168-71, 173-4, 176-7, 186-7, 202, 205, 207, 213, 219, 229, 243, 254, 260, 263, 266, 269-70, 279, 282, 292

New York Herald, The, 131, 149

New Zealand, 86, 202

Newcastle Chronicle, The, 85

Newcastle Weekly Chronicle, The, 150

Newdegate, C.N. (1816-87), Tory MP,

198, 204, 206-8, 218-9, 222, 226, 248

Newman, F.W. (1805-97), man of letters, 55, 89

Nine hours movement, 128

Nineteenth Century, The, 212

Nonconformists, 15-6, 70, 72, 79, 103, 105, 108, 111, 152, 184, 190, 274, 297

North American Review, The, 269

North, Sir Ford (1830-1913), High Court judge, 224

Northampton, 62, 69, 79, 94-5, 104-11, 128, 149, 152, 155, 178, 184, 186, 189-90, 198, 201-2, 205, 209, 214-5, 235, 247-8, 256, 275, 285, 289-91, 294, 296-7

Northcote, Sir Stafford (1st Earl of Iddesleigh) (1818-87), Tory statesman, 192-3, 197, 205, 213, 215, 223, 231-2, 235, 247

Northcote, Sir Stafford (1st Baron) (1846-1911), Tory statesman, 287

Oath, 16, 48, 71, 75, 192-223, 231-2, 235-6, 249-51, 268, 271, 274, 282, 298, App. 4

Oaths Act (1888), 274-5, 277

Obscene Publications Act (1857), 180

Obscenity, 10, 54, 173, 178, 181-5

O'Brien, Bronterre (1805-64), republican journalist, 239

O'Connor, Feargus (1794-1855), Chartist militant, 132, 155

O'Connor, T.P. (1848-1929), journalist, 251, 265

Odger, George (1813-77), radical shoemaker, 89, 105, 107-8, 111-2, 121, 124, 128-9, 131-2, 136, 141-2, 144, 155, 160

O'Donnell, F.H. (1848-1916), Irish MP, 209, 215, 232, 248

O'Donoghue, Daniel (The) (1833-89), Irish MP, 97

Olcott, H.S. (1832-1907), US theosophist leader, 149, 270, 278

Olivier, 1st Baron (1859-1943), civil servant, 245

On the Deity of Jesus of Nazareth, A. Besant, 157

Oracle of Reason, The, 18, 38, 40

Orsini, Felice (1819-58), Italian patriot, 55-7, 119

O'Shea Parnell, Kitty (1845-1921), political hostess, 157, 285

Otis, F.N. (1825-1900), US medical practitioner, 163-4

Our Corner, 230, 242

Owen, R. D. (1801-77), birth control advocate, 175, 181

Owen, Robert (1771-1858), utopian socialist, 25, 40, 42, 59, 60, 151, 239

Owenism, see Socialism, utopian

Oxford Movement, 16

Packer, J.G. (1812-83), clergyman, 17-20, 24-5, 35, 38, 43

Paine, Thomas (1737-1809), Anglo-American writer, 16, 21, 23

Pall Mall Gazette, The, 222, 264, 269

Palmer, Elihu (1764-1806), US deist, 25

Palmerston, 3rd Viscount (1784-1865), Whig Prime Minister, 38, 56, 84

Pankhurst, Emmeline (1858-1928), suffragette, 289

Parker, Theodore (1810-60), Unitarian theologian, 150

Parliamentary Oaths Act (1866), 194, 204, 212, 216, 222, 225

Parnell, C.S. (1846-91), Irish leader, 114, 157, 191, 197-8, 202, 214, 246, 285, 296

Parris, Annie (fl. 1880s), wife of Touzeau, 180, 183, 253

Parris, Touzeau (1839-1907), secularist, 173, 180-1, 183

Parry, J.H. (1816-80), sergeant-at-law, 79

Patriotic Society, 115, 143, 211

Peace movement, 89, 185, 278, 289, 298

Pease, Edward (1857-1955), Fabian socialist, 245

Pease, Joseph (1799-1872), Quaker statesman, 16, 89

Peel, Sir A.W. (1st Viscount) (1829-1912), Commons Speaker, 247, 249-50, 287

Peel, Sir Robert (1788-1850), Tory Prime Minister, 107, 247

Pensiero ed Azione, 79

People's League against the Hereditary Principle in Legislature, 243

Perceval, Spencer (1762-1812), Tory Prime Minister, 104

Percy, Earl (7th Duke of Northumberland) (1846-1918), Tory MP, 206, 249

Perfitt, P.W. (fl. 1860s), independent pastor, 76-7

Perjury, 236, 264, 268

Permissive society, 10, 70, 299

Perpetual pensions, 193, 205, 211, 254, 256-7, 261, 270-1

Perry, P.P. (fl. 1870s), civic leader, 128, 161

Peters, Samuel (fl. 1880s), Tory protectionist, 252, 264, 266, 268

Phillips, Wendell (1811-84), US abolitionist, 150, 152, 164

Philpot Street Hall, 22, 24-5, 50, 64, 103

Phipps, Pickering (b. 1827), Tory MP,

152, 190

Picton, J.A. (1832-1910), Liberal MP, 274, 289

Place, Francis (1771-1854), reformer, 39, 175

Plea for Atheism, A, C. Bradlaugh, 159

Plimsoll, Samuel (1824-98), Liberal MP, 198

Polish Committee, 84-5

Poor Man's Guardian, The, 25

Positivists, 120-1, 228

Presbyterians, 108

Pride, Thomas (d. 1658), Puritan colonel, 218

Prince of Wales (Edward VII) (1841-1910), Hanoverian King of England, 88, 123, 128-9, 131-2, 148, 213, 261, 265, 267, 287

Principles of Nature, The, Elihu Palmer, 25

Progress, 230, 242

Promissory Oaths Act (1868), 194, 212, 216

Proportional representation, 90, 105, 299

Protestant Alliance, 206, 215

Purser, Thomas (fl. 1880s), civic leader, 108, 198

Quakers, 15-6, 99, 114, 160, 194, 274

Queensberry, 8th Marquess of (1844-1900), sportsman, 248, 289

Radical, The (Bates's), 160

Radical, The (Standring's), 258

Radicalism, 10-1, 25, 41, 104-5, 107, 136, 144-5, 149-50, 155-7, 159, 161, 184, 188-9, 191, 211, 213, 221, 242-3, 258, 264, 272, 277-8, 289, 297-8

Raikes, H.C. (1838-91), Tory MP, 249, 251

Ramsey, W.J. (1844-1916), secularist publisher, 176, 182, 213, 219-21, 224-6, 258, 260

Rationalism, 24-5, 38, 157, 159, 164

Rationalist Press Association, 281, 296

Razor, The, 109-10

Reasoner, The, 25, 40, 42-3, 51-4, 62, 67, 75, 81, 102

Reclus, Élisée (1830-1905), French geographer, 88

Reddalls Junior, George (1846-75), secularist journalist, 134, 138, 140, 163

Redesdale, 1st Earl of (1805-86), Tory peer, 215

Redistribution Act (1885), 243, 247

Redshirts, 68

Reed, Mary (fl. 1880s), Bradlaugh's secretary, 263, 285-6

Reform Bill, Great (1832), 15, 39

Reform League, National, 88-9, 93, 95-7,

107, 113, 244

Reform, Parliamentary, 9, 11, 15, 18, 62, 68, 75, 89-90, 92-5, 110, 145, 153-4, 169, 243, 290

Reform Union, National, 88

Reform Union, Northern, 55, 67

Reformer, see National Reformer, The

Reply to Brindley's Reply, C. Bradlaugh, 23

Representation of the People Act (1867), 97-8, 103

Representation of the People Act (1884), 243, 261,

Republican, The (anon.), 118, 127, 132-3

Republican, The (Carlile's), 133

Republican, The (Standring's), 186, 258

Republican Brotherhood, 55

Republican Brotherhood, National, 138-41, 143, 145, 148, 154

Republican Chronicle, The, 162, 184, 186

Republican Club, London, 122-3, 137, 139, 143, 145

Republican Herald, The, 143, 154-5

Republican League, National, 145-6, 148, 154

Republican League, Universal, 127-8, 145

Republicanism, 9, 11, 21-2, 24-5, 38, 55, 67, 76, 78, 97-9, 104, 113, 118-56, 162-4, 184, 186, 188, 191, 209, 211, 243, 258, 276, 299, App. 3

Reynolds, William (1844-1911), secularist, 188, 293-4

Reynolds's Newspaper, 265, 267

Richard, Henry (1812-88), Liberal MP, 274

Richards, H.C. (1851-1905), Tory MP, 235, 248

Riley, W.H. (fl. 1870s), radical journalist, 133, 138, 140-1, 143, 154-5

Ripon, 1st Marquess of (1827-1909), Liberal statesman, 282

Risorgimento, 24, 78

Ritchie, 1st Baron (1838-1906) Tory statesman, 262, 287

Roberts, W.P. (1806-71), solicitor, 99, 157

Robertson, J.M. (1856-1933), Liberal statesman, 242-3, 245, 264, 281, 290, 292, 294, 297

Robespierre, Maximilien (1758-94), French revolutionary, 9

Rogers, J.T. (1823-90), economist, 246

Rogers, Thomas (fl. 1850s), solicitor, 41, 43, 48, 61, 64

Rollin, see Ledru-Rollin, A.A.

Roman Catholics, see Catholics, Roman

Rooke, Henry (fl. 1880s), civil servant, 289

Ross, W.S. ('Saladin') (1844-1906),

secularist journalist, 164, 248, 258-60, 264-8, 288

Rossetti, D.G. (1828-82), poet-painter, 168

Rossetti, W.M. (1829-1919), critic, 168

Rothschild, L.N. (1808-79), financier, 62-3, 91, 144, 167

Rousseau, J. Morley, 212

Row (Rao), Sir Madhava (1828-91), Indian statesman, 280

Roy, Raja R.M. (1772-1833), Indian reformer, 16

Russell, 1st Earl (1792-1878), 93

Saladin the Little, T.E.Jacob, 260

Salisbury, 3rd Marquess of (1830-1903), Tory Prime Minister, 215, 247, 256, 264, 268

Salvation Army, 286

Samuel, 1st Viscount (1870-1963), Liberal statesman, 297

Santos e Silva, Geraldo dos (Barão de Ferreira) (1830-70), Portuguese diplomat, 99, 115-7, 146

Saturday Review, The, 54, 96

Savage, James (fl. 1840s), radical freethinker, 18, 22, 41

Savage, John (do), do, 18

Schreiner, Olive (1855-1920), South African writer, 114

Scott, Thomas (1808-78), radical publisher, 157-60

Seamen, 198, 278, 289

Secret Doctrine, The, H.P.Blavatsky, 270

Secular Benevolent Society, General, 76, 94

Secular Chronicle, The, 134, 172, 186

Secular Review and Secularist, The, 181, 186

Secular Review, The, 168, 172, 176, 186, 221, 248, 258-60, 264, 267

Secular Society, East London, 50

Secular Society, London, 42, 48, 50, 57

Secular Society, National, 94, 100, 112, 128, 144, 156, 158-9, 162, 167, 169, 174, 176-7, 181, 184, 186-8, 201, 229-30, 244, 258-60, 264, 269, 280-2, 285, 290, 292-3, 296

Secular Song and Hymn Book, The, A. Besant, 163

Secular Union, British, 181, 184-6, 228, 248

Secular World, The, 77, 82, 86

Secularism, 39-40, 43, 50-1, 53, 64, 68-9, 72, 75, 77, 86, 94, 112-4, 129, 134, 141, 145, 154, 167-8, 172, 184-5, 204, 213, 227-9, 237, 241, 243-4, 248, 251-3, 258-60, 264, 269, 278, 280-2, 285, 294

Secularist, The,, 164, 167

Secularist's Manual of Songs and Ceremonies, The, A. Holyoake and C. Watts, 130

Security Laws, 101-2, 144

Selborne, 1st Earl of (1812-95), Lord Chancellor, 225

Self-reliance, 26, 151, 271, 273

Settlement, Act of (1701), 123, 137

Seymour, W. Digby (1822-95), judge, 62

Shaen, William (fl. 1850s), solicitor, 52, 82

Sharman, W. (fl. 1880s), radical pastor, 72, 206, 220

Shaw, G.B. (1856-1950), dramatist, 114, 181, 230, 243, 245, 252

Shelley, P.B. (1792-1822), poet, 23

Shipman, J.G. (b. 1848), Liberal MP, 297

Shipman, John (fl. 1860s), secularist, 62

Shoemakers, 89, 104-5, 110, 112, 161, 184, 235

Simon, 1st Viscount (1873-1954), National Liberal statesman, 297

Simon, Sir John (1818-97), Liberal MP, 223, 249, 251, 274

Singh, Maharaja Pratap (Partab) (1850-1925), Indian prince, 276

Smiles, Samuel (1812-1904), biographer, 42

Smith, A. Headingley (fl. 1870s), republican, 125

Smith, B.B. (do), US senator, 150

Smith, Montagu (1809-91), High Court judge, 74, 99-100

Smith, R.O. (fl. 1880s), secularist, 113, 186, 247, 294

Smith, W.H. (1825-91), Tory statesman, 81, 260, 270-1, 282, 287, 296

Snell, 1st Baron (1865-1944), Labour statesman, 114

Social Democratic Federation, 237, 252, 257, 272, 297

Social Science, National Association for the Promotion of, 49, 67, 113

Socialism, Christian, 39-40, 162, 181

Socialism, marxist, 11, 106-7, 119, 133, 143, 213, 229 236-45, 248, 251-3, 263-5, 269-73, 277, 281, 293, 297, 299

Socialism, utopian, 22, 38-9, 67, 141, 236-8, 241

Socialist League, 237

Soir, Le, 126

South Place Chapel (Ethical Society), 55, 159, 163, 181, 281, 293

Southwell, Charles (1814-60), atheist journalist, 38-40, 43 48, 59, 86, 96, 109

Sozial Demokrat, 265

Spain, 146-8, 153, 214

Spencer, 5th Earl (1835-1910), Liberal peer, 274

Spencer, Herbert (1820-1903), sociological pioneer, 42

Spiritualism, 113, 269, 293

Spottiswoode, William (1825-83), publisher, 226

Spratt, John (1797-1871), Irish reformer, 32

Spurgeon, C.H. (1834-92), evangelist, 46, 114

St Stephen's Review, 268

Standard, The, 96

Standring, George (1855-1924), secularist journalist, 162, 169, 177, 186, 206, 211-2, 258, 294

Stanley, A.P. (1815-81), Anglican dean, 110

Stead, W.T. (1849-1912), radical journalist, 264, 269-70

Stephen, Sir J.F. (1829-94), High Court judge, 203, 221, 231, 277

Stephen, Sir Leslie (1832-1904), man of letters, 203

Strachey, Lytton (1880-1932), biographer, 265

Stuart, J.J. (fl. 1880s), solicitor's clerk, 198, 207-8, 215

Stuart, W.G. (do), solicitor, 198

Suez Canal, 167, 185, 299

Suffrage, see Reform, parliamentary

Sumner, Charles (1811-74), US statesman, 150, 161

Sunday League, National, 46

Sunday observance, 109, 198, 291

Sunday Observance Act (1677), 44, 272

Sunday Trading Bill, 44, 46

Swaagman Darwen, J. (fl. 1880s), secularist, 201, 212

Tablet, The, 74

Tait, A.C. (1811-82), Archbishop of Canterbury, 197

Talandier, Alfred (b. 1823), French revolutionary, 87, 183

Taunton, 1st Baron (1798-1869), Liberal statesman, 189

Taxation, C. Bradlaugh, 184

Taylor, Robert (1784-1844), heterodox clergyman, 20-1, 23

Taylor, Sir Peter (1819-91), Liberal MP, 55, 63, 85, 97, 113, 122, 128, 136, 138, 188

Temperance 14, 18, 21-2, 24, 31-3, 36, 66, 70, 89, 111, 116, 142, 152, 297

Theosophy, 269-70, 281, 293, 296

Thiers, Adolphe (1797-1877), French President, 123-5, 144, 147

Thomson, James ('B.V.') (1834-82), poet, 34-6, 43, 62, 83 85-7, 90-1, 112, 116-7, 135-6, 148, 152, 159, 162-3, 168, 177, 180, 186, 211

Tillett, Ben (1860-1943), dockers' leader, 278

Times, The, 20, 30, 35, 62, 97, 131, 182, 192, 204, 220, 264, 276, 280

Tinworth, George (1843-1913), modeller, 294

Tissot, Charles (1828-84), French diplomat, 120-1

To-Day, 237

Tories, 67, 95, 102, 108, 111, 144, 152, 154, 160-1, 163, 185, 188, 190-223, 235, 243, 246-9, 251-2, 255-8, 260-5, 268, 282, 285, 289, 297

Tottenham and Edmonton Weekly Herald, 92

Toynbee Hall, 289

Trades Council, London, 67, 89, 188

Trades Union Congress, 105, 109

Trades unions, 59, 67, 83, 109, 133, 155, 184, 269, 271-3, 278, 281, 289-90

Trafalgar Square, 93, 96, 209, 222, 251-2, 264, 270

Trelawny, Sir John (1816-85), Liberal MP, 71

Trevelyan, Arthur (1802-78), secularist patron, 54-5, 129, 183

Trevelyan, Sir G.O. (1838-1928), Liberal statesman, 130, 246

Tribune, The, 293

Truck, 254, 289

Truck Amendment Act (1887), 261

Truelove, Edward (1809-99), secularist publisher, 42, 49, 51, 55-6, 64, 68, 73, 101, 108, 158, 174-5, 181-2, 289, 294

Truth, 189, 205, 264

Turberville, Henry (d. 1876), secularist, 178

Turner, Richard (b. 1826), civic leader, 161, 256

Turner, Sir Ben (1863-1942), trade union leader, 95, 114

Tyler, Sir Henry (1827-1908), Tory MP, 196, 219-20, 222, 225, 244, 254

Tyndall, John (1820-93), physicist, 226

Tyrannicide: is it Justifiable?, W.E.Adams, 55

Ulster, 255

Uncultivated land, 106, 123, 187-8, 226, 251, 254, 257, 271, 286

Unionists, Liberal, 255-6, 258

Unitarians, 26, 42, 48, 67, 72, 103, 108, 122, 150, 160, 180, 189, 220, 226,

228, 251

United States, 38, 67, 75, 98, 108-9, 118, 133, 135-6, 148-52, 160-2, 164, 172, 175, 214, 240, 251, 279, 293

University College (London), 226-7

Unwin, Jane Cobden (fl. 1890s), 293-4

Vaccination, Royal Commission on, 277-8, 288-9

Varley, Henry (fl. 1880s), propagandist, 202, 205, 213, 215, 222, 263

Vatican, 56, 78, 99, 202, 204, 299

Verheyden, F. (fl. 1890s), sculptor, 294

Verinder, Frederick (fl. 1880s), Christian socialist, 211

Vestry, Tottenham, 88

Vice, Society for the Suppression of, 175, 181

Vickery Drysdale, Alice (1844-1929), birth control advocate, 181, 183

Victor Emmanuel II (1820-78), King of Italy, 83

Victoria (1819-1901), Queen of England, Empress of India, 55, 122-3, 128-32, 137, 148-9, 155, 184, 191, 194-5, 197, 215-6, 258, 277

Victoria Park, 16-7, 149

Voltaire, Arouet de (1694-1778), 92

Voysey, Charles (1828-1912), heretical clergyman, 96, 157, 228

Walewski, Count (1810-68), French diplomat, 56, 63

Wallace, A.R. (1823-1913), evolutionist, 107, 113

Wallas, Graham (1858-1932), political scientist, 245

Walpole, S.H. (1806-98), Tory statesman, 97, 193

Walter, Arthur (1846-1910), barrister, 182

Walter, John (1818-94), publisher, 182

Walton, Izaak (1593-1683), angling writer, 64

War of Independence, American, 149

Warpath of Opinion, The, G.J. Holyoake, 296

Warrington Observer, The, 268

Washington, George (1732-99), US President, 147

Waterlow, Sir Sydney (1822-1906), Liberal MP, 112, 198

Watson, James (1799-1874), freethought publisher, 24-5, 39, 42, 55, 101, 173

Watson, W.H. (1827-99), Law Lord, 225

Watts, C.A. (1858-1946), agnostic journalist, 221, 267, 281, 296

Watts, Charles (1836-1906), secularist journalist, 48, 91, 94, 108, 112, 122, 130, 134, 138, 140, 145, 152-3, 155, 159-60, 162-4, 169, 173-82, 198,

228, 248, 288, 296

Watts, John (1834-66), secularist printer, 48-9, 77, 81, 84-5, 91-2, 94, 228

Watts, Kate (fl. 1870s), wife of Charles, 134, 152-3, 157, 174-81

Waugh, Edward (fl. 1880s), Liberal MP, 214

Webb, Sidney (1st Baron Passfield) (1859-1947), Labour statesman, 245

Webster, Sir Richard (1st Viscount Alverstone) (1842-1915), Lord Chief Justice, 256

Wedderburn, Sir William (1838-1918), civil servant, 280

Wedgwood, 1st Baron (1872-1943), Labour statesman, 296

Weekly Dispatch, The, 188

Wesleyans, 48, 108, 122, 192

Westminster Review, The, 77

What does She do with it?, G.O. Trevelyan, 130

Whigs, 15, 97, 104-5, 107-8, 144, 154, 245, 251, 263, 297

White Anglo-Saxon Protestants, 149-50

Whitehall Review, The, 216

Wife or Mistress?, anon., 170

Wilberforce, William (1759-1833), abolitionist, 16

Wilkes, John (1727-97), polemicist statesman, 10, 205, 253, 282, 287

Wilks, Thomas (fl. 1850s), secularist newsagent, 52-4, 142

William the Conqueror (1027-87), Anglo-Norman king of England, 137

Williams, Sir C.J. Watkin (1824-84), High Court judge, 206, 212, 217

Williams, Sir E.V. (1797-1875), High Court judge, 74

Wilmot, Sir J.E. (1810-92), Tory MP, 201

Wilson, Henry (1812-75), US Vice-President, 150, 152, 164

Wilson, James (fl. 1860s), radical shoemaker, 110-1, 294

Wiseman, N.P.S. (1802-65), RC cardinal, 58

Wolff, Sir H.D. (1830-1908), diplomat, 193, 195, 247-8, 254, 261

Women's suffrage, 94, 113, 159, 164, 289, 298

Wood, Sir Evelyn (1838-1919), field marshal, 157

Wood, Sir Matthew (1768-1843), Lord Mayor of London, 157

Wood, W.P. (1st Baron Hatherley) (1801-81), Lord Chancellor, 99, 157

Working Classes, National Union of the, 16

Working Men's Club and Institute Union,

390

83, 289

World, The, (London), 168

World, The, (New York), 147-8

Worms, Henry de (1st Baron Pirbright) (1840-1903), Tory statesman, 196, 223, 288

Wortley, J.A. Stuart (1805-81), Whig statesman, 45

Wycliffe, John (?1320-84), heresiarch, 104

Yates, Edmund (1831-94), publisher, 168

Young, Frederick (fl. 1850s), secularist bookseller, 48

Young Italy, 24

Young Men's Christian Association, 73